The magnetic era

Video art in the Netherlands 1970–1985

Editors:

Jeroen Boomgaard

Bart Rutten

Authors:

Ruth Bellinkx and Marga van Mechelen

Jeroen Boomgaard

Anne van Driel

Heiner Holtappels

Hinke Kappert

Sebastián López

Rob Perrée

Bart Rutten

Jorinde Seijdel

NAi Publishers, Rotterdam

Netherlands Media Art Institute, Montevideo/Time Based Arts, Amsterdam

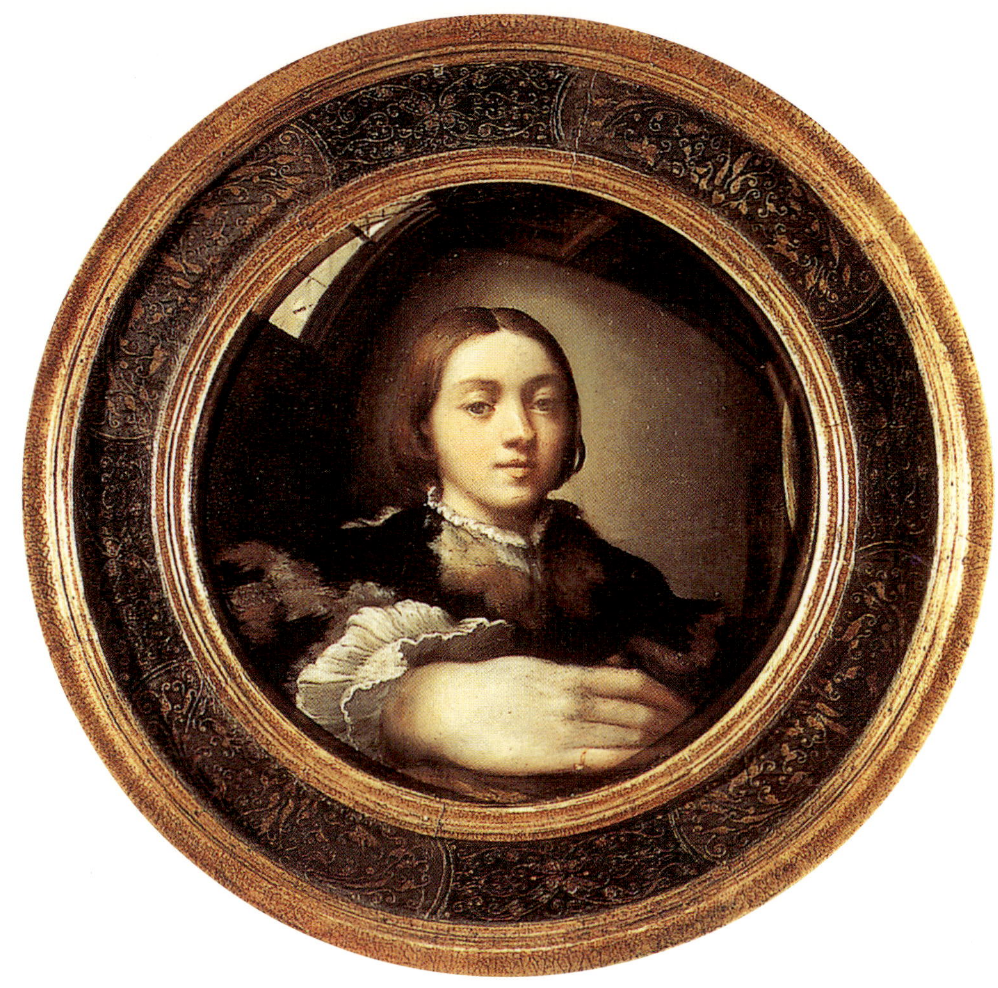

Parmigianino, *Self-portrait in a convex mirror*, 1523, Kunsthistorisches Museum, Vienna

From Portapak to WebCam

Point of view

Since the late 1970s, the *Zeitgeist* has shown an existential uncertainty, a crisis of management and of consciousness. The centrifugal forces once unleashed by Copernican ideas now confront us inexorably with a world view which the art historian Sedlmayr described as 'the loss of the centre' and which according the philosopher Lukács leads to the 'metaphysical alienation of man'. Cast into an infinite emptiness, drifting apart at ever greater velocity and surrounded by the ever-shrinking fragments of a once coherent world, we perfect our long-distance communications to compensate for the loss of proximity. In political jargon this is called the individualistic society, while the thinkers and doers see a gap in the market into which they can sell yesterday's neo-Ptolemaic ideas as a New Age tranquillizer.

It is from this point of view, if from different angles, with different objectives and a changing narrative, that I wish to plot the contours of art in general and of video art in particular. In other words, what you are now reading is the scenario for a history in the form of a film plot. The highest ideal in this is to turn the fiction into reality.

The establishing shot or the twentieth century in bird's eye view

The twentieth century surpassed the cultural riches of all preceding centuries from the Renaissance until today, not only in the abundance art and the profusion and diversity of its works, but also in the broad awareness of aesthetics as a touchstone of civilization. Never before have people held the past in higher esteem, cherished the present more warmly or invested more in the future, than now. The past century was, however, also the most atrocious, ravaged by two world wars and countless regional ones, by holocaust and the merciless exploitation of people and of nature. 'The need for art is indicative of increasing barbarism in society.' Whether or not this statement by Peter Sloterdijk is true, is not the point. It at least expresses the need for coherence between aesthetic and ethical progress at a time when thinking in linear, hierarchical structures is in continual decline.

If we are to understand the history and development of media art, we must take into account the diversity of conceptions, which differ in their scientific, religious or philosophical background, which are backed up by psychological, sociological and political arguments and are presented with much rhetorical elan. He who looks back is in search of continuity. A review of the progressive tendencies in the twentieth century shows that the 1920s, the 1960s and the 1980s were the creative milestones of the century. They were an answer to the conservative, reactionary movements that flourished in the intervening periods.

The 1920s were marked by the vigour and the rapidly ensuing crisis of the social revolution. Constructivism and Futurism interpreted the pervasive technological euphoria as communist and capitalist utopias, as reactions to the industrial revolution and the political liberalism of the nineteenth century. But every euphoria was followed by a *petit mort*: the betrayal of totalitarian hopes by Stalinism and Fascism.

The 1960s saw the peaceful revolution and the struggle for the autonomy of the individual, which was still embedded in a collective longing. The establishment was swept away by peaceful uprisings in Berlin, Paris and Washington. Instead of continuity, experiment now became the standard. The visual arts disclosed their full range in Fluxus and Conceptual Art: from a maximum of ethical and social aspiration to a minimum of aesthetic weight.

The 1980s took the form of a transformation of political, economic, scientific and cultural systems, all of which tended in one direction – the fuzzing of boundaries. Major technological advances in the communicative media, in biotechnology and applied computing made it into an optimistic decade. In the euphoria, many walls fell. Speculation, notably in the art market, was rife, and the infrastructure was laid down for the new complexity of the network society. What was once thought of as an integral whole now appeared as a miscellany of individual findings interlinked through chat rooms. The media-saturation and aesthetization of the individualized world was a reflection of contemporary philosophy. 'When interpretation flourishes and works of art are practically unable to escape the shadow of their own hermeneutic advertising, this is primarily the fault of a modern philosophy – a philosophy that has lost touch with the truth because there is no longer a single entity one can describe as the successful union of the true, the beautiful and the good. Contemporary philosophy needs aesthetics and uses the roundabout route of aesthetic theory to say what a "real philosophy" would have to say, if it still existed. Aesthetics is a crutch on which an untenable philosophy drags itself through the twentieth century.'[1]

Medium shot, or how twentieth-century technology conquered the arts

The most important art form of the twentieth century was film – not because of its primary economic status, but because of its capacity for being understood as a universal language, any-where in the world, without an arduous translation. The visual grammar of film was evidently simple enough to take root in every culture, while being complex enough to portray the main human narratives.

Technically speaking, film is reproducible without loss of information (like books, graphic art, photography, radio and television). Upgrading presents no difficulty: the transition from analogue to digital is easily made. The technology of film might have remained no more than a fairground attraction had it not proved its capacity as a mediator of traditional, current and future content. It transposed theatre (tragedy, drama and comedy), music (from opera to videoclip), literature (epic, novel, novella, reportage and poetry), visual art (all genres, from self-portrait to still-life and landscape). It has used every accepted style, from realism to minimalism. In other words, film satisfies practically all the criteria of classic art forms: being able to render reality through representation, expression and reflection. But film's most decisive success has been to render the chang-ing time and space experience of modern man, through accel-eration and deceleration, and the discontinuous experience of space (montage and camera angle). Film prepares the way technologically for what we later observe as social change: the fragmentation of reality, based on a discontinuous experience of time and space. Video technology adds real-time rendering to this, a feature widely used by artists in the early years of video art in closed-circuit installations and performances.

The rise of the personal computer brought an opportunity to tempt the consumer into becoming a producer, by means of interactivity. The consumer is no longer a passive spectator but

1
Peter Sloterdijk, *Kopernikanische Mobilmachung und ptolemäische Abrüstung*, Frankfurt am Main 1987.

a designer of reality. The real world changes from a datum into a potential, an actuality to be created.

Close up, or the introduction of the subject

The establishing shot dissolves into an 800-year long zoom from feudalism to civil society, from the collective to the individual granted fifteen minutes of stardom (the contemporary counterpart of nobility) by Andy Warhol. The camera zooms in farther, from palaces to towns, to glass towers where, in an over-designed living or working environment, a person comes into view. The gaze concentrates first on his face, then on his eye (as the place of recognition of the human, of expression and reflection) finally to disintegrate into the here and now, the realm of pixels.

The self-portrait in a convex mirror by Parmigianino (1503-1540) perhaps just expresses the vanity of a young artist eager to show off his painterly skills. But the unending stream of self-portraits produced by artists introduces the emergent belief in individualism as a pacesetter of history. In painting, however, the self-portrait remains a representation of a mirror-image, a visible proof of the impossibility of really seeing oneself. The camera puts an end to this. The representation of yourself is no longer a mirror image but an authentic, 'objective' image. The camera allows you to see yourself as through the eyes of a spectator. Every artist since the start of modernism has been a poseur, an actor playing himself in the hope of making a convincing impression. The claim of autonomy, the cult of genius and of the modern artist's star status, can be read as nothing other than an attempt to compensate for the lost paradise of the monopoly of visual representation.

Epilogue, or video art as deceleration

Video art has, during the last thirty years, recapitulated the history of art from its origins to the present. This may be expected of any new art form: testing the new aesthetic capability by reproducing the past. Only once this test has been accomplished can the phase of developing the new begin.

Media art is in the same stage of development as film was in 1895. Socially, media art has not progressed since 1975, when individualism became common property. Technically, we have reached 1995, the point where the Internet became available as an infrastructure. Digital coding brings the promise of a new cultural revolution, comparable to that inaugurated by typography, which mechanized information and liberated it from interpersonal communication.

The modernism of the last 200 years shows changing styles with a shorter and shorter duration, accompanied by a simultaneous increasing annexation of new areas. Visual art colonizes the media (photography, film, video, computers), design (graphics, product design and fashion) and the performing arts (theatre, music, dance). It also seeks new

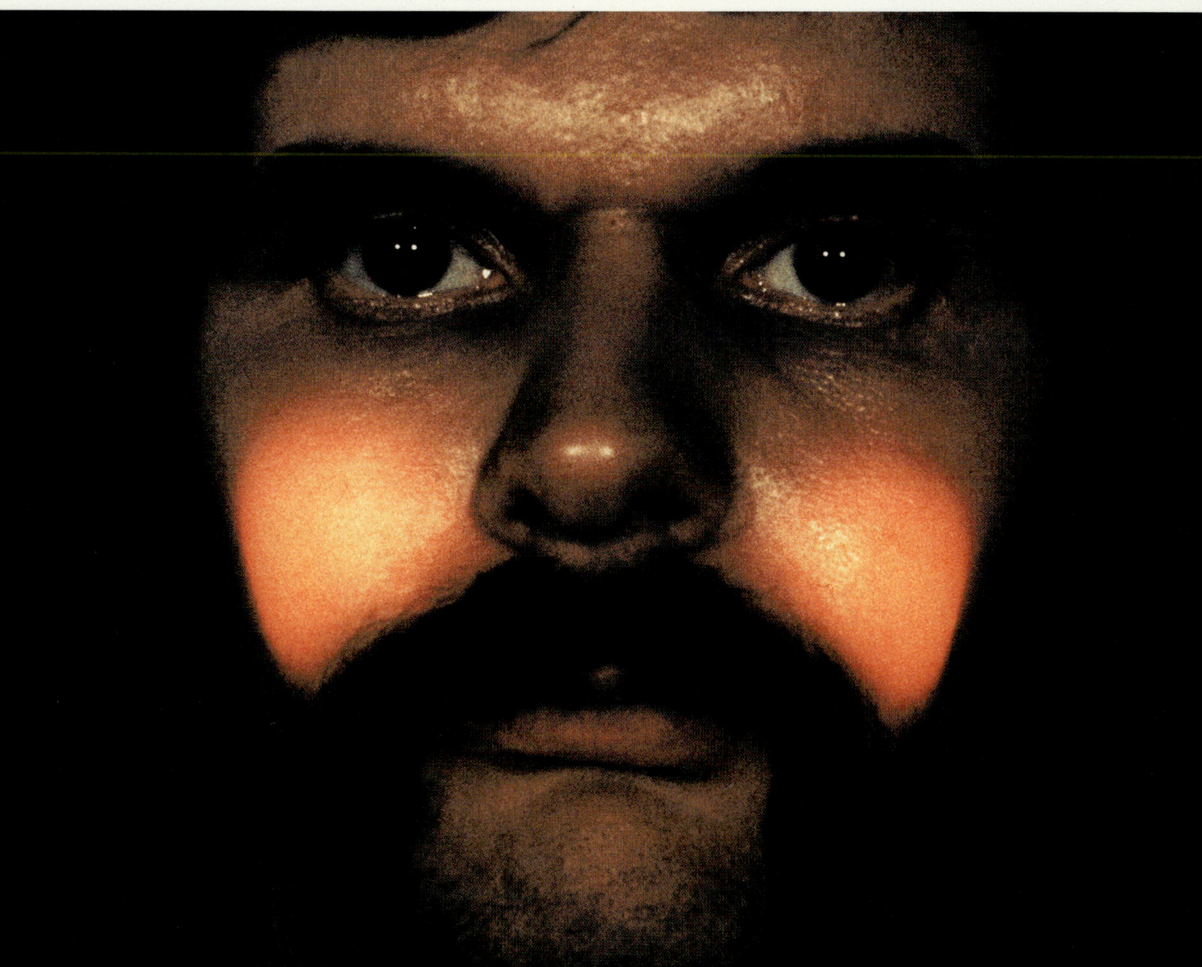

Jan van Munster, *Self-portrait I*, 1972, 16 mm film, colour, no sound

territories in non-Western cultures. Media art since the 1960s has shown a similar course of development. It reacted to the aesthetics of television, and tries to lay claim to television's production and distribution possibilities – first by disruption, and later by the failed attempt to run its own broadcasting organization. The artists of *Aktionskunst* and happenings which emerged from the Fluxus movement annexed the aesthetics of theatre and disseminated their work increasingly by documentation on video as well as film. The next stage, in the 1980s, was for artists to occupy the narrative domain of experimental film. By the end of that decade, this movement had expanded to take in the aesthetics of bad taste – pornographic film and kitsch. The anthropological/political documentary appeared and completed the erosion or liberation of the last remnants of the canon of modern art.

From the late 1980s onwards, Postmodernism was the new utopia which aimed to realize the aesthetic ideals of the French Revolution: *égalité, liberté, fraternité*. The digital camera and digital montage has put everyone in a position to produce his own images and stories, and the arrival of the Internet in the 1990s has opened up the possibility worldwide distribution,

and to find kindred spirits for even the most private wisps of
fantasy. It is inherent to every utopia that it can have only one
fate: that of failure, the incapacity to conclude the story with a
happy end. Perhaps this is the real difference between visual art
and film, in which case we can concur with Peter Sloterdijk:
'The need for happy endings is indicative of increasing
barbarism in society.'

Heiner Holtappels is an artist, a teacher at the Arnhem Institute for
the Arts and is also Director of the Netherlands Media Art Institute,
Montevideo/Time Based Arts, Amsterdam.

Jeroen Boomgaard

Bart Rutten

Introduction

Video is now a full-fledged medium within the visual arts. Though not all museums of modern art seem to be adapted for it yet, video is a trend-setting presence at important national and international exhibitions. Once a marginal and avant-garde experiment, it has become a 'mainstream' medium for artistic production. This almost universal acceptance overshadows the shaky beginnings, and the seminal hazy and long-drawn-out tapes disappeared a long time ago, but in this process we have also lost sight of the ideals that video initially seemed to fulfil. Unlike more traditional art forms, video was regarded as a democratic medium, and video art seemed to be capable of turning the old avant-garde ideal of the integration of art and life into a reality with the aid of leading-edge technology. Video was not primarily an art form, but a registration of reality. The video camera offered an alternative for mind-numbing television. Using video, the artists themselves could instantly test out their work while it was still 'in production', so that everything they did became art without it having to be concretized as an object.

This book is about these early experiments. We have tried to recapture the enthusiasm with which video artists set to work. We explore the territories where they dared to tread, we visit the centres that were set up throughout the country in order to propagate video, and we look at the ways in which the new medium was presented to the public. However, this book also describes the stumbling blocks and failures. The waning enthusiasm at the end of the 1970s, when the first generation of

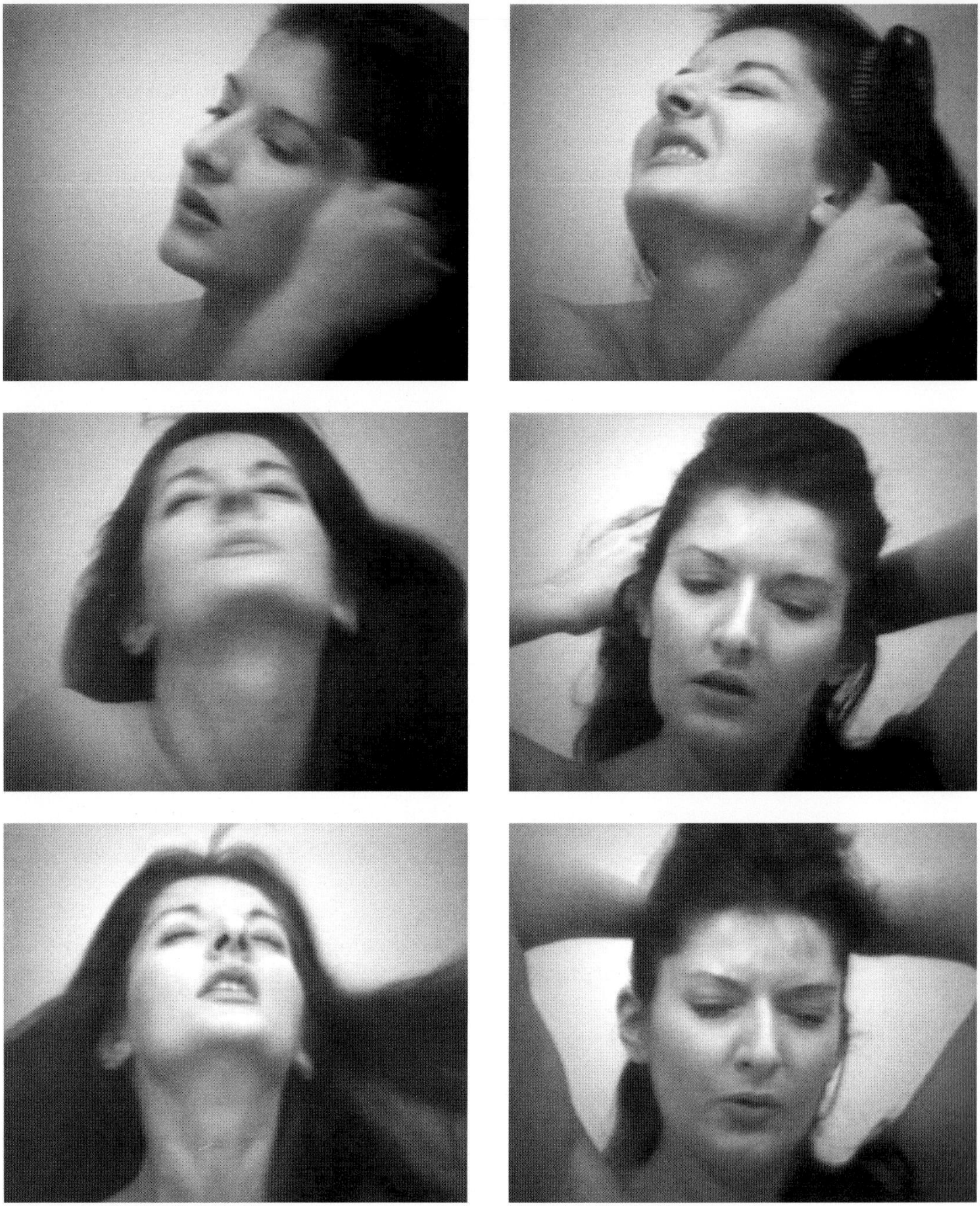

Marina Abramovič, *Art is beautiful, Artist must be beautiful*, 1975, video, b/w, sound, 55'00"

video makers had already turned their attention elsewhere, was followed by a period in which video endeavoured to find a narrative form in order to forge a link with the postmodern mentality. These were also the years in which a wavering government policy primarily succeeded in playing off the various institutions in the video world against each other. The period covered by this book comes to an end in the mid-1980s, when the initial ideals seem to have been completely worn down and video, like an ironic gesture of history, first started to gain a foothold on the museum circuit in the form of large-scale installations and presentations. It was also the era when people were taking their first tentative steps on the digital highway, which would lead to the unprecedented flourishing of new video experiments in the 1990s.

We decided to organize the book's content in more or less chronological order. However, video cannot be captured from a single perspective, as the medium is far too heterogeneous. The onward march of history is therefore subdivided into discrete 'shots'. The text does not simply tackle the artists and their work, but also the institutions, the press and the presentation. In doing this we have tried to spread the examples over the various chapters. Certain crucial moments and pioneering productions return on more than one occasion, as some overlap is unavoidable, but on each occasion it is to turn the spotlight on a different facet. The book does not offer an inventory, and being encyclopedic was not our objective. For this reason there are perhaps some exceptional artists, and also important works of art, which regrettably go unmentioned. This book does not signal the end of the history of video art in the Netherlands, but presents the groundwork for further study.

Looking back over the first 15 years we see a familiar picture on the screen. During this era, Dutch art strode forward in the vanguard of the newest developments, experimenting with verve and examining all the possibilities presented by the new medium of video. The large number of artists from abroad who contributed to that first wave of video is remarkable. The generous Dutch subsidy climate was undoubtedly a factor in this, but at least as important was the tolerance that made the Netherlands such an exceptional spot on the world map during these years. The country fostered a vibrant art world in which guests from abroad were welcome and everything seemed possible. However, there was another aspect, possibly a characteristic feature of Dutch art, which continued to predominate the picture: the majority of video works speak of humour and honest personal relativism. Insofar as this is not evident in the texts in this book, the illustrative material picks up this story, emulating the flow of early video.

Jeroen Boomgaard

Bart Rutten

Early days
Dutch video art in the 1970s

16   Video was born old. The ability for people to make their own
video recordings which became available in the mid 1960s,
caused little excitement. After all, the video recorder was
preceded by a whole range of different types of equipment,
all capable of recording reality. The camera, the super-8 camera
and the tape recorder had already brought reality into reach,
and video was no more than another logical step in the same
direction. The images created by the medium were no different
from those that found their way into millions of living rooms,
evening after evening: the amorphous greyish recordings of
events, providing living witness to life in some other place.
Within a decade television had become the most influential of
the mass media and had established a way of viewing, a pattern
of expectations, into which video fitted almost perfectly.

Artistically speaking too, video was essentially just the next
step along a well-trodden road. Experiments with all kinds of
techniques and materials, combinations of types of art which
had previously been strictly separate, emphasis on daily life and
the integration of art into society, had all been launched from the
late 1950s onwards in movements like Happening, Fluxus and
Pop Art. The use of video as a way of approaching daily life and
as a critical reflection on the power of the medium of television
was a logical step in this development, and for a public

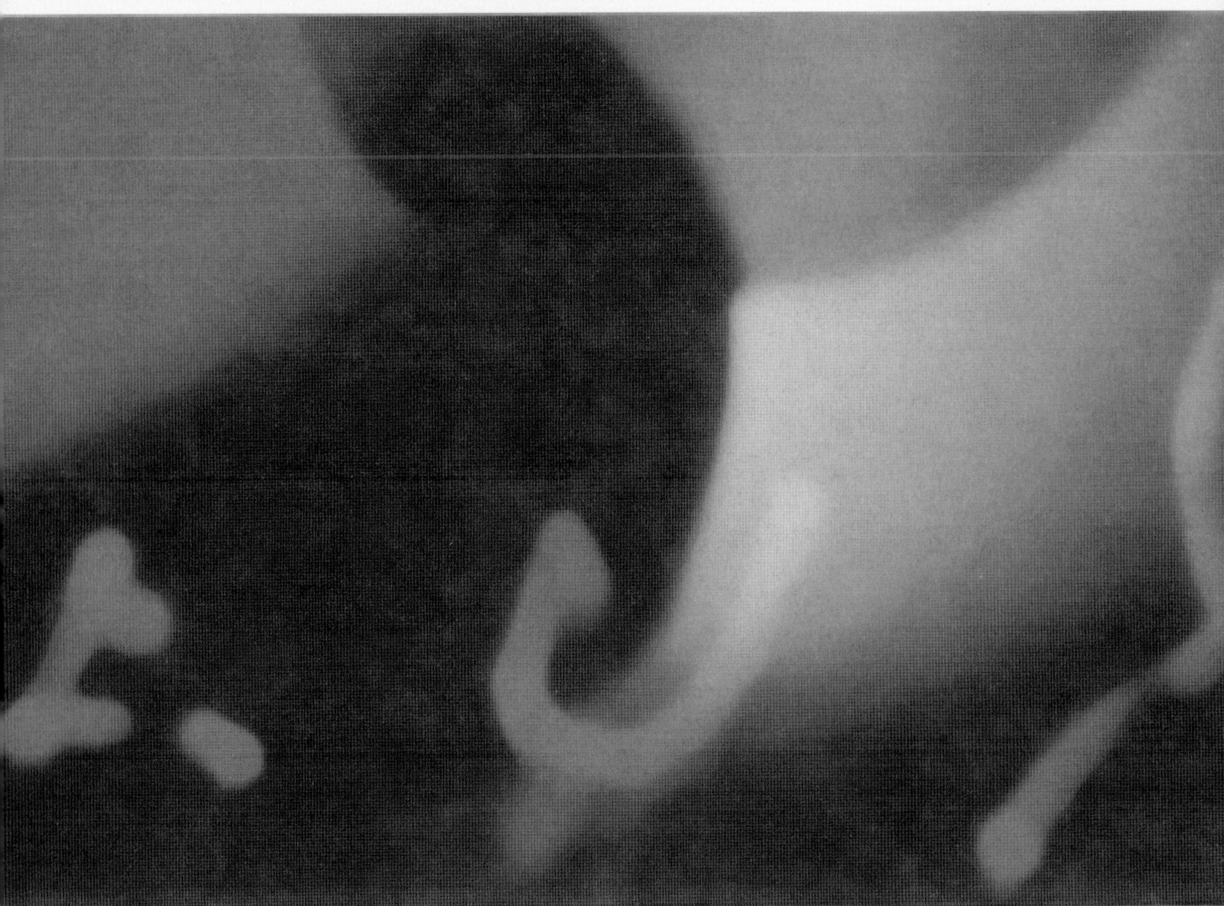

Livinus, example of a *fotopeinture*, 1964

thoroughly trained in strange and pioneering forms of art the endless grey tapes which characterized the early days of the medium were simply part of the spectacle provided by progressive art. While the admission to the art world of earlier mass media like photography and film took many decades, it took little effort for video to force its way in.[1] But precisely because video went so well with all kinds of different trends, the medium became charged with expectations which had a lasting effect on its use. It seemed to bring closer the possibility of achieving nothing less than the democratization of art and, with no extra effort, society. The pursuit of heterogeneity within art, the fusion of image, sound, time, space and movement seemed to be coming to fulfilment. These expectations laid a heavy burden on the shoulders of this new kind of art, and in some sense contributed to its emphasis on immediate use. Video was expected to fulfil its promise immediately, with the result that reflection on the possibilities and limitations of the medium remained limited. The heterogeneity was applauded, but its consequences were never investigated.[2]

[1] Burris 1996. Available online at www.mfjonline.org/journalpages/MFJ29/Jburrisportapak5319.html

[2] See also Krauss 2000, pp. 30-31.

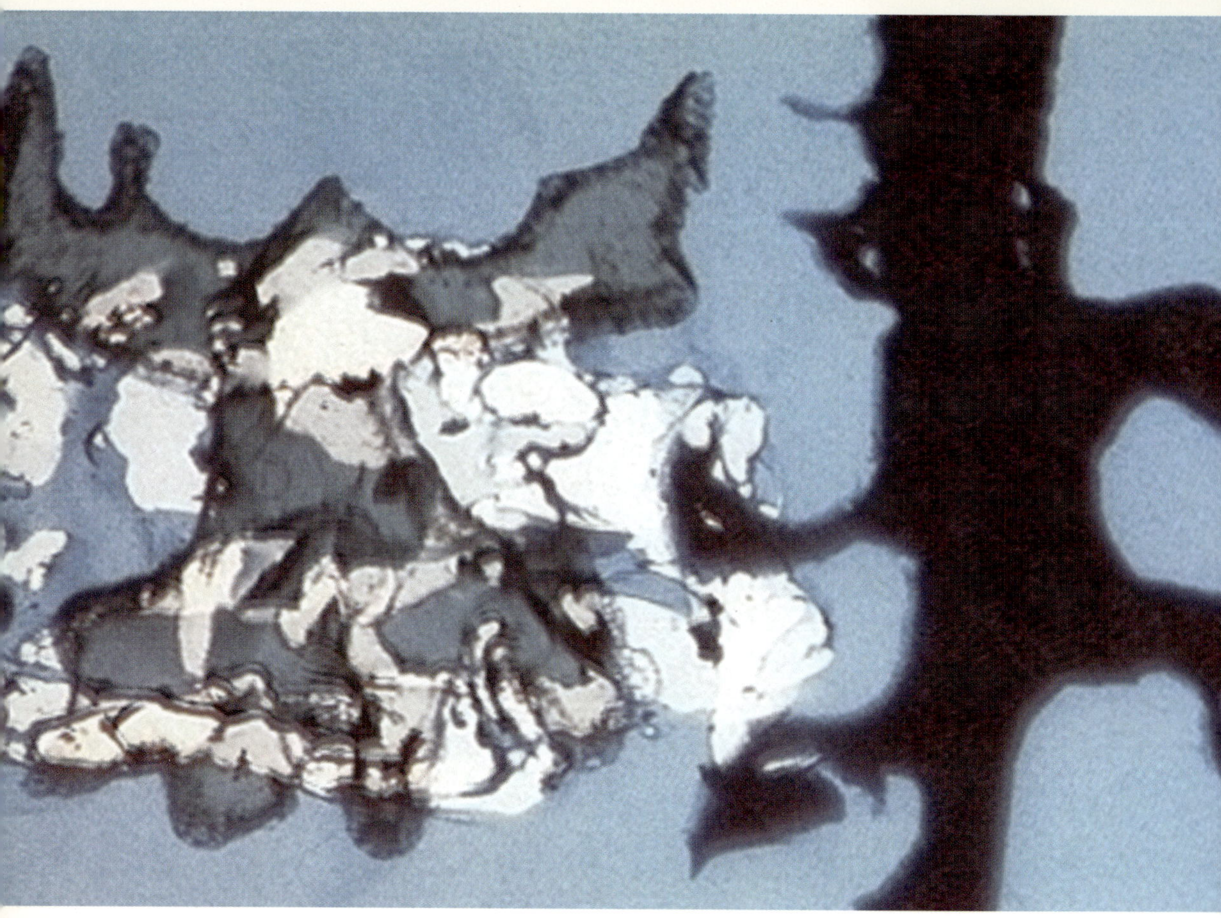

Livinus, example of a *fotopeinture*, 1964

18   Anyone who goes deeply into art produced by video, only too
soon finds himself involved in the shadowy discussion of video
art, in which it looks on itself as a specialty. Here authors, who
often come from the video world themselves, seem to go to
great efforts to treat video art as a discipline distinct from other
media like film and television. Even the documentary use of
video is excluded, whether the work of artists or socially
involved collectives and political organizations.[3] It seems to
resemble a pursuit of purism, in no way malicious, in a voyage of
exploration into the creative possibilities that lie hidden within
the medium. But it can also be seen as justifying the existence
of those organizations which specialize in video.[4] Video art
began to distinguish itself from art made with video and tried to
present itself as an 'ism', an art form with its own formal laws
and so its own judgement system. This may have been a
necessary phase in the emancipation of the new medium,

[3]
For an extensive discussion of the position occupied by video art, see Hall/Fifer 1990.
[4]
Sturken 1990, pp. 115-118. This method of exclusivity reached its zenith in the 1980s, in which
organizations were increasingly well provided with equipment and had their own places to display
work. Treating the medium as distinct from others made it possible for them to find finance. This
was the period in which the first collections were built up, a time when a personal view would
determine which works of art should be kept for the future. Sturken discusses the American
situation, where the responsibility for determining the way things went lay mainly with the major
museums. In the Netherlands video was largely ignored by the museums, so the small organizations
were able to make video art their exclusive property.

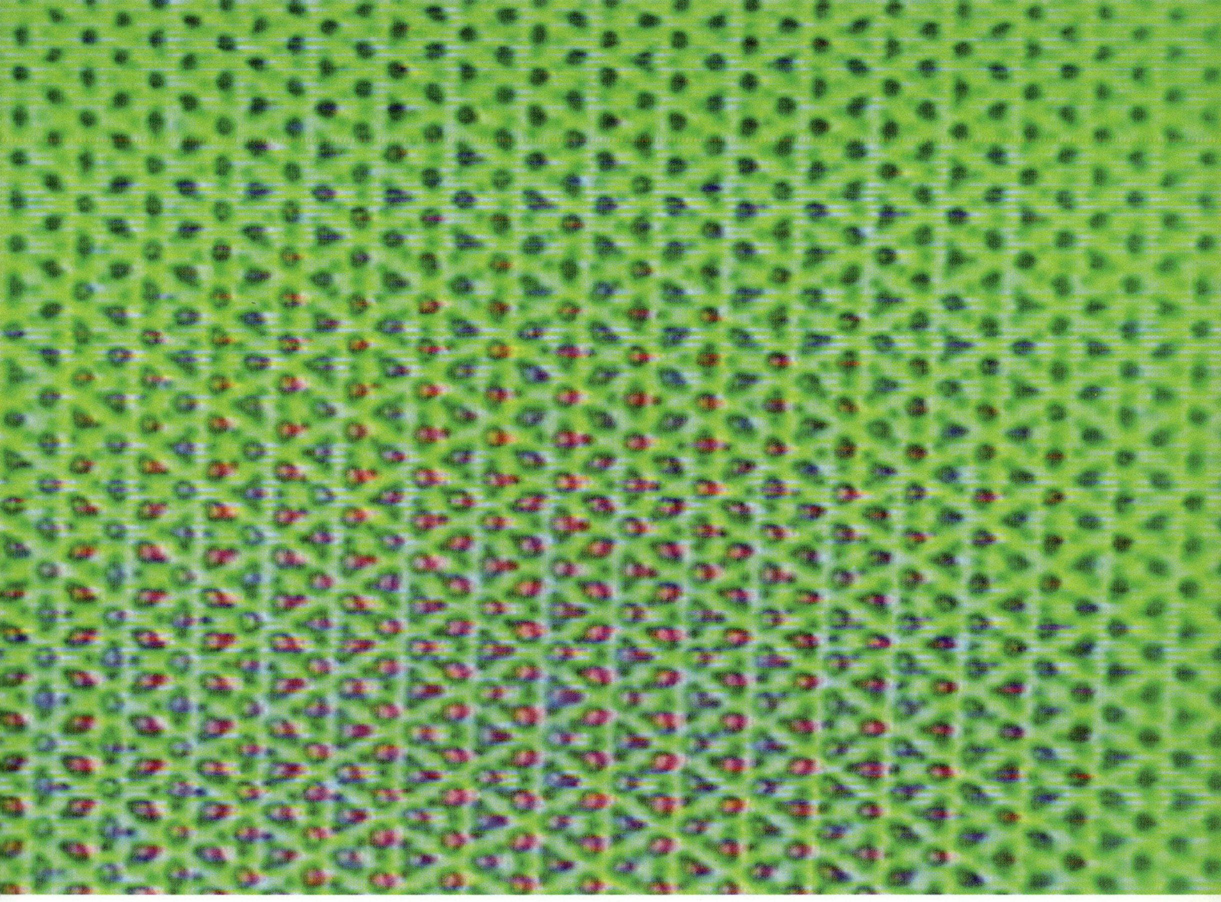

Livinus and Jeep van de Bundt, *Moirée*, 1975, video, colour, sound, 6'12"

but in the literature it led for the most part to introspection and the creation of ghettos, in which the same artists were always the centre of attention and everyone else was excluded.

The starting point for this chapter on the very earliest Dutch video art is provided by those works which were shown on video and which can still be seen today. This selection mainly involves those artists who are represented in the country's most important video collections, and whose works, thanks to preservation, will still be available for viewing in years to come, but who are hardly discussed in the context of video.[5]

The collection belonging to the former Lijnbaancentrum plays an important role here, because of the way it threw open its doors to a highly pluriform use of video and so was willing to provide a home for the very earliest Dutch videos, without worrying too much about their medium-specific character. Video art had no need to wait for the arrival of the Portapak camera.[6] Even without a camera, artists were already using television sets and 16 and 8 mm film in their work.

[5]
Inclusion in a collection gives a greater chance of survival, because people there have the means to replace old video tapes on which the work is recorded with new ones. Works dating from the early 1970s which failed to find a their way into collections can no longer be viewed, either because the signals have deteriorated through age or because suitable players are no longer available.

[6]
Burris 1996. Available online at www.mfj-online.org/journalpages/MFJ29/Jburrisportapack5319.html

Video went well with their method of working and so was
applied as one means amongst many, without anyone thinking
too much about working with a new medium. Many of the artists
discussed here were only concerned with the medium for a
short time and were not really 'converts'.[7] This essay is an
attempt to show, by reference to the first Dutch video users, the
straightforward place that video came to occupy in the 1970s,
as one new method amongst the many other art-making
methods and processes, like film, television and performances.
This has a striking resemblance to contemporary artistic
practice, where, because the equipment is within reach of
everyone, video no longer needs to treat itself as special.
The present chapter chronicles the early history of the medium,
but can also be read as an ode to the medium. Video is an
unknown quantity.

Electronic painting
In the very early days, before the Portapak set going the
production of independent videos, the main thing that attracted
artists' attention was the equipment, the first Dutch artist
deserving mention in this connection being Livinus van de
Bundt.[8] From the mid 1950s Livinus van de Bundt (generally
known simply as Livinus) carried out experiments with a type of
photography, invented by himself, which used a glass fibre rod
to point light in the desired direction, allowing him to work
directly on light-sensitive material. This he called 'painting with
light', in which the rod replaced the paintbrush. The resulting
works, which became known as *fotopeintures*, were unique
images, a direct reproduction of the artist's movements on
transparent sheets, which could be stretched over light boxes
for display purposes. The discovery of this way of working with
light changed his life because they allowed him to apply the
achievements of science and technology to the field of art. In
the years which followed, Livinus used light to experiment in
many fields: light was used as a 'live medium', became an
architectural component (he ascribed a curative effect to light in
the context of the modern city) and was applied in various light
machines. He experimented with series of transparencies with
moving abstract figures, and built steel cases (*chronopeintures*)
in which he created a colourful illuminated display, as in a
kaleidoscope. Technology played an increasingly important role
in his experiments. In 1958 he produced a projector which used
an adapted slide projector, combined with a turntable to make it
possible to read images. The necessary electronics he
developed himself. The projector was later expanded into the
Lumodynamic machine, which allowed the composition

[7]
Reedijk 1984.
[8]
'The ultimate pictorial art of Livinus (1909–1979), the grandfather of Dutch video, put him far ahead
of his time.' In: Delft 1988. And: 'Paint with light, paint with light, roared the grey-bearded old man
like an impressive prophet. Livinus had actually replaced canvas with the television screen.' In:
Luijters 1997, p. 1; Rajandream 1986 provided the basis for this piece on the work of Livinus. Also
published in abbreviated form as 'Livinus en het licht', *Mediamatic*, December 1985.

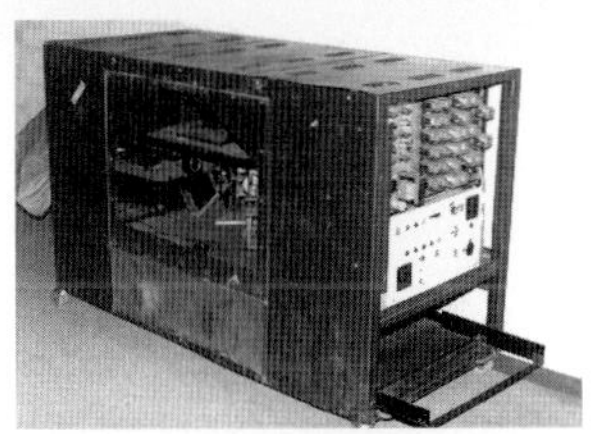

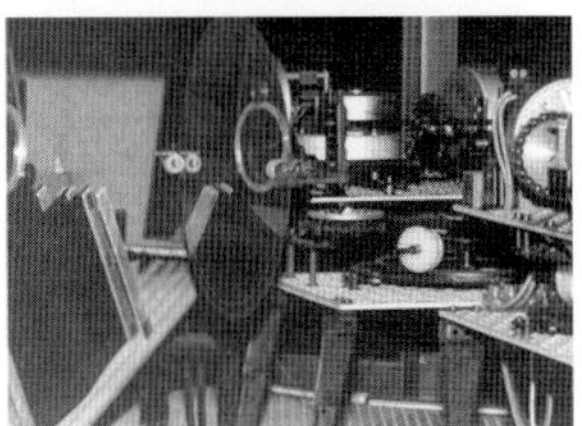

Livinus, Lumodynamic machine, 1958

displayed on the screen to be changed by pushing various buttons. Speaking about this work Livinus said: 'I use a keyboard on a projection unit that I designed myself to improvise my chronopeintures like moments in time.'[9]

When Livinus came into contact with Nam June Paik and Karl Heinz Stockhausen at the end of the 1960s he discovered the possibilities that the medium of video could provide for perfecting the well trodden road leading to the integration of sound and image. His first opportunity to work with video came in 1970 when, accompanied by his son Jeep, he went off to Vancouver to experiment at Intermedia, an artists' collective that had video equipment available. The first thing he had to do was, in his own words, to get to know the equipment inside out.[10] His efforts from 1972 onwards resulted in a handful of video tapes, mostly prepared in cooperation with Jeep. These were abstract works, with a large number of images which, like his *fotopeintures*, were created without a camera. Here too Livinus turned out to be an artist who worked in the modernistic idiom. The fact that Livinus was using equipment for the purpose whose wide ranging reproducibility was to halt once and for all the modernists' pursuit of essence, did not mean that his experiments were about anything other than such an essence. His emphasis on the artist's movements, on abstract formal vocabulary without reference to any recognizable representation and his attempt to get to know the new medium inside out, showed that his work was much more closely related to the modernistic painting of the 1950s and 1960s and with the experimental cinema than with the bulk of the video works produced in the 1970s.

Livinus' method of working is reminiscent of that of Nam June Paik, the pioneer and self-crowned king of video art. No one disputes Paik's pioneering role in video art, but his work to some extent displays the same limitations with respect to the medium as Livinus' work. Paik's work was characterized by a greater emphasis on form than on content, though tradition has it that on 4 October 1965 he became the first user of the Portapak when he recorded the visit of the Pope to New York from a moving taxi, then showed the tape that same evening in Café A Go Go, a meeting place for performance artists.[11]

As someone coming from the field of electronic music, Paik's original concern was mainly with enlarging the possibilities of sound. In the first exhibition at which he used manipulated television sets, the frequently cited *Exposition of Music – Electronic Television* in Galerie Parnass in Wuppertal in 1963, the emphasis was on acoustic equipment; TV sets formed only

21

[9] Rajandream 1986, p. 19.

[10] Rajandream 1986, p. 25.

[11] For the mythical history of the first tape, see: Ross 1976/1977, pp. 109-110. Paik always played the prototypical role of the avant-garde artist who task was to be far ahead of the rest; see Rossler 1990. Paik himself was happy to reinforce this image. In an interview in 1984 he said that if you want to be number one, the best thing is to choose something that no one else is doing. That is why in 1961 he decided to try video art, a field in which nobody else was active at the time. Documentary by Stefan Decostere, produced for the BRT in 1984.

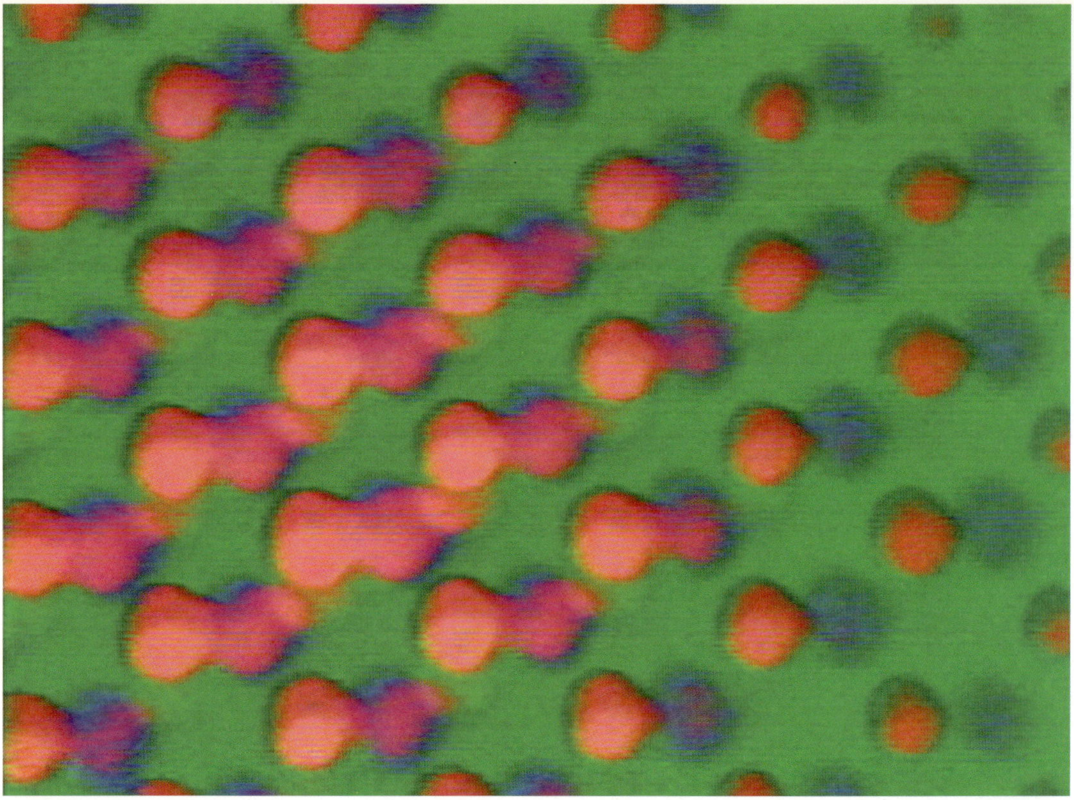

Livinus, *Fifty out of Two*, 1973–1978, video, colour, sound, 7'30"

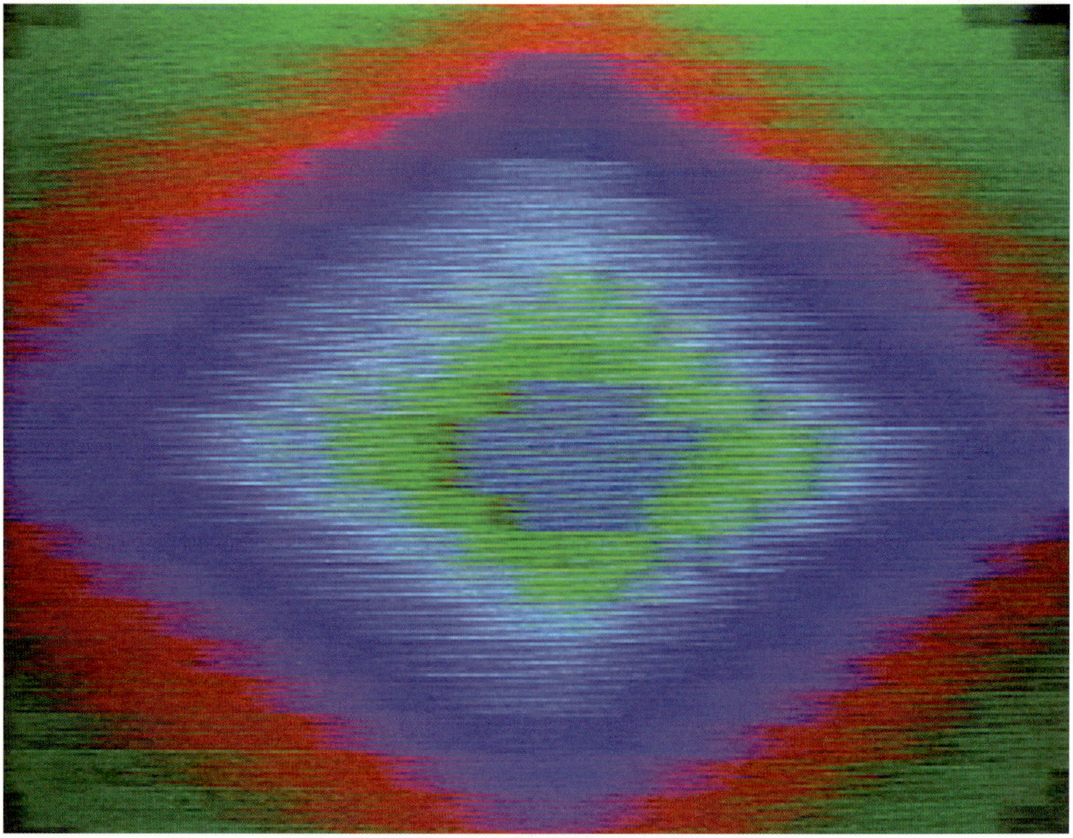

Livinus, *Percussion a till e*, 1973–1978, video, colour, sound, 31'50"

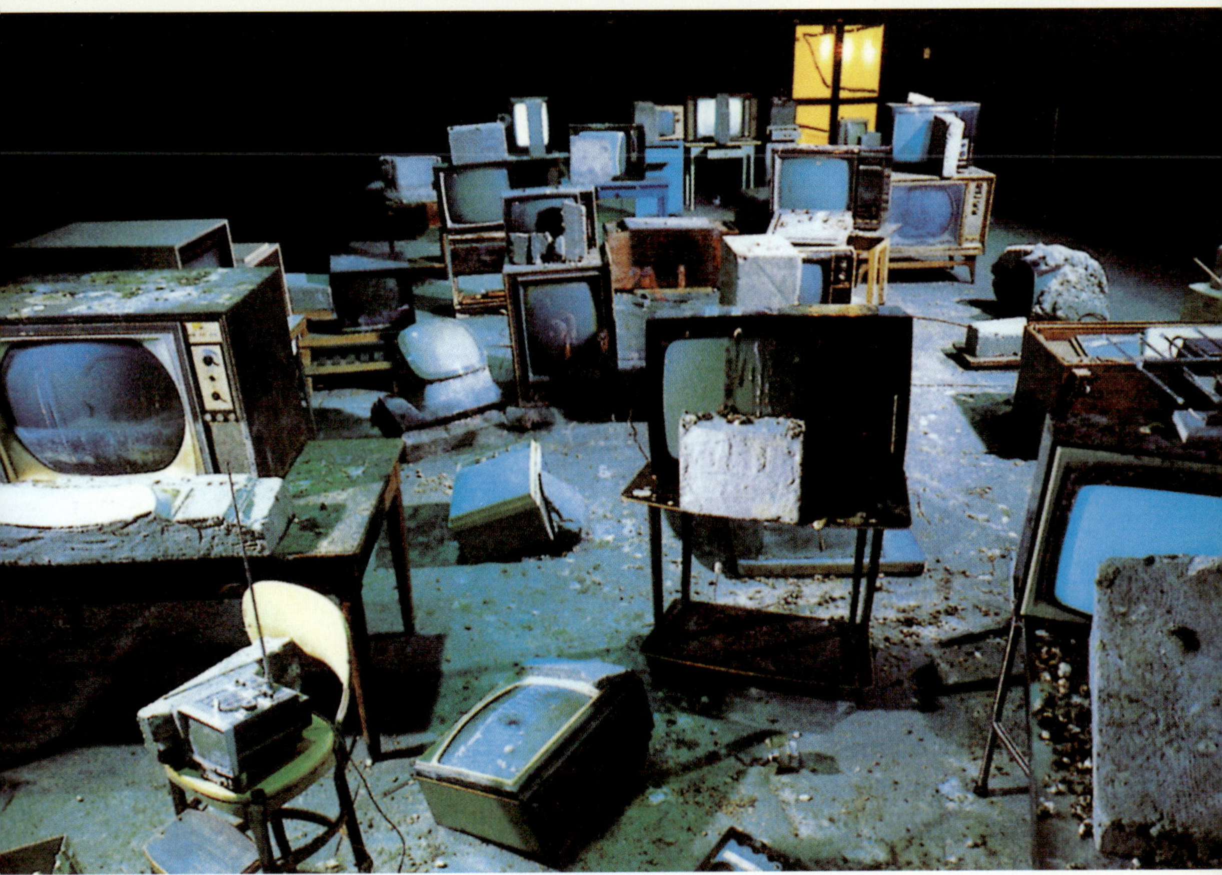

Wolf Vostell, *Endogene Depression II*, 1980, video installation at the 'Elektra' exhibition, Musée d'Art moderne de la Ville de Paris, 1983

a minor element. And, like Livinus's sets, Paik's sets too produced abstract images.[12] However, two of the twelve sets deviated from this pattern, and if we look at this more closely it becomes apparent that Paik's work always involved an analysis of the equipment as a whole, rather than being exclusively focused on the graphic possibilities of an electronic signal. One set lay with its screen facing the ground, its plug disconnected. This simple operation made clear how much TV depends on external input: if the flow of energy is interrupted, the flow of images stops and the equipment becomes a sad dead thing with nothing left to offer.[13]

In the second case a television set was stood on its side, with the signal distorted to produce a bright white strip dividing a black screen vertically into two sections. Here Paik indicated much more emphatically than with the other sets at the exhibition the particular perception of time associated with TV. The work extends through time, continuing to send out a signal as long as the set is plugged in, generating a certain sense of anticipation in the viewer, who watches and waits to see if

23

[12]
Decker-Phillips 1998, pp. 36-40.
[13]
When Paik again displayed this equipment in the 1970s, he again carried out the complete exercise in the ready-made tradition. This time it was given the title *Rembrandt-TV*, because this type of equipment was called Rembrandt. In fact the title considerably increased the number of possible meanings of the work.

something will happen. The stripe in the middle acts like a
curtain, which can open at any moment to allow the
performance or the programme to begin. But in fact nothing
begins, not even an abstract graphic pattern. In this way Paik
could be said to have let the working of television be seen
clearly for the very first time. His concern with the specific way
in which the medium works became apparent when in an
interview he compared it with film. In Paik's view, film involves an
image and a specific place, but television involves neither.
TV consists exclusively of electronic lines which are essentially
linked with time.[14]

Acts with equipment

Paik was certainly not alone in the way he manipulated his
equipment. TV's conquest of the living room encouraged many
artists to take out their distaste for middle-class society
symbolically on the new mass medium.[15] TV had to face up to
this kind of behaviour particularly from members of Happening
and Fluxus. The work of the German artist Wolf Vostell, who had
links with both Happening and Fluxus, makes clear what it was
all about. 'A genuine Happening is a not a form of exhibitionism
but an expression and sensitization of experiences with an
absurd reality', he wrote.[16] Art needs to make people aware of
the absurdity of daily life. The consumption-oriented, zombie-
like way in which people generally move through life, should be
broken down and replaced by 'genuine' experience.
This emphasis on genuine experience was precisely why
television was never the favourite medium of the artists
belonging to these groups. In this same context, from the end of
the 1950s onwards Vostell put on with some regularity
tv-dé-collages, short performances in which a TV image was
interfered with in front of an audience. These performances
invariably ended by blowing up, shooting to bits or otherwise
sacrificing the hated TV set. The basic thinking which underlay
these acts was not a longing for the pre-technological era, but
an attempt to make the public aware of the manipulative effect
of the medium, and to show that it can be used to suit one's
own ends. In the case of Vostell this ambition led him in the mid
1960s to create laboratory-like installations in which the visitor,
as he should be called, could operate interactively.[17]

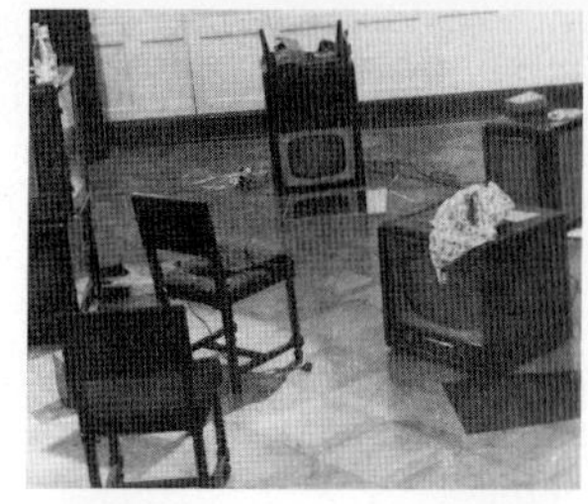

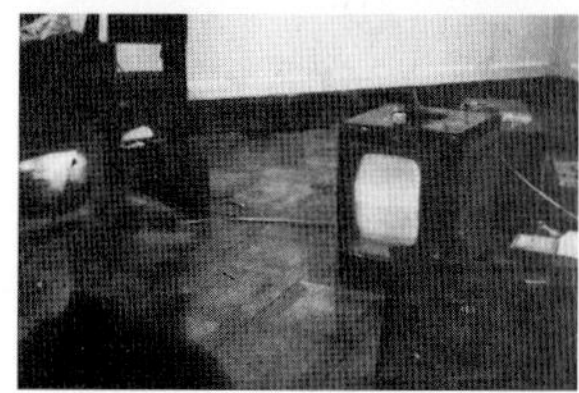

Nam June Paik, exhibition
Wuppertal, 1963

24

[14]
Cassagnac/Fargier/Van den Stegen 1979, pp. 10-15. This work too was later produced again and
given the title: *Zen for TV*. The fact that the two works treated here came about by accident – in fact
the two sets were broken on their way to Galerie Parnass – bears witness to Paik's talent for
improvization. See also: Boomgaard 2000.
[15]
See also: Van Berkum 1988, p. 115.
[16]
Vostell 1973, p. 53.
[17]
Berghaus 1995, p. 326. The struggle to be seen as the prime mover formed part of the mythology of
the early days. Thus Vostell long maintained that his very first television works dated from before
1963. However further research showed that he was not ahead of Paik, but followed the course of
the development immediately behind him. For further details, see: Decker-Phillips 1998, pp. 41-53.

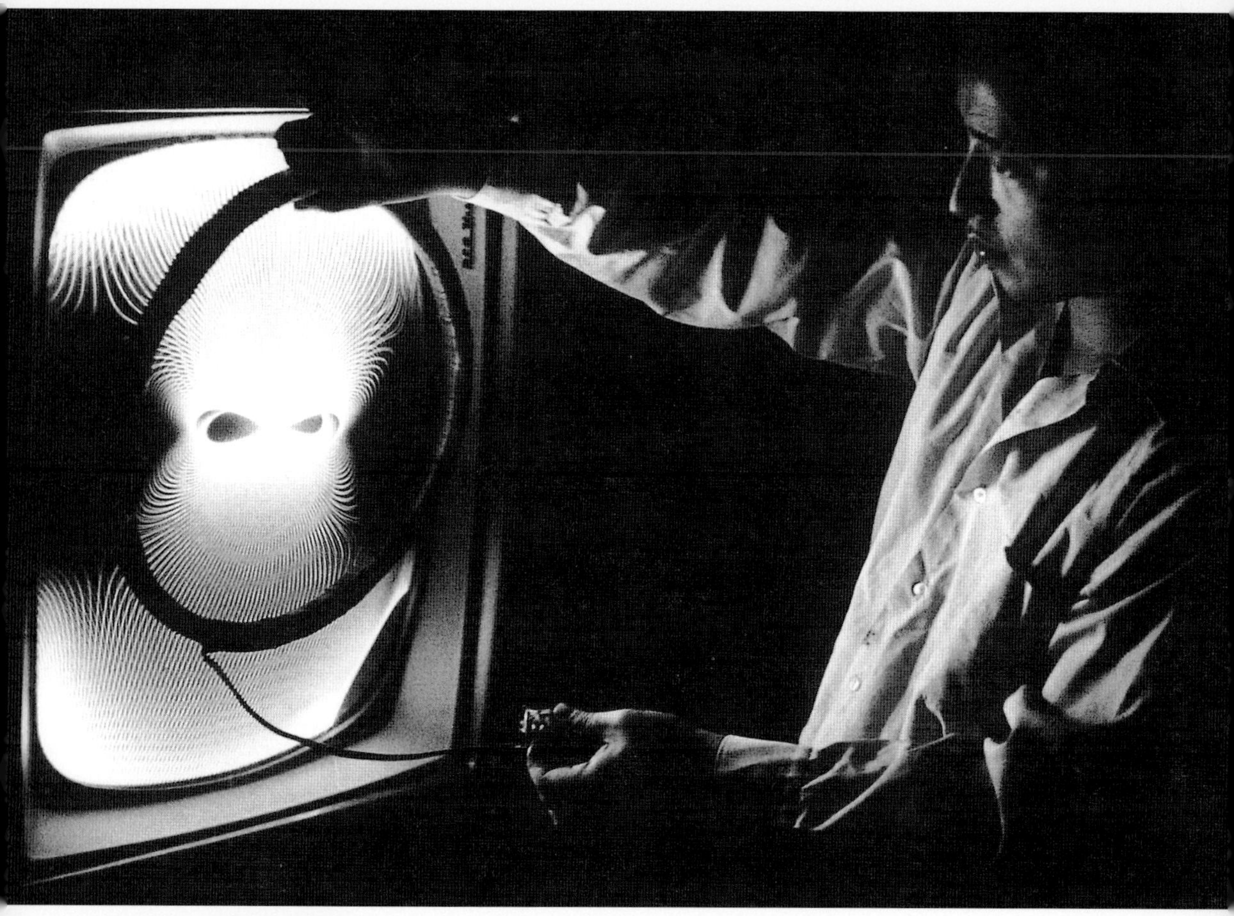

Nam June Paik, with *Demagnitizer (Life Ring)* in his Canal Street studio, New York, 15 October 1965

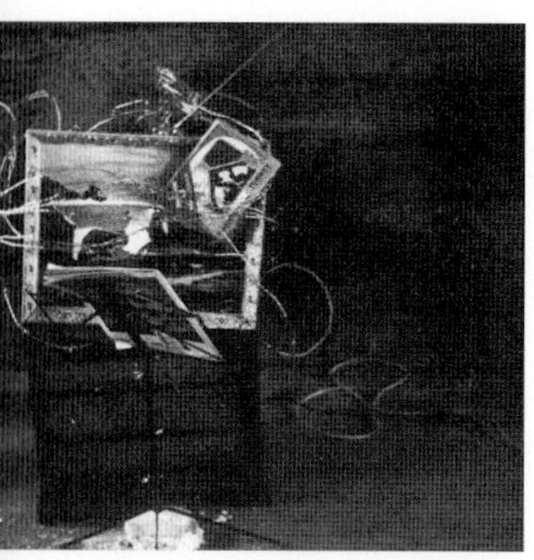

Wolf Vostell, *TV Burial*, assemblage realized during the YAM Festival, New Brunswick, 19 May 1963

This frequently violent method of settling accounts with the TV set seems to have largely passed the Netherlands by. Seems is the right word, since it is entirely possible that experiments in this direction were not preserved and so were hardly handed down. In the early days many artists became involved with the medium almost incidentally, producing small practice exercises, often with splendid results still worthy of a place in history. But there also turn out to be artists none of whose video work are to be found in any collection. One reason for this is that installations composed using the television equipment itself were less easy to keep than tapes. Not for nothing did Paik produce his TV sets again, a decade later. In the Netherlands the same thing could be said of JCJ van der Heijden, who was also briefly involved with the medium of video and who influenced the development in the Netherlands of art produced with video, more particularly during his appointment as visiting lecturer to the Jan van Eyck Academy in Maastricht.

JCJ van der Heijden is mainly known as a painter, more specifically as a painter who problematized painting, exhibition and even what it means to be an artist. His work with video was limited to a few experiments, whose value can only be judged as part of his work as a whole. In 1978 Locher wrote of the way Van der Heijden worked in the 1960s: 'What it was about was

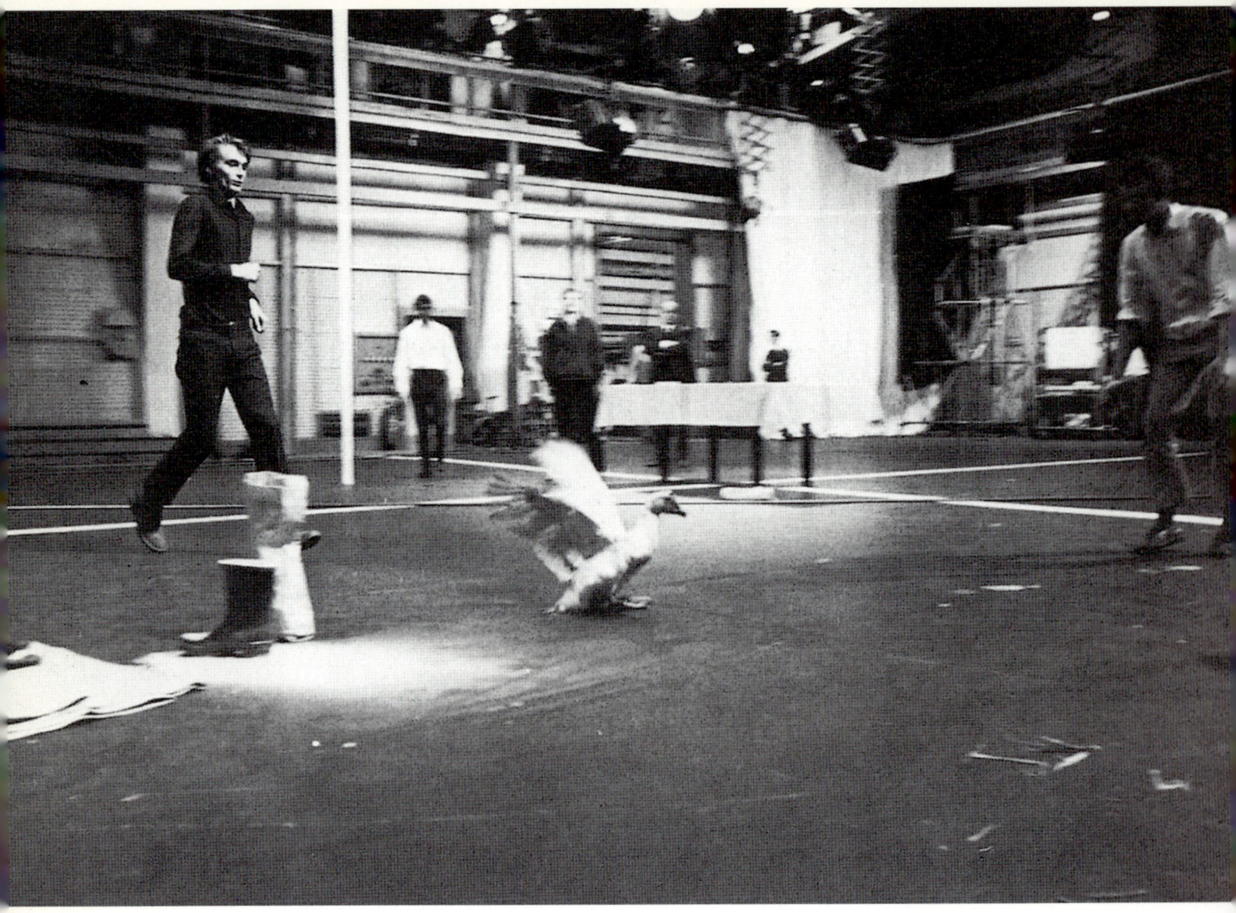

Studio recording of *Die Fundamente de la Tour Babel*, JCJ van der Heijden, H. van de Rijdt, R. Menken, 1970

26   the adventure of making himself open, in his immediate environment, to every kind of possibility to be found within himself.'[18]

During a short period in which he gave up painting, Van der Heijden produced a number of experimental works with TV sets. For example, one dull day in 1971 he put a television set out in the garden, its screen facing the sky, so that raindrops could fall on the broadcast weather bulletin. This poetic operation also served to point out the way in which television distances the viewer from a genuine experience of the weather. Another example involved an experimental arrangement of four television sets in his studio. The thing that really fascinated Van der Heijden was the diversity and multiplicity of images provided by this arrangement. 'For me the most important thing was the way the images converged. For example, every now and then it could happen that the horizons on two neighbouring television images coincided, creating a single new image [...] In such a situation I would always tell people who had no idea what they ought to be looking at, to look at the middle of the cross. Sometimes they had no idea how to deal with a multiplicity of images.'[19]

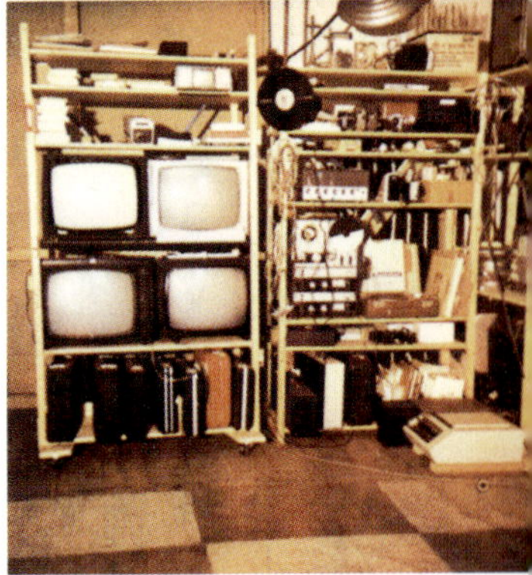

JCJ van der Heijden, arrangement of four televisions in atelier, 1971

[18]
The Hague/Eindhoven 1977/1978, p. 25.
[19]
Conversation with JCJ van der Heijden, 17 July 2002.

In the closed world of the artist's own studio the power of television to force its images into the room is reinforced and emphasized. These works correspond with research the artist carried out into lenses and windows. Van der Heijden was fascinated by the way lenses and windows provide a fundamentally different experience of space. In parallel and allied to this, he became absorbed in the operation of the eye, the camera obscura, the still camera and the movie camera. The use of video made no significant change to his method of working but rather provided a new application for that method.

Van der Heijden also came in touch with television through electronic music. In 1969, looking for inspiration, he attended a course at the 'studio for electronic music' where, with Peter Struycken, he became acquainted with computer technology. The course had a sequel in Cologne, where under the direction of the composer Mauricio Kagel he and his artist friends H. van de Rijdt and R. Menken were given the opportunity to make a television production in which the central features were experimental montage and the relationship between sound and image. The resulting work was in fact seen by the outside world when it was broadcast by the German station WDR 3 as *Die Fundamente de la Tour Babel*, on 30 August 1970, the same year in which Gerry Schum amazed the world with his *Identifications*.

The time of reality

When in 1970 Van der Heijden was asked to become visiting lecturer at the new Mixed Media department of the Jan van Eyck Academy – 'Because there were awkward students around who didn't want to paint' – he immediately arranged for the purchase of video equipment.[20] With the first group of students many experiments were carried out in a separate room. Hardly any of this work has been retained, because the tapes, which were in limited supply, were constantly being reused, and because people were more interested in dealing with the medium live. The result was the first workplace where video was used exclusively to create art.[21] All the equipment was of course stolen and the experiments performed by the video class were followed by the academy with Argus eyes, but in spite of that the second year brought a new set of students who were no longer fixated exclusively on the technical possibilities of the equipment, but used it for their own purposes. Artists who worked there went on to specialize in video art and share in determining the shape of future developments.

In those years the academies not only of Maastricht but also of The Hague and Enschede began to come up with the first definitions of what later came to be known as video art.

20
Conversation with JCJ van der Heijden, 17 July 2002.
21
It was not long afterwards that the Vrije Academie in The Hague, an interdisciplinary workshop which Livinus set up in the 1950s but left in 1968, made video equipment available to participants.

However understandable these attempts at definition may have been, defining video art turned out to be quite difficult and many attempts did less than justice to the way in which the medium was used. Video, or really its parent, television, is a medium that does not allow easy definition. Its most important characteristic seems to be heterogeneity. Despite the attempts of Paik and, to some extent, Van de Bundt, its origins in radio, the way it followed in the footsteps of electronic music, its fascinating ability to show life as it really is, the way it is used to provide a miscellany of information and straightforward entertainment, all made the medium unsuitable for any kind of modernistic self-analysis. TV was an entertaining mass medium that seemed hardly to have a specific language of its own. The thing that was to concern artists the most was its ability to show everyday reality and to bring people closer to life as it really is. This expressed itself in two distinct but inseparable ways, always present in experiments and contradicting every later distinction or definition.

The possibility of recording reality encouraged students at the various academies who were able to get their hands on the necessary equipment to record artistic activities. This sub-ordinate position, which turned out to be important mainly in connection with the rise of performance art, is dealt with at length later in this book. Here however we are concerned with works in which the recording of reality is presented as an art in itself. Of course the possibility of direct recording had long existed in photography and film, but video seemed capable of providing something which the other two media lacked. Video was able not only to achieve real-time reproduction, eliminating any delay between recording and playback (a feature that was to play a major role in video performances), but also to show the actual time. Or, as Van der Heijden expressed it: 'If you record something and play it back immediately, what you are really doing is investigating the element of time, breaching its hegemony, its condition.'[22] This possibility makes the medium extraordinarily suitable for carrying out real life experiments, of the kind set up by Fluxus and Happening.

Fluxus, the loose association within which Paik too presented his work, shared with television not only the vaudeville character which maintains a balance between amateurism and slapstick, but also subjected its audience during its Fluxus evenings to a temporal experience which could in no way be compared with the structured time of a concert or a normal stage or film performance. The plays, sound poems or musical pieces presented at such evenings were either extremely short (over before anyone had realized that they had started), or awfully long (in some cases because even the participants had no idea in advance how and more particularly when the work would finish). The preference for genuine unmanipulated time reached its

28

22
Conversation with JCJ van der Heijden, 17 July 2002.

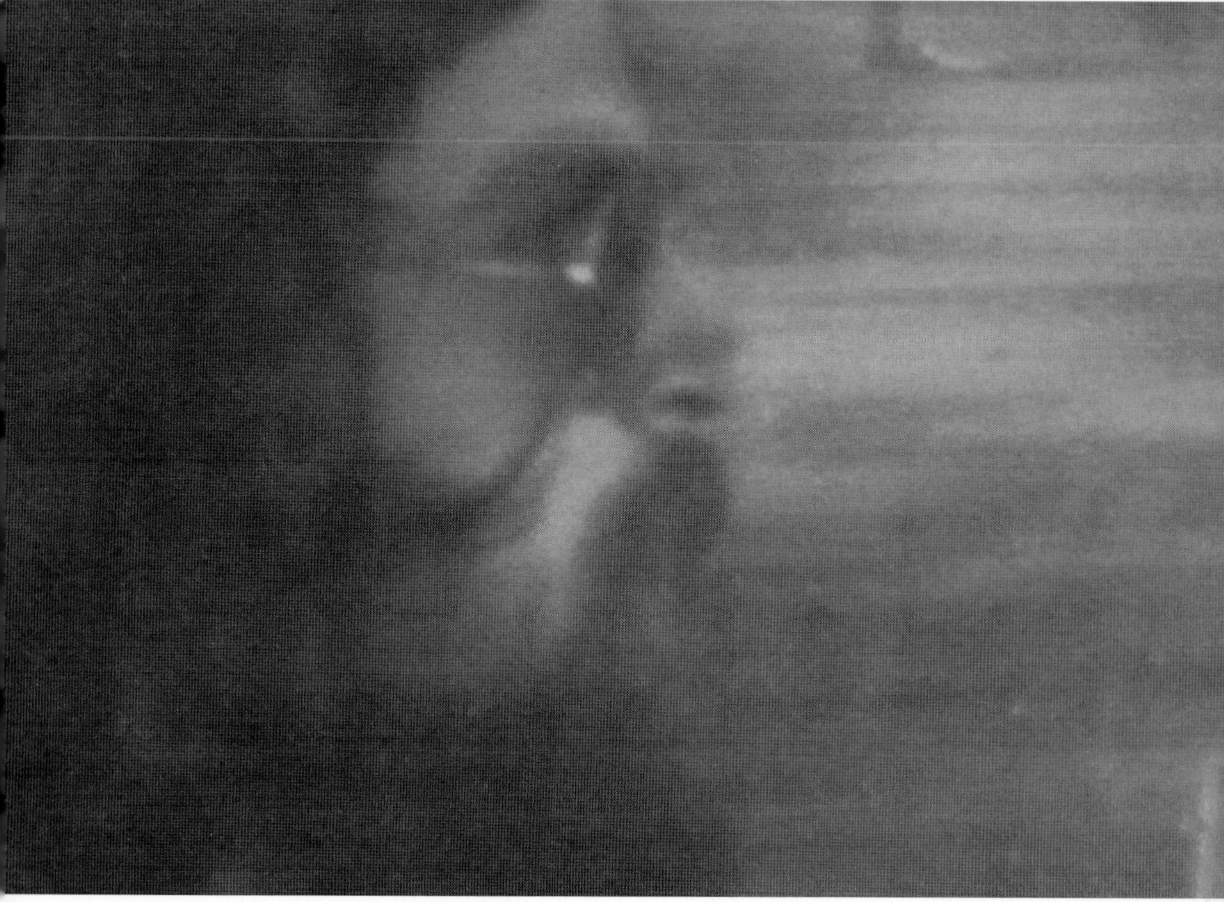

Raul Marroquin, *The Driver*, 1974, video, b/w, sound, 5'00"

climax in John Cage's work *4'33"* (1960), a musical piece which involved the pianist closing the lid of a grand piano and then looking straight ahead, in absolute silence, for 4 minutes and 33 seconds.[23]

On a pictorial level the effect of this preference for true unmanipulated time could be observed in the early films of Andy Warhol, who in works like *Sleep* (1963), *Kiss* (1963), *Eat* (1963) and *Empire* (1964) made time visible by the unedited recording of slow events. But equally strong, particularly amongst the members of Fluxus, was the almost televisual emphasis on the insignificant gesture, the small everyday action, which when singled out and magnified suddenly becomes an event. These trends and intentions combined in the videotapes made by Raul Marroquin, a Colombian artist who in 1971 was given a bursary to study at the Jan van Eyck.

The Driver and *The Listener*, both dating from 1974, share the same treatment. The viewer sees a recording of someone carrying out a not particularly spectacular operation (e.g. driving a car or listening to the radio) unedited, in black and white, with the sound of a real radio as accompaniment. For Marroquin this way of allowing the unimpeded influx of everyday reality was a

23
There is also an earlier version of the work, dating from 1952. It actually consisted of three parts.

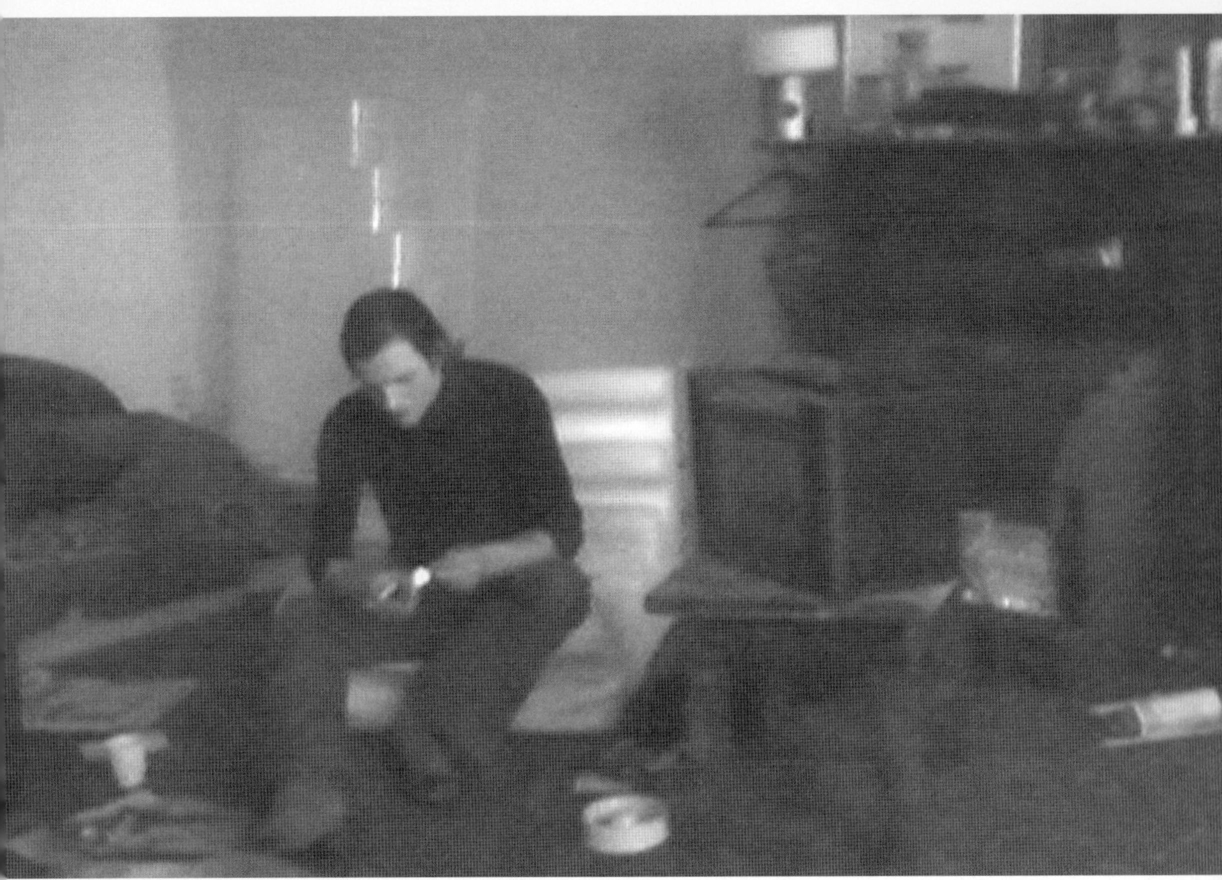

Raul Marroquin, *The Listener*, 1974, video, b/w, sound 5'00"

30   reaction to the way reality is manipulated by television.

At that time ideas about the medium of television were beginning to be influenced by the writings of Marshall McLuhan, the first media guru. His 'The Medium is the Message' (1964) in particular, was enthusiastically received. As is often the case with prophetic writings, the character of the reception owed nothing to the clarity of the statements included in the writing. On the contrary, McLuhan's way of piling metaphor on metaphor created such a mixture of keen insights and bizarre ideas that anyone could extract from it whatever he wanted. Although in the 1970s, under the influence of Jean Baudrillard, his central thesis, that the medium itself is the message, was interpreted as meaning only that it is impossible to transmit critical content, at the beginning of the 1970s the general view of the thesis was much more optimistic. When McLuhan used a quotation from Shakespeare to characterize the medium of TV, his meaning remained unclear. 'Some might quibble', he wrote, 'about whether or not he was referring to TV in these familiar lines from *Romeo and Juliet*: But soft! What light through yonder windows breaks? It speaks and yet says nothing.'[24]

24
'The Medium is the Message', in: McLuhan 2000 (1964), p. 9.

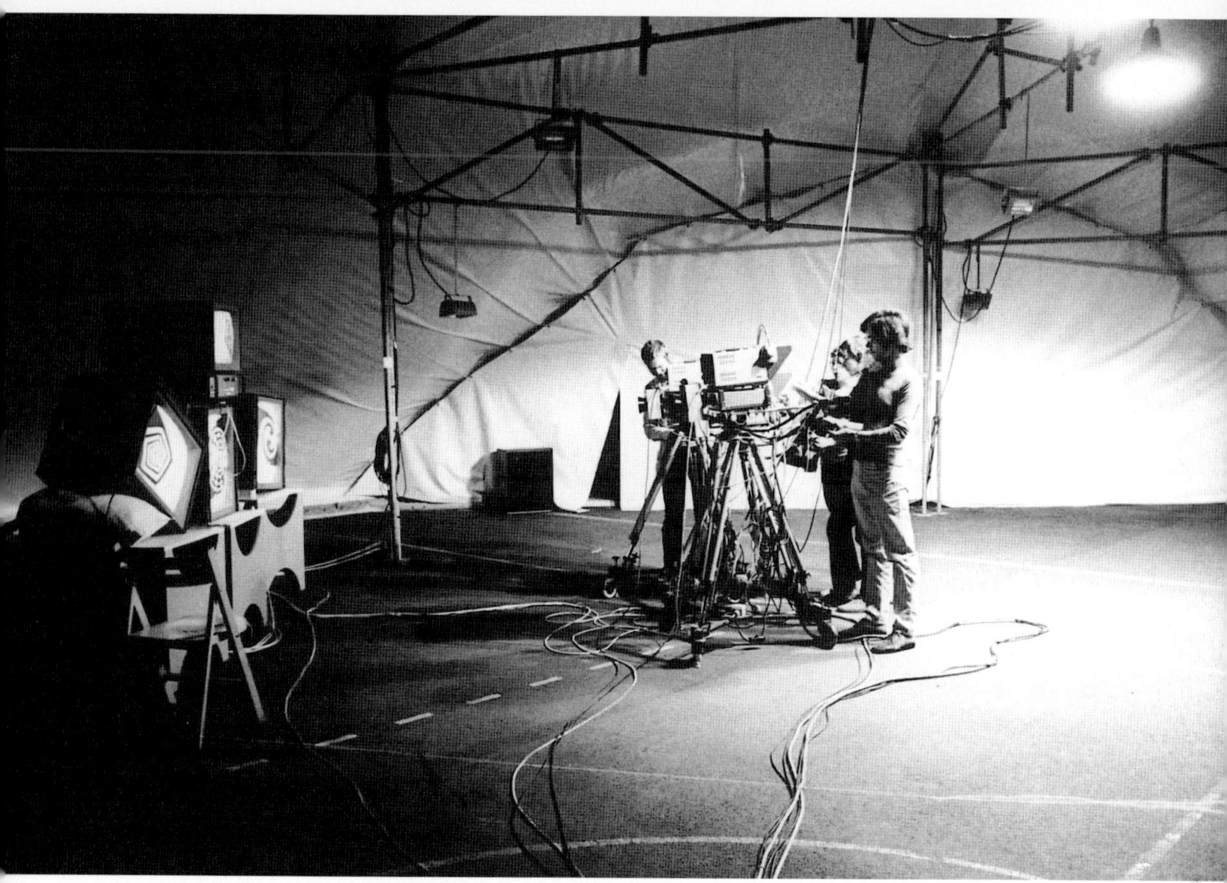

'Sonsbeek beyond the pale', video tent, Arnhem 1972

Whatever McLuhan may have meant, for many artists of the period the conclusion was that light had to be made to speak and that TV had still to find its true voice.

The improvement in TV envisaged by Marroquin implied the direct recording of life as it really is, in all its endlessness. Art should be every bit as exciting and every bit as dull as life itself. This basic principle had always encouraged video artists to use boredom as a stylistic device. The exasperating timing that makes much of the early video work so indigestible today, was the result of a deliberate decision to present an unmanipulated time stream, in radical contrast to the fragmented, speeded up time of film and television.[25] The decision made by this early video work to present an almost unmediated recording of reality was, without knowing it, in line with one of the most fascinating aspects of television and anticipated the way in which video would force its way so radically into daily life. For what gave television its great attraction was its power to record life and then let it be seen without visible intervention in a paradoxical combination of predictability and fortuity. What television transmits is not a succession of staged photographs, like a film, but a stream of images originating somewhere else and flowing

[25]
See also Haase 1983, p. 36. In this connection the author introduced the brilliant concept of the 'Rastlosigkeit der Langeweile'.

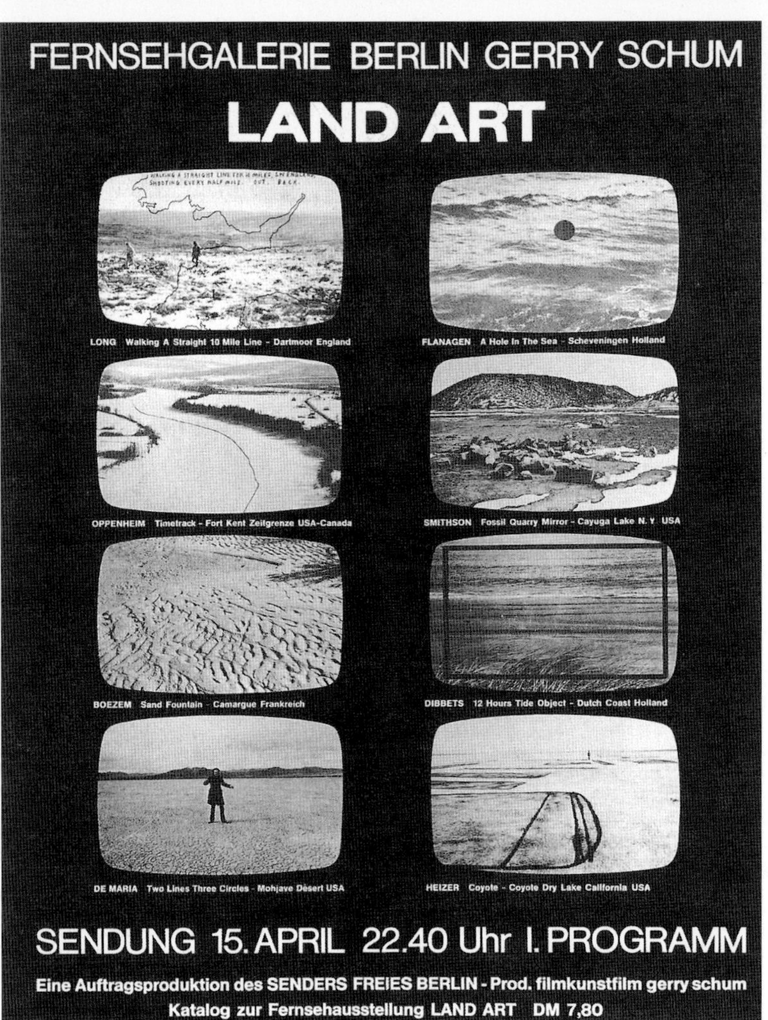

Fernsehgalerie Gerry Schum, announcement of the transmission of *Land Art*, 1969

unhindered to the viewer, via the television screen.[26] It allows the viewer to look at something continuously, even though hardly anything is happening and there is no visible reason to concentrate on that particular point. Television is the prototype of the surveillance camera, constantly keeping its eye on a particular spot. But this very watchfulness tells the viewer that something could happen, for surveillance would be pointless without the possibility of an offence being committed. Although these implications are present but hidden in works like those produced by Marroquin, they are not worked out in any detail. Moreover they lack precisely that feature which is always present in television: the stream they present may well show life but is not *live*.[27]

[26] Raymond Williams referred to this permanent signal, filled with a stream of images, as *'flow'*. See Williams 1990. See also Dienst 1994, p. 18.

[27] As far as is known, the surveillance character of the video/recording does not occur in Dutch art of the 1970s. It could however be seen in 1975 at an exhibition of the work of Dan Graham in the Stedelijk Van Abbemuseum in Eindhoven. For further details, see: Levin/Frohne/Weibel 2002.

The masses as a target

Video was given a powerful boost at the beginning of the 1970s by the exhibition 'Sonsbeek buiten de perken' [Sonsbeek beyond the pale]. This exhibition introduced Minimal and Land Art on a grand scale, but also included a programme of artists' films and videos. A tent set up in the grounds of Sonsbeek park contained a studio for carrying out experiments in the new medium. Although the effect of those experiments was relatively modest – the expense of the equipment and the lack of expert assistance impeded direct use by the public – it indicated that video was considered to form part of the great process of democratization that had yet to be set in motion.[28] This attempt not only spawned a stream of different initiatives, but also showed how in the beginning video art was not distinct in the strictest sense from documentary, social acts and interaction with the public generally.

Characteristic of the use of video in this period was the presence at Sonsbeek of Shinkichi Tajiri, an artist who used a large number of different media and employed a varied pictorial language. By the mid 1950s he had already made a number of 16 mm films, including the prize-winning *The Vipers*[29], which portrayed, in a rough documentary style, very associatively edited (in the camera), the smoking of marijuana. This was followed by *Bikers,* an ode to the use of the bicycle in the Netherlands. These films were in the tradition of the experimental film and showed signs of contact with Johan van der Keuken. Besides film Tajiri did a good deal of photographic work, but the main thing for which he has become known is his sculpture. Tajiri found video an intriguing new medium and was one of the first Dutch artists to own his own video camera. For him the documentary expressiveness of the medium was always more important than its artistic force, and not surprisingly his work at 'Sonsbeek 71' consisted mainly of recordings. The tapes however were not retained.

In 1972 he made *Berlin Wall*, a work on video in which once again the essential aim was to create a record. The basic idea was: 'To contain 43 kilometres of wall in coded form on approximately 200 meters of half inch magnetic video tape'.[30] The pilot of the helicopter was instructed to remain at a height of 200 meters, 200 meters to the west of the Wall. The quality of the recording material was extremely important. After all, what concerned him was the continuous track of signals on the magnetic tape, not a collation of still photographs (the process which produces film) which makes the work a good example of the *flow* mentioned above.

33

Shinkichi Tajiri, *The Vipers*, 1955, 10'16"

Shinkichi Tajiri, *Bikers*, 1960, 16 mm film, b/w, sound

Shinkichi Tajiri, *Berlin Wall*, 1972, video, b/w, sound, 21'00"

28
Boomgaard, Van Mechelen, Van Rijsingen 2001.
29
The film received the Golden Palm award at the Festival for Amateur Film in Cannes for 'Best Use of Film' in 1955.
30
Introductory text on the tape. This video work is often shown outside the country but rarely in the Netherlands.

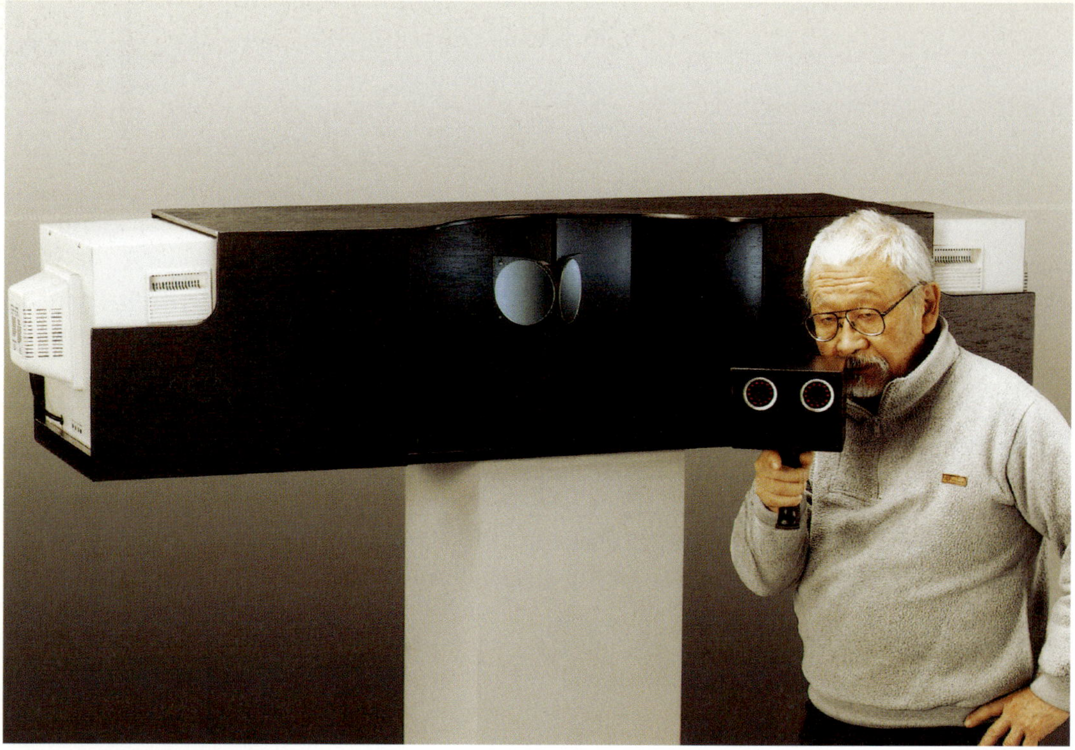

Shinkichi Tajiri, *Three Dimensional Video*, 1976, reconstruction 2003

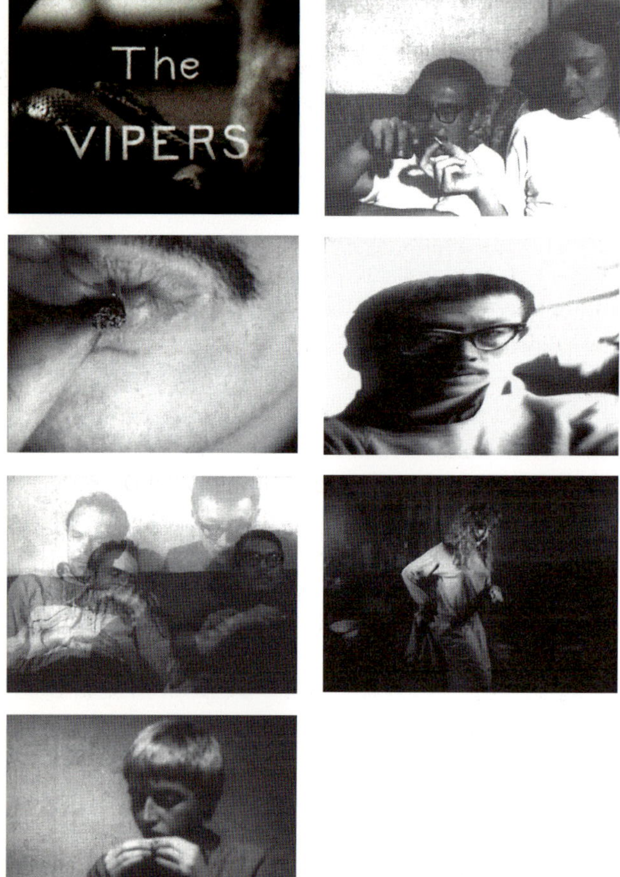

34

Shinkichi Tajiri, *The Vipers*, 1955, film, b/w, sound 10'16"

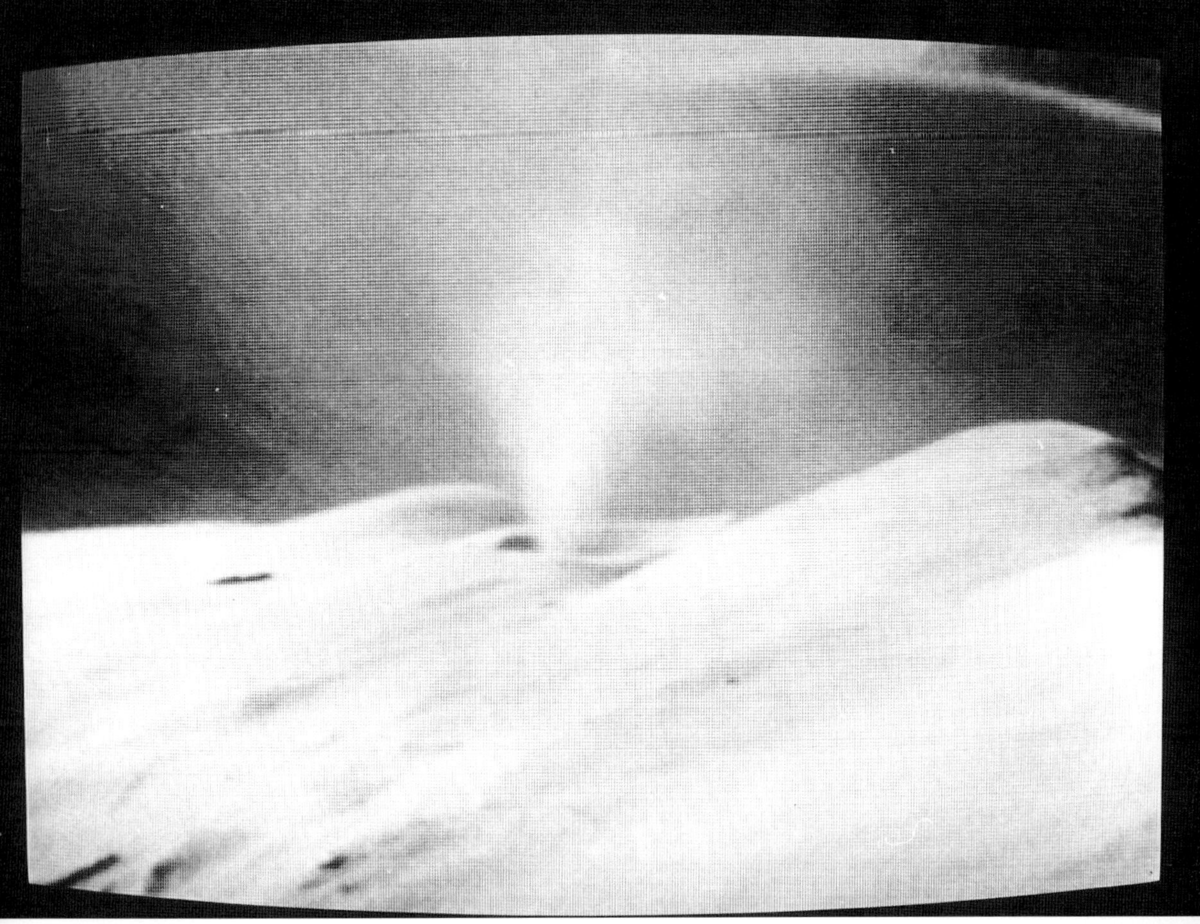

Marinus Boezem, *Sand Fountain*, 1969, TV and video, b/w, sound, 4'12"

Also shown at 'Sonsbeek 71' were films by the German artist Gerry Schum made with television in mind. For the two episodes *Land Art* (broadcast on 15 April 1969) and *Identifications* (broadcast on 30 November 1970), he asked a large number of artists from Europe and America, including from the Netherlands Jan Dibbets, Stanley Brouwn, Marinus Boezem and Ger van Elk, to come up with ideas which would subsequently be recorded by him. Only Van Elk had any previous experience with audiovisual media. For *Land Art* Boezem produced the work *Zandfontein* [Sand Fountain] and Dibbets *12 hours tide object with correction of perpective*. These were both conceptual works, in which camera movement was kept to a minimum to ensure that the process was portrayed as objectively as possible. For the second broadcast Van Elk produced the short work *The Well-Shaven Cactus* and Stanley Brouwn *Een stap* [A step]. From later interviews it emerged that it had been Schum's ideas on television and art that had persuaded the artists to contribute. So for example for Boezem the reason for participating was the chance to display his work in a new setting.[31] All the works in the *Identifications* series could be described as documentary, mainly exploiting the

Stanley Brouwn, *A step,* film for tv, b/w, sound, 10'00"

31
'Statements, vragen en antwoorden', Amsterdam 1979, p. 17.

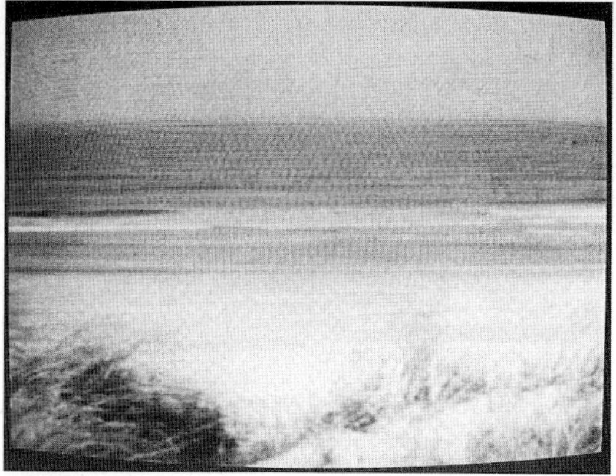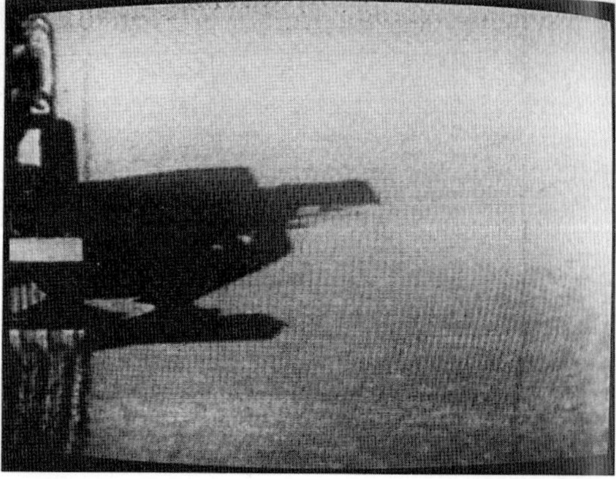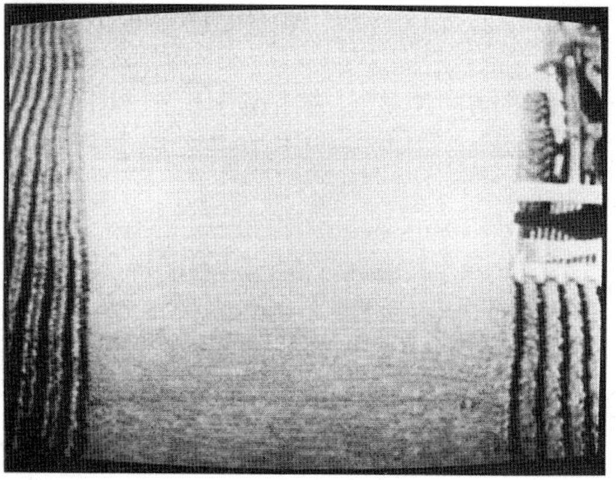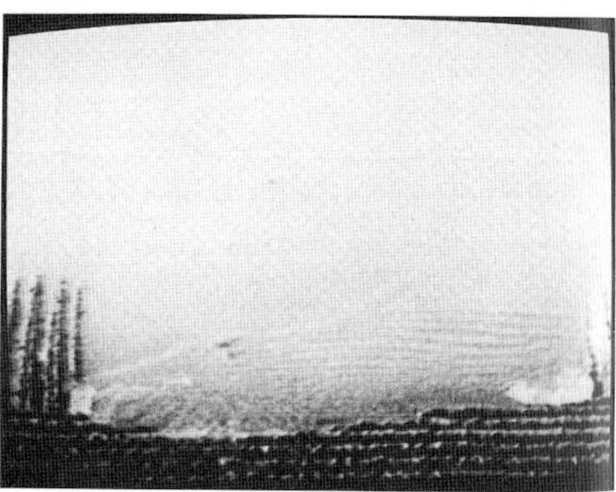

Jan Dibbets, *12 hours tide object with correction of perpective*, 1969, film for TV, b/w, sound, 7'33"

intangible character of television. The work was only made to be recorded and only existed by the grace of broadcasting. Nothing remains of it.[32] Yet the individual character of the televisual recording in these works is much less obtrusive than for example in the tapes by Raul Marroquin mentioned above. An idea was portrayed, but the length of the performance appeared to be determined by the length of the reel.

Not surprisingly the main aim of the broadcast was to bring art to the attention of the general public. Reflections on the medium of television were completely absent. It was a completely different story with the separate work that Schum produced in cooperation with Dibbets. *TV as a Fire Place*, a 24 minute recording of a crackling open fire, three minutes of which were transmitted daily between 25 and 31 December at the end of the WDR's official programme, was a typical piece of television art which not only used the medium as its mouthpiece, but was also about television itself. What it showed was that the TV had displaced the fireplace as the centrepiece

Jan Dibbets, *TV as a Fire Place*, 1969, film for tv, b/w, sound, 8 x 3'00"

[32] A reminder of the broadcast can of course be preserved as a videotape, but its significance is fundamentally different when viewed outside the context of the television broadcast. In: Amsterdam 1979, pp. 17–19.

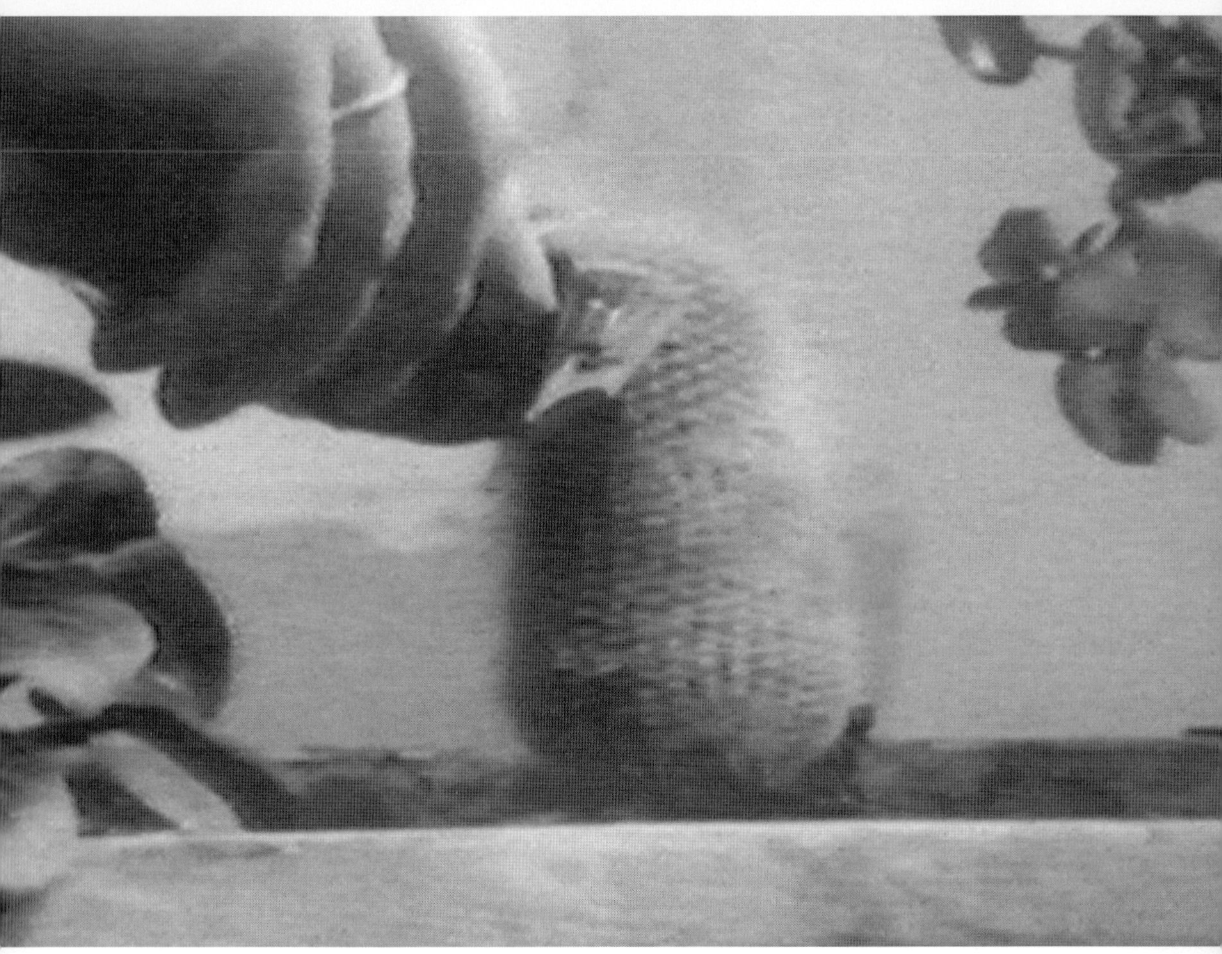

Ger van Elk, *The Well-Shaven Cactus*, 1970, film for TV, b/w, sound, 1'25"

Marinus Boezem, *Breathing up on the Tube*, 1971, 16 mm film for tv, colour, sound, 3'00"

Jan Dibbets, *Paintings 1 & 2*, 1970, film transferred on to videotape, colour, no sound, 4'20"

Jan Dibbets, *4 diagonals*, 1971, film transferred on to videotape, b/w, no sound, 2'00"

of the living room, but at the same time it went along with the dismissive attitude with which many artists from the early days of video viewed the mass medium.[33]

Dutch television followed Schum's example by producing *Beeldend kunstenaars maken televisie* [Graphic artists make television], directed by Frans Haks. In three broadcasts in 1971, Boezem, Brouwn, Dibbets and Van Elk were again given the opportunity to display their art on television. After the broadcast Boezem's contribution in particular, *Het beademen van een beeldbuis* [Breathing upon the Tube], became a permanent feature of Dutch video history.[34] In it Boezem, looking impassively into the camera, is shown blowing on the glass in front of (or forming part of) the camera, after which the artist, and with him the viewer, have to wait for the condensation to disappear so that his intent gaze can be seen again. This performance not only demonstrates the tangibility of air, but

[33]
Followed in 1970 by the work *Paintings 1 & 2* (shot on film, but published as a video in an issue of four copies) and in 1971 by the work *4 diagonalen*, that elaborated on the perspective correction in *Land Art*. After this video work Dibbets did nothing more with television or video.
[34]
The artificial respiration of the television screen was included in a collection published by Time Based Arts, later Netherlands Media Art Institute, Montevideo/Time Based Arts.

makes television seem less intangible and transparent than is often suggested.[35]

The fifth artist invited to contribute was Peter Struycken. This was his first black and white film to record moving abstract compositions. Since 1968 his main interest had been 'making non-figurative time sequences of images', taking his inspiration from the composition of electronic music. Until 1971 the results had only been presented in museums. As he put it himself, television 'did nothing to disturb my earlier interest in structuring colour and form, but was an extension of that interest to working in time. For me working for locations other than museums stemmed not from any protest against presentation in museums, but from an interest in those architectural spaces for which my work was suitable. Since the beginning of the 1960s I had been extremely interested in increasing the refinement and variety of visual impressions as a component of architectural public space. Working for TV provided a way of presenting work in a style somewhere between a style suitable for a museum and a style suitable for a public space.'[36] Like Van de Bundt, Struycken was mainly interested in the new opportunities which technology could offer art. But whereas Livinus was mainly concerned with the materials, light and the videotape as carrier of that light, for Struycken the purpose of video and film was to record a process.[37] The computer and the computer program formed the heart of the work.

Other work totally in line with the use of video as bearer of a conceptual message was produced by the Amsterdam artist Pieter Engels, who in 1972 produced a variety of works on video and film. According to him the decision to work with video came about more or less logically. First he started to include photography in his work, then film and finally video.[38] At 'Sonsbeek 71' the combination of his conceptual approach with the use of mass media emerged from the placing of an advertisement in which he let it be known that he would use his fee to buy a colour television. This ridiculing of the art world was something that he would continue to do in many of his early works. Notorious examples include his *Suicide* objects, in which the visitor was challenged to set foot in his works. Anyone foolhardy enough to do so received an electric shock. Later on he made *Verbrande Meesterwerken* [Burnt Masterpieces], small cases in which he kept the carbonized remains of his work.

35
After this work Boezem also made *Een briesje in mei* [A light breeze in May] (1971) on video. This is a modest black and white recording of a curtain dancing softly in the wind, in which the viewer's attention is increasingly drawn to the patterns of light and dark in the room as time passes. Boezem too could only be said to have worked for a brief period with a video and film.

36
E-mail correspondence with Peter Struycken, 21 October 2002.

37
The basis of the choice whether to work with film or video was mainly technical. 'In my case, making films instead of videos was purely a matter of technical necessity, since in fact all the monitor images that I worked out on the computer were made with the same colour mixing technique (R, G, B) that is used for TV. Interestingly enough, it has now long been possible to have a computer, processing in real-time, produce a TV signal which can be transmitted at once. All attempts by me, over the years, to get this technique accepted by the broadcasting companies have so far come to nothing. The people there seem quite simply unable to appreciate the potential.' E-mail correspondence with Peter Struycken on 21 October 2002.

38
Telephone conversation with Pieter Engels, 25 October 2002.

Marinus Boezem, *A light breeze in May*, 1974, video, b/w, sound, 13'50"

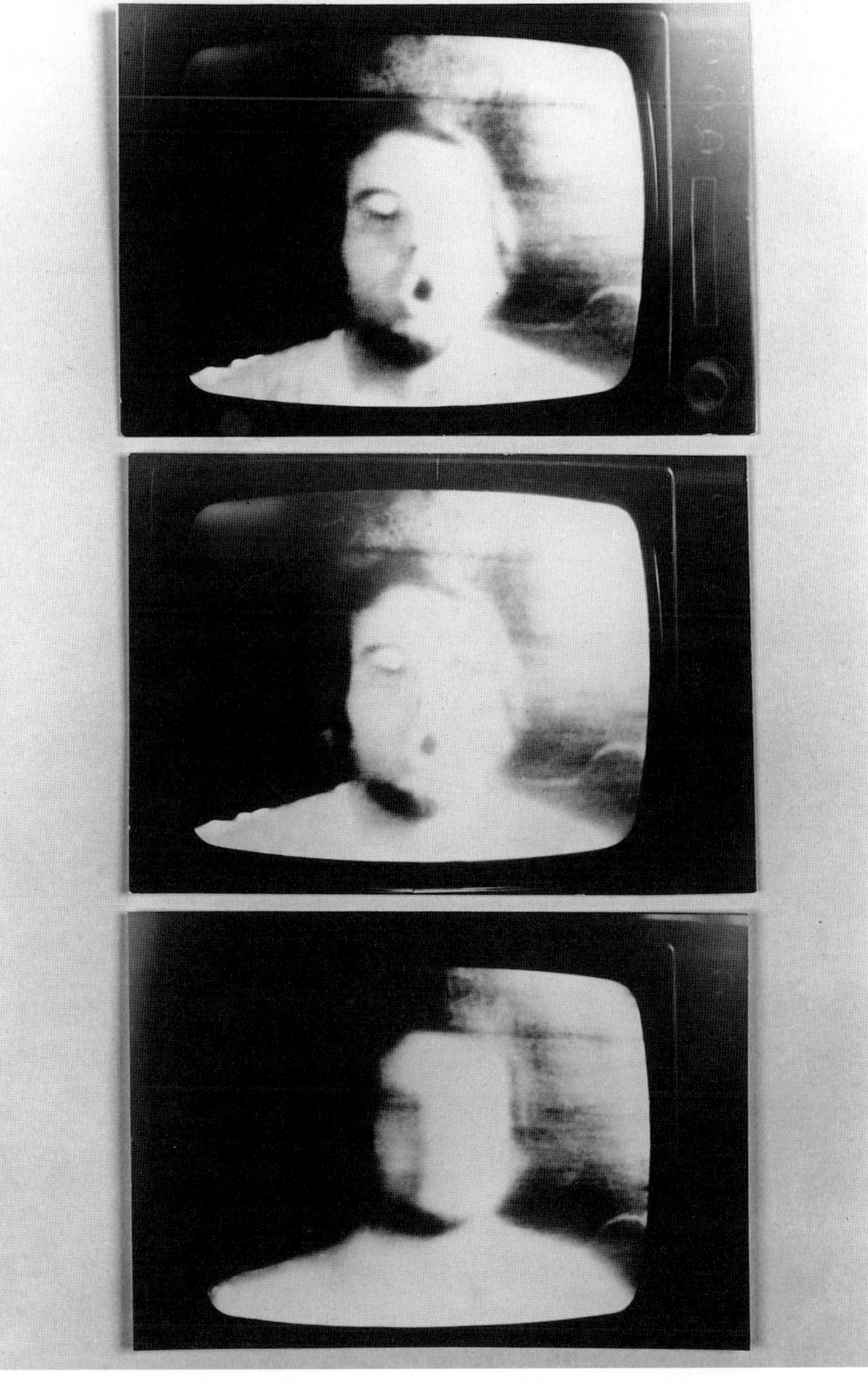

Marinus Boezem, *Breathing upon the Tube*, 1971, 16 mm film for TV, colour, sound, 3'00"

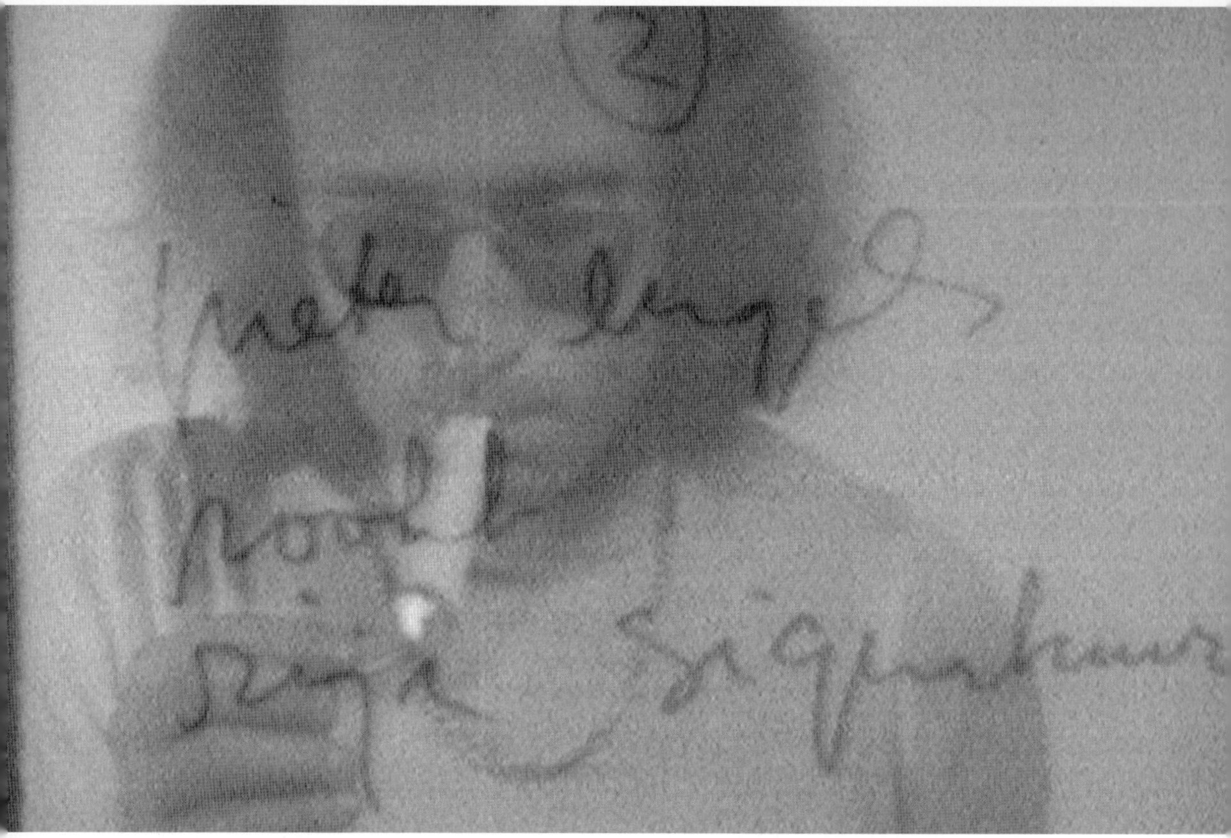

Pieter Engels, *Engels smokes his signature, signing the universe*, 1972, video, b/w, sound, 2'33"

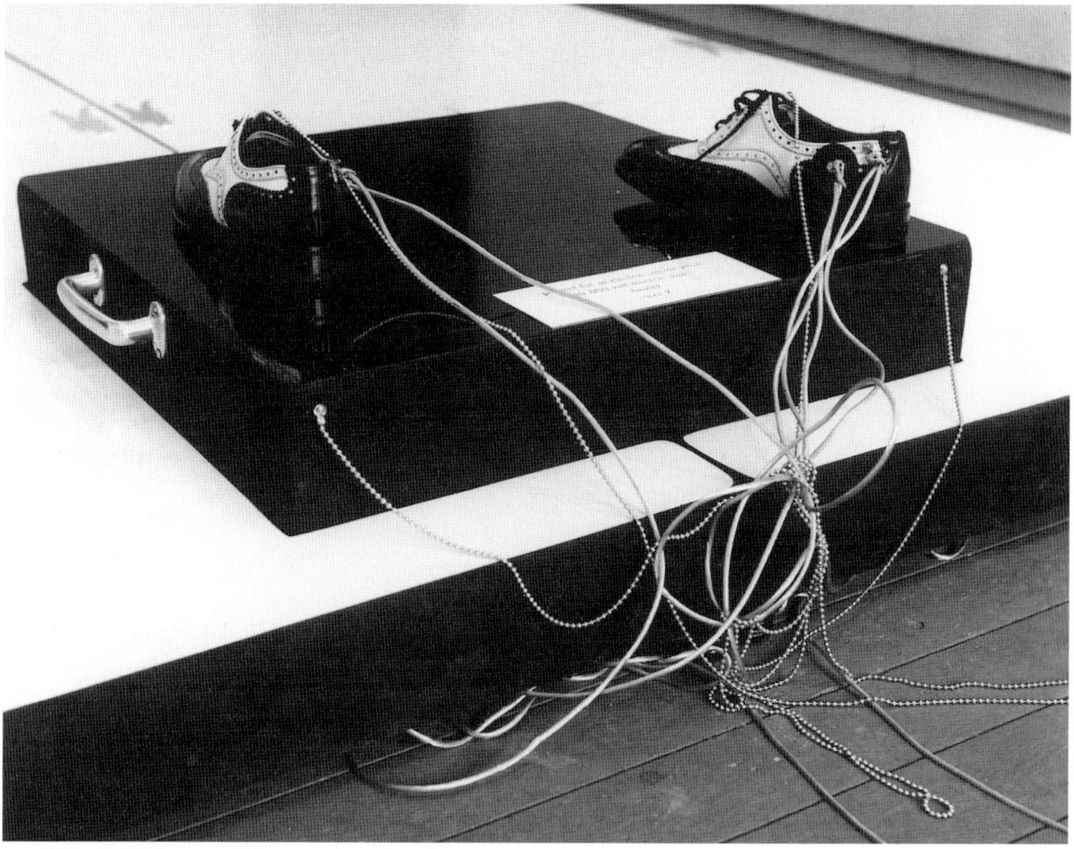

40

Pieter Engels, *Project for an electric suicide piece*, 1968

The status of art also took a knock in the video *Engels smokes his signature, signing the universe* (1972), in which he wrote his signature on a sheet of paper, which he then rolled up into a cigarette and smoked. This was his first video, and was made at one of the Lijnbaancentrum's video workshops.
The tape was a sequel to his earlier film *Mondelinge Ondertekening* [Oral Signature], a close-up of his lips pronouncing his own name. Afterwards a voice over added in three languages that this was a way of signing the film. The film *Para Marche* demonstrated the functionality of a perversely designed pair of shoes (with high soles and low heels). The artist tries to demonstrate that it is actually possible to use such shoes by laboriously walking backwards and finally disappearing into a wood. Although Engels clearly sought to ally himself with the mass media, television remained beyond his reach. Nor was that particularly strange, given the nature of his work: like most conceptual artists he was mainly concerned with the boundaries of art.

Living experience

Many artists thought to have found in TV the natural medium for disseminating their work, without giving any thought to the nature of that medium and the requirements it might impose on their work. As indicated above, producing work for television was considered a challenge because the truly democratic character of the medium was still to be expressed. But television had always had a bad reputation and producing work in its service would require concessions. In particular the medium's educational possibilities, once valued so highly, soon turned out to be swallowed up by the preference for vulgar entertainment.[39] Not surprisingly the earliest experiments with TV were often not followed up. So for example despite the positive reactions to *Die Fundamente de la Tour Babel*, Van der Heijden never did any more work on developing a pictorial language for television, 'because as a graphic artist you really have no chance of making an individual contribution'. Apart from that it was difficult and above all extremely expensive to come by the right equipment, particularly 'if you wanted to develop something technically which was not available as standard'.[40]

Yet at that time there were artists who not only wanted to use television as a medium for distributing conceptual images, but also got involved in the character of the medium. A good example is Wim Gijzen, whose decision to work with video was inspired by Gerry Schum's broadcasts. 'And since at the time we happened to have the Lijnbaancentrum in Rotterdam, it was quite simple for me to put my ideas into practice.'

Pieter Engels, *Para Marche*, 1971, film transferred on to video tape, 5'00"

41

39
'What is to prevent television from degenerating into an interminable and unrelieved variety show?', wondered an Amerikaanse critic in the early 1950s. Boddy 1995, p. 54.
40
Conversation with JCJ van der Heijden, 17 July 2002. Though he has continued his experiments with film (under the influence of the experimental film maker Frans Swartjes), photography and, in the 1990s, with the surveillance cameras at exhibitions.

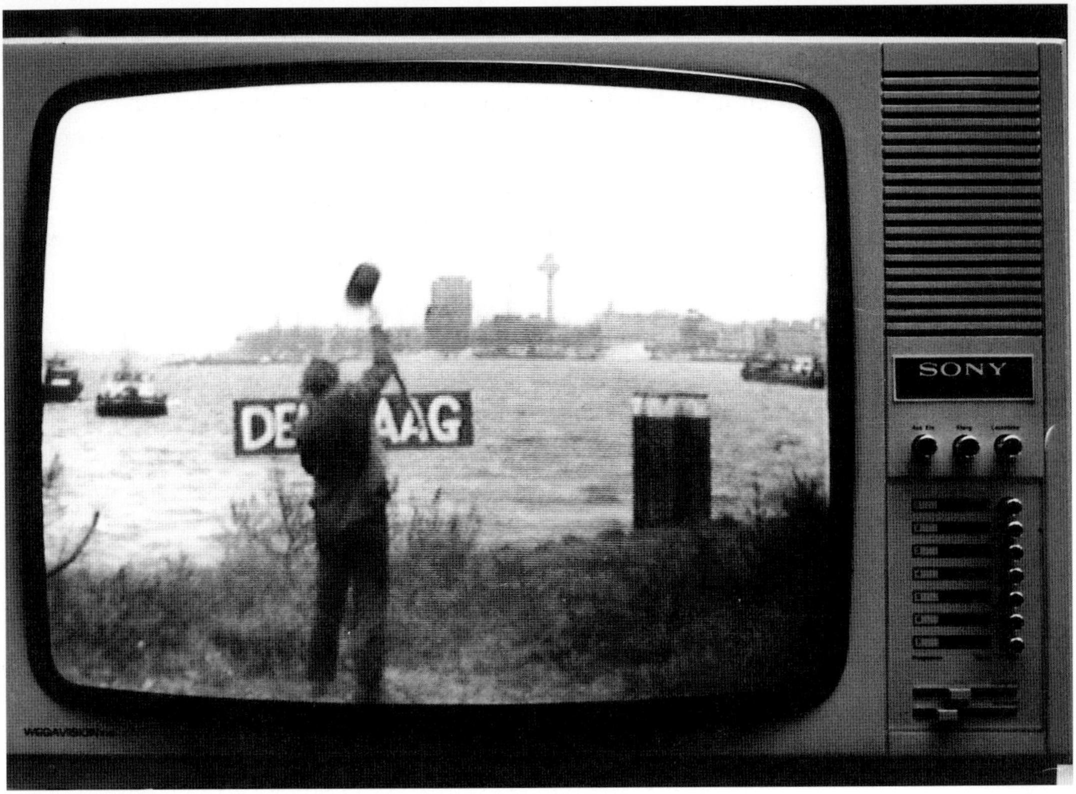

Wim Gijzen, *Rotterdam–The Hague Interchange*, 1970, video, b/w, sound, 2'00"

42   The result was a 'series of mistakes', in which a transposition of place and name gave an image an entirely new meaning. In one example Gijzen goes before the camera and draws a copy of the map of Italy with minute precision, but then goes on to place Athens amongst the cities of Italy. Another variation involved Rotterdam and The Hague. The camera is trained on the characteristic view of the harbour and Rotterdam's highly recognizable skyline. Gijzen walks into the picture displaying a board bearing the name 'The Hague'. 'My concern was mainly with the claimed truth of the television image', he said.[41] What Gijzen was challenging was in fact the suggestion of an immediately present reality. A large part of television's power to convince consists in the end of its ability to send a distant reality into the living room 'unfiltered'.

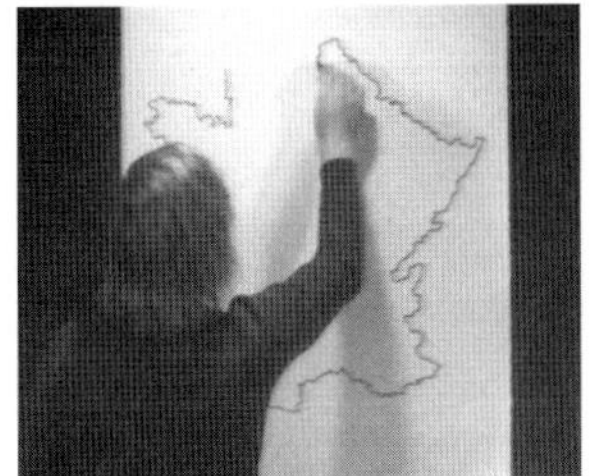

Wim Gijzen, *Mistakes*, 1970–1972, video, b/w, sound, 7'15"

Another property of the medium, and perhaps indeed its greatest attraction, was inaccessible to most artists. Not only does television allow us to see something happening somewhere else, it enables us to witness these events as they happen. The medium literally makes it possible for the viewer to be present on the spot, to experience something immediately at the very instant that it happens. This *rhetoric of liveness*, as it is

41
Telephone conversation with Wim Gijzen, 4 November 2002.

known, is one of the key characteristics of television and the medium goes to extraordinary lengths to maintain the suggestion of an immediacy which, since the introduction of the videotape, has largely been a sham.[42] Taken together, reality TV programmes, candid camera, 'funniest home videos', and the many Dutch variations on the same themes make up the most banal but also the most crucial side of the medium. What makes us go on watching is the possibility that in this continuous stream of sound and images something unexpected might suddenly happen, something that we would want to share. The same structure of unpredictability and fortuity turns everything at which television directs our eyes into an event. The simple fact that we are watching means that something has got to happen, that apparently there is – or will be – something to see, that some event lurking just round the corner will jump out at us if we don't watch out.[43]

It is however precisely this element that was unattainable by many video artists. A tape is a completed work, incapable of showing anything going on in front of the camera anywhere else at the same time. Artists only make use of this presence in video performances, but in such cases they are more interested in the possibility of feedback, an immediate reaction to their own image, then with the voyeuristic satisfaction with which we endlessly view everyday happenings.

Only one artist ever really understood what TV was about, and he succeeded in exploiting this understanding in the course of the 1970s. Wim T. Schippers has never produced any video art, but has drawn the most extreme conclusions from the relationship between art and television. When in the early 1960s Schippers poured a bottle of fizzy water into the sea near Petten, it was not a conceptual work – the expression did not yet exist – nor indeed a performance. The presence of television made it a media activity, an event which was an event only because it was watched by the eye of the TV camera. This direct use of the medium was extended and developed by Schippers in the shows he put on for the VPRO in the 1970s, which showed the keenness of his insight into the character of television in those years. The chaos, the combination of information, games and somewhat rancid song and dance numbers, and the deliberate amateurism of Schippers' television work was a magnified form of what television had to offer evening after evening. The cardboard sets, the almost constant presence of an audience, the errors and mistakes, all these elements were used to evoke the atmosphere of domestic intimacy and presence which constitutes the medium's greatest strength. Television works because it constantly gives the impression, very often false, that the broadcast it is transmitting is live. To some extent video art heads off in the opposite

42
Feuer 1983. See also Boomgaard 1999.
43
For the way in which TV turns everything into an event, see: Doane 1990.

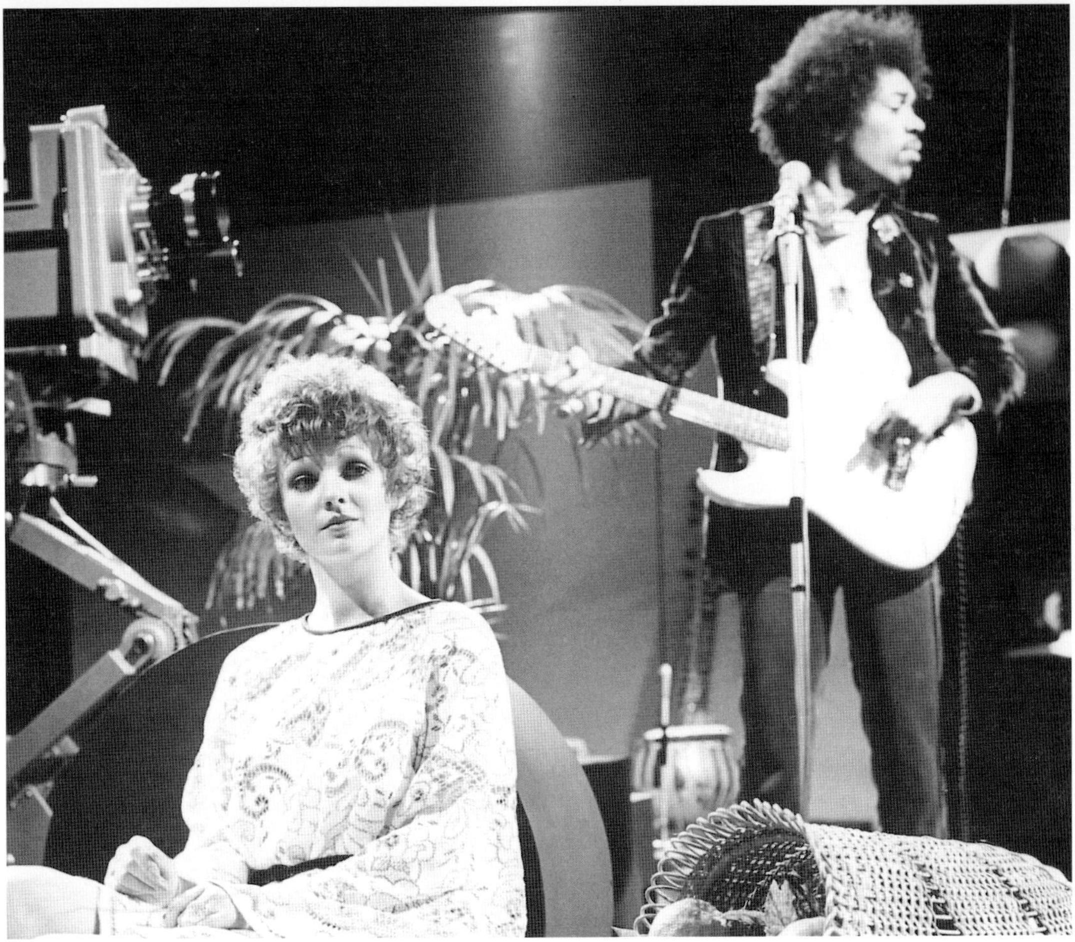

Wim T. Schippers, *Wintershow/Waldolala*, VPRO, 13 March 1978

direction. Live performances are recorded and then played back
later, with the result that they lose the unpredictability of the
original performance. In this case however video plays a
different role, which has precious little to do with its relationship
with TV.

The eye of the observer

The video camera is a witness, which is why its arrival marked
an important development in the graphic art of the 1960s and
1970s. The transition from art as personal expression directed
at individual experience to art as a public appearance directed
at a public subject, the sort of thing that took place in minimal
art at the end of the 1960s, found its logical sequel in the
videotape. The anonymous neutral installations of the minimal
artists created a public observer for the first time in the sense
that the only thing they actually made visible was the process of
looking at art. 'Anyone who takes the effort to allow these works
to get through to him', wrote Camiel van Winkel, 'is constantly
confronted by a heightened awareness of himself.'[44] The birth of
the viewer inevitably led to the emergence of the viewer *in*

44
Van Winkel 1999, p. 71.

absentia: the video look. The video recording is the eye of the viewer even when he is not or can not be present. It represents public availability in advance, even without any work being produced, even without any need for work to be produced. In America this development can be seen in the work of Bruce Nauman and Vito Acconci. Starting from the idea that art is a public activity, they were converted to the idea of recording their activity as artists (originally on film and later on video), so that that activity itself became a work of art. Nauman's basic idea was that art is what the artist does in his studio, and what the artist does there – pacing to and fro, flicking two balls up and down, or playing a violin without knowing how – is a matter of small importance.[45]

In the Netherlands this development can clearly be seen in the work of Jan van Munster. In the tradition of Minimal Art, Van Munster originally used light to make abstract sculptures, some of which were explicitly intended for public open spaces. Between 1972 and 1974, after seeing Bruce Nauman's early film and video work in New York, he produced ten short works for film and video. These were short performances (without an audience) in which he used fluorescent tubes and light bulbs to investigate the influence of light and dark on the perception of space and his own body. He would for example swing a lamp round on its lead, creating a circle of light, fill up his mouth with small light bulbs or fix two light bulbs to his ears. Although it might be possible to detect a conceptual approach in these works, it seems that the main thing the artist was trying to do in his studio was to investigate the limits of his capability. Thus the recording was not itself a work of art, nor indeed did the tape serve to reveal a particular idea, but the recording had the effect of turning what was going on into a work of art. This new direction in his work turned out to be short-lived, for after producing these works in the early 1970s he never worked with film or video again. As he said himself: 'I saw no reason to go on with film and video, because I'd had enough. I decided to use a different material to express myself. The decision to stop working with film and video had in itself nothing to do with the medium. It could be that in future I shall start to use it again.'[46]

Some years later Bert Schutter took this approach a stage further in a number of video productions. In *Producing Lines no. 1* we see the artist leaping up and down in front of a wall as a way of drawing lines on it. Even more strikingly than in the case of Van Munster, the effect produced is inversely proportional to the force applied. The artist goes to enormous lengths to draw his lines and the only way this can become a work of art is by converting it into the lines which make up a video image. Schutter's next work, *Producing Lines no. 2*, went a step further. In it the artist used his own brain activity to produce lines

Bert Schutter, *Producing Lines no. 1*, 1978, video, colour, sound, 8'00"

Bert Schutter, *Producing Lines no. 2*, 1978, video, colour, sound, 2'52"

45

45
Van Winkel 1999, p. 83.
46
Telephone conversation with Jan van Munster, 6 November 2002.

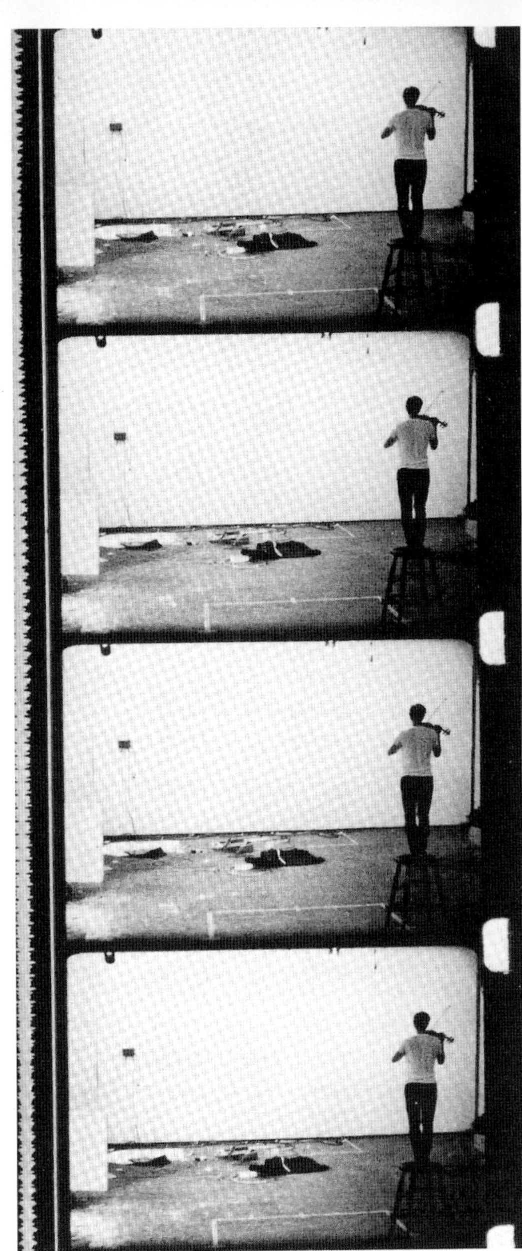

Bruce Nauman, *Playing a Note on the Violin While I Walk Around the Studio*, 1968, 16 mm film, b/w, sound, 10'00"

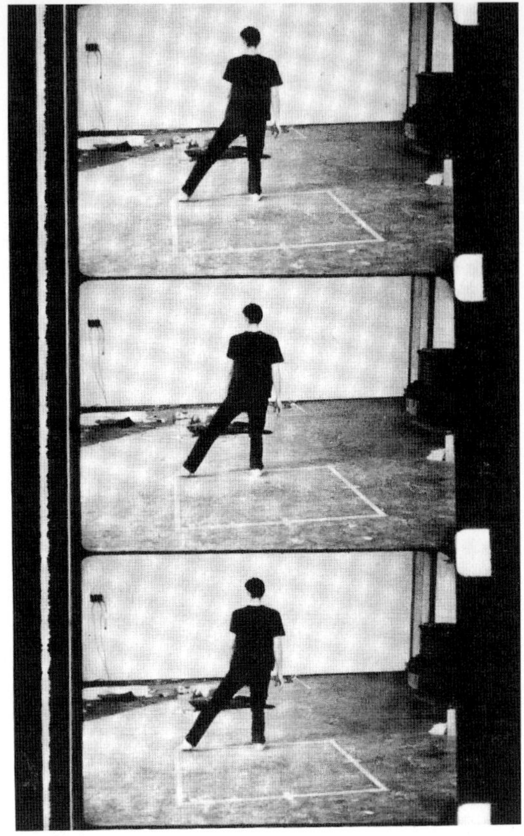

Bruce Nauman, *Dance or Exercise on the Perimeter of a Square*, 1968, 16 mm film, b/w, sound, 10'00"

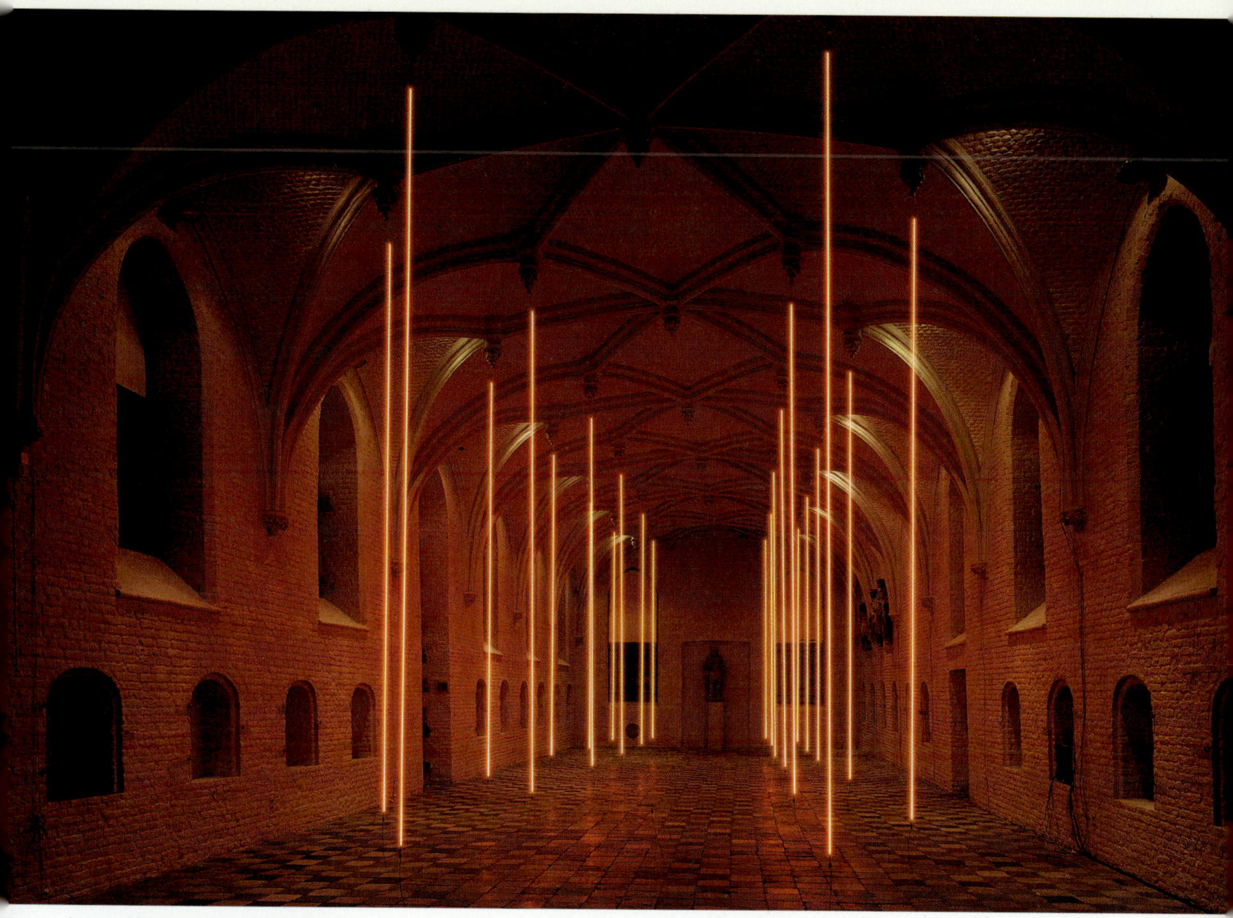

Jan van Munster, *Heat Installation, 100,000 Watt*, installation, De Vleeshal, Middelburg 1989

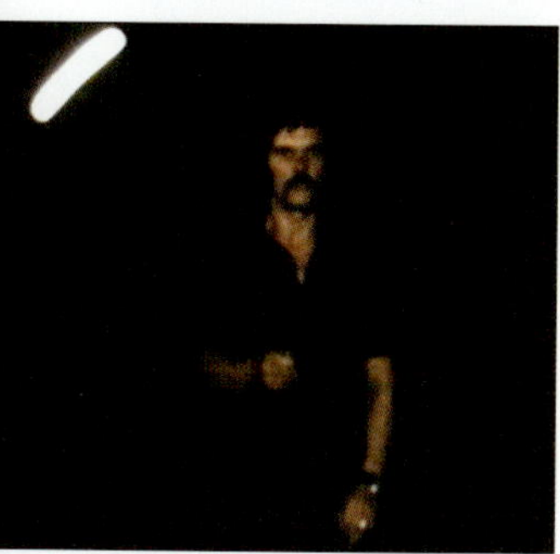

Jan van Munster, *Circles*, 1973,
16 mm film and video, 5'04"

by creating an encephalogram. Here the effort was minimal, but the effect was every bit as meaningless. Once again it was only the fact of the video recording that turned it into a work of art. These works again made clear how strongly, with the help of video, the eye of the artist was directed at himself in the art of the 1970s. The feedback provided by video allowed to the artist to see himself producing at the exact instant he did so. This reflexive capability was thought to lie at the heart of video: in this sense the artist stood for mankind in general which, confronted by itself, would come to a better awareness of its own existence. This in contrast to television, which has nothing to offer but illusions. This observing eye by and large led to a total neglect of content in favour of simple recording. Quality, meaning, reproduction, all these issues were pushed aside by a fixation on recording 'reality'. The reflection of the artist himself led to a lack of reflection on the medium.[47] Remarkably enough the reflection of the artist himself brought him no closer to his public. The recreation of himself as a media image only increased his remoteness from the observer.[48] Only when the observing eye was properly installed, when it became clear

[47]
See Burris 1996.
[48]
See also Rosalind Krauss, who in this context termed video a narcissistic medium. In: Krauss 1978.

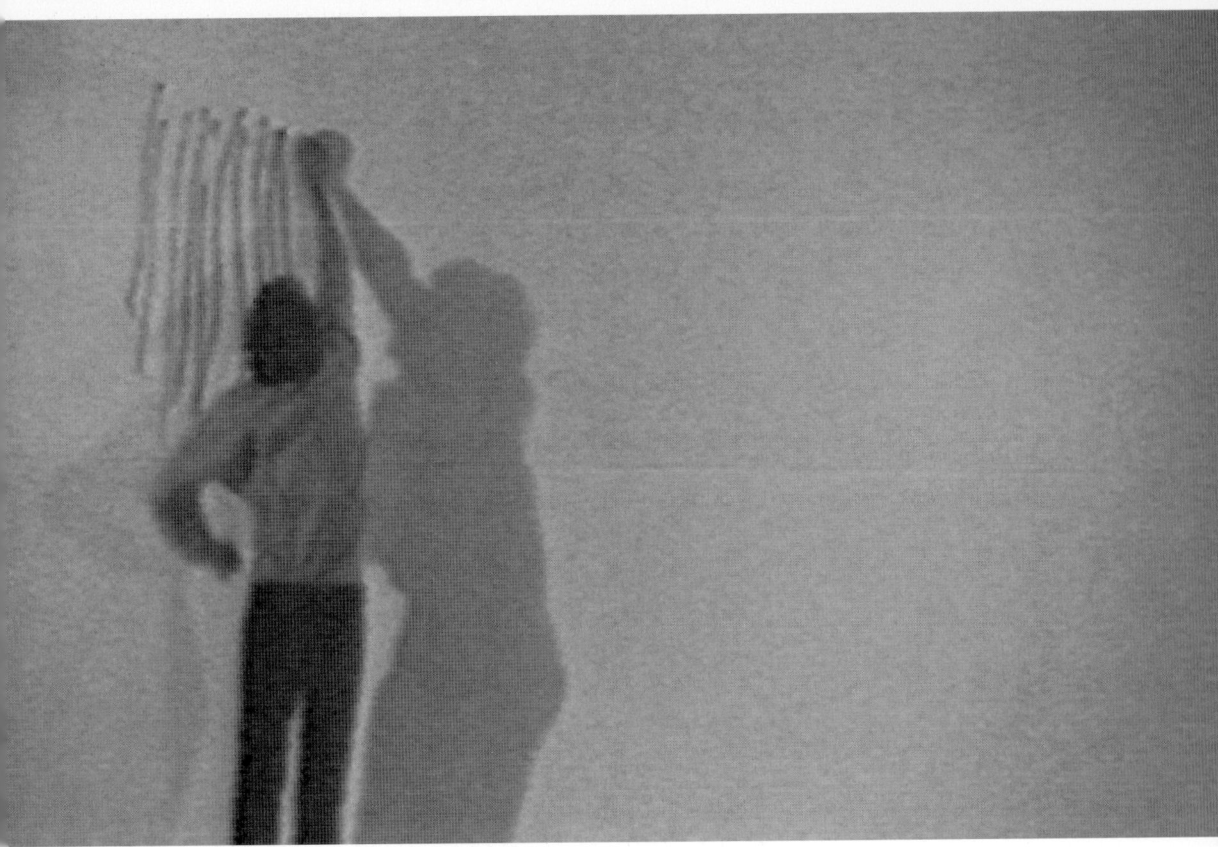

Bert Schutter, *Producing Lines no. 1*, 1978, video, colour, sound, 8'00"

48 even to the public that looking at art was no longer a matter of empathy and immersion but of patient and watchful observation, did it become possible to reflect on the medium that made this possible.[49] Reflection on the medium itself was also stimulated by the fact that towards the end of the 1970s belief in 'reality' and the possibility of transmitting it without mediation was beginning to show clear signs of faltering.

This turnaround was plain to see in works produced by Stansfield and Hooykaas from the late 1970s onwards. Installations like *Split Seconds* and *Tidal Flow* duplicated and interrogated video images. The rise of the tide was linked to the flow of images transmitted by the monitor. The work *Au Deo Vi Deo* investigated the relationship between image and sound, while yet another work confronted the lines on the screen with lines occurring in nature. This form of art still involved observation, but the observation itself had now become the object. The simple monitor was doubled or even tripled; it became clear that reality was a video image.

Video had lost its innocence.

Stansfield/Hooykaas, *Tidal Flow*, 1979, video, b/w, sound, 6'00"

Stansfield/Hooykaas, *Au Deo Vi Deo*, 1978–1979, video, b/w, sound, 10'00"

[49]
The specific way of watching which arose here, was developed by Samuel Webber with the help of the verb *to watch*. It is a way of observing which he links with the phenomenon of television. The televisual look gives the viewer the feeling of being present somewhere while at the same time remaining at a distance. It is not so much that events are presented, rather they happen at the same moment that we watch them, at the place from which we are watching, although we are radically separated from them in both time and space. The look is continuously moving, searching, currently zapping, always on guard in case something might happen. It is a look that can never settle on one object, but which must always take care to keep hold of a never-ending stream. Webber 1996.

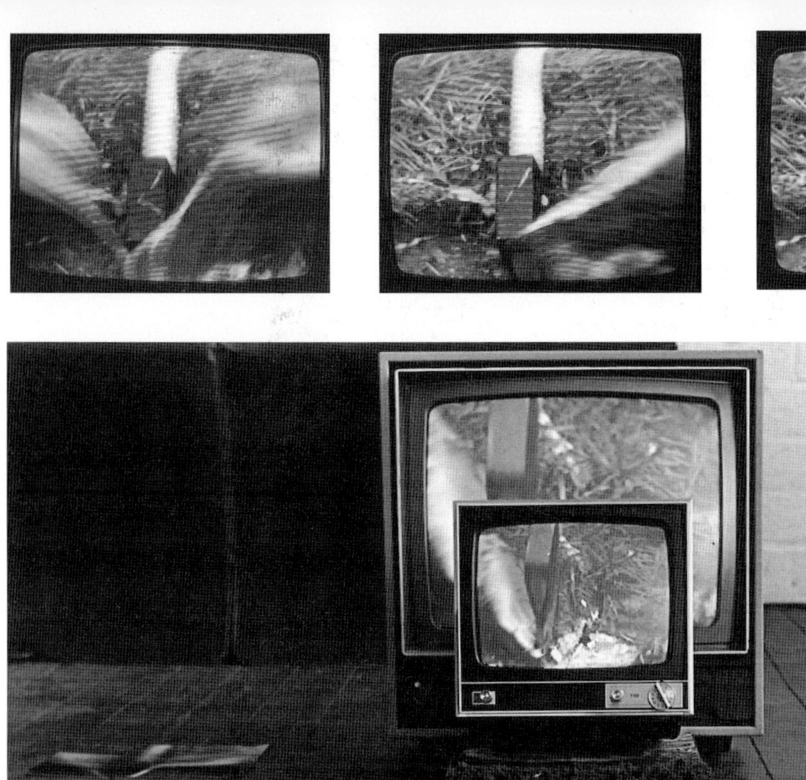

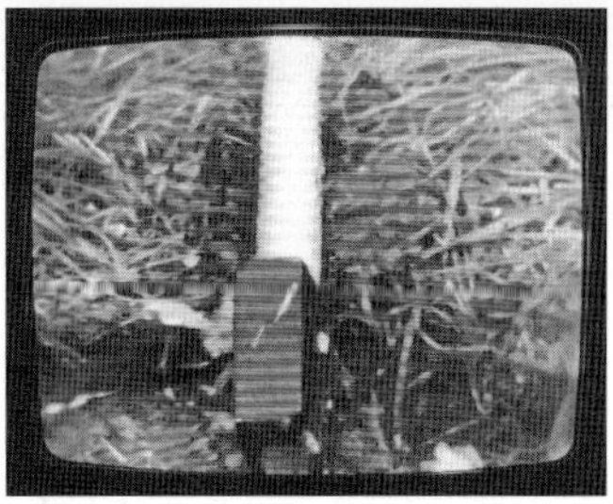

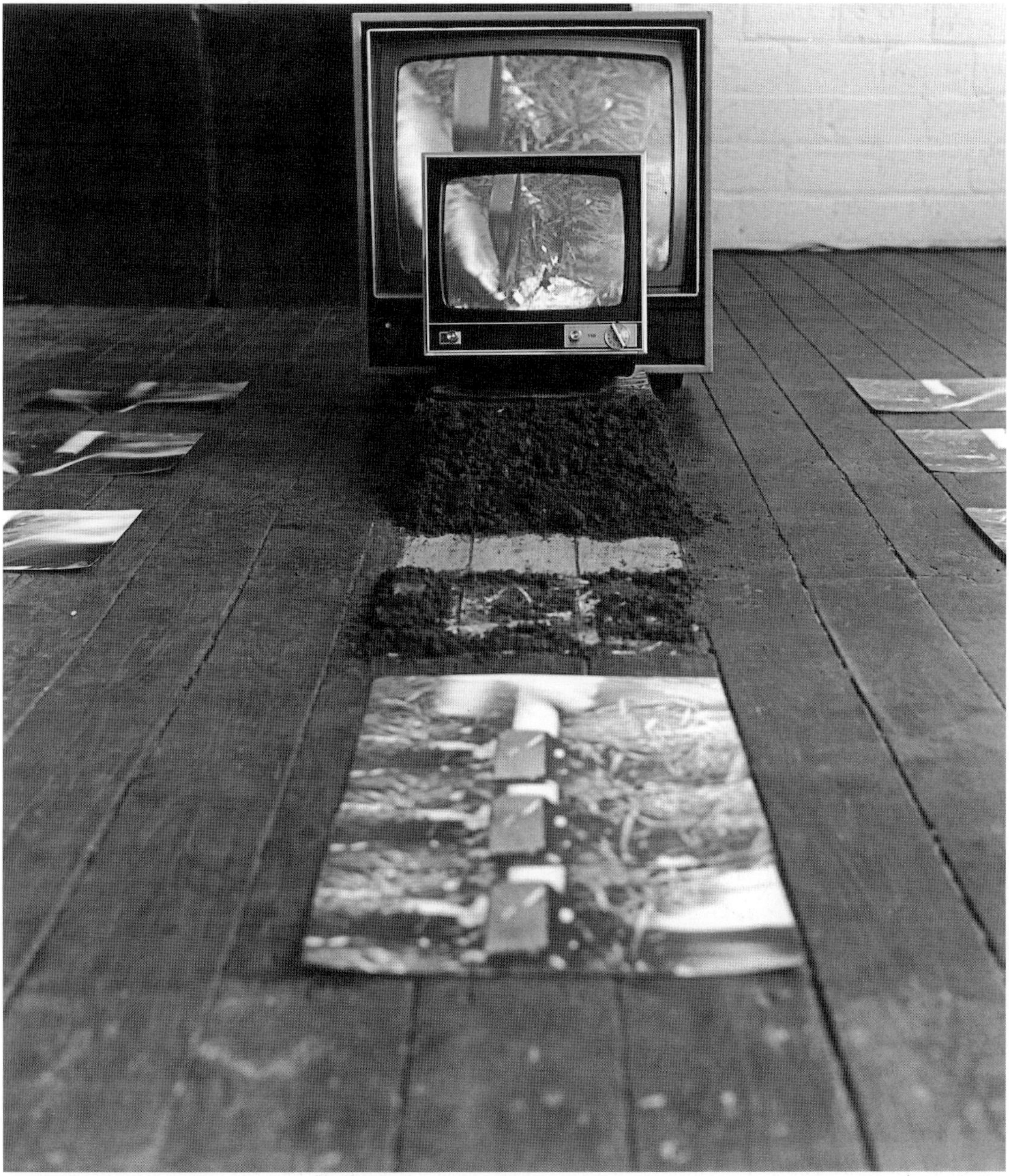

Stansfield/Hooykaas, *Split Seconds*, installation, De Appel, Amsterdam 1979

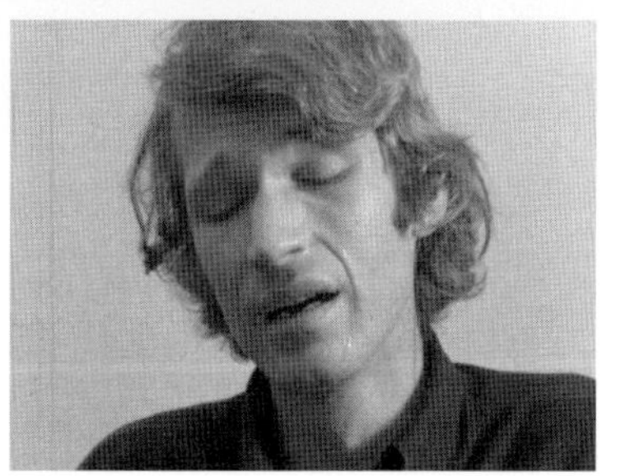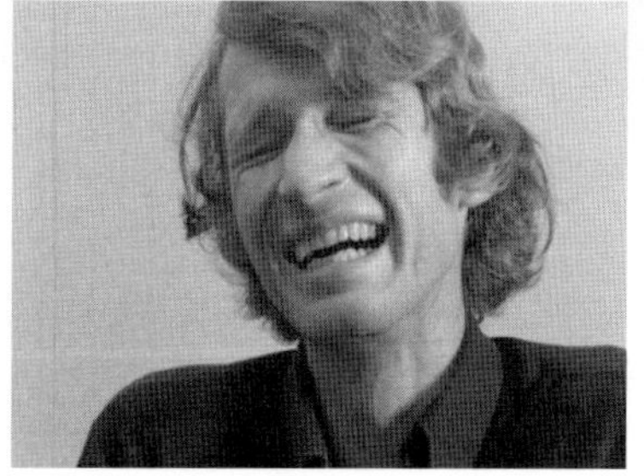

Bas Jan Ader, *I am too sad to tell you*, 1970–1971, 16 mm film, b/w, silent, 2'30"

Jeroen Boomgaard is Professor in Art and Public Space at the University of Amsterdam and Rietveld Academy. He also works at the Technical University Eindhoven as an art historian. He was awarded his Ph.D. in 1995 for *De verloren zoon. Rembrandt en de Nederlandse kunstgeschied-schrijving* [The lost son. Rembrandt and the historiography of art in the Netherlands]. He was co-editor, with Marga van Mechelen and Miriam van Rijsingen, of *Als de kunst er om vraagt. De Sonsbeektentoonstellingen van 71, 86 en 93*, published in 2001. He also writes on contemporary art.

Bart Rutten studied the history of art and cultural history at the University of Utrecht and the University of Wisconsin, Madison (USA). He has been working at the Netherlands Media Art Institute, MonteVideo/Time Based Arts since 1997, where he started out as an art history researcher into the collections of Time Based Arts, De Appel and the Lijnbaancentrum and managed the mediatheque. In 2002 he became the head of presentation.
He has been a guest lecturer at various art academies and at the University of Utrecht. Rutten has written about video art for the periodicals *Skrien* and *Metropolis M*.

Rob Perrée

From Agora to Montevideo
Of video institutes, the things that pass

Introduction

Conclusions from the present have the tendency to turn rapidly into history. In 1990 the Amsterdam Boekman Foundation commissioned Volkskrant journalist Pauline Terreehorst to conduct an inquiry into 'how national and local government, the advisory boards and the institutions have reacted to the phenomenon of video art'.[1] The result was published in the following year in *Kunst en beleid in Nederland 5* [Art and policy in the Netherlands 5]. Although the article is sometimes confusing and bitty, the conclusions leave little scope for interpretation: 'The enthusiasm of the basis could not be communicated to the remote national administrators. That is one of the reasons for the disappearance of a video culture.'[2] And: '[...] the government has had great difficulty with the phenomenon of video. Decisions were postponed time and again. But no policy is also policy. The permanent delaying tactic, whether deliberately intended as such or not, has left institutions and artists dependent on those institutions – because of the particular properties of video art – completely

[1]
Terreehorst 1991, p. 12. This article, the result of extensive research among video institutes, is an important source of information for the history of video art in the Netherlands. I have made grateful and critical use of it.

[2]
Terreehorst, p. 31.

out in the cold. [...] We have to conclude that it is above all the national government that is responsible for the stagnation in the development of video art and has failed to see how important the institutions were for the phenomenon to flourish. [...] Local government proved to be better informed and much better able to respond adequately to the new trends than national government. It fulfilled a reconnaissance role. That role is not appreciated by national government. In fact, it was up to local government to clear up the mess after the heavy-handed decisions.'[3]

I think that today, in 2002, Terreehorst would have written a different text. Video culture has not disappeared. On the contrary, video and photography are the most widely used media among artists at the moment. It is debatable whether those government bodies, advisory boards and institutions have played a part in this. At any rate, the link that once existed between video institutions and artists has disappeared, the inconstancy of national government seems to a large extent to have been kept under control by a system of long-term subsidies, and the specialized advisory boards of the past have now been incorporated in the Council for Culture. Video has become one of the means of artistic expression, video art no longer exists as such, and institutions exclusively devoted to video have disappeared or changed their format.

Video has become both outdated and up to date. That is the paradox within which the story of the different video institutes is situated.

Open studios

Wim Beeren organized the exhibition 'Sonsbeek buiten de perken' [Sonsbeek beyond the pale] in 1971. Until then, Sonsbeek had been an interesting but rather conventional and low-threshold sculptural exhibition. That conventionality changed drastically under the responsibility of Beeren.
He invited a group of international conceptual artists who, in the words of Ger van Elk, wanted to break with 'that dismal beret art of the Fifties'.[4] Most of them made works in situ that were related to the landscape. One of the features of the exhibition was a tent in which videos were shown and where it was also possible to make videos. Philips had provided the equipment free of charge for this improvised studio. Entirely in the democratic spirit of the time, the cameras were available not only for the artists (who included Shinkichi Tajiri, Nam June Paik and Stanley Brouwn), but also for the public. The basic idea behind it was setting up communication, a form of idealism that had not yet earned the label 'naive'. Although not a lot came of it (and a lot of what did come out of it has been lost), for many this introduction to the new medium was an exciting and stimulating

3
Terreehorst, pp. 64-65.
4
Interview with Van Elk by Hans den Hartog Jager, *NRC Handelsblad*, 3 September 1999.

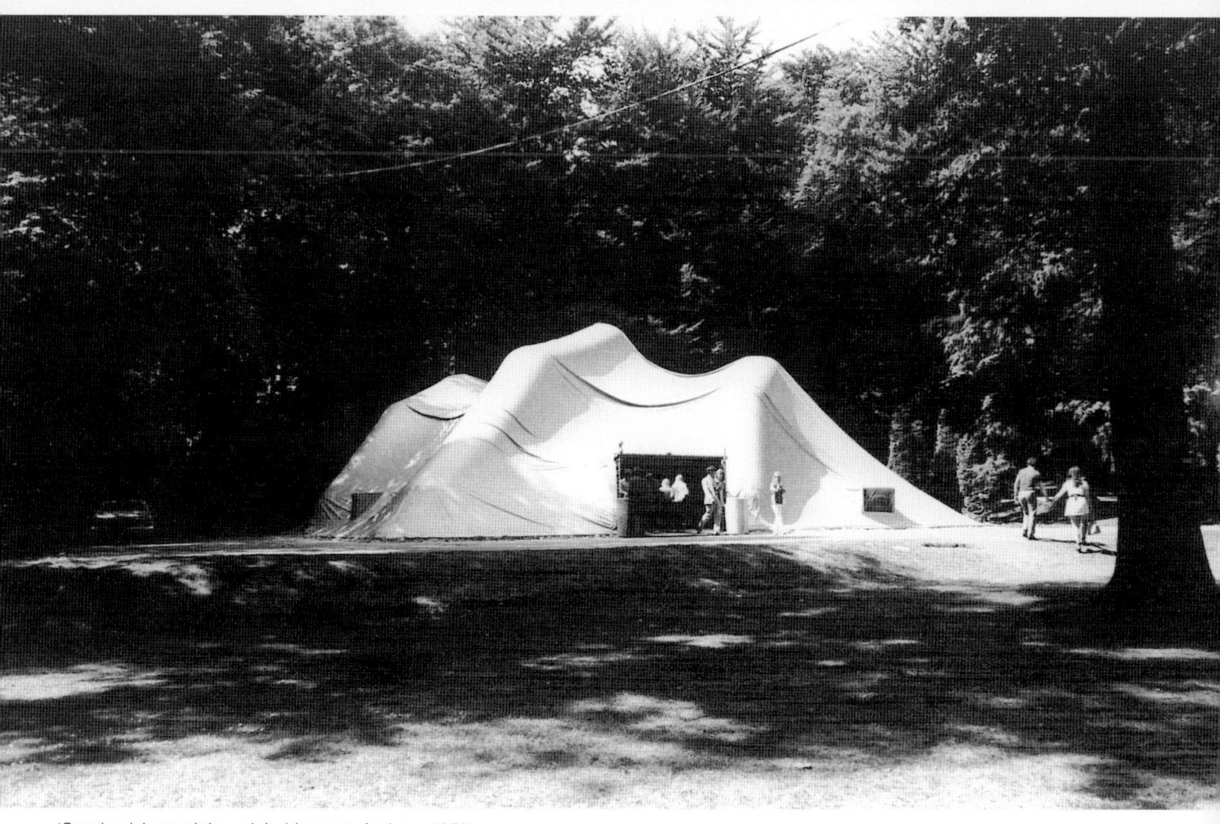

'Sonsbeek beyond the pale', video tent, Arnhem, 1972

experience. That excitement led to a number of initiatives that marked the start of a notable development.

53

In the year after Sonsbeek, Theo van der Aa and Ger van Dyck set up the Maastricht Agora Studio (renamed Agora Foundation in 1978 when it received a subsidy). Beeren had provided the final push. They wanted a sort of open studio for artists with ideas. Precise definitions of the objectives were out of the question: whatever happens happens. It is not the institution that determines the art, but the artist. Agora Studio was also an information centre. International contacts played an important role in it, not only with artists but also with comparable centres in Paris, San Francisco, Buenos Aires and elsewhere. Van der Aa and Van Dyck no longer regarded art as tied to a location; the video tape, book, cable, satellite, telephone and magazine made it possible to transcend every boundary. There were close contacts with the Bonnefantenmuseum and with the Jan van Eyck Academy in Maastricht, which was well equipped from the 1980s on. So the use of (video) equipment rarely created problems. Theo van der Aa and Raul Marroquin founded the periodical *Fandangos*, and there were mass media projects with Ulises Carrión, Servie Janssen, Michael Gibbs, Martha Hawley

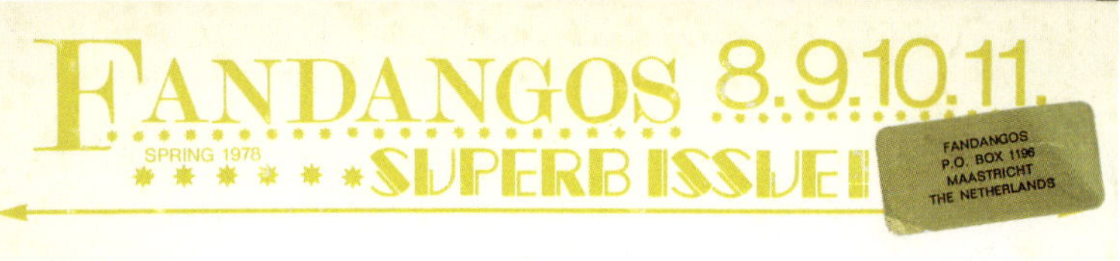

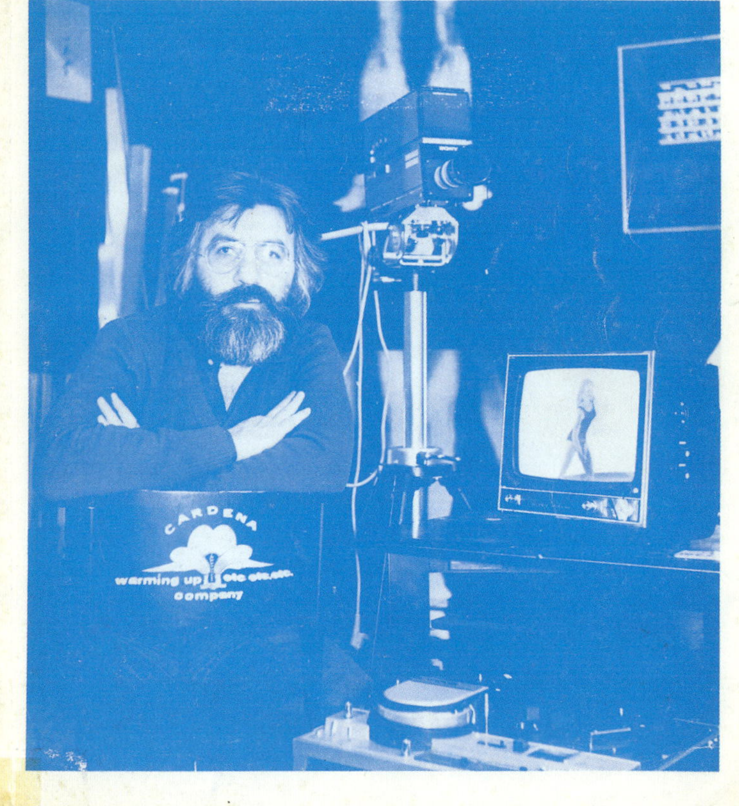

Raul Marroquin et al., cover of *Fandangos 8.9.10.11 SuperIssue!*, Spring 1978

and many others. The exhibitions followed one another in rapid succession in the exhibition space. Multimedia, a concept that had not yet been invented, was already being implemented in Agora.

Although Agora still exists, it has not had the function of a gallery and open studio since 1986. It has undoubtedly played a role in the careers of various (video) artists.

There was another initiative that followed directly from Sonsbeek. The designer Rien Hagen had been commissioned by Wim Beeren to make a visual record of the exhibition (though the result has been lost). Hagen had been fed up with the 'advertising kids' for some time and the commission went very well, so he decided to stop with his Checkpoint design agency in The Hague and in 1972 founded Meatball (the name is borrowed from a cartoon by Robert Crumb).[5] Meatball aimed at audiovisual productions intended to bring about social change. It wanted to investigate new forms of communication and to

5
Interview with Rien Hagen, July 2002.

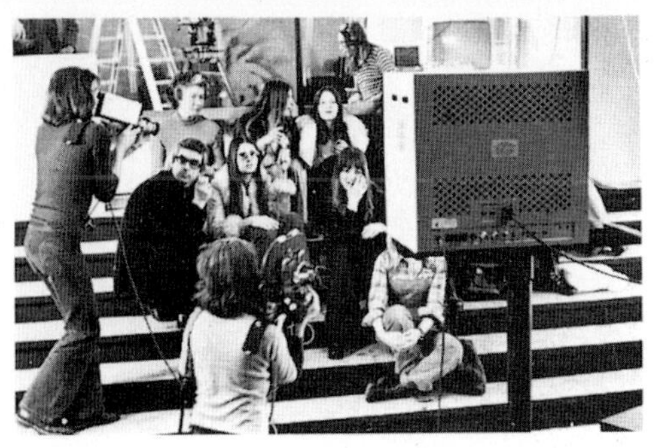

Begin 1972 werd te Den Haag stichting Werkgroep Video Meatball opgericht. In de statuten van deze stichting staan de algemene doelstellingen aldus omschreven:
● het onderzoeken, stimuleren en evalueren van het gebruik van audio-visuele middelen als instrument van sociale veranderingen in grote zowel als kleine samenlevingsverbanden,
● het onderzoek naar nieuwe vormen van kommunikatie en informatie-overdracht, in het bijzonder op basis van elektroniese beeldregistratie,
● het begeleiden en adviseren en verrichten van onderzoek op het gebied van ontwikkelingen met betrekking tot lokale televisie en andere vormen van distributie van audio-visuele informatie.
De stichting geeft een internationale videokrant uit Meatball geheten.

Stichting werkgroep video 'Meatball', Hartogstraat 5a Den Haag. Tel: 070 183557

Working Group Video Meatball Foundation

ensure that non-commercial productions got a showing via presentations and distribution (the later Kijkhuis). There was no money – it was only years later that a structural subsidy freed their regular girl friends from the obligation to fund it –, no bureaucracy, and no shortage of ideals. Meatball made a name for itself above all with social documentaries and programmes (for the VPRO broadcasting company) like *Ik ben even weg, Tuig, Huilend Beton, Koninkrijk voor een huis*, which were made on the initiative of Meatball itself or were commissioned. All the same, there were always links with art and artists. Meatball recorded, for instance, the performances organized by De Appel. To celebrate its tenth anniversary, four artists (including Marie-Jo Lafontaine and Lydia Schouten) were commissioned to make a video work. Individual artists (such as Ineke Smits) made use of the facilities. In addition, Meatball helped to organize exhibitions with the Rotterdam Arts Foundation (RKS). For years it maintained close links with Het Kijkhuis, and the first World Wide Video Festival would never have been held without the initiatives and efforts of Rien Hagen and his team. In the last resort, although Meatball probably contributed more to video and the documentary as media (with their docudramas, for instance), it deserves a place in the history of video art.

Video Heads/The Bank Foundation

Meatball went bankrupt in 1992. Rien Hagen got a job at the Haags Filmhuis, and eventually became director of the Netherlands Film Museum in Amsterdam.

Video Heads (1971, Amsterdam) was primarily aimed at artists. The founder and director was the US artist Jack Moore. In the early years he was assisted by the Canadian engineer David Jones, who was later to become a sort of inventor in the field of electronics (the Jones Colorizer is a household name to insiders). Moore was also involved with Sonsbeek, where he had helped to devise and set up the video tent. Video Heads started life in the premises of The Milky Way, primarily to create video productions. The ideas for them came from the artists themselves in almost every case. Moore was not concerned about the content, nor did he have a clear policy. His main criteria were what and who appealed to him, and he displayed a measure of unpredictability in his choices. The main task of Video Heads was to provide the necessary equipment for each plan. In 1980 Moore wanted to expand his activities with

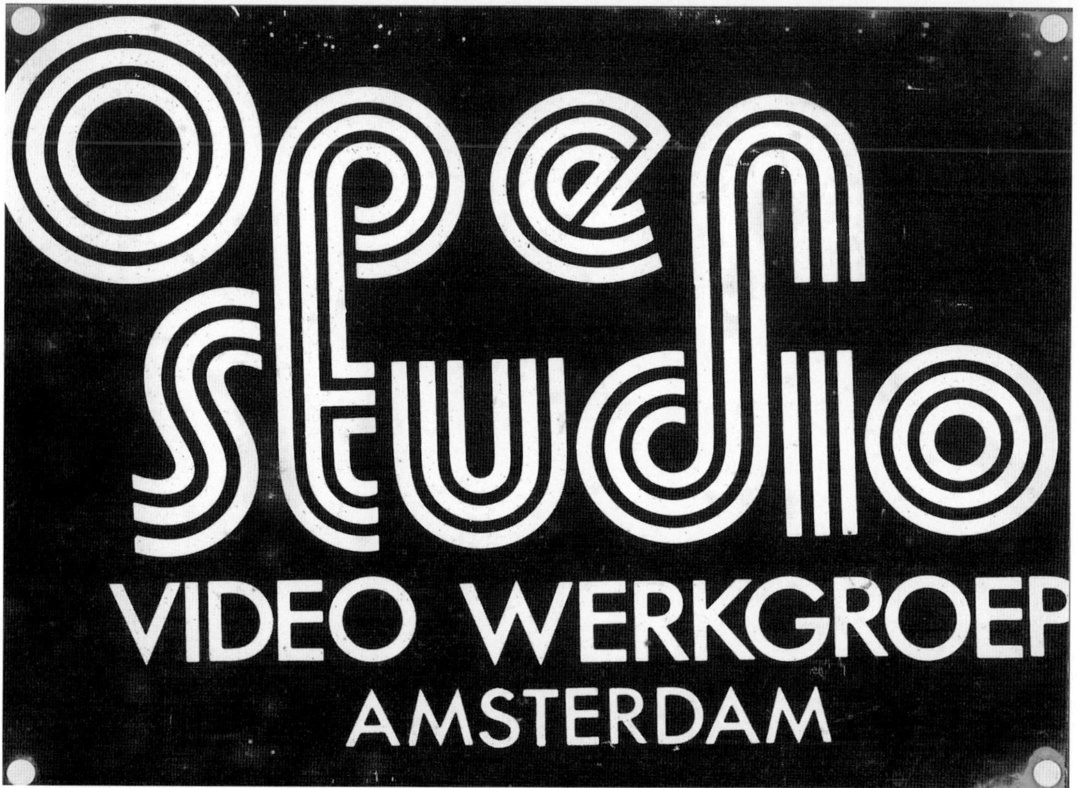

Logo Open Studio

presentations and exhibitions. The Bank Foundation was set up for this purpose. It was in a large building in the Haarlemmerstraat in Amsterdam that the pretentious and rather amusing ambition was to be achieved: '[...] a social video concentration for breaking through the anti-social homecentred effect of monolithic mass-communication'.[6] The plans received the backing of a government grant.

Three years later The Bank went bankrupt. The board members were held personally liable for the debts it had run up, and Jack Moore disappeared abroad. It is difficult to tell what importance Video Heads has had. Video artists from the first generation (Raul Marroquin and Nan Hoover) often used the facilities. Others of those involved react with amusement when the name Video Heads is mentioned. Probably Jack Moore's unorthodox way of working was not Dutch enough to be taken completely seriously.

Although the Open Studio, founded by Lily van den Bergh, opened its basement doors in Amsterdam one year after Sonsbeek too, there is no need to seek a causal connection.

6
International Media Meeting, report of a media conference held at the University of Maastricht from 19 to 24 April 1982 on the initiative of the Agora Foundation in collaboration with the General Studies Department of the University of Maastricht.

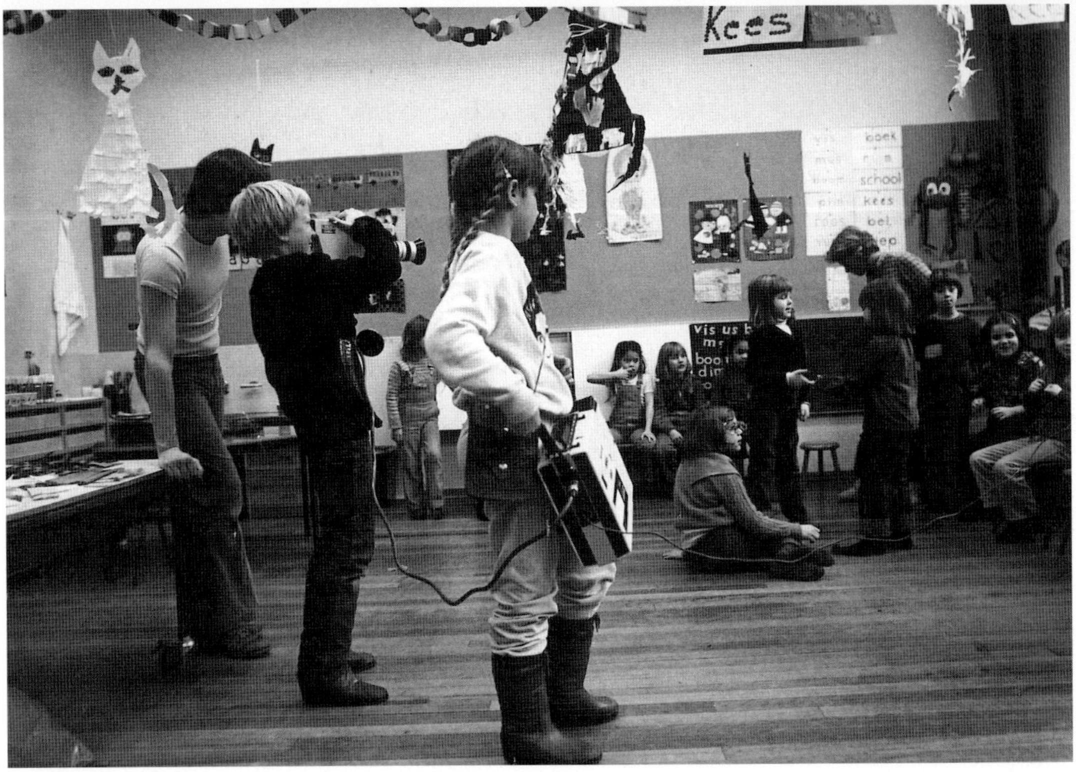

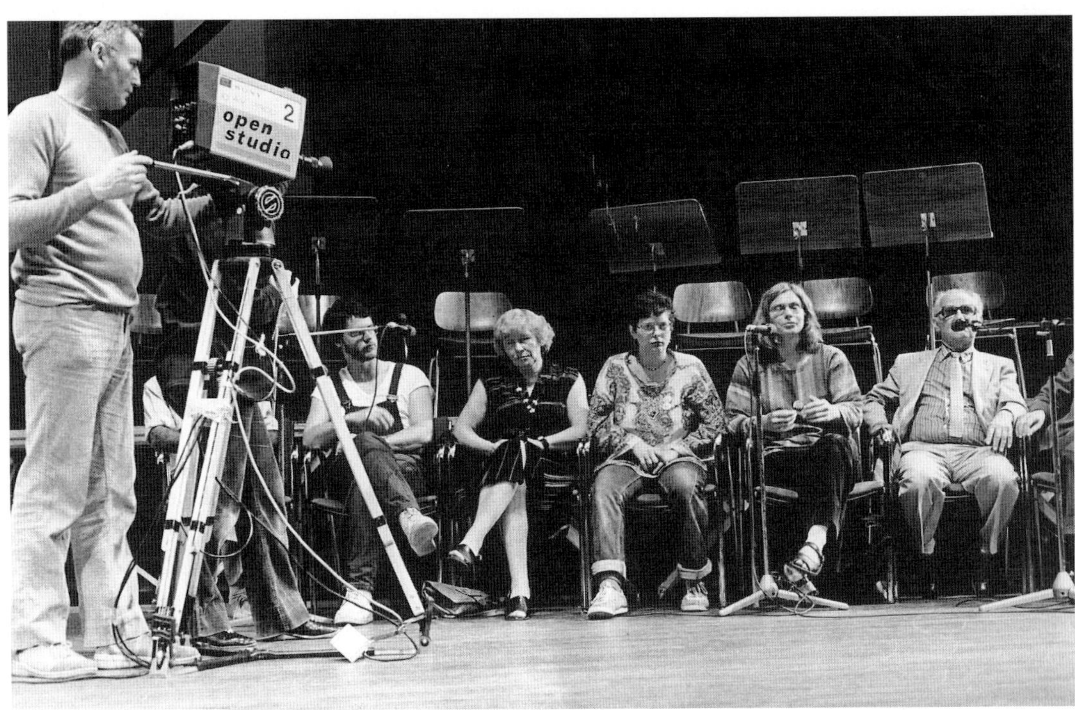

Open Studio at school

Open Studio at the Waarheidsfestival, cameraman Jan Oonk, September 1980

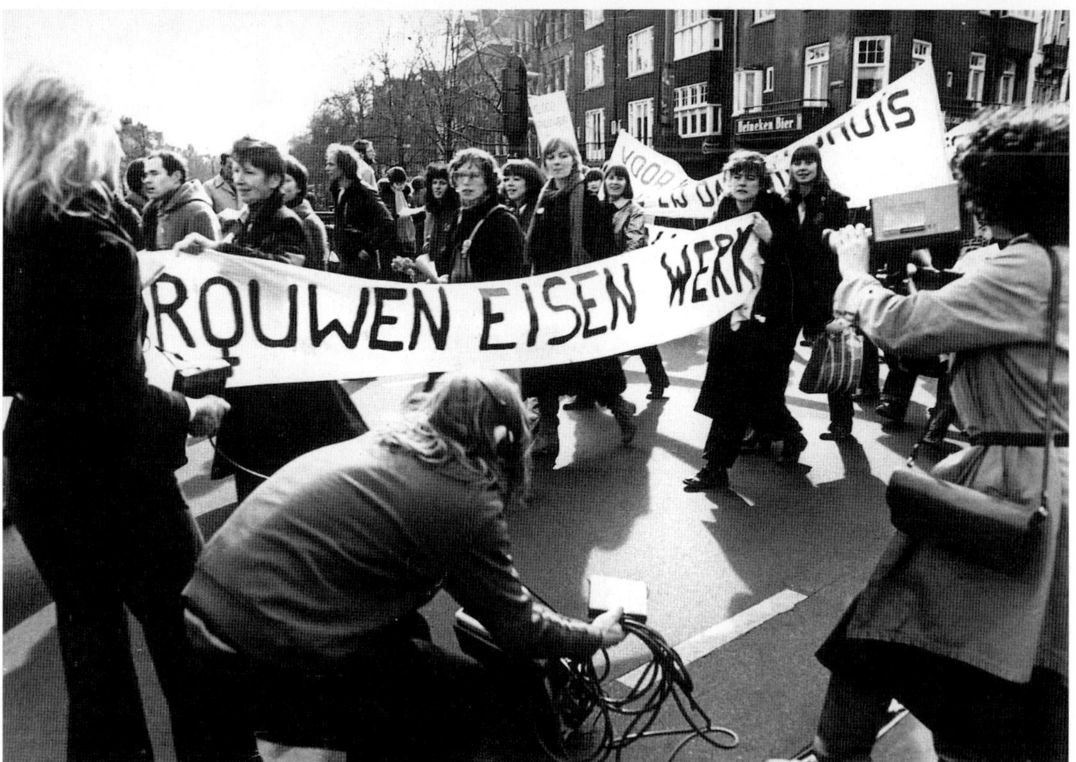

Open Studio in action during a demonstration, Amsterdam

Its origins clearly lie in social ideals. The objectives were
unambiguous on this score. Open Studio wanted to make
audiovisual resources accessible to people who worked with
communicational, educational and informative projects.
The ability of the video makers to work on their own and their
creativity had to be encouraged.[7] The aim was to advise
institutes on acquisition, use and maintenance, as well as
facilitating documentary productions or creating them itself.
Open Studio's broadly defined purpose made it difficult for
subsidizing bodies to place it - a welcome obstacle that they
cleverly exploited by means of the well-known system of passing
the buck. The result was that it had to make do with small, one-
off subsidies, so that most of the personnel were volunteers.
Open Studio occasionally worked with artists. Stansfield/
Hooykaas and Ulay/Abramovič, for example, have made videos
with Van den Bergh or in her studio.

In 1985 Open Studio became a commercial production
company that also started to offer courses and workshops.
That was when Lily van den Bergh decided to become an
independent maker of documentaries and programmes.

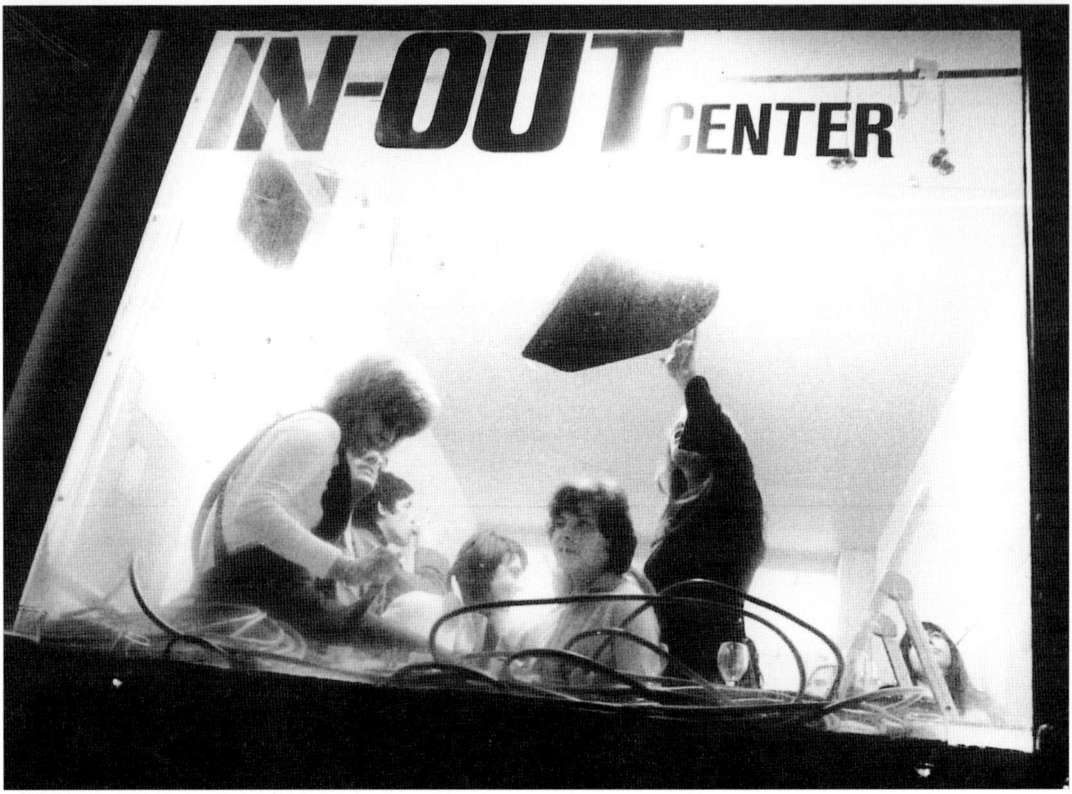

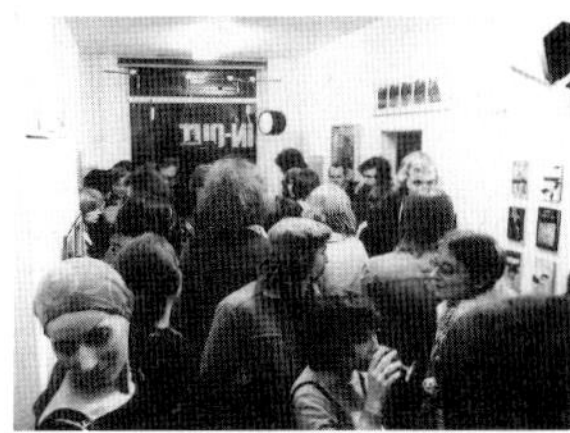

Vernissage, In-Out Center, Reguliersgracht 103, Amsterdam 1972

60   A special place was occupied among these early initiatives by the In-Out Center. Michel Cardena, a Colombian who had lived in the Netherlands for a number of years and had already built up something of a reputation as an artist, founded the centre in 1972. Raul Marroquin, Ulises Carrión, a number of Icelandic artists (including Gudmundsson) and a few Dutch ones (including Hetty Huisman) were also involved. With a high frequency they presented work in a small venue in the centre of Amsterdam that did not stand much of a chance in the regular circuit, so that meant a lot of video work. They may have only reached a limited audience, but what is more important is that they represented a growing group of foreign artists who felt drawn to Amsterdam for its tolerant, artistic and grant-friendly climate, and whose innovative and refreshing presence had a stimulating effect on developments, particularly in Dutch video art.

The In-Out Center lasted little more than a year. It was closed down in 1974, though for no apparent reason. Probably the artists' own work was demanding more attention. The arrival of De Appel in Amsterdam in 1975 was of great importance for the artists who presented or were presented. De Appel was clearly inspired by Cardena's initiative.[8]

8
See too Amsterdam 1992.

The role of the government

All of these institutions were the result of private initiative, the idealism of a few. The Lijnbaancentrum in Rotterdam, that was founded as early as December 1970, was an initiative of the local authority. The advantage of this is that, since the city assumes responsibility, it is in principle prepared to provide funds and an infrastructure. The disadvantage is that the bureaucratic road has to be followed. It is not only by definition long and wearisome, but it also lacks the unpredictability or the unorthodoxy that make institutions interesting. The Lijnbaancentrum was set up as a low-threshold exhibition space in the centre of the city, so that shoppers would feel free to come and go. It was run by the Exhibitions Department of the Rotterdam Arts Foundation. The video section limited itself to recording exhibitions, interviewing artists, and assisting artists who wanted to show videos in exhibitions. This limited use of video was not so much ideological as it was the result of the absence of an ideology. A video working group set up by the local

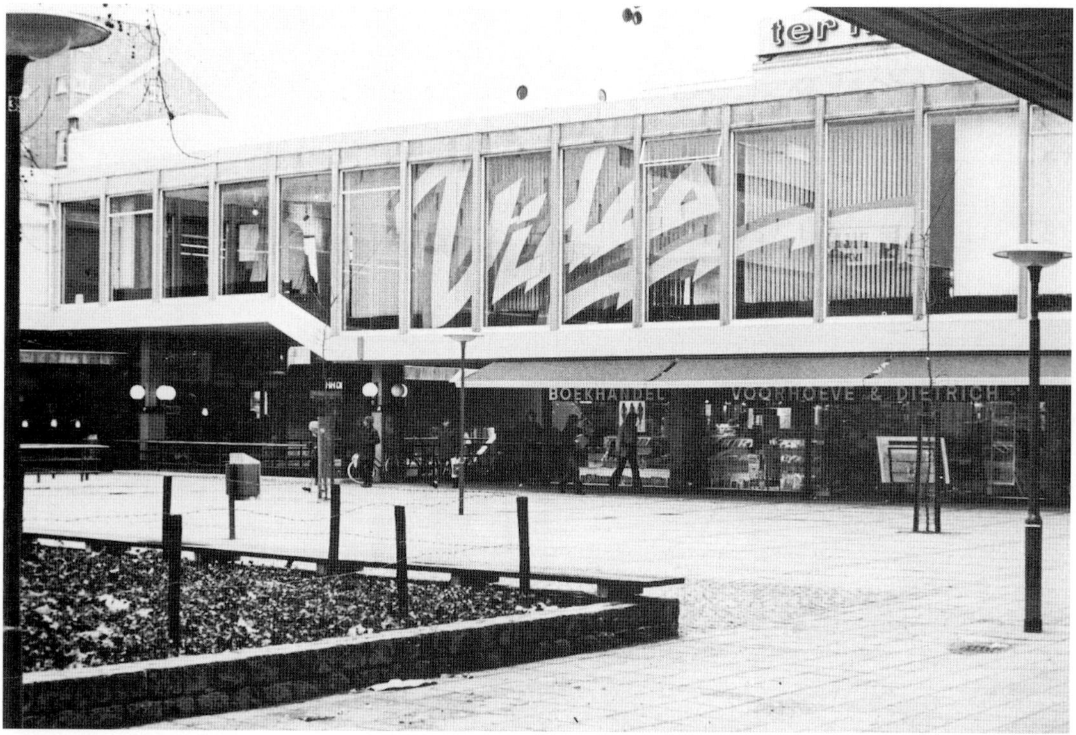

Lijnbaancentrum, Rotterdam 1973

Lijnbaancentrum staff

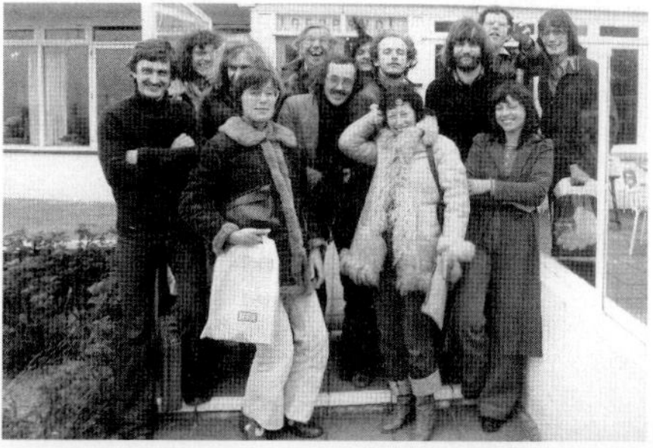

authority tried to draw up a video policy for years – in vain, because the aim was to arrive at an overarching policy. This was unrealistic, because the social function of the medium in a slum neighbourhood cannot be weighed up against the importance of the individual artist looking for opportunities to make his or her own work. The setting up of the Video Centre in 1976, which was primarily concerned with the making of productions for neighbourhoods, education and art, and that was able to offer a studio facility, was unable to break the impasse. Even the plans for an international video festival as an extension of the Film Festival and Poetry International - an initiative of Tom van Vliet, researched by Rien Hagen – failed to come off; it was successfully pulled off in The Hague in 1982.

These gloomy developments do not imply that the Lijnbaancentrum has not played a role at all. It was one of the first places where video equipment was available (free of charge). Various artists have made welcome use of it over the years. A number of foreign artists who had taken part in 'Sonsbeek buiten de perken' stayed on in the Netherlands and made new work in Rotterdam. In 1973 the Lijnbaancentrum organized an important video exhibition, showing not only documentaries but also video works by Livinus van de Bundt, Dennis Oppenheim, Henk Tas and others. In addition, the exhibition charted all of the video and cable activities in the Netherlands.

The Lijnbaancentrum disappeared long ago. Low-threshold exhibition spaces are out of fashion. In 1988 the Rotterdam Arts Foundation released a report recommending that video presentations should be linked to existing institutes (for example, theatre-like video works in Lantaren/Venster). The video and film showings in De Unie appear to be the only surviving result of that.[9]

Soon after its launching in 1975, De Appel became one of the most important art institutions in the Netherlands. An initiative of Wies Smals, this location beside the Brouwersgracht was the international centre for those forms of art that knocked on the doors of the museums in vain: 'performances, environments and situation art', as they were called in the objectives.[10] De Appel is the first location on the track lists of a respectable number of major international artists, such as Laurie Anderson, Charlemagne Palestine, Jenny Holzer, Nan Hoover, Marina Abramović, and Ben d'Armagnac. As Ruth Bellinkx and Marga van Mechelen show in more detail in their contribution to this volume, however, the significance of the Amsterdam foundation for video art was ambiguous. On the one hand, video functioned primarily as a supporting medium: performances, lectures and exhibitions were recorded by it. Smals deliberately aimed at

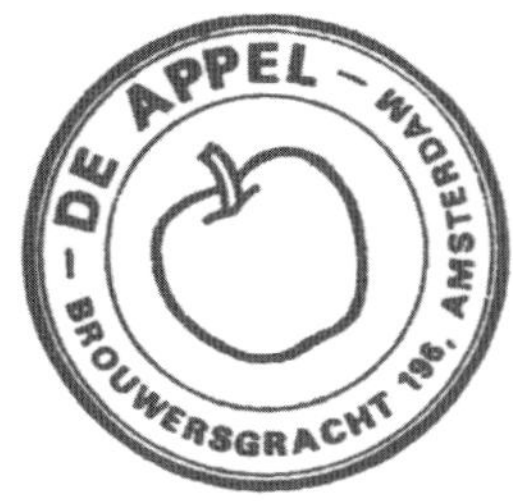

Logo De Appel

[9]
Notitie over Film en Video in Rotterdam, Rotterdam Arts Foundation, May 1988.
[10]
From a report by the Amsterdam Art Council on De Appel, drawn up in 1977 and published in 1978, compiled by Walter Barten, Antje von Graevenitz, Frans Haks, Rob Huisman and Rob van Tour.

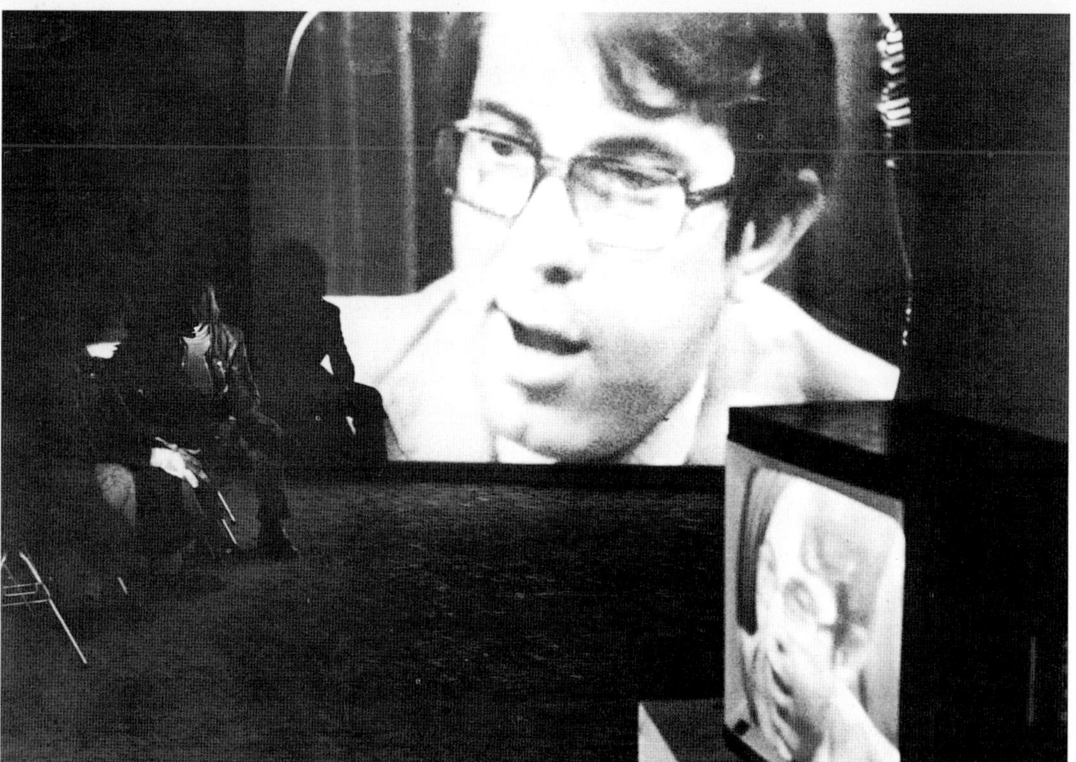

Video exhibition at the Lijnbaancentrum, Rotterdam 1973

forming the largest possible collection of this kind of document- 63
ary material. On the other hand, in a number of cases video was
a part of the performance (as in the work of Nan Hoover). On the
evenings open to the public, independent video productions
were shown by artists like Ulrike Rosenbach, Michel Cardena
and Tony Morgan, but they only accounted for a small percent-
age of the total number of presentations. Video gradually came
to occupy a larger place, but that trend was deliberately called to
a halt. In 1980 Wies Smals took the initiative of setting up an
independent institute for video. This eventually became Time
Based Arts (TBA), which took over the video collection of De
Appel.

The year in which De Appel was founded, 1975, was also the
year in which Het Kijkhuis commenced operations in The Hague.
It was eventually to become one of the three main institutes for
video art. Together with Montevideo and Time Based Arts in
Amsterdam, it also (especially later on) became the international
point of contact for interested viewers, artists, producers and
exhibition curators. The policy of the various government bodies
was to target these three institutions above all.
Het Kijkhuis occupied premises in Noordeinde that a private
individual made available free of charge. At first it concentrated

on distribution, presentation and the forming of a collection.
During the first few years it focused on social documentaries
that set out to improve the world and were produced by people
with more idealism than money. The neighbouring Meatball was
the main supplier, so the presentations consisted largely of
socially engaged tapes and documentaries broadcast (usually
by the VPRO) on television. However, quality film, photography
and musical performances also formed an important part of its
activities. In addition, visitors could request tapes from the
video library and view them by themselves. From 1977 to 1982
the activities were accompanied by a monthly magazine with
background information on the programme and announcements
of the new acquisitions, sometimes with brief comments on
them. Entirely in accordance with the Zeitgeist, Het Kijkhuis
also organized political evenings, for example on atomic energy.
There was little scope for art in them.

The first, rather hesitant and tentative article on video art
appeared in the magazine for the first time in 1981. The same
issue announced a video festival. It took place in the following
year, gradually bringing about a sea-change in the nature and
structure of Het Kijkhuis. Video art really appeared on the scene
at the World Wide Video Festival, although many of the tapes
shown there still had a strong social component. The term
'independent video' enabled the organizers to present a wide
range of tapes. Director Tom van Vliet stated in an interview with
Johan Pijnappel that it was particularly the light that he found so
exciting in video as a medium, but in all of his other replies there
was no mistaking the importance that he attached to social
commitment in video art.[11] With the arrival of the festival, Het

64

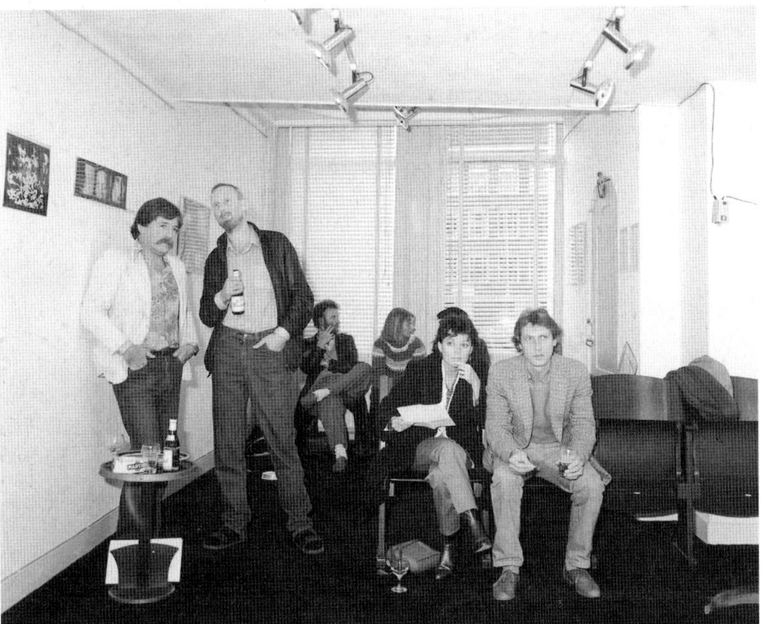

Opening of the Servaas exhibition at Montevideo, 1984. Standing: René Coëlho and Servaas

11
Art 1993.

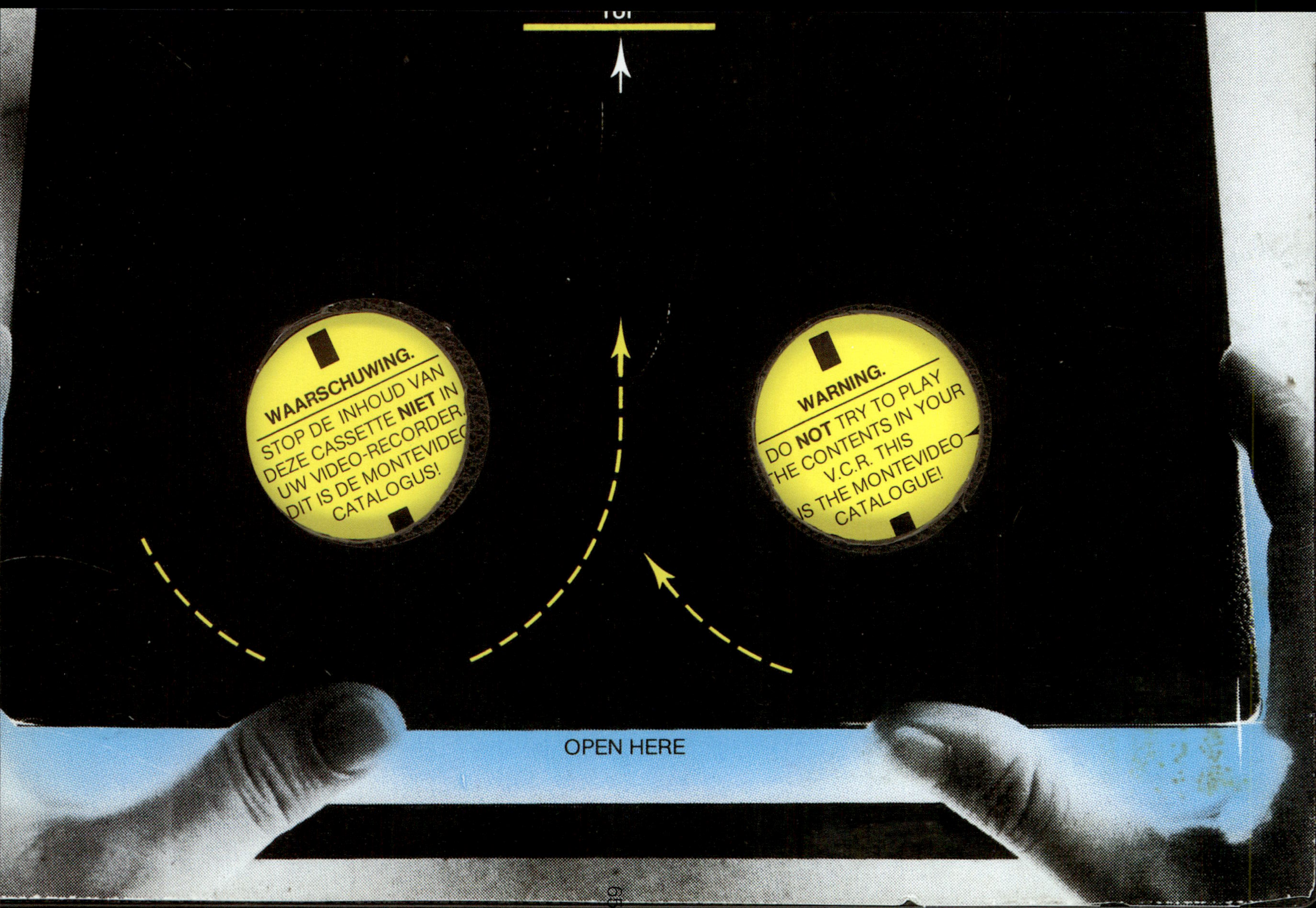
TOP
OPEN HERE
WAARSCHUWING.
STOP DE INHOUD VAN
DEZE CASSETTE NIET IN
UW VIDEO-RECORDER.
DIT IS DE MONTEVIDEO
CATALOGUS!
WARNING.
DO NOT TRY TO PLAY
THE CONTENTS IN YOUR
V.C.R. THIS
IS THE MONTEVIDEO
CATALOGUE!

Kijkhuis increasingly interpreted its role as that of facilitating
video productions (often in collaboration with Meatball). There
was an attempt at market research on the interest in
independent productions, and writing about video was
encouraged. It also mediated in the lending of equipment.
The first festivals were already marked by cooperation with
other institutions, such as the Haags Gemeentemuseum.
This was to happen more and more in the later period, when Het
Kijkhuis had disappeared as a physical institution.

When the government suddenly came up in 1986 with the
idea of a national video institute, designated Time Based Arts as
such in principle, and closed the subsidies to the others, Het
Kijkhuis managed to survive thanks to the relatively high level of
funding it received from the local authority in The Hague and the
growing success of the festival. Plans were even being made for
a new building at the time. Videoline (video tapes broadcast on
the cable in The Hague) was set up, and the ideas about a
regular programming of exhibitions took on a more specific
shape. The publication of a new video catalogue supported the
task of distribution. It showed, incidentally, that Het Kijkhuis
began the European distribution of the collection of its big
brother in New York, Electronic Art Intermix.

Things went wrong when the local authority in The Hague
breathed new life into the Haagse Filmhuis. The new building in
Spui, the World Wide Video Center, which was so enthusiastically occupied in 1993 and which at last provided the sorely
needed space for a regular programming of installations and
other activities (Dan Graham was the first artist to make use of
it), suddenly had to be shared with that Filmhuis. In the end a
large portion of the subsidy went to it as well. At this, Tom van
Vliet and his team decided to leave The Hague, to move their
festival to Amsterdam, and to drop their other activities. Moving
had become a realistic option now that the Stedelijk Museum in
Amsterdam was prepared to accommodate the festival. When
that cooperation came to an end after three years, as had been
agreed, the organization intensified its links with all kinds of
other institutes in Amsterdam to enable its wide range of
programmes to be accommodated somewhere. The switch to
Amsterdam increased the numbers of visitors significantly.

Het Kijkhuis/World Wide Video Festival has certainly had an
influence on the interest in video art. At first the festivals had a
high in-crowd component and appeared more of a meeting
place for artists and others directly involved, but later on they
became more open and attracted a growing audience.
Moreover, the festival has always had an international allure and
attempts to bring new (technical) developments to the public
eye. As a result of the festival practice, the unambiguous
concept of video became outdated long ago. Although Het
Kijkhuis has disappeared as an institute, the WWVF has
become one. Incidentally, Dutch video artists never played a

major role in the presentations or programming. 'Sooner an unknown Chinese than a well-known Dutch artist', as one frustrated Dutch artist once put it.

Het Kijkhuis was a model of how a local authority can contribute to the promotion of art and culture. It was able to function for years thanks to the generous support that it received from the local authority of The Hague, making it less vulnerable to the unpredictable and arbitrary policy of the national government.[12]

Rivalry

Montevideo, the second major player in the Dutch video field, started up in 1978. Its founder, René Coëlho, had worked as a cameraman for years and had received the necessary impulses from his mentor Livinus van de Bundt: the latter's ideas and his videos had made such an impression that they were to be a permanent source of inspiration. Coëlho was never very keen on theory. In one of his many interviews he said: 'Feeling is more important than theory. You read a lot of bla-bla in art criticism. You write in pompous terms about what you ought to judge intuitively.' In the initial stage, Montevideo was no more than a private studio that had got out of hand: just some equipment, a space to show work, and a little documentation. Coëlho's aim was equally modest: 'To contribute something to video art'.[13] He was already in contact with artists like Bert Schutter and Servaas, and others were soon to follow. In the next few years, as a tutor at the AKI in Enschede, Coëlho had at his disposal an arsenal of potential video artists. That direct link with the academy provoked a lot of criticism. He was accused of assuming too much of the role of a paternalistic tutor towards 'his' artists, which made it difficult for them to evade his control. Moreover, it was alleged, the large influx from Enschede led to the creation of a one-sided picture. However, criticisms of this kind often arose from the animosity between the different institutes, which clouded awareness of the fact that the link between Montevideo and the AKI was a logical one.

Montevideo was soon able to rent out many works by artists. It was also not long before it felt the need for financial support. This materialized in 1983, at which the video centre moved to North Amsterdam, where there was enough space to put on regular presentations (accompanied by a bulletin). Artists were invited from abroad as well as from the Netherlands to show their videos or installations. The space and the resources were also sufficient to expand the production facilities and to run them more effectively. The particular relation with Sony was very important in that process. Coëlho had personal contacts with Sony Nederland (represented by Brandsteder), which for years provided him with inexpensive equipment of the latest kind.

[12]
Discussions that I had with Tom van Vliet and Rien Hagen in July 2002 provided a large part of the information about Het Kijkhuis and the WWVF.
[13]
E-mail interview with René Coëlho, July 2002.

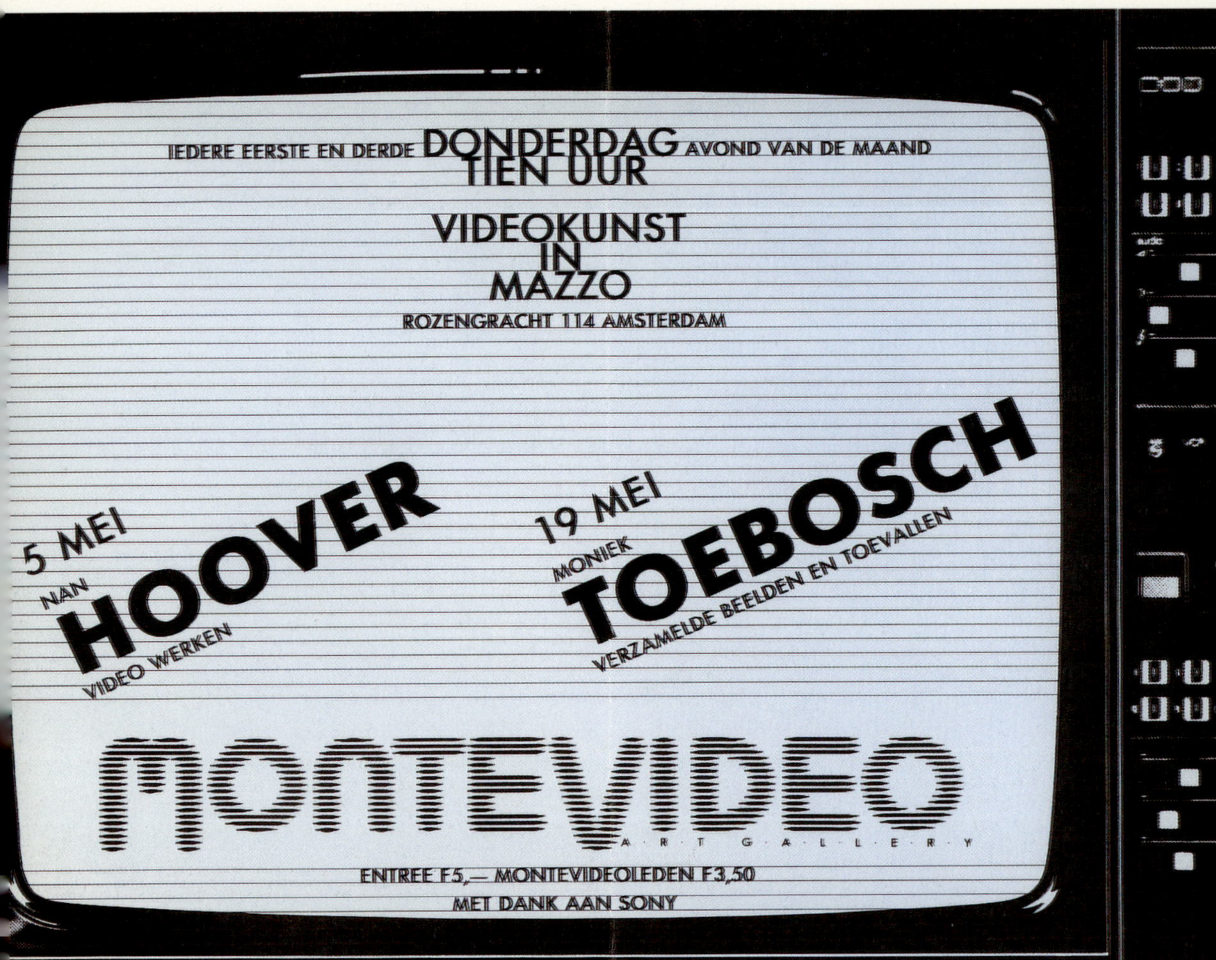

68   Video art in Mazzo, organized by Montevideo, Amsterdam 1982

On 22 March 1982 the Dutch and foreign video artists living in
the Netherlands received a letter from De Appel. It was an
invitation to attend a meeting for the setting up of a new
institute for video art. It was a known fact that De Appel wanted
to drop its video activities because they took up too much time
and because the foundation wanted to concentrate more on
site-specific projects. All the same, it was a remarkable
document, as Montevideo had already been in existence for four
years. It gives the impression that Montevideo, and in particular
its director, were not taken very seriously by the art world.
Coëlho described his position: '[...] I came from the world of
television, which a sizeable proportion of the video artists tend
to rebel against'.[14] De Appel, on the other hand, was at that time
an institute with a very high reputation among artists in the
Netherlands and abroad and among a small, élitist public of art-
lovers. So some arrogance could be expected from it.

It was at that meeting that the Association of Video Artists
was set up, with Madelon Hooykaas as the first chairperson.
There was no subsidy available for an association, so they were

14
E-mail interview with René Coëlho, July 2002.

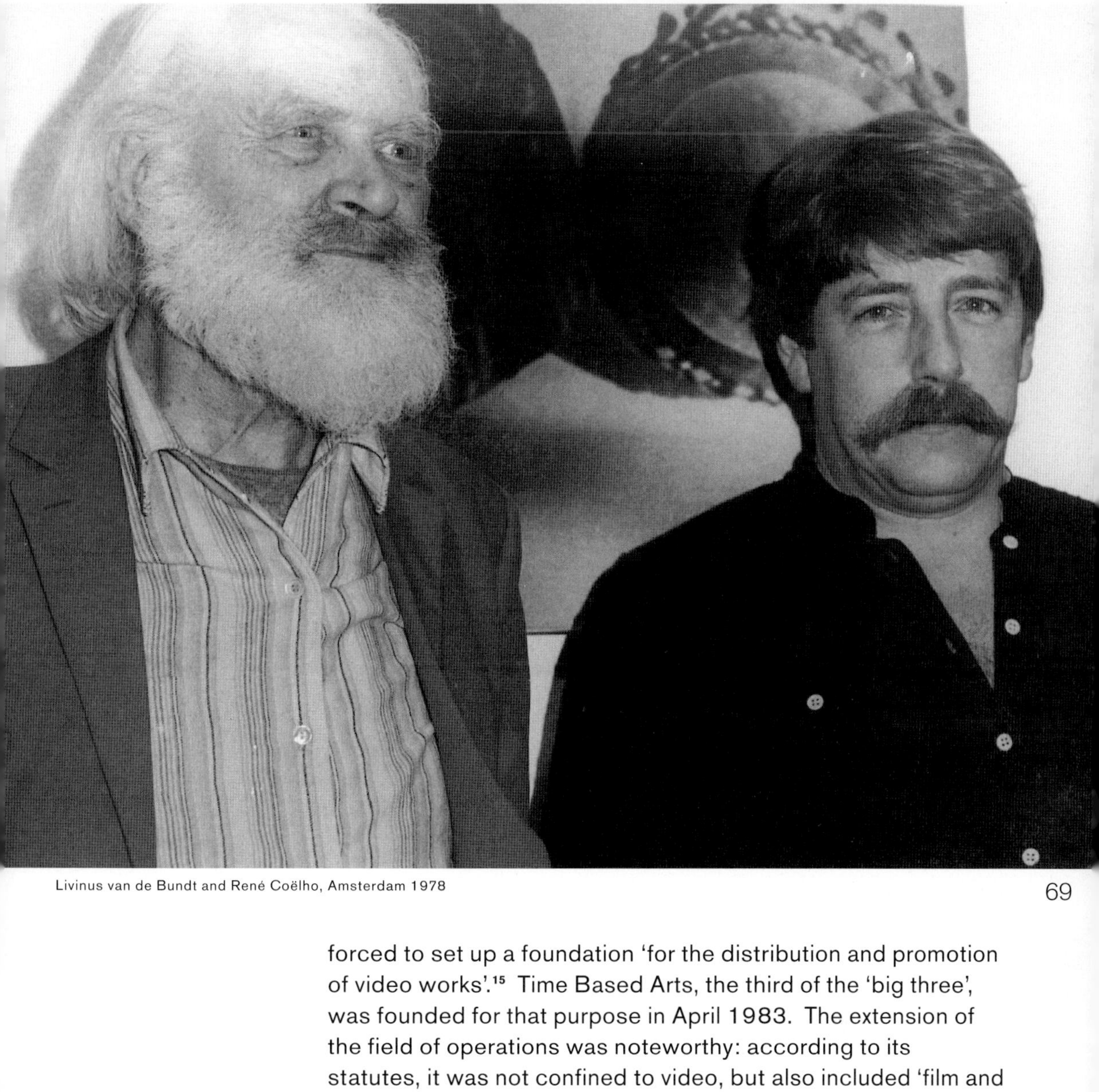

forced to set up a foundation 'for the distribution and promotion of video works'.[15] Time Based Arts, the third of the 'big three', was founded for that purpose in April 1983. The extension of the field of operations was noteworthy: according to its statutes, it was not confined to video, but also included 'film and audio works (and combinations of them)'. Aart van Barneveld was appointed as director of the new institute. Unlike Van Vliet and Coëlho, Van Barneveld had a background in art. Through his friend Ulises Carrión, he had been involved in Other Books and So, a kind of gallery that focused on artists books and other artists publications.

It was unfortunate that TBA was set up as a rival to Montevideo, but even more unfortunate was its structure. An association of artists, whose number rapidly rose to a few dozen, set up a foundation of which they remained in charge. The practical consequence was that the TBA staff were not free to get on with the job. There was always the threat of conflict situations. That well-intentioned but unworkable construction was eventually to herald the demise of TBA as an independent

[15]
Cited from the charter.

institute. Many viewed in a positive light the fact that from now on work would always be based on an artistic perspective – there would be no commercial interests in the setting up and implementation of projects, no water with the wine when it came to presenting work. That is also the reason why TBA never paid any attention to technical production and only mediated to facilitate that production. Thinking commercially and basing your policy on it was not done at TBA.

TBA concentrated on the presentations, which took place at least once a month. On Van Barneveld's initiative a video circuit was set up in 1984 to show videos on a monthly basis in different parts of the country (including Mediamatic in Groningen). Many Dutch video works could be presented abroad thanks to the old contacts with De Appel and Other Books.

TBA initiated and organized a large number of large-scale projects. In 'Talking Back to the Media' (1985), an international group of artists responded via various mass media to the representations disseminated by those same media. Aorta, the Rijksacademie, De Appel, Shaffy Theater, the Amsterdam cable and VPRO radio collaborated on the project. A year later 'The Box' was organized, a project by the artist Daniel Brun. Artists and others involved debated the new technologies and their consequences live on the cable. 'Geluid herzien' (1986) was a large-scale international audio art project, once again involving a number of other institutes too (such as Christofori in Amsterdam and the Apollohuis in Eindhoven). TBA had the lowest threshold of the three. It was easy for the public to walk in and ask something or to view tapes (TBA had an extensive archive). This was because the premises beside the Bloemgracht had always had the atmosphere of a place where all kinds of people could meet, almost a kind of club.

In 1986 TBA received the dubious honour of being elevated to the status of the single institute of the future. In itself this was a compliment, because the decision was taken on the basis of quality of content, but at the same time it set TBA up as a rival to the other institutes, the losers.[16] That was not what TBA itself wanted at all. The fact that the new situation would put an end to the permanently meagre level of subsidies from the Amsterdam local authority and from the national government was an attractive side-effect. The main loser from all this was Montevideo, which was still a flourishing institute at that time. Montevideo received a small transitional subsidy, and that was the end of it. The destruction of capital was the least of the damage that this astonishing decision was to cause. René Coëlho showed the determination that is in his nature. First of all he created a big fuss – never has video art received so much coverage in the press – so that everyone knew what the

---

[16] What exactly was meant by 'quality of content' was not spelled out in more detail. It was and still is unclear why preference was given to TBA. Perhaps the choice was motivated by the emphasis that the institute put on its presentations and on providing information to the public.

Ulises Carrión,
Twin Butlers,
Time Based Arts,
Amsterdam 1983

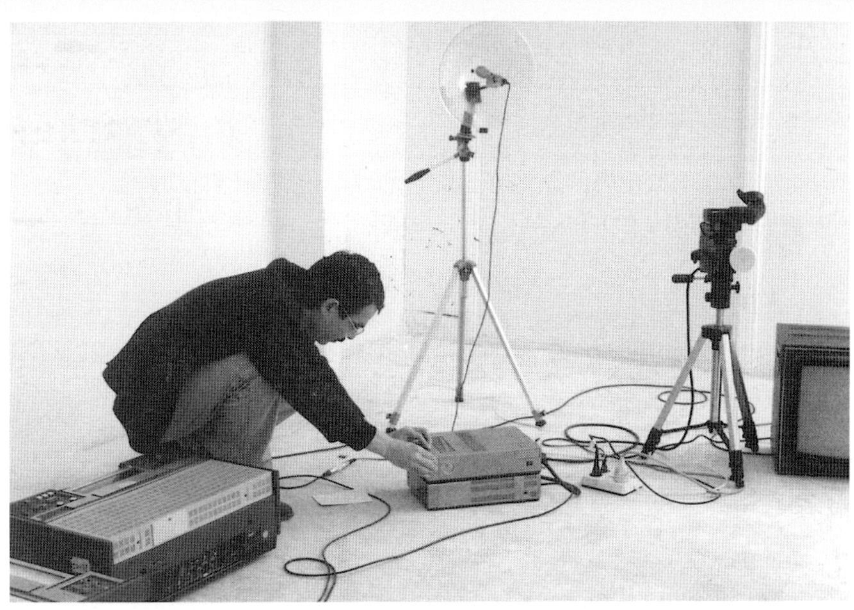

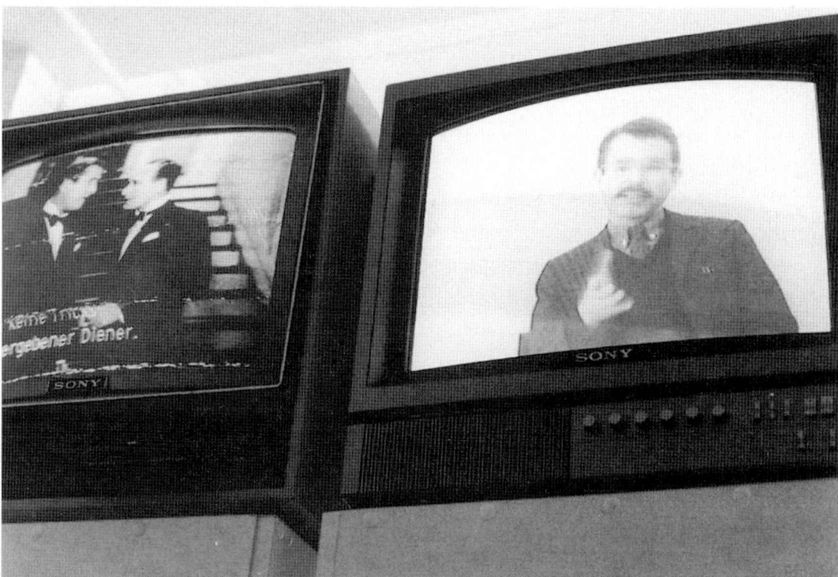

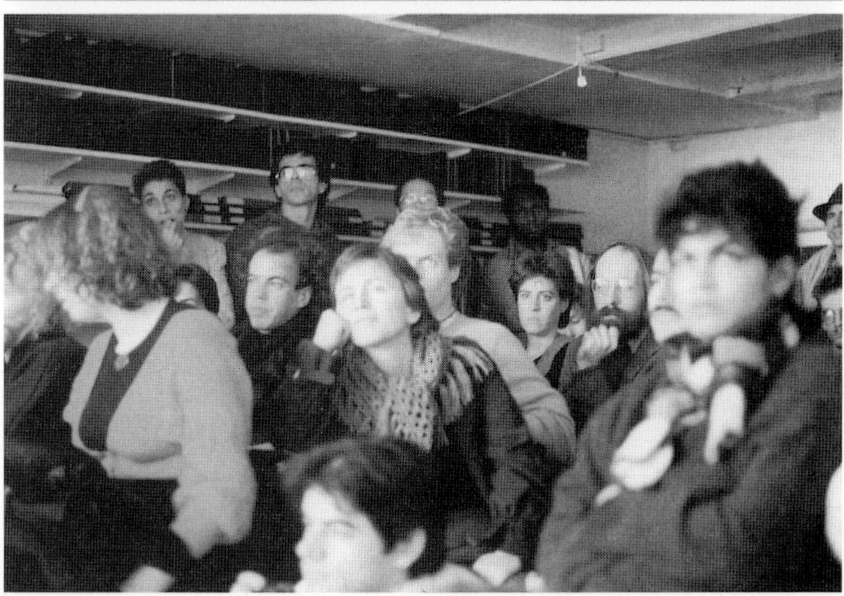

situation meant. Then he went back to the Singel, where he had originally started, and continued his activities on four cramped floors. It continued to function as a vital and affordable production facility for many artists (and was now open to others as well). Distribution, documentation and promotion were simply carried on. In 1987 the front of the premises was turned into a gallery. Nan Hoover was the first artist to show there. Some of the staff continued on their own with Media Art Development, an institute that reacted to the new electronic developments that went beyond video art and brought the wider field of media art closer.

Montevideo managed to survive on its own income, some money from the Amsterdam local authority, and by setting up large-scale projects that were useful and interesting, as well as having the banal function of keeping the business going. For a time it cooperated with the Amsterdam audio institute Steim. In 1993 Coëlho was given a commission that he had initiated himself: to conserve the total body of Dutch video art on disk.[17] In addition he developed and produced 'Imago', an exhibition of Dutch video installations that travelled around the world for five years, starting in 1990. These and other projects helped Montevideo to get through the no subsidy era.

In the meantime its colleague Time Based Arts had got into deeper and deeper trouble because the government went back on its original plans - though only after it had let all the institutes, particularly TBA, plod on for a couple of years and make plans. This gave the unfortunate structure of the institute the chance to play up. It was like an unhappy marriage that runs on the rocks during a recession. The Foundation and the Association did not end up in the street, but only by the skin of their teeth. To make matters worse, Aart van Barneveld, to whom acting as a mediator had become second nature, died in 1990. It became increasingly clear that, now that the TBA had no subsidy and was riven by internal conflicts, it had no chance of survival. Wary approaches were made to Montevideo, delicately steering clear of old wounds. The first specific joint project was Kanaal Zero, a monthly art programme on the Amsterdam cable, with the artist Claudio Goulart as series editor. With the aid of a project subsidy from the Amsterdam local authority, it was eventually able to transmit seventy-five broadcasts. It provided a venue for many artists, particularly Dutch ones.

In 1993 Time Based Arts was incorporated in Montevideo. Although it was called a merger, insiders knew how the roles were divided: the TBA collection was transferred to Montevideo. From then on Montevideo adopted the name of the Netherlands Media Art Institute, Montevideo/Time Based Arts, a tactical and polite mouthful, but the 'real' name Montevideo

72

17
This proved to be a brainwave in more than one respect. The rise of digital technologies constantly makes the existing equipment redundant. Transferring the existing video material to disk was a forward-looking and natural step that activated and encouraged thinking about 'what next?'.

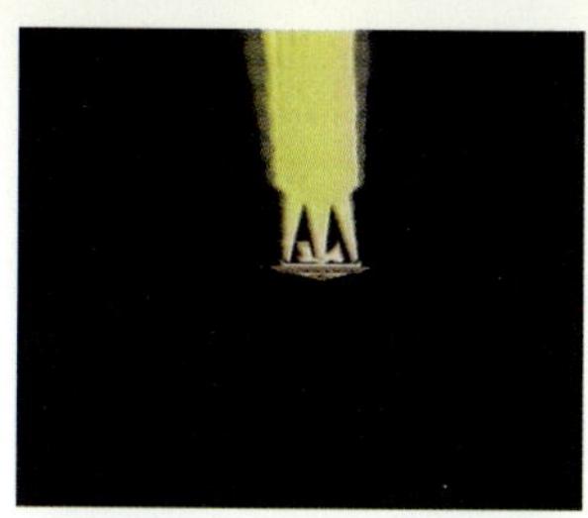

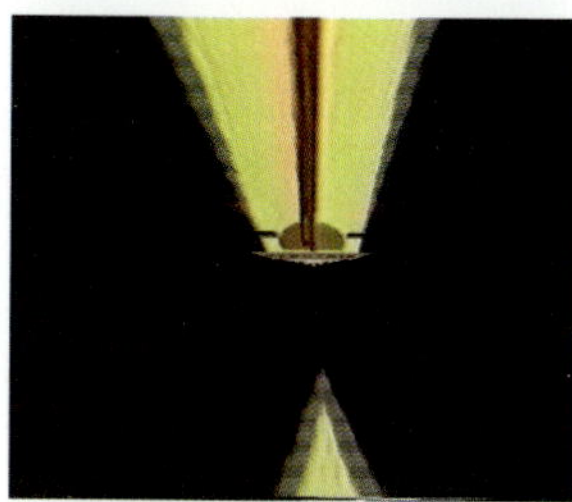

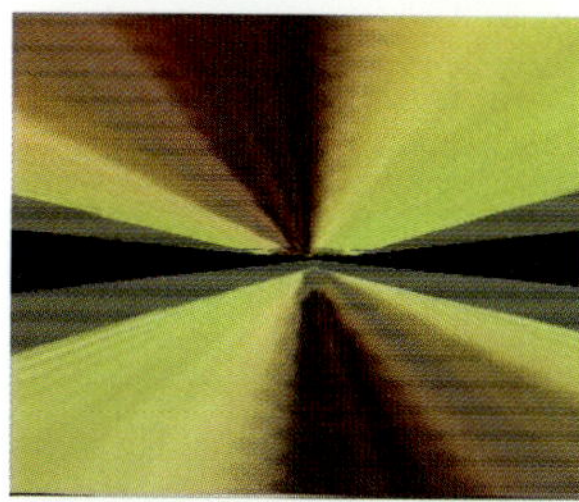

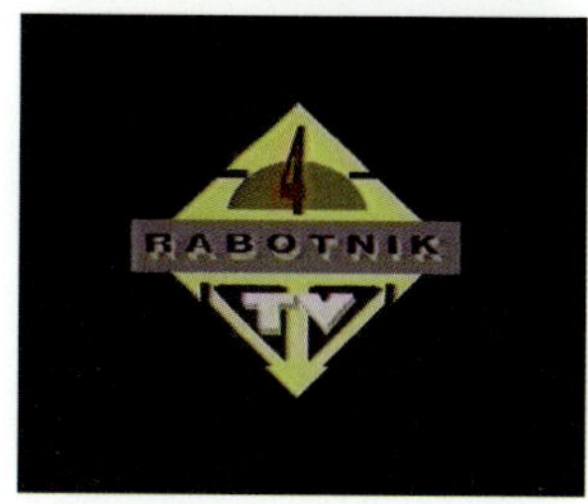

Leader, Rabotnik TV

has never disappeared from popular parlance. As a result of the merger, the national government reopened the flow of subsidy. It was increased in 1997 and, again, in 2001, and was turned into a four-year subsidy. The objectives were wider too: production, presentation, documentation, research, and education. In 1994 Montevideo moved to Spuistraat, and in 1997 to the present premises beside the Keizersgracht. In January 1998 the artist Heiner Holtappels took over from René Coëlho. The private studio of the past had by now become a large, established institute.

Conclusion

It is impossible in one article to do justice to all the initiatives that have played a role in Dutch video art, but I would still like to mention a few of them. Mediamatic in Groningen, and later in Amsterdam, which was founded in 1983, was important, particularly through its international journal, which made serious attempts to promote theoretical discussion. The Stedelijk Museum in Amsterdam (personified in its curator Dorine Mignot) demonstrated its willingness to take the medium seriously, at a time when colleagues showed a general lack of interest in it, with the exhibitions 'The Luminous Image' (1983) and 'Kunst voor tv' (1987), its one-man exhibitions by Gary Hill and Bill Viola, and its video screening space, the so-called 'video stairs'. Without a doubt, the unconventional programmes that Rabotnik TV was transmitting on the cable in the 1980s, 'postpunk, Dadaist Modernist, from God to trash'[18] (with Peter Klashorst, Gerald van der Kaap, Menno Grootveld and others) contributed to a new visual idiom of its own and a different approach to the medium of television. The VPRO tried the same thing with programmes like Tape TV and Neon. The Amsterdam Arts Channel, Amsterdam C, has been presenting weekly programmes on the cable since 1987 (in Rotterdam and The Hague too); intended above all to reflect topical cultural events, they regularly include work by (video) artists. The AVE Festival in Arnhem profiled itself on various occasions in the 1980s as the art academy students' alternative to the World Wide Video Festival. Finally, the more recent 'Impakt' presents itself as the somewhat recalcitrant, unpredictable offspring of the sometimes more settled parent World Wide.

More than thirty years of video institutes, mini institutes or initiatives yield an exciting picture. It is almost moving to consider the amount of enthusiasm, dedication, idealism and good intentions that went into launching each institute. It was very often a noble sort of craziness. There was no money, and there was not usually a suitable space available either. If the term 'to do something for love' had not already been coined, it could have been devised with this situation in mind. It is

73

18
Mediamatic, 1988, 2 (1988) 3, p. 138.

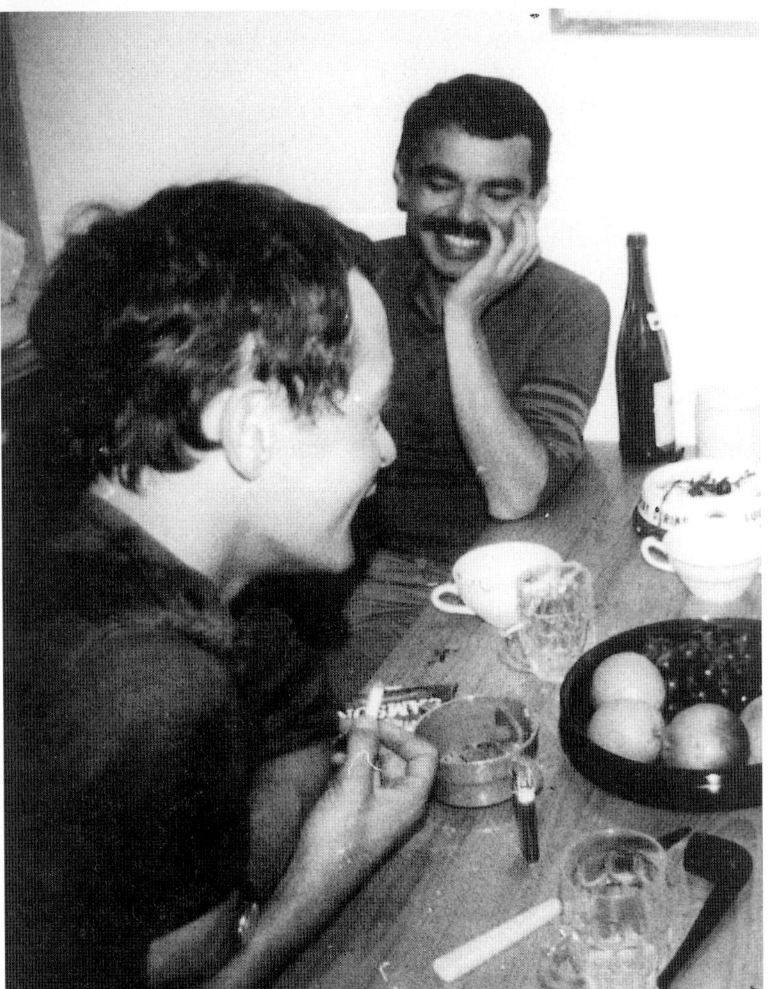

Ulises Carrión and Aart van Barneveld (former TBA director), Ten Katestraat, Amsterdam 1980

therefore extremely doubtful whether the inconsistent, ill-conceived and unpredictable subsidy policy of the various levels of government really had much influence on the various activities. Montevideo has risen from the ashes three times without its content or qualities being impaired. The World Wide Video Festival has survived all the political madness for twenty years. Time Based Arts did not go under from the lack of funds, but from the lack of a strong leadership when the funds were withheld. Other initiatives have been stopped because they had become outdated or because the original energy and motivation had run out. It is perhaps comfortable to work when money does not have to be a cause for concern, but no matter how much of a cliché or conversation-stopper it has become, it does not usually promote creativity.

It is difficult to say whether these institutions have had an influence. There are no criteria by which it can be gauged. If they had made an impact, then it is primarily the big three that have done so. And that influence could have been greater if the relations between them had been better.

Although those directly involved do not have much to say on this score or, in the case of TBA, have lost their voice, it was a public secret that Coëlho from Montevideo and Van Barneveld from TBA would not go through the same doorway. This was due to huge differences in character, but also to differences in background, perspective and the frustrations connected with the emergence of TBA. The third, Tom van Vliet, always kept his distance, refused to take sides, and kept out of reach, which made him a force to be reckoned with. Besides, he operated (for a long time) in The Hague, and there is a tendency in Amsterdam to regard everything outside Amsterdam as inconsequential. Neither Montevideo nor TBA took him very seriously. Those poor personal relations meant that there was very little or no cooperation, not even at times, as in 1986, when there clearly was a common 'foe': the government. There was no effective division of labour at all. Neither was there a healthy competition because of the lack of mutual respect.

But these considerations and judgements become less significant when set against the turbulent developments of video as a medium since the mid-1990s. What had proved impossible after years of struggle suddenly succeeded without any effort. Among art academy students and young artists video grew to become one of the most popular media. They had no links with video or media institutes, and knew nothing about their less successful predecessors. Unfettered by any past, 'filmpjes' were made (a casual term that was taboo during the emancipation era of the medium). Galleries and museums were not slow to jump onto the bandwagon. Artists of the first hour, many of whom had already given up the struggle, now saw 'kids' making a name for themselves without much difficulty with a medium whose qualities they, the older generation, had had to demonstrate time and again. It would take another article to explain this sudden miracle. I can only note with an undertone of bitterness that there is no room for video institutes in this perspective.

It will be unnecessary and impossible to write another article like this one in thirty years' time.

Rob Perrée studied Dutch language and art history at the University of Amsterdam. He works as a freelance writer and exhibition curator, specialized in American art and new media. Perrée is on the editorial staff of the dutch art magazine, *Kunstbeeld*. His other books include *Image on the Run: Dutch Video Art of the 80s* (1985); *Into Video Art: De karakteristieken van een medium* (1988); *Bakelite: The Material of a Thousand Uses* (1996); *Postcards from Black America: Hedendaagse Afrikaans-Amerikaanse kunst* (1998); *Dialogue: About Nan Hoover* (2001); *Cover to Cover. The Artist's Book in Perspective* (2002). Rob Perrée lives and works in Amsterdam and Brooklyn, New York.

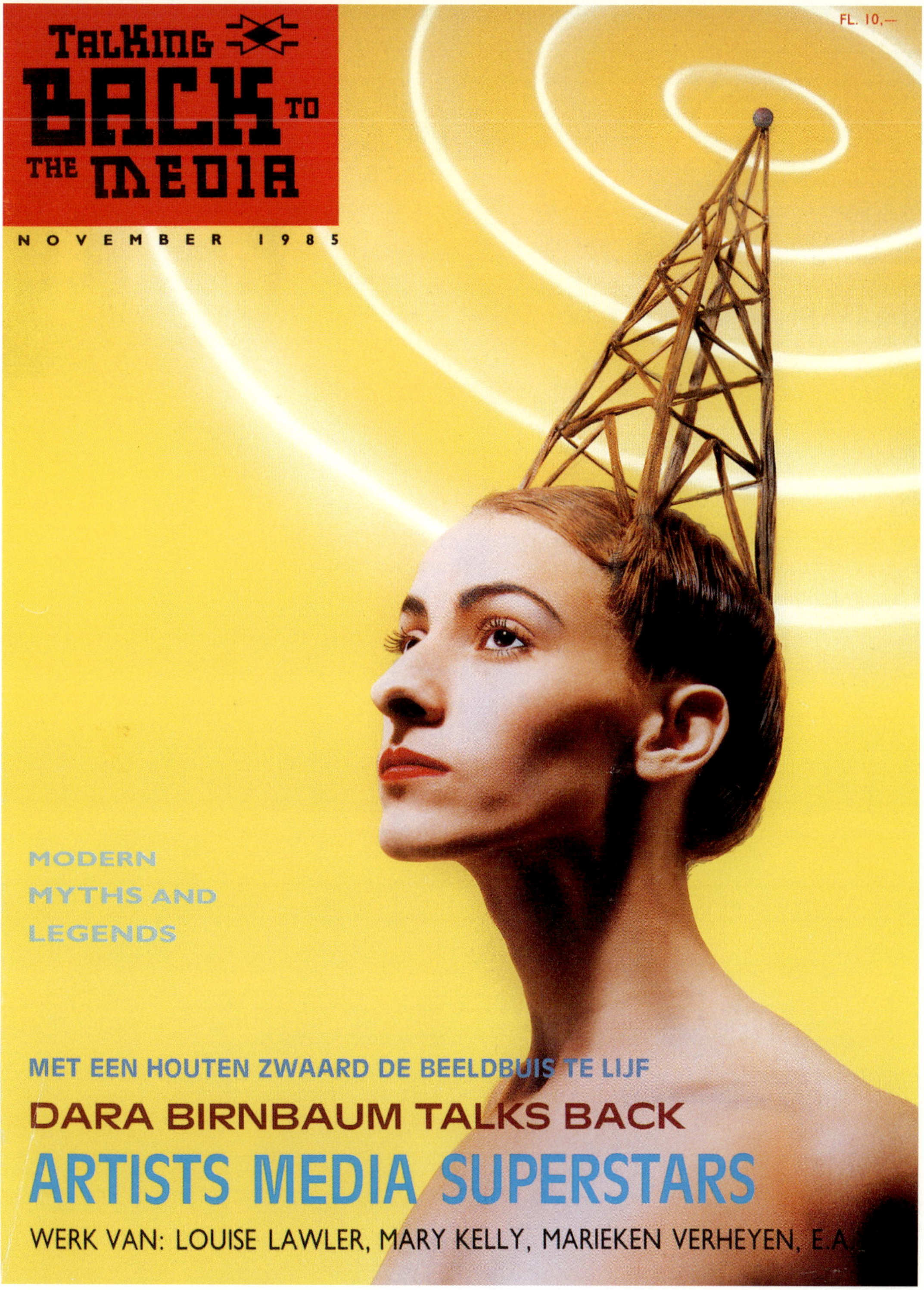

'Talking Back to the Media', Time Based Arts, Amsterdam 1985

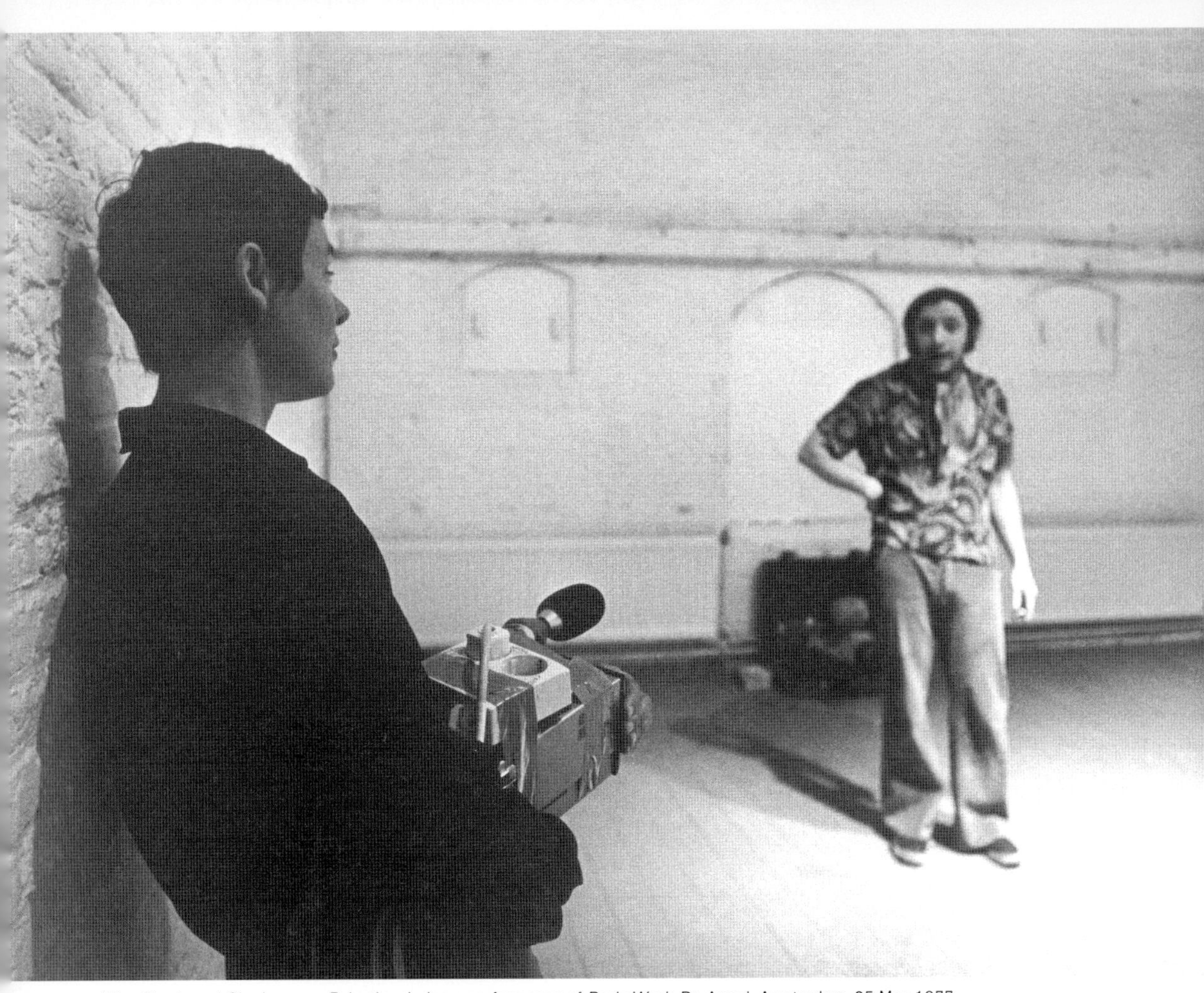

78   Wies Smals and Charlemagne Palestine during a performance of *Body Work*, De Appel, Amsterdam, 25 May 1977

Ruth Bellinkx and Marga van Mechelen

Instrumental and autonomous
Video in De Appel

Introduction

Video played simultaneously both an essential and a secondary role in De Appel (1975–1983):[1] essential because without video De Appel would never have been able to give a good picture of the history of performance art nor of the performances that took place on its premises or elsewhere at its instigation; secondary because Wies Smals, the founder and director of De Appel, was primarily interested in performances and environments and initially regarded video purely as a recording medium.[2] Moreover, she felt that video art did not need an institution like De Appel. In her view, the museum would be an ideal venue to present it because she regarded video as an art form that still had a traditional object character. The lesson of reality, however, was that museums were not very active in this field in the 1970s and that many video artists welcomed the opportunities offered by institutions like De Appel. Smals was thus obliged to revise her position and although performances dominated during the first years of De Appel, the use of video in

[1]
De Appel was inaugurated on 4 April 1975 under the directorship of Wies Smals and Josine van Droffelaar, which ended with their sudden death in 1983. After some time the board asked Saskia Bos to assist with the current projects. She charted a new course under the same name. De Appel was first housed in a former warehouse of that name beside the Brouwersgracht in Amsterdam. Later it moved to the Prinseneiland. The present premises are in the Nieuwe Spiegelstraat in the centre of Amsterdam.

[2]
See the interview with Ton Haak: Omdat 1978.

all kinds of forms became an intrinsic part of the institution's activities soon after its foundation. As a time-based medium, video proved in practice to be an invaluable resource for approximating to the experience of a performance. In retrospect we can conclude that De Appel has played an important role in the history of Dutch video art and that almost all of the artists living in the Netherlands who worked with video in that period were included in the programme of De Appel.

The present article deals not only with the use of video but also with projects intended for television. It is noteworthy that right from the start De Appel considered one of its responsib-ilities to be to promote and (co)produce television programmes made by artists. In the early days video was regarded at De Appel as a training ground or as a stepping-stone to the larger scale of work for television, and although the institution also had to change its view on this too, working with a mass medium like television was still a priority on the agenda.

The preliminary stage: performance on video
De Appel was founded at a moment when performance art already had a history. Names spring to mind like Yayoi Kusama, whose first performance was in 1962, or Carolee Schneemann, whose name is associated with body art and performance art. Around 1965 the term 'actions' was still in use in Europe for performances by artists like Hermann Nitsch or Joseph Beuys, who were both of great importance for the development of performance art. The programme of De Appel focused on such actions right from the start, as well as on 'gebeurens' – events or performances linked with the names of Gerrit Dekker and Ben d'Armagnac, and on music performances that harked back in some respects to Fluxus-like forms. Wies Smals regarded video recordings as an excellent way of introducing the Dutch public to the prehistory of performance. During an orientation trip in early 1973, she visited the video gallery Studio Oppenheim in Cologne, and in Florence she met Maria Gloria Biccochi from Art/Tapes/22, a newly founded centre for the production and distribution of artists' videos for Europe, the United States and Japan. Smals made an agreement with her for the sending of video tapes on consignment, which made it possible to present the history of performance art to the Dutch public in De Appel.

Video was a natural medium for the recording of perform-ances. Video and performance art had already made inroads in the alternative circuit in the 1960s as brother and sister. After all, they are both based on the possibility of working in real time. Wies Smals had a portapak at her disposal right from the start, which could be used for every live activity in De Appel. She soon assumed the role of camerawoman, and in a short time built up a sizeable and highly rated video collection. Video was a fixed component of De Appel from the start. Most of the 1,800 visitors to De Appel in its first months took advantage of the

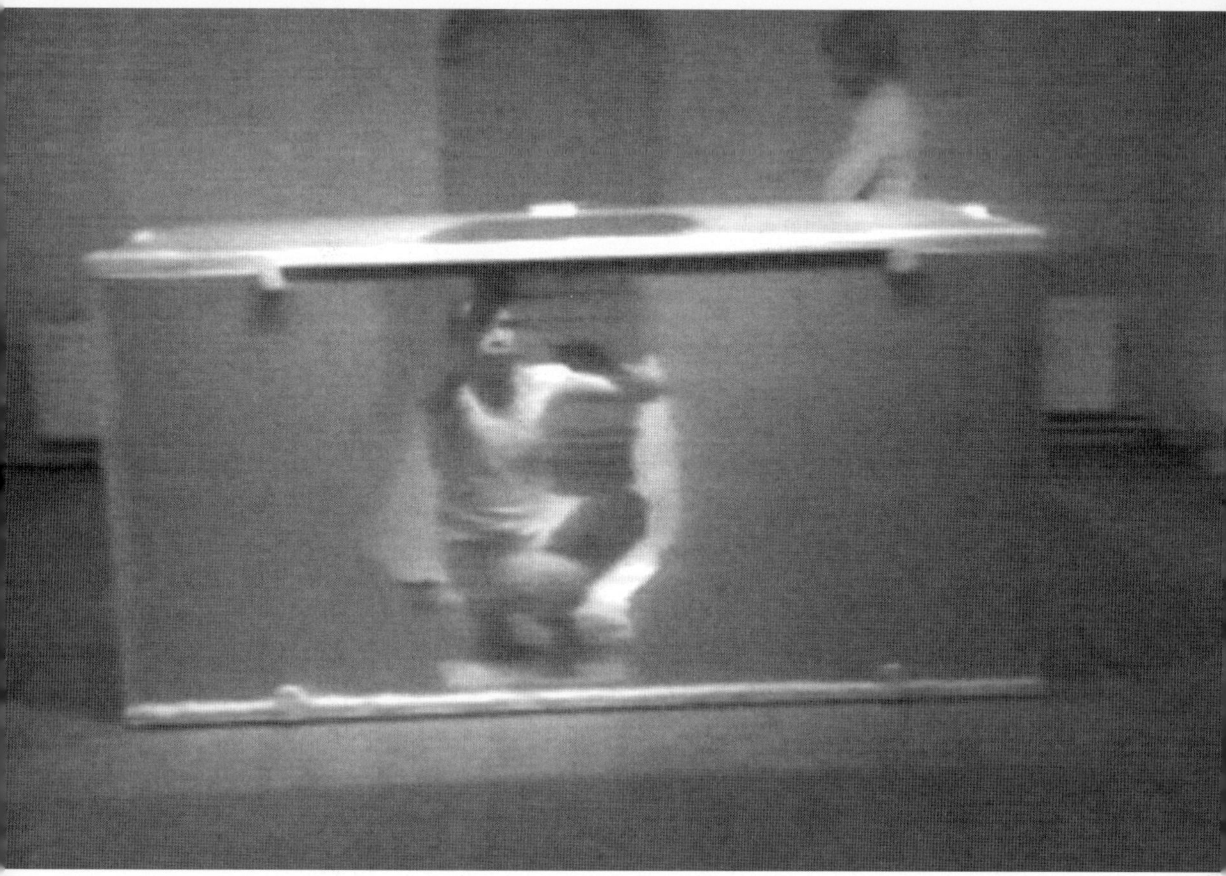

Ben d'Armagnac, performance in De Appel, Amsterdam 1975, video, b/w, sound, 15'30"

opportunity to watch videos. If you missed a performance, you could see it on video afterwards and thus keep up to date. There was an opportunity to view video tapes every Thursday evening, and there was usually documentation on the performances, which often consisted of video tapes. For instance, during a performance by Urs Lüthi in early April 1975, the showing of his *Self Portrait* and *Morir d'amore* from the previous year was also announced. A little over a month later the first video performances appeared on the programme: *Playbox Amsterdam* by Michael Druks. A television set stood in the performance space in De Appel. Druks performed all kinds of activities around the television set in front of the video camera, so that the picture was partially or completely hidden from view. Work by Gerrit Dekker and Ben d'Armagnac, two artists who had previously done performances that had been recorded on video or been performed in front of the video camera, was presented in the summer of 1975. In this case they were performances that had been done elsewhere, in Galerie De Mandelgang in Groningen and the Neue Galerie in Aachen.

Besides Wies Smals, Marina Abramović and Uwe Laysiepen also saw the importance of recording their performances on video or film. A first anthology of the seventeen performances

Urs Lüthi, *Self Portrait*, 1974, video, b/w, sound, 7'30"

Urs Lüthi, *Morir d'amore*, 1974, video, b/w, sound, 9'00"

Michael Druks, *Playbox Amsterdam*, 1975, video, b/w, 22'45"

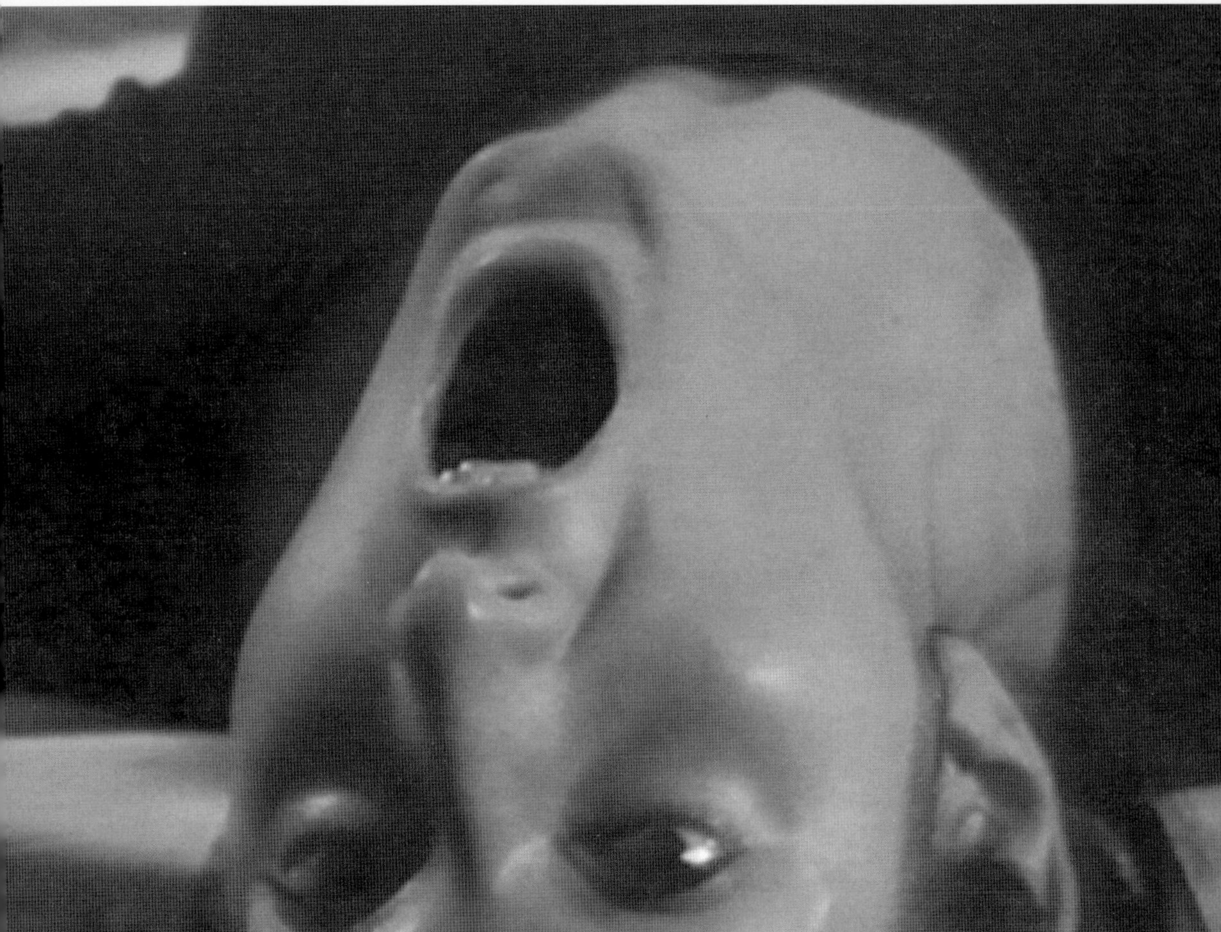

Abramovič / Ulay, *Freeing the Voice*, 1976, video, colour, sound, 38'20"

that the two of them did between 1976 and 1980, produced by
Time Based Arts, was released in 1980, followed in 1988 by a
more extensive anthology that the artists issued with
Montevideo.[3]

Marina Abramovič (Belgrade, 1946) and Uwe Laysiepen
(Solingen, 1943), also known as Ulay, met in De Appel in 1975
during Marina Abramovič's first performance in the Netherlands.[4] As well as a performance, Abramovič also presented a
video installation, under the title of a performance that she was
later to do in Belgrade: *Freeing the voice*. This was not the first
time that she worked with video. In 1973, when she was still
living and working in Yugoslavia, she presented her first video
work, *Sound Ambient White*, a follow-up to *Sound Environment
White*, a work consisting of the recording of the silence on a
tape recorder. The influence of John Cage on these two works
was obvious, as was that of Nam June Paik, especially his 1962

[3]
This discussion of the role of video in the work of Marina Abramovič and Ulay draws on several
publications on their work, monographs and exhibition catalogues, as well as additional information
provided by Uwe Laysiepen.

[4]
Abramovič's move to the Netherlands was the pretext for the programme *Beeldspraak* to draw
attention to her work, but she was ahead of her time. The prior announcement of the programme
mentioned the performance *Lips of Thomas*, in which Abramovič cuts a five-pointed star in her belly.
The scene was so controversial that the broadcast planned for 18 January 1976 was cancelled out of
'political caution'.

Abramovič / Ulay, *Lips of Thomas*,
1975, film and video, colour,
no sound, 10'00"

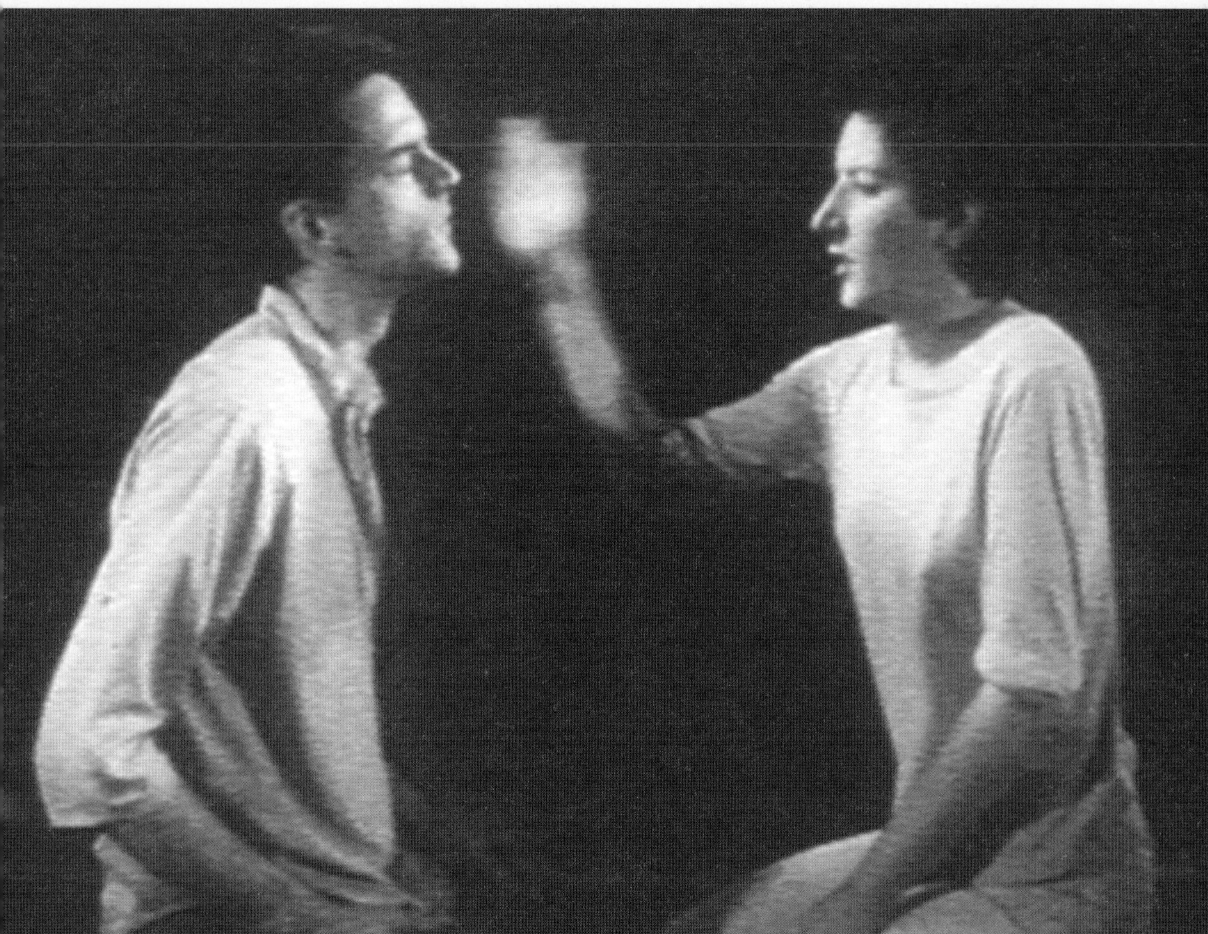

Abramovič/Ulay, *Light/Dark*, 1977, film and video, colour, b/w, sound, 9'18"

Nam June Paik, *Zen for film*, 1962-1964, 8mm film, b/w, no sound, 8'00"

video *Zen for film*, which shows nothing but the light of the projector. Abramovič and Ulay came back to Paik's work in 1984, when they made a parody of his 1974 *Buddha* installation in the Stedelijk Museum in Amsterdam. This video installation, *The World is my Country*, shown at the Biennale in Venice, consisted of a stone with a pair of eyes painted on it, which observed the stone ruins of Sicily on the video monitor. This installation was a follow-up to *The World is my Country*: *The Sex Life of Flowers* (1982), an equally humorous installation in Time Based Arts, which the spectators had to watch hanging upside down in special shoes. If they accidentally moved, the tape stopped which, as the title indicates, presented the sex life of flowers on the monitor.

At first Marina Abramovič and Ulay had a clear preference for film as a medium for recording their performances. During the first years of their joint performances they asked famous directors to make recordings of their performances. For instance, three performances were filmed by Maarten Rens and Louis van Gasteren: *Breathing out/Breathing In* (1977), *Light/Dark* (1978) and *AAA-AAA* (1978). They chose these directors not so much for the specific qualities of their films, but above all because they considered that they were capable of

Abramovič/Ulay, *Breathing out/Breathing in*, 1977, film and video, b/w, sound, 11'00" / Abramovič/Ulay, *AAA-AAA*, 1978, 16 mm film and video, colour and b/w, sound, 13'00"

grasping their ideas and of making a 'dry' recording of their performances. So Abramovič and Ulay were looking for a way of recording for which the medium of video was actually ideal. When a durable recording in colour was required, however, film was the best choice. All the same, they still made regular use of video. The first part of *Breathing in/Breathing out*, a perform-ance which was done in Belgrade in 1977, was recorded on video by Jack Moore of Video Heads.

We have called video and performance brother and sister because they both work with real time, but the experience of a video recording was essentially different from a live perform-ance, especially when the performances by Marina Abramovič (and Ulay) were concerned, characterized as they were (to a certain extent) by the indeterminacy of the process and duration. The patience of the audience was sometimes put severely to the test during a performance, but this was even more the case when it came to watching videos. In compiling their anthologies, Abramovič and Ulay therefore used a limited number of minutes from the actual recordings, though long enough at any rate to conjure up the sensation of its really happening for the viewer.

Video as an art medium played a much less important role in the period covered in this article, although Abramovič and Ulay did make a number of single screen tapes and a few video installations in 1982 and 1983. It is striking that their video works from those years have a completely different character from the performances, such as the series *Nightsea Crossing*, which covered a period of four years. During these perform-ances they sat for days, often seven hours a day, opposite one another like living sculptures. The videos from this period were made during their travels and often show the daily life of the places they visited. One of the best-known was *City of Angels* (1982), a video featuring five people: a rickshaw driver, a beggar, two fruit vendors and a little girl. They are filmed for five minutes, at sunrise and sunset without any cut, in real time, in a motionless pose of their own choosing. Although this work is no longer concerned with the actual physical and spiritual experiences of Abramovič and Ulay, at the same time it matches the silence and tableau character of the performances. In the following year they made *Crazed Elephant*, an installation with a colour video lasting sixty minutes, which has not been shown so often.

Structural attention for video

By August 1975 the financial resources of De Appel were exhausted. A letter was sent to the subscribers to the bulletins asking for a donation of 100 guilders. In her next circular, dated January 1976, Wies Smals announced that at the end of 1975 both the Ministry of Culture, Recreation and Social Work and the Amsterdam Art Fund had allocated a subsidy for the year 1976 and that there was still 2,600 guilders left of the donation.

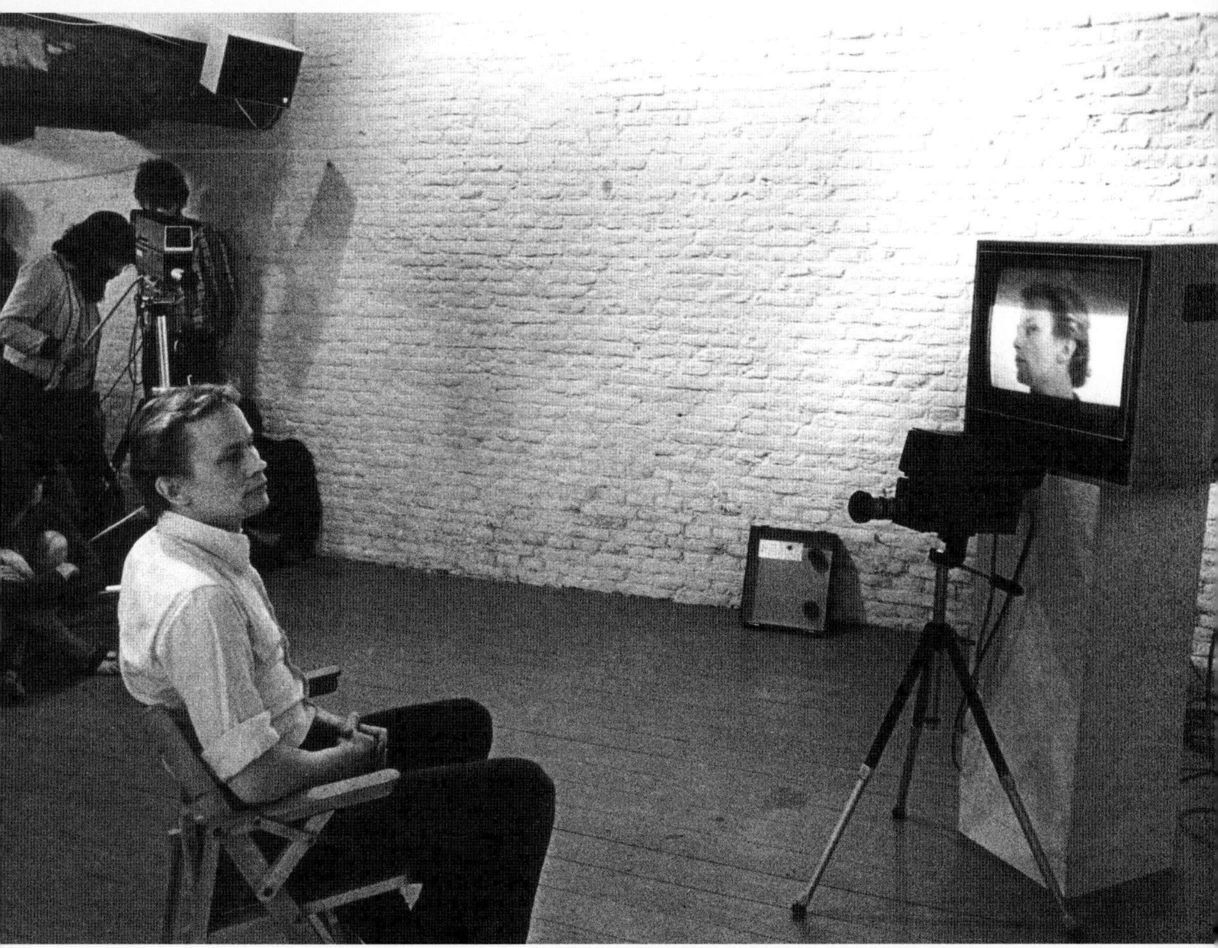

Harrie de Kroon, during the Dutch Week in De Appel, Amsterdam, 5 June 1976

It would be used to finance a video week programmed for the following month (7 to 14 February), to be followed by a number of video evenings. De Appel would be open for a week from 14:00 to 22:00 hours. The video tapes were from Studio Oppenheim in Cologne. They could be viewed by request, which was typical of the personal approach to the public that De Appel favoured. The video evenings were continued in the following months, though they were moved to Wednesday evenings and were at first focused on a single artist.

The successive videos shown were by Nan(cy) Hoover, Michel Cardena, Gina Pane and Joseph Beuys. The contribution of Dutch artists to the programme was small, too small, as the board agreed. The Dutch Week planned for early June 1976 was to change that. Video played a role in two parts of the programme by artists living in the Netherlands, Raul Marroquin and Nan Hoover. Despite the attempts to provide Dutch artists with a platform for performances and video performances, the number of Dutch artists remained small. Attracted by the artistic climate and the financial schemes for artists, a number of foreign artists settled permanently in Amsterdam or Maastricht, where the Jan van Eyck Academy had a well-known experimental department.

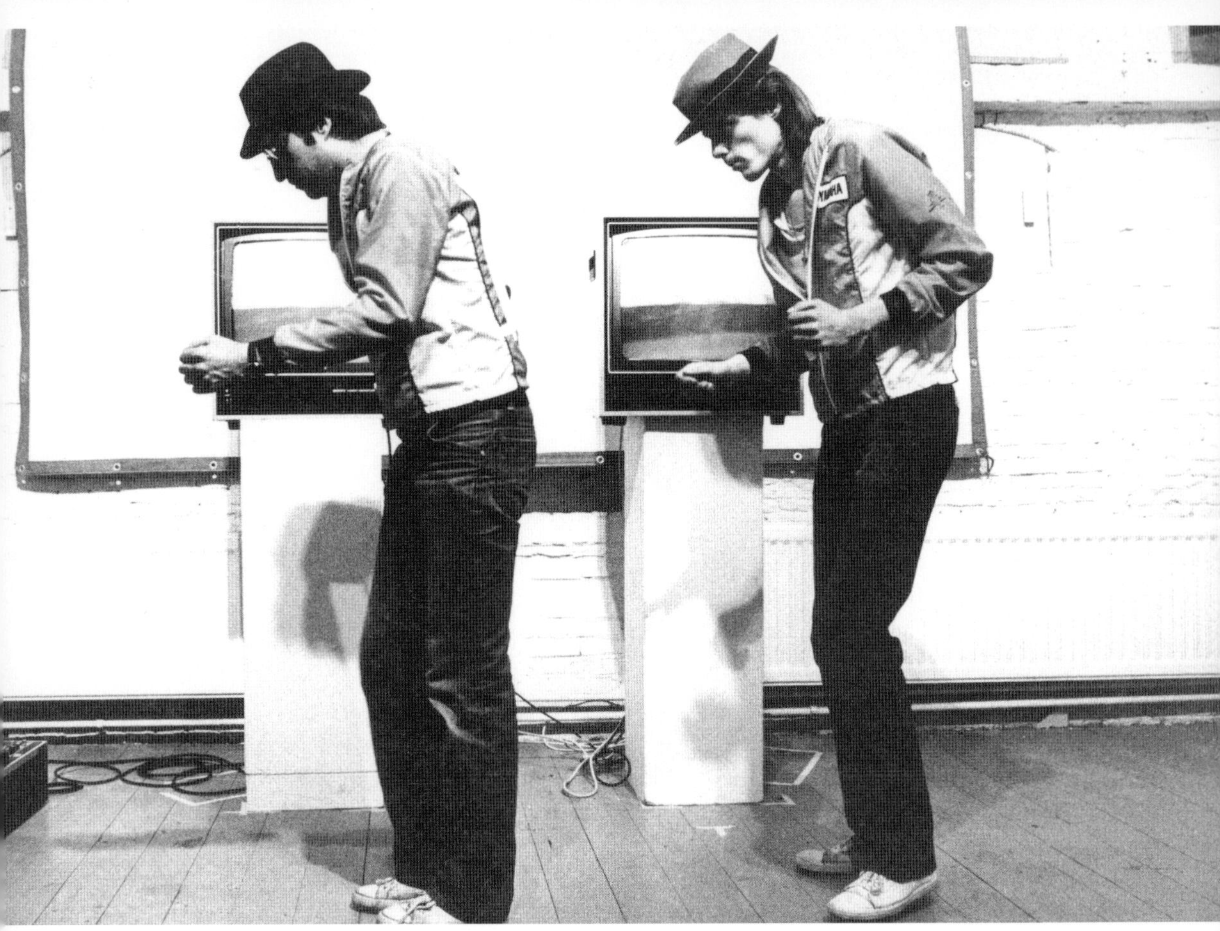

Raul Marroquin, *6'. Dollars Men*, during the Dutch Week in De Appel, Amsterdam, 5 and 11 June 1976

86   Nan Hoover (New York, 1931), originally a painter, had settled in Amsterdam in 1969. Spurred on by fellow painter Richard Hefti, she started to experiment with video in 1973. After this discovery, she worked in total isolation for eighteen months on producing a number of videos without being aware of what was going on in this field. Since there was no suitable exhibition space available, Hoover showed her first tapes in 1974 in the Amsterdam bars Het Paleis and De Prins, where she worked part-time.

The contact between Wies Smals and Nan Hoover really got under way in 1976, and from then on Wies Smals devoted herself unconditionally to introducing Hoover's video art and video performances in the Netherlands and abroad. The basis of Hoover's work was formed by a fascination with the contrast between light and dark, and in her early works she used the body to show this contrast. The initial reaction of the viewer at seeing the tapes is to be struck by the abstraction of the images. Hoover used only her body, a neutral décor like white paper, a light source, and the camera, which she operated herself. She recorded herself moving a single part of the body very slowly, such as a hand. The gradations of light in the black and white video recordings of the time form greys and nuances between black and white. They create an abstract play of light

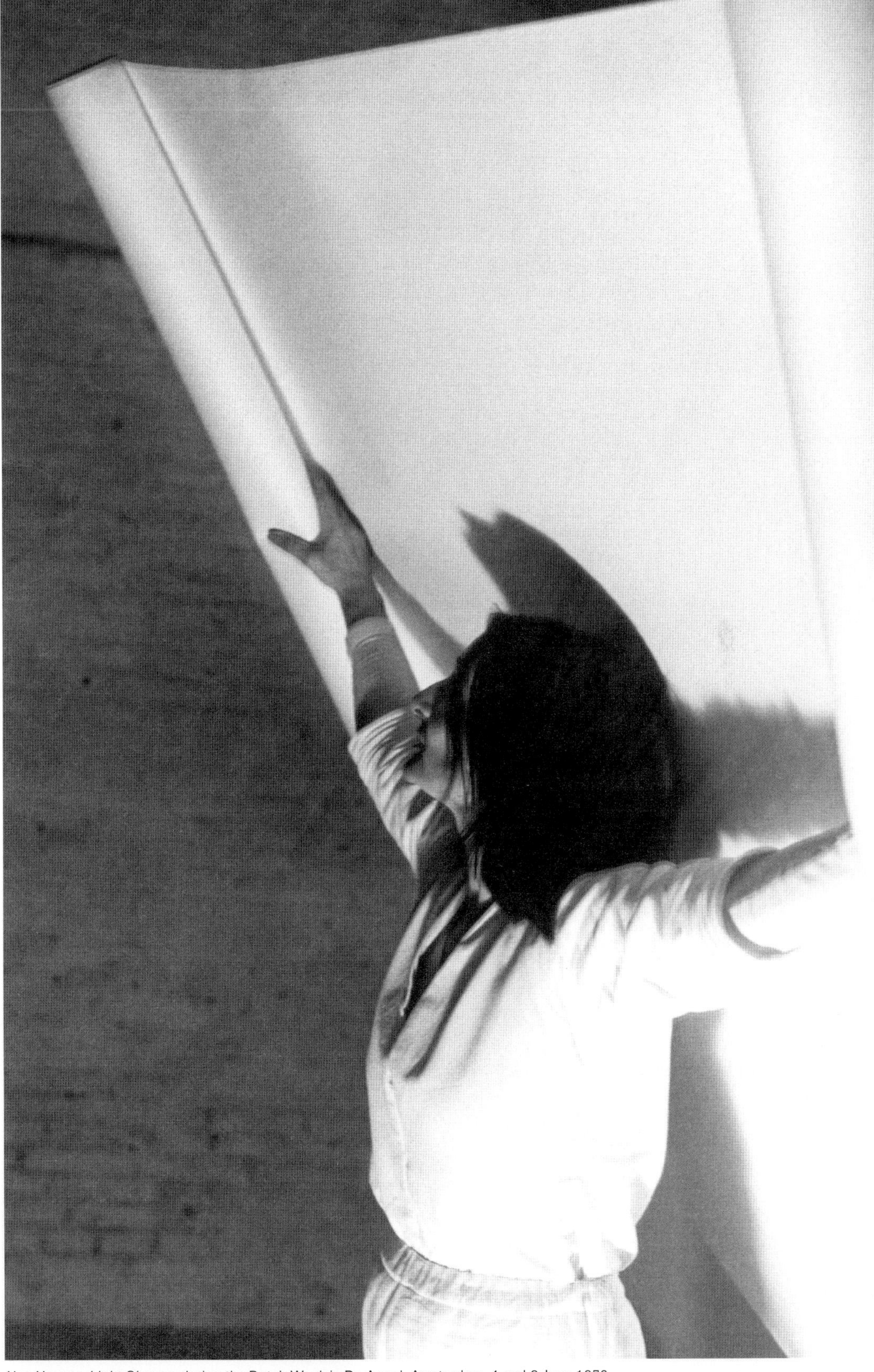

Nan Hoover, *Light Shapes*, during the Dutch Week in De Appel, Amsterdam, 4 and 9 June 1976

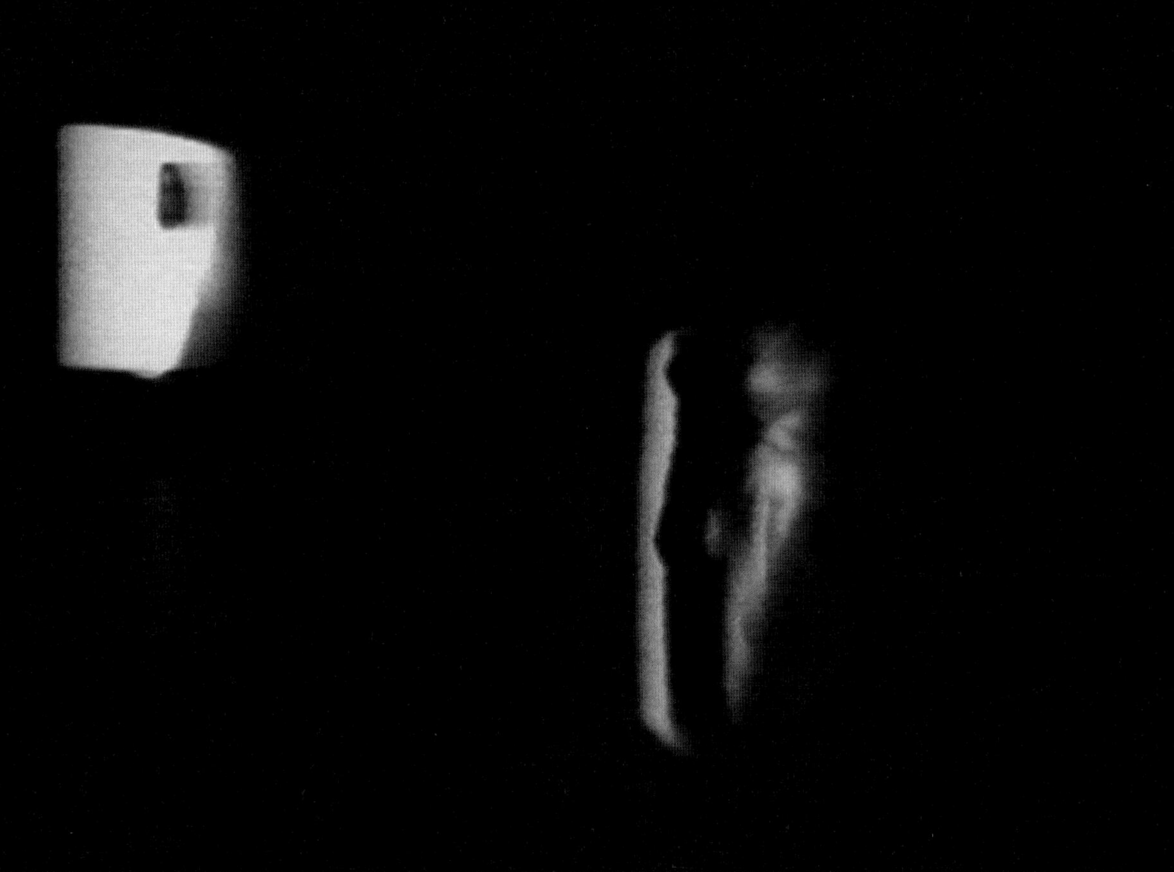

Nan Hoover, *Body Light*, 1977, video, b/w, 13'16"

88   with endless possibilities. The camera films from a single point, and the shot is not interrupted, so that a determinate process can be taken through to the end. Hoover also plays with the transition from reality to abstraction. At a certain moment the picture seems to be pure abstraction, while at the next moment it may be possible to distinguish a real part of the body such as a hand or a back.

Nan Hoover distinguishes clearly in her work between video art and video performances. She compared the making of video tapes with drawing – holding the camera was like holding a pencil. The recordings were made in the closed and intimate space of the studio. This called for extreme concentration, as any mistake would be immediately visible and could not be touched up. A video performance, on the other hand, was like painting for her. Paintings generally have a more monumental character than drawings. In the case of a painting the illusion of space plays an important role, and a mistake in the elaboration of the details is not so important. In her video performances Hoover worked with both existing video tapes and live recordings. The presence of a number of cameras and monitors made it possible to create a hyper-real reality that the eye cannot compose because it does not have so many options for perception.

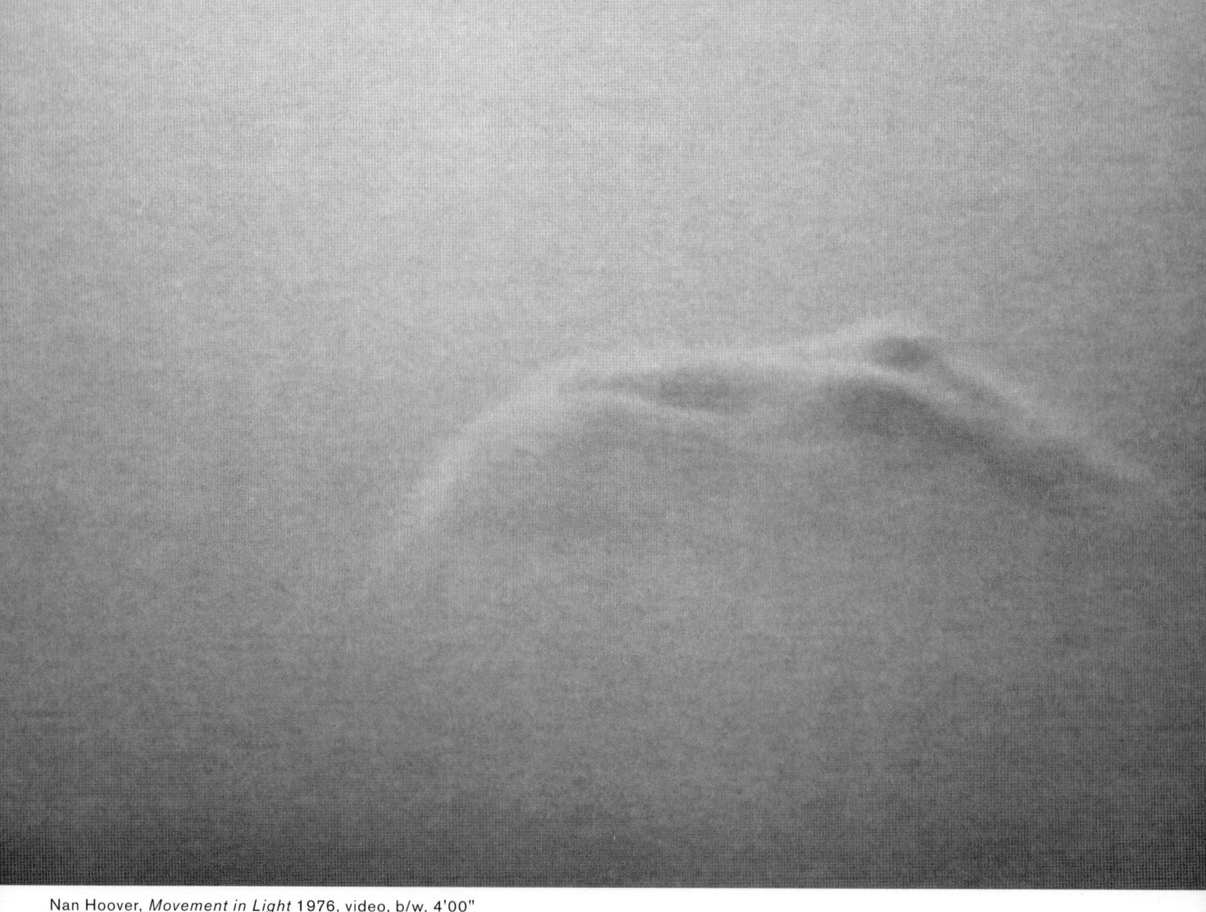

Nan Hoover, *Movement in Light* 1976, video, b/w, 4'00"

Hoover showed her first video performance, *Light Shapes*, during the Dutch Week of June 1976. For the performance she had positioned herself between two monitors with a large sheet of paper and a light source. The camera recorded only details of her movements, so that the monitor presented nothing but an enlarged abstraction of reality. Under the auspices of De Appel, Hoover did another two video performances in 1977: *Body/Light* during the Dutch Art Fair in the Sonesta Koepelkerk, and *Light Dissolves no. 2* in Museum Fodor, both in Amsterdam. She made a large number of video tapes during these years, only in black and white until 1978, generally using a macro lens, and in colour too from that year on. *Impressions*, her first colour tape, shows her manipulating an intense beam of light with her fingers to break it. At the end of the tape, when she withdraws her hand, the ray of light resumes its original shape.

Nan Hoover, *Light Dissolves*, 1975, video, b/w, sound, 10'00"

Nan Hoover, *Impressions*, 1978, video, colour, no sound, 10'30"

Michel Cardena, one of the founders of the In-Out Center, had already been working with video for a number of years before the founding of De Appel.[5] When Wies Smals invited him to show a number of video tapes one evening, he had already established a certain reputation and had been asked to do a

5
This discussion draws on Amsterdam 1984, Rotterdam 1981, an interview with Cardena and other sources. See too Bellinkx 2001.

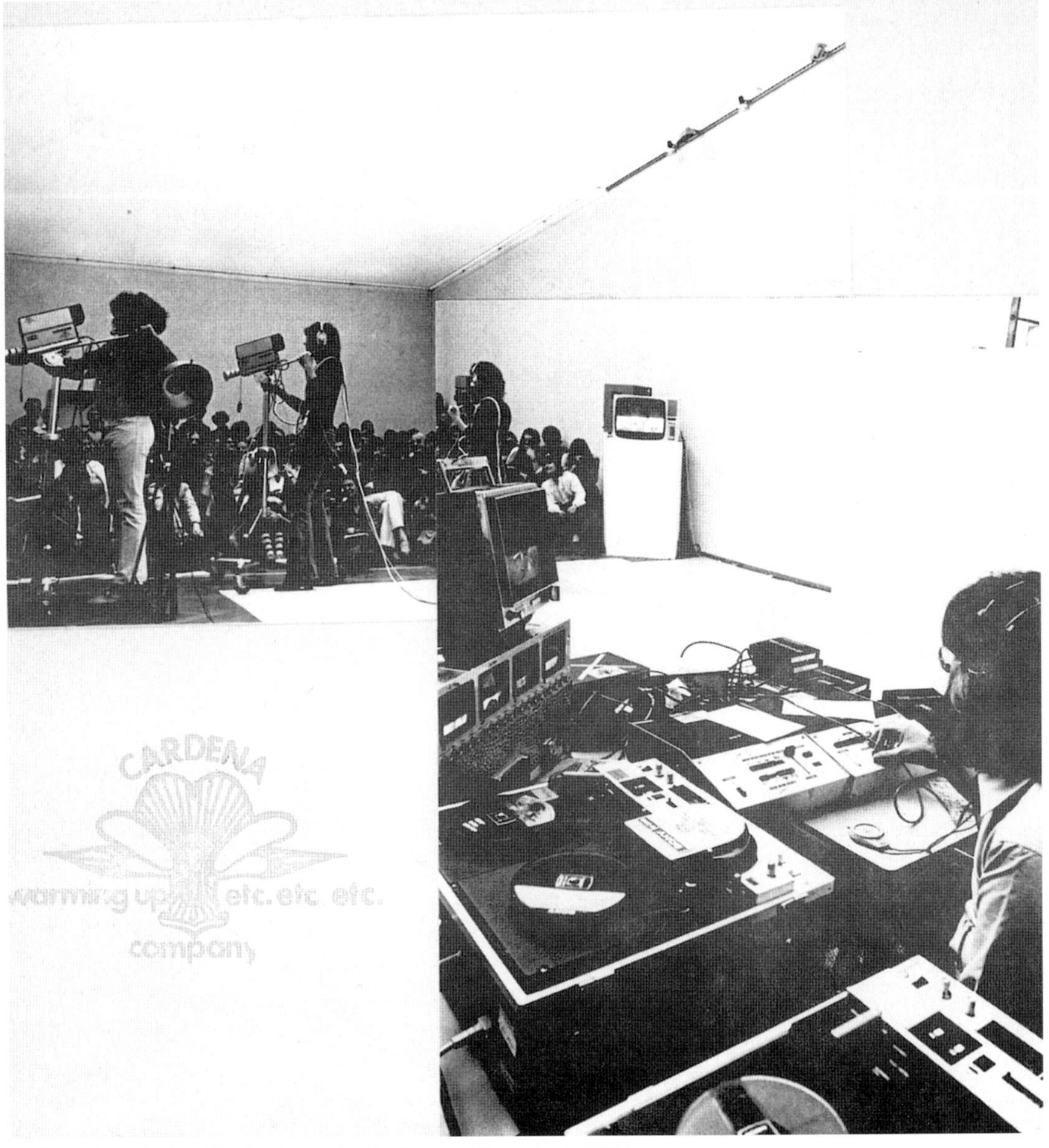

Michel Cardena, Cardena Warming Up etc. etc. etc. Company, *My name is beautiful*,
live video performance, Museum Fodor, Amsterdam 1978

video performance by the Stedelijk Museum in Amsterdam.
In spite of the fact that Wies Smals did not usually make efforts
on behalf of artists who could already show their work in other
places in the Netherlands, she entered into an intense
collaboration with Cardena and regularly asked his advice on the
programme. In 1968 Cardena had founded the Warming up etc.
etc. etc. Company, a company that was a permanent part of his
image as an artist. Warmth was an essential aspect of his work.
Drawing on his strict Catholic background in South America, he
had developed a concept in which the psychological and
metaphysical aspects of warmth were emphasized. In an
interview he explained: 'An artist has to be religious, since it is

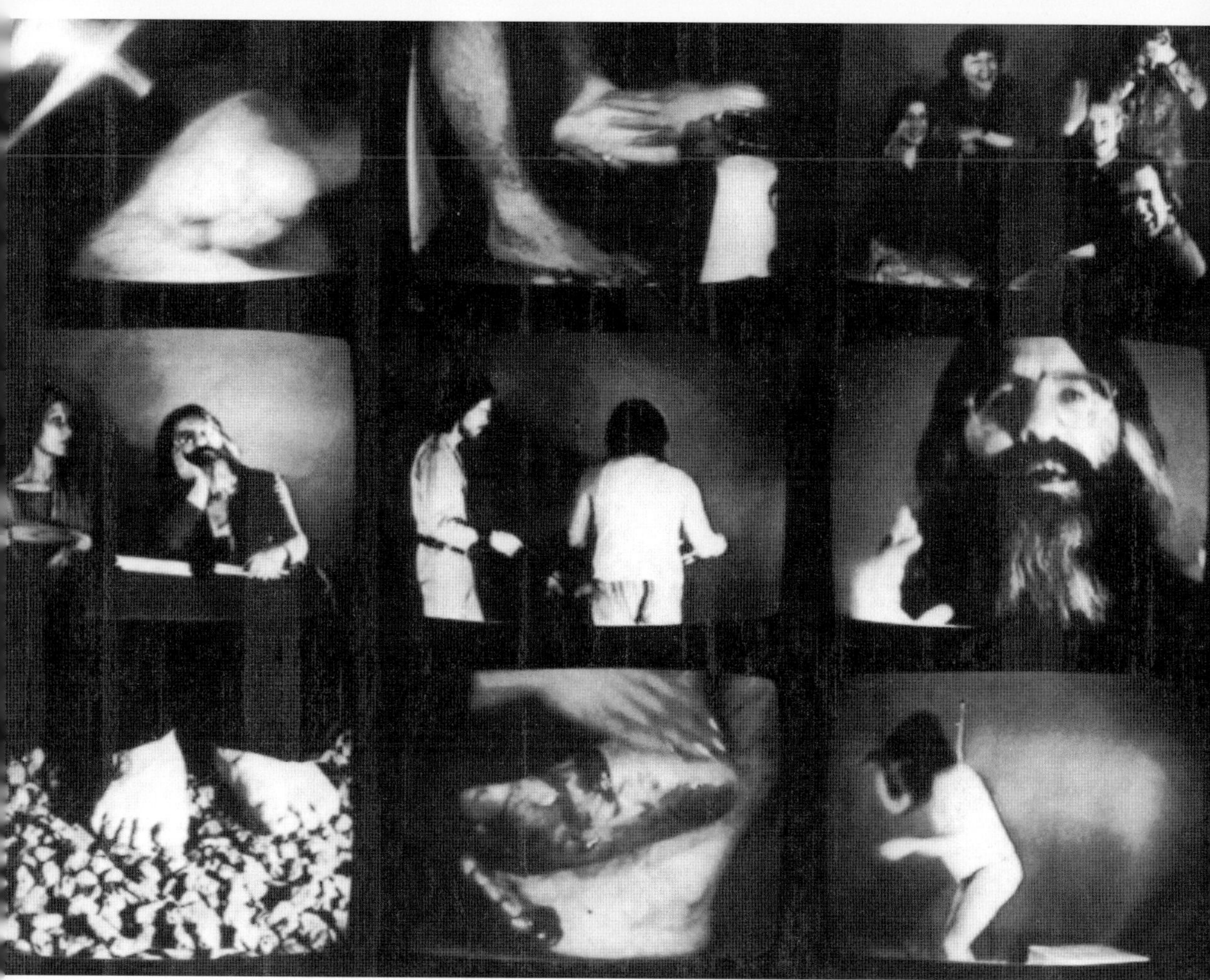

Michel Cardena, *Smiling and Barefoot Cardena walks on burning coal*, 1977, video, colour, sound, 17'15"

Michel Cardena, *Searching for Unity*, 1976–1977, video, b/w, 59'14"

the task of the artist to work on the changing of values...'[6]
This change could only be brought about by the use of warmth
as a kind of catalyst.

Cardena's concept of warmth as the basic energy for human
existence has a lot in common with the theories of Joseph
Beuys. The result in the case of Cardena, however, unlike
Beuys, is a large amount of humour and self-mockery. This can
be seen clearly in the video performance Cardena; *smiling and
barefoot, Cardena walks on burning coal* (1977), presented
during the Dutch Art fair mentioned above. The artist walked
barefoot on a construction of so-called glowing coals as an
ironic commentary on the self-mutilations carried out by body
artists. In the same year he presented the video performance
Searching for Unity during the K45 art market in Vienna, where
De Appel had been offered a stand free of charge. For these
performances Cardena had fixed two cameras to the two ends
of a plank. By balancing carefully, he tried to combine the two
different images supplied by the cameras. Unlike other video
performers, Cardena did not regard his own body as essential.

6
W. Barten, 'De video-kunst van Michel Cardena', *Het Financieele Dagblad*, 29 May 1981.

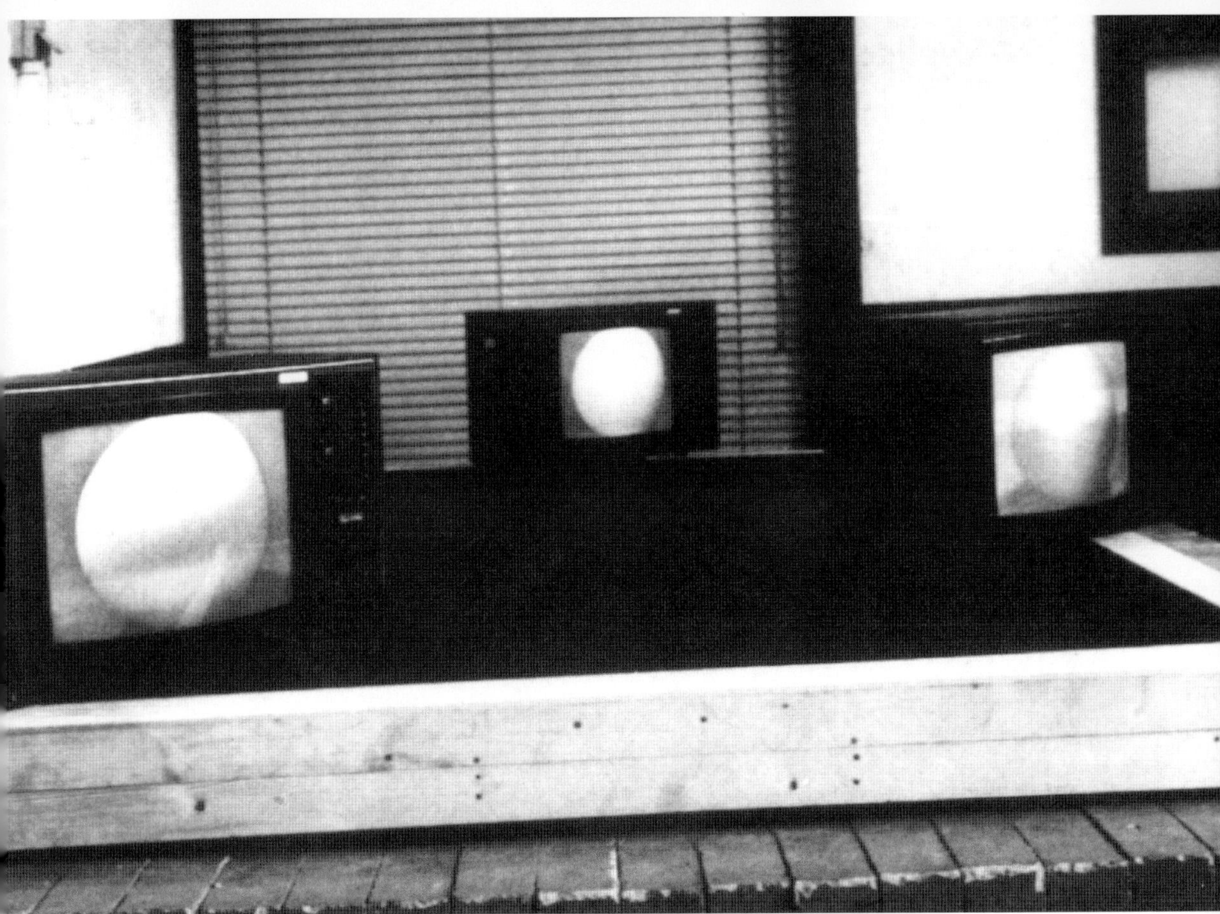

Michel Cardena, *25 Caramboles and variations*, installation in Café De Sport, Amsterdam, October 1979

92 Inspired by Fluxus-like ideas, he tried to break down the boundaries between the different artistic disciplines. He worked with
dancers, cooks and musicians in different situations. His first
videos were usually recordings of interventions carried out or
directed by him in a public place, such as the street or a railway
station.

Between 1976 and 1979 Cardena concentrated on video
performance. Like Nan Hoover, he was fascinated by the
possibility of using a number of cameras as different means of
perception to collect as much information as possible about the
real world. The simultaneity of the recording and the screening
which enabled the creation of a hyper-real reality was an important part of the video performance *25 Caramboles and
variations*, which was presented in a bar in Amsterdam in 1979
in collaboration with De Appel. For this performance Cardena
had positioned three cameras near a billiard table. During the
shooting he manipulated the recording and screening by
montage, thereby creating variations on reality.

These were the years in which not only video performances but
also video installations were gaining in importance. A good
example of this is the work of Elsa Stansfield and Madelon

Hooykaas, who formed an artistic duo at the beginning of the 1970s.[7] They started to concentrate on the production of videos in 1975. Stansfield had trained as a film director, and Hooykaas as a photographer. At the beginning of their collaboration they made a number of films, but film production was expensive and the distribution possibilities were limited. The artists discovered at a relatively early stage that their films belonged to the context of a museum or gallery and were not suitable for screening on television. Working with video offered them more possibilities and did not involve the restrictions that film entailed. One of the most important elements was the direct influence that could be exerted on the image. The result of a recording was immediately visible, unlike film, which required a few days for developing and could thus lead to a loss of concentration.

In September 1977 Stansfield and Hooykaas showed two video environments in De Appel entitled *Memory Window*. On the ground floor they had assembled four monitors like a window with four panes of glass. Three different tapes were shown on three of the monitors. The first tape was the recording of the building of a house in the Jordaan district of Amsterdam. The second tape, on the monitor beside it, showed details of the building process. The simultaneous showing of a single event taken from two different angles prevented the viewer from forming a single picture of the whole. The third monitor showed interviews with people from the neighbourhood where the building was going on. The sound consisted of building noise alternating with the voices of the interviewees. On the fourth monitor the visitor saw himself or herself live. Photographs of the building process were hung in the exhibition space upstairs, where there was also a monitor with the video with the interviews. The sound consisted of a number of fragments of the building process. The whole environment set out to give the viewers a sort of memory training. By being confronted with the same visual material for a second time, the visitors were confronted with their incapacity to store images for long in their memory.

Many artists associated with De Appel were invited to perform-ance festivals in countries in Eastern Europe, especially Poland, in the period from 1978 to 1980. The largest event by far was 'I am' in Warsaw, organized by Henryk Gajewski, who was later to move to the Netherlands. The organization of the Dutch contribution was in the hands of Jan Brand. He was also in charge of a presentation in the same year, 1978, in collaboration with the Brooklyn Museum in New York. A number of New York artists were involved, as well as a group of artists from the Netherlands including Ben d'Armagnac, Marina Abramovič, Uwe Laysiepen, Reindeer Werk, Gerrit Dekker and Hans Eykelboom. In spite of the fact that De Appel did not

---

[7]
This discussion draws on an interview with the two artists and (video) documentation from the archive of De Appel. See too Bellinkx 2001.

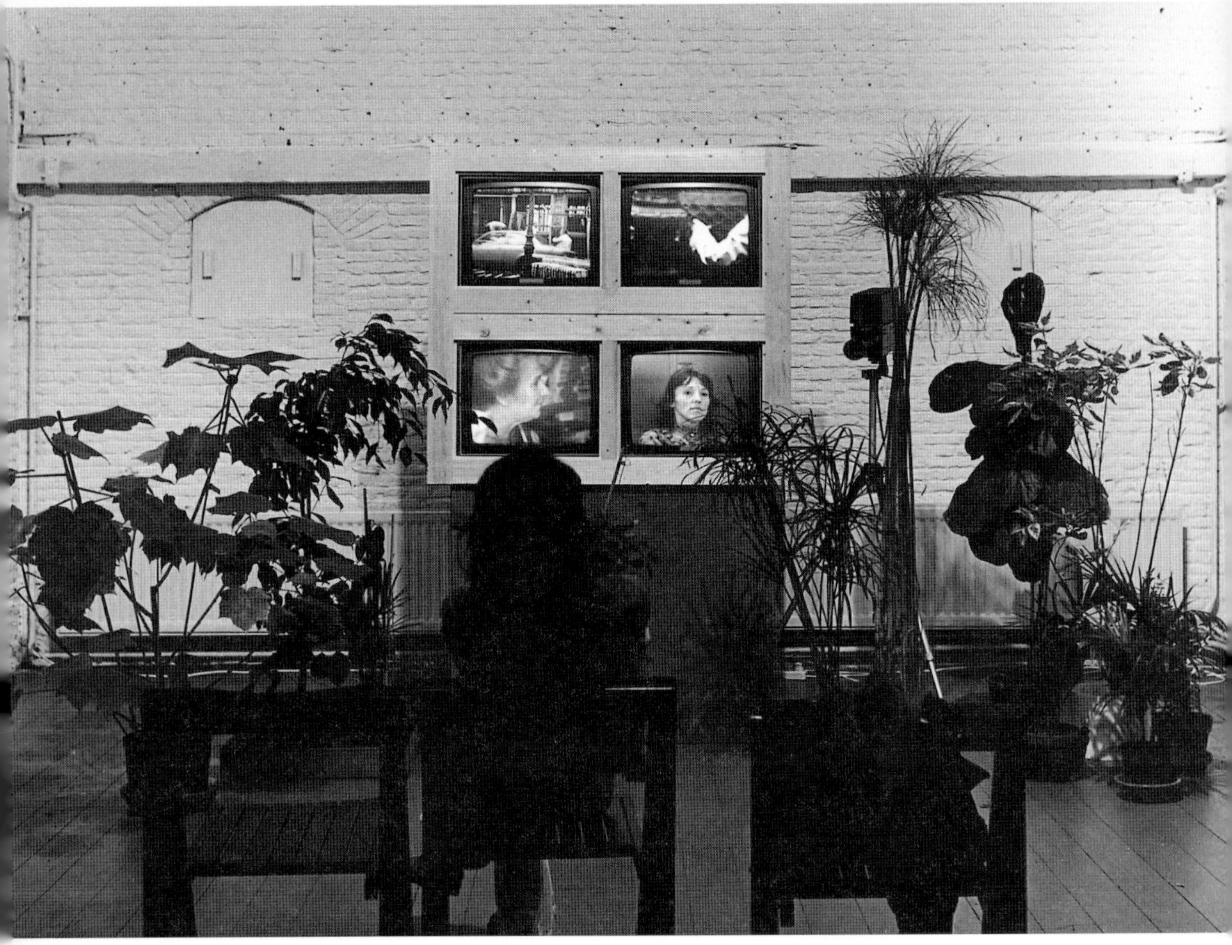

Stansfield/Hooykaas, *Memory Window*, video environment, De Appel, Amsterdam, September 1977

operate directly as a mediator, most of the artists from the Netherlands were performance artists who had been launched onto the international art world by De Appel. Wies Smals herself travelled to New York with a number of Dutch artists two years later. She made contact with Franklin Furnace Archive, which put its space and facilities at her disposal for a period of six weeks in the autumn of 1980. The space of the famous performance institute The Kitchen was also made available for a weekend. Wies Smals made sure that as many different aspects of performance, installation and video as possible were represented in the selection of artists. Gerrit Dekker and Nikolaus Urban constructed an installation that was shown for ten days, while other artists, including Harrie de Kroon, Servie Janssen and the duo Stansfield/Hooykaas, did a (video) performance and an exhibition at the same time. Moniek Toebosch and Marja Samson only put on a performance.

Although it was only a one-way exchange, the project was important because it enabled a group of Dutch artists to present their work in a number of places in New York. All the same, Wies Smals was rather disappointed when she returned from this trip, not only because the reactions in New York had not been so enthusiastic about what was going on in Europe, and particu-

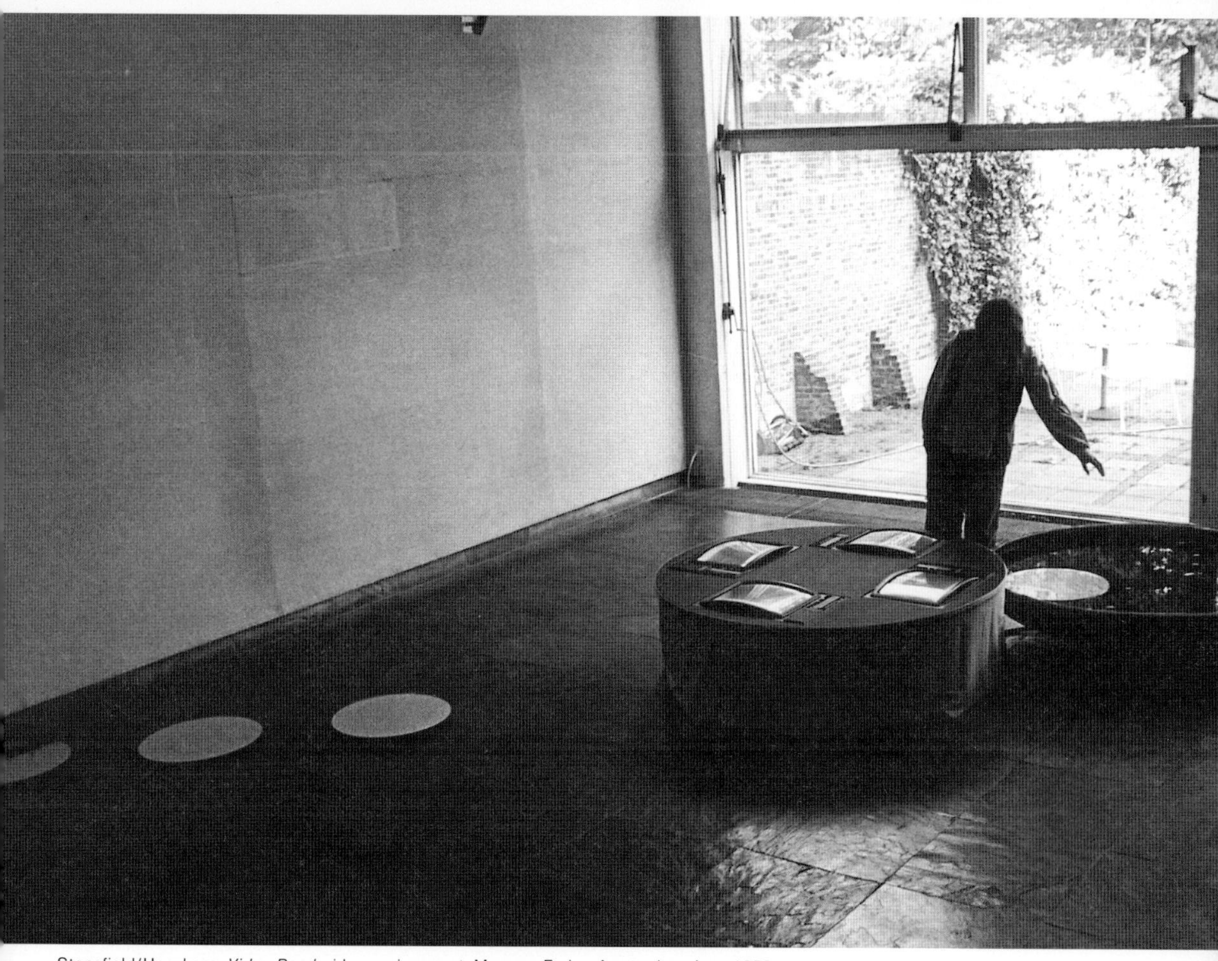

Stansfield/Hooykaas, *Video Pond*, video environment, Museum Fodor, Amsterdam, June 1978

larly in the Netherlands, but also because the relation with the public was completely different from what De Appel favoured. But that would soon change at De Appel too.

Video as a stepping-stone to television productions
With the arrival in 1978 of Josine van Droffelaar, who in the previous years had joined with Dorine Mignot in advocating the presentation of video work in the Stedelijk Museum in Amsterdam, the emphasis shifted in De Appel toward performances and installations in which sound played a central role. For a short while the attention spent on these seems to have been somewhat at the expense of video works, although De Appel was still active outside its walls in showing videos during lectures at universities, polytechnics and art academies. Several special tapes were made for that purpose. De Appel also organized special events elsewhere, such as a video week in the Mickery Theatre in November 1979, and it was closely involved with 'The performance phenomenon in Amsterdam' held in Museum Fodor in 1978 with *Videovijver* [Video Pool] by Stansfield/Hooykaas and the eight-hour performance-video-installation by Marroquin entitled *Oh, I left the TV on*. Video came in for rather more attention in 1980, although the plans

Raul Marroquin, *Oh, I left the TV on*, 1978, video, b/w, sound, 56'15"

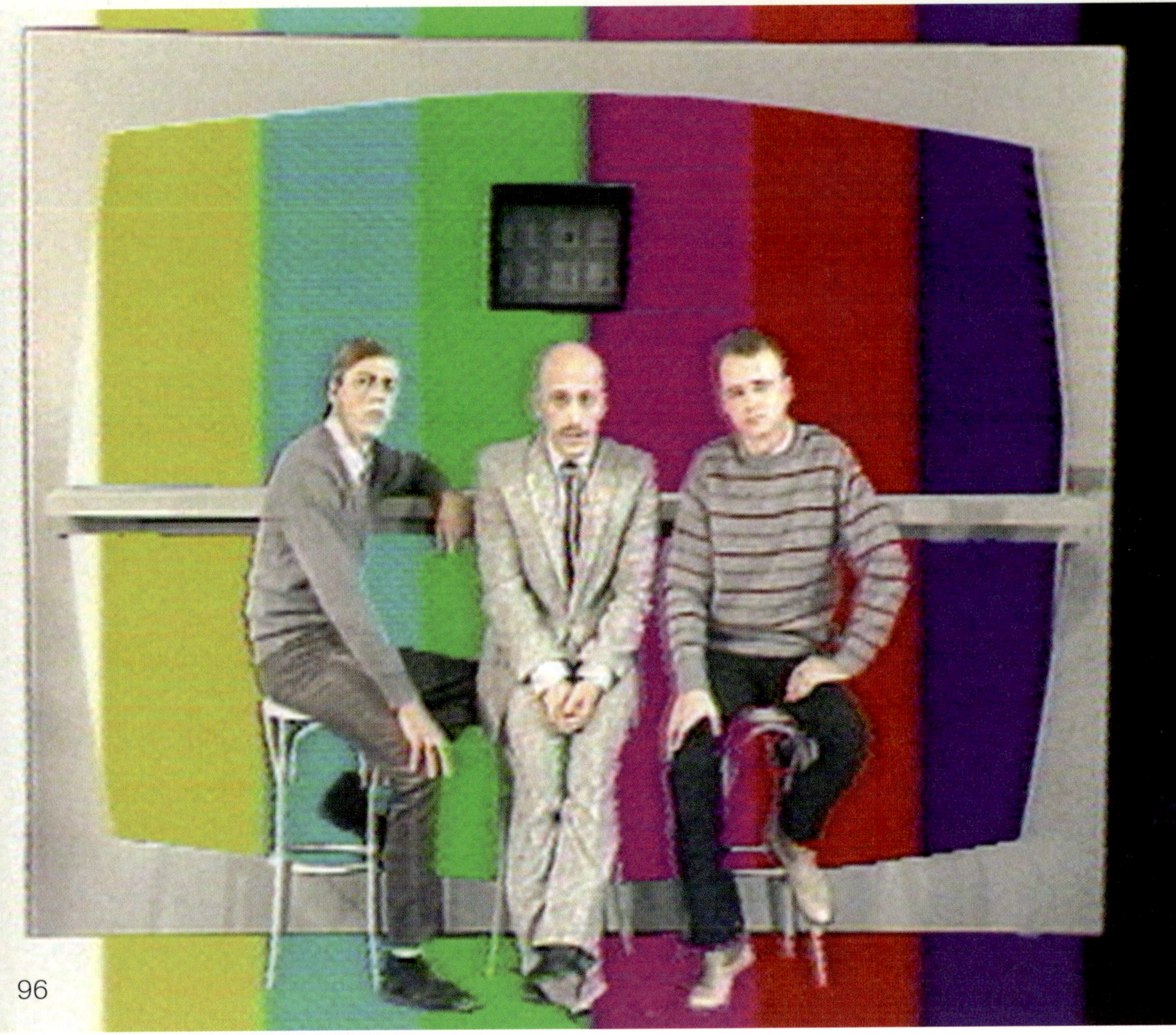

General Idea, *Test Tube,* 1979, video, colour, sound, 28'15"

were already in the making to alter the course of De Appel
drastically. De Appel had always attached a lot of importance to
its public function, and the educational importance of video for
that purpose was evident. With the change of direction that took
shape in the course of 1981, the direct communication with the
public more or less disappeared, the video evenings were
scrapped, and less attention was paid to video as an
independent artistic medium. De Appel continued to fulfil its
role as a sort of mediator and impresario, but its main efforts
were now directed towards initiating projects that were no
longer tied to a specific locations like De Appel, including films
and television productions.

Elsewhere too video art was regarded as a medium that
could function as a pendant to television. This idea lay behind
the setting up of the group The New Electric TV in 1968.
It consisted mainly of technicians and worked on video and
television experiments. Gerry Schum opened his Fernseh-
Galerie in 1969. In the following year Jack Moore opened up his
production studio Video Heads in The Milky Way in Amsterdam,

followed by the Lijnbaancentrum in Rotterdam, which from the very start was closely involved with the video activities that took place under the direction of Wim Beeren during 'Sonsbeek buiten de perken' [Sonsbeek beyond the pale].[8] That exhibition focused on forms of indirect communication with the aid of such media as telex, conference telephone, photography and video. The exceptionally conceptual, ephemeral and non-commercial character of many of the works in the Sonsbeek exhibition in 1971 must have appealed to Wies Smals, although that only really found proper expression during the last few years of De Appel, after it had changed course. Everything seems to indicate that 'Sonsbeek buiten de perken' was still making an impact ten years after the event.

De Appel already took steps to breath new life into the initiatives of Gerry Schum and Wim Beeren in 1978. In an interview with Gea Kalksma and Lydia Schouten, Wies Smals stated that 'it still proved to be the case that the people who were deliberately working with the medium (video) were actually making video tapes with the intention of showing them on television. If that does not happen, there is something lacking in the work.'[9] She also explained that every effort had been made to change this situation, for instance by improving the technical quality of the videos, but that this had not (yet) been achieved. A working group was set up in the same year to look into the possibilities for De Appel to act as producer in the making of programmes for television.[10] After several vain attempts to get the traditional broadcasting companies and producers to cooperate with artists, De Appel decided to make a number of high-quality productions itself. By acting as the producer, De Appel hoped to forestall the criticism that video artists would not provide an acceptable technical quality.

The first commission for the making of a television production was given to the Canadian trio of artists General Idea, who were a permanent presence in Amsterdam in the early 1980s.[11] General Idea, which had been founded in 1968 by Felix Partz (1945-1994), Jorge Zontal (1944-1994) and AA Bronson (1946), used performances, films and objects to construct a fictional world to poke fun at how art and artists functioned. They were inspired by the image that Warhol created around The Factory and the relation that he maintained with the world of art and commerce. Their work set out from the idea of a 'Miss General Idea' beauty contest to be held in 1984, the year of the novel of the same name by George Orwell. The whole oeuvre was organized around this fictional event. Annual beauty contests were held starting in 1969 to prepare for the contest to be held in 1984. The public also received training in reacting

[8] This exhibition is described and documented in Boomgaard/Van Mechelen/Van Rijsingen 2001.

[9] The text of this interview can be found in the archive of De Appel, dossier 1980.

[10] Report of the TV Programme Advisory Group, 14 September 1978.

[11] This discussion draws on Basel 1984, Trescher 1996 and other sources.

in the right way to the instructions issued by the trio. Scale models of the Miss General Idea Pavilion with a grand stairway and the Colour Bar Lounge were exhibited as artistic objects. They wanted to use techniques derived from the world of advertising and the mass media to criticize artists, fascism, capitalism, discrimination against homosexuals and the position of women.

Test Tube, commissioned by De Appel, was filmed in 1979 with the assistance of producer Joes Odufré in the Cinevideo Group Holland studios. It is considered one of the 'mature' video works of General Idea because it had more of the characteristics of a work of art than their earlier work. In the course of the production, which lasts almost thirty minutes, television techniques were used to sketch a complex picture of the position of the artist. General Idea concentrated on the form of the medium, leading to not just a flirtation with but above all a parody of the medium television. However, the structure of the programme ensured that the layers of meaning remained virtually inaccessible to a wider audience. Although the formulae of the talk show, comedy mini-series, interruption for commercials, etc. were supposed to be familiar to everyone, the effect of the whole, which was based on a collage principle rather than on a filmic narrative, was puzzling. *Test Tube* premièred in De Appel, but it was never broadcast on Dutch television. That was a serious blow, not only for the artists but also for De Appel as producer. Despite the negative response to its first own production, the role of independent producer became very important to De Appel. Its policy between 1980 and 1983 was increasingly directed towards making its own productions.

In 1980 Michel Cardena was asked to make a film for television in cooperation with De Appel. This was a new experiment for Cardena. His work until then had been marked by its rough, sketchy character and its technical imperfection. The new production called for a precisely formulated plan and cooperation with professional camera crews and technicians. The film, *Somos Libres!?*, charted the journey of two homosexuals who escape from the stifling Catholic climate and the military dictatorship of a country in South America in search of freedom. Their final destination, an imaginary homosexual paradise, could only be reached via different stations symbolising the deadly sins. The exclamation and question marks in the title, 'Are we free!?', are an ironical allusion to the fact that there is no absolute freedom in paradise either. The film was presented in 1981 within the framework of a retrospective of Cardena's work in Museum Boymans-van Beuningen in Rotterdam. This production was also the subject of arduous negotiations with the Dutch broadcasting companies. Only one organization, the Humanist Society, was prepared to include the video in its programme in 1982.

The desire to make its own productions was continued in

Michel Cardena, *Somos Libres!?*, 1981, video, colour, sound, 23'00"

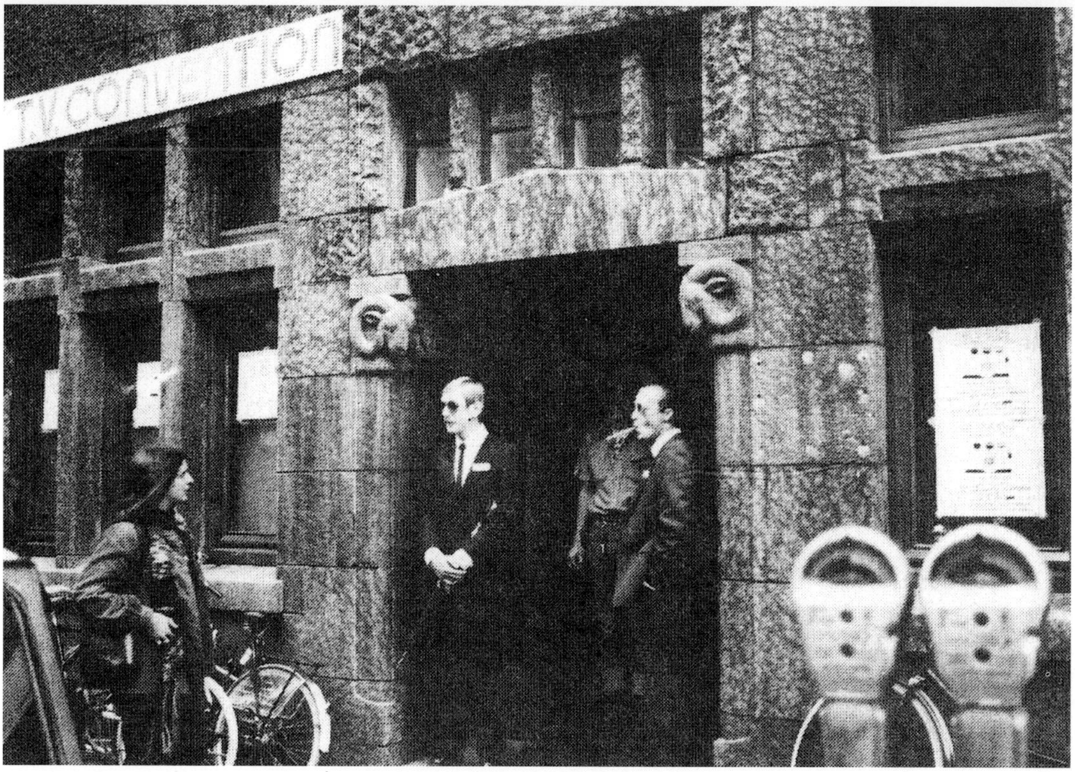

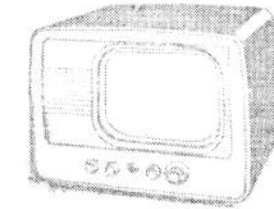

World's First TV Convention, reception at the The Bank, Amsterdam, June 1980

cooperation with Raul Marroquin, an artist who has always been fascinated by the application of new means of communication.[12] He was one of the first artists to work with colour video, but he also experimented with the possibilities of art via the cable, with the Slow Scan, a predecessor of later digital techniques like View Phone, CuSeeMe, Video Conferencing, Streaming Media, and recently I-Mode, and with the Bulletin Board System, that enabled the exchange of ASCI characters, a form of communication that would later be taken over by the internet.

Right from the start, Marroquin's work was characterized by satirising the US consumer and media culture. He set up Mad Enterprizes for that purpose. Marroquin put Marshall McLuhan's

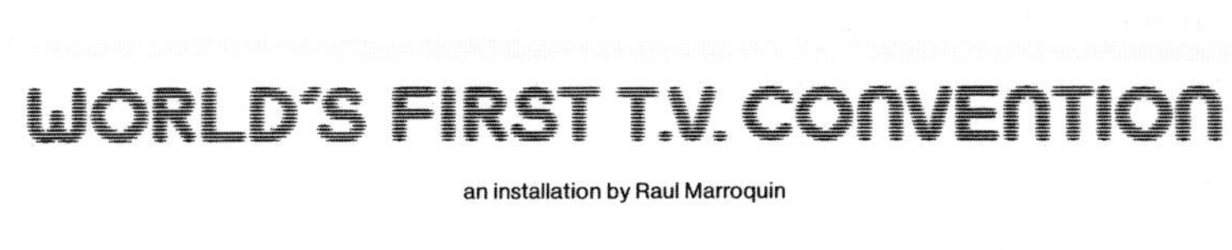

WORLD'S FIRST T.V. CONVENTION

an installation by Raul Marroquin

June 23 - 27 1980
The convention is open to public
from 8 to 10 p.m

The Bank
Haarlemmerstraat 118
Amsterdam 020 - 26 53 92

Raul Marroquin, invitation for *World's First TV Convention*, The Bank, Amsterdam, June 1980

12
This information is taken mainly from e-mail correspondence with Raul Marroquin and the videos from the collection of the Netherlands Media Art Institute.

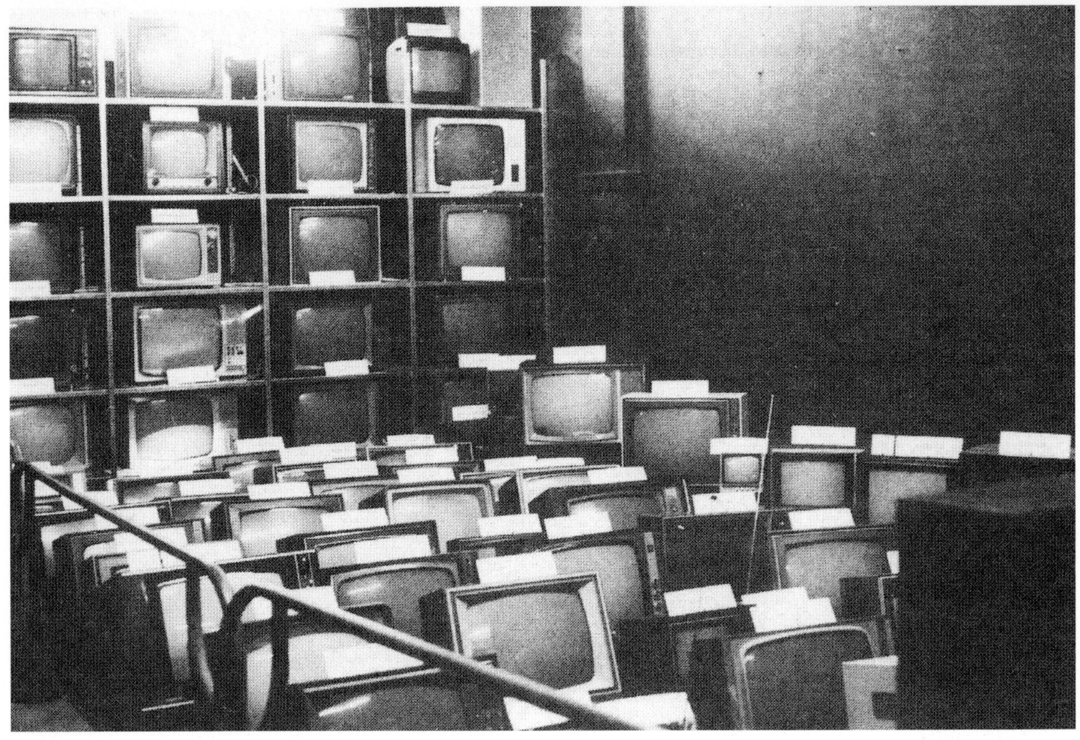

Raul Marroquin, *World's First TV Convention*, The Bank, Amsterdam, June 1980

 slogan 'the medium is the message' into practice in an extremely literal way. The television is a medium with specific codes, with clear-cut idols who penetrate the living room and settle there. In 1977 Marroquin started *Fandangos Evening News*, a satire on television interviews under the name of the magazine that Marroquin had set up a few years earlier with students from the Jan van Eyck Academy in Maastricht. The same idea would be used again later on, for a real broadcast via the cable.

The cable television studios on the Bijlmer housing estate in Amsterdam, the first district in the country to have cable television, were very important for Cardena's career. In 1977 there were ten broadcasts of half an hour each. Wies Smals recognized the importance of this new means of communication and assumed responsibility for the production of a new episode in the series *Superbman's Last Adventures*, a series of works on which Marroquin's reputation is above all based. Titus Muizelaar played the role of Superman, alias Clark Kent, who races through space, is constantly called in to help, but who otherwise seems little concerned about the major problems in the world. Although Marroquin continued to implement large-scale projects in the Netherlands, including his *World's First TV Convention*, a video installation in which monitors took the

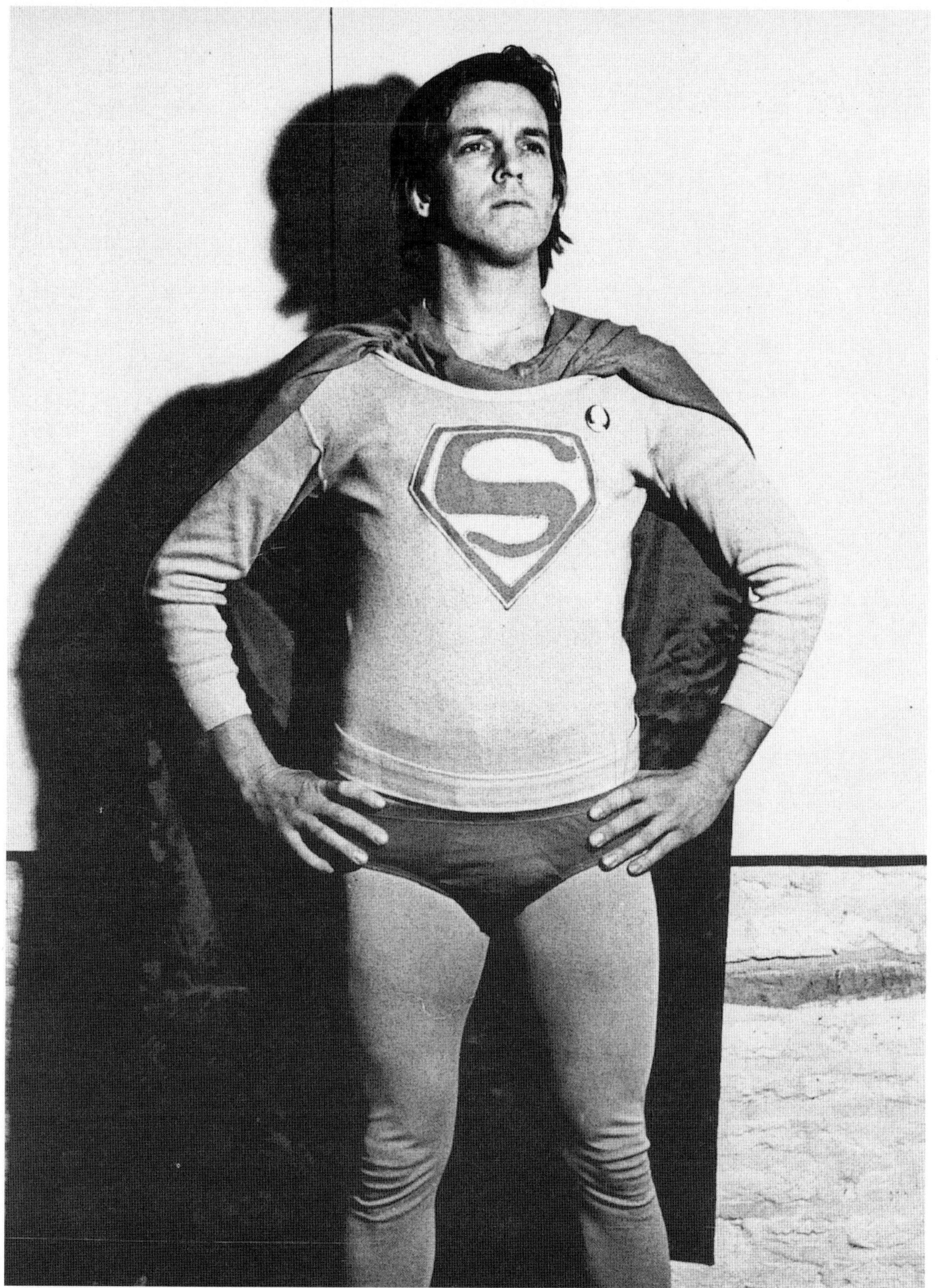

Raul Marroquin, *Superbman's Last Adventure*, 1978, video, b/w, sound, 28'00" and 85'00"

place of the delegates to the United Nations, he has worked
primarily in New York with cable television. One of his projects
was *The Link*, a live television programme produced by
Manhattan Cable and Amsterdam Cable Television in 1981.
Once again De Appel was a partner in this project, though it
was a fiasco thanks to the enormous bureaucracy and red tape
in the Netherlands. As a result, the planned satellite link could
not be made, and *The Link* was only broadcast on the New York
cable.

Conclusion

This article is limited to the period during which De Appel was
directed by Wies Smals and Josine van Droffelaar. After their
death, their work was continued for a while by Sabrina Kamstra,
Frank Gribling and Saskia Bos, who have also initiated and
assisted with video projects. A few years later Saskia Bos was
to chart a new course in the new location on the Prinseneiland.
The disappointing experiences have meant that projects with
television are given a low priority. But video, in all its guises, is
here to stay.

Ruth Bellinkx is an art historian specialized in contemporary art. She
is currently working at Galerie Paul Andriesse in Amsterdam. She is
preparing a monograph about De Appel Foundation 1975–1983 in
association with Marga van Mechelen.

Marga van Mechelen is a member of the Contemporary Art History
faculty at the University of Amsterdam. She is preparing a monograph
about De Appel Foundation 1975–1983 in association with Ruth
Bellinkx. Her writing is published regularly, primarily in foreign
semiotics journals and conference volumes on performance art and
new media. She was a contributing editor for the recently published *Als
de kunst erom vraagt. De Sonsbeektentoonstellingen van 71, 86 en
93* (Amsterdam and Arnhem, 2001), along with Jeroen Boomgaard and
Miriam van Rijsingen.

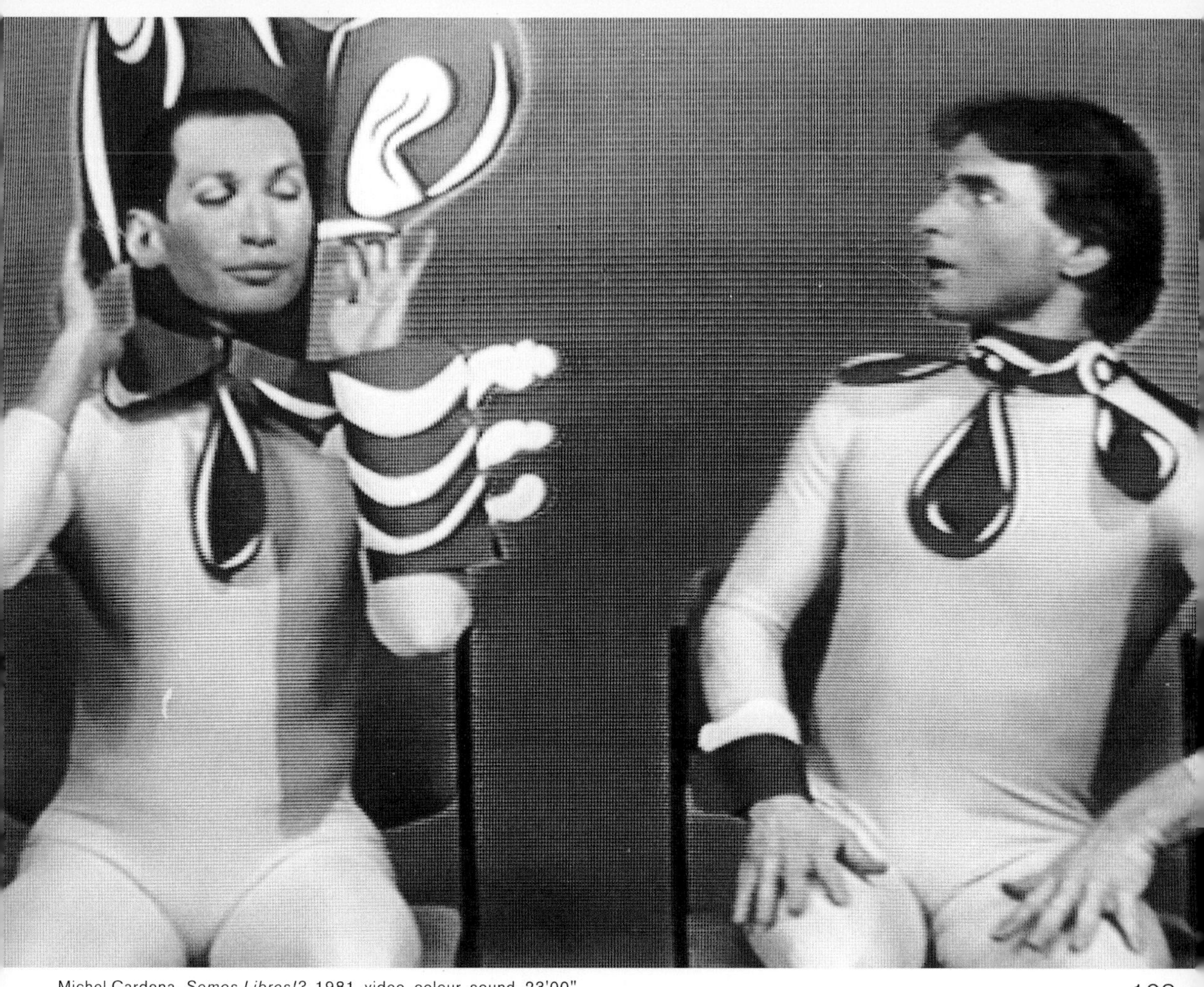

Michel Cardena, *Somos Libres!?*, 1981, video, colour, sound, 23'00"

Hinke Kappert

The image in word
Trends in the Dutch response to video art

Introduction

In 1996 the publicist Julia Knight, in her book *Diverse Practises. A Critical Reader on British Video Art*, stated the following about video art in the 1970s: 'In North America, Germany and Holland, video art has achieved artistic recognition. But the British video art remains in obscurity.'[1] While we were thinking that conditions for video art in the Netherlands were bad at the time, in the eyes of foreigners they were okay after all.[2]

What was Knight's view actually based on? While she did not elucidate further on her viewpoint, from closer study of the footnotes it appears that this was based on a 1976 issue of *Studio International*.[3] It is highly likely that this magazine prompted Knight's statement since the issue was the ideal starting point for a comparative study of video art in western countries. For this special theme number writers from Austria, Belgium, Britain, the Netherlands, West Germany, Canada and the United States were invited to give an insight into the development of video art in their own country. And indeed when comparing these responses the Netherlands came better off than Britain, even though the Dutch contributor, Hein Reedijk, had certain reservations.[4]

[1]
Knight 1996, p. 2.

[2]
P. Terreehorst, 'De videowereld is vol van verdriet en miskenning', see Terreehorst 1991, p. 15.

[3]
Studio International, no. 981 (1976).

[4]
Reedijk 1976.

This contribution examines articles on the medium from the 1970s and 1980s. How was the situation in the 1970s when Dutch artists first began experimenting with video? When was video art no longer seen as 'special' or 'new'? How do various publications on the medium from the 1970s and 1980s on the medium differ from each other?

Publications about the medium fall roughly into three categories: reports on developments in the video world, reviews of exhibitions and thoughtful articles about the past, present and future of video. The more interest for video increased in the Netherlands, the greater the number of articles from the first two categories, especially in the daily press, but in contrast to what you would logically expect, the last category did not only occur in the early 1970s. Over both decades overviews and 'stocktaking' articles appeared regularly in the written media.

Hardly novelty value

While a few art historians had undoubtedly become acquainted with video art via institutions like the Lijnbaancentrum in Rotterdam, the Stedelijk Van Abbemuseum in Eindhoven, Galerie Agora in Maastricht, Art & Project, Mickery and Video Heads in Amsterdam, video acquired a clearer image for a wider group via the influential *Museumjournaal* in 1974. In the article 'Is video kunst voor allen?' [Is Video Art for All?] journalist Hein Reedijk pitched into one of the issues that had been central to an open circuits conference organized by New York's MoMA, also in 1974. Reedijk described the close link between video and television – the power for social change it was ascribed by scholars like René Berger and by artists working with the medium. At the end of the article he stressed the 'shroud of newness' surrounding the medium which impeded the art world from forming a balanced judgement. However, he promised readers that more attention would be given to this in a follow-up article.[5]

Hein Reedijk began his career at the Van Abbemuseum – then under the directorship of Jean Leering – which in the 1970s organized the high-profile exhibition 'The Street'. Leering's aim was to make art and exhibitions accessible to a wide an audience as possible. This approach was shared by the policymakers and exhibition organizers of the Rotterdam Arts Foundation (RKS), where everyone – taking up Berger's ideas – believed that video could play a role in this.[6] Reedijk further explored his vision with 'de Kijkkist' [Looking Box], a travelling exhibition in Rotterdam – and a RKS initiative – where anyone who wanted to could make a video.

Two issues after his first article appeared in *Museumjournaal*, Reedijk discussed video art in the Netherlands, triggered by what was widely regarded as an unsuccessful showing of the

[5]
Reedijk 1974.
[6]
For more information see the magazine *Hollands Diep* for a discussion on museum policy, the book *Museum in Motion*, and a review of museum policy in the 1970s in *Metropolis M*, 8 (1987) 5/6.

medium at the 'Sonsbeek buiten de perken'[Sonsbeek beyond the pale] exhibition, which proved controversial due to the content and dubious quality.[7] Beginning his article with the opening line 'Is video the new star in the firmament?', Reedijk and his co-writer, Gijs van Tuyl, attempted to put the innovative aura surrounding video into perspective by comparing it to the emergence of photography and polyester in art – two media which were originally ascribed earth-shattering attributes, but later turned out less than anticipated after all.[8] They then described and defended the specific attributes of the new medium. Based on its formal and technical characteristics, Reedijk and Van Tuyl argued that video should not be linked to film. Not only were both media different in the way they were presented, but unlike film, video could be played back almost instantly and in that sense was faster. Film first had to be developed, then positive images made from the negatives, thus making it a much slower medium than video. As far as presentation was concerned, the writers opined that 'A large image in a dark space places looking completely differently than a small image in a half-lit room. Moreover it makes quite a different impression whether a light source projects images on a screen, or that you experience a light source and image as an entity. For both situations the perception is conditioned in a quite different way'.[9] Reedijk and van Tuyl believed that the Dutch museum world only offered video art a small platform and both argued that the museums should provide more opportunity for its development and wider use. The fact that the gallery circuit gave slightly more attention to video is apparent from the list of names subsequently mentioned, although the writers note that the experiments to be seen there were often little more than playing around with technical possibilities.[10] The article gave a reasonable overview of platforms for video in the Netherlands, but aside from the opening line it hardly referred explicitly to video as a 'novelty'.

The idea that video was not seen as 'new' is heightened by reading other articles that appeared in the 1970s and – noteworthy enough – also written by Reedijk. His 'Video in the Netherlands. It Takes a Long Time to Grow Up and Be Recognized' is very similar to the *Museumjournaal* article: the situation for video is poor and from a summary of organizations bringing video, still too few museums had anything to do with the medium.[11] In 1978, Reedijk and Marga Bijvoet wrote an article for the *Openbaar Kunstbezit* [Public Art Collection Foundation] from a slightly different angle and with

more objectivity towards the subject. They outlined the use of
video in the United States and compared the situation there with
the Netherlands. There then followed a summary of video events
in the Netherlands with a list of names. The two writers made a
distinction on the Dutch scene between anecdotal tapes and
video performances. Only a few artists used video professionally,
including Livinus van de Bundt, Peter Struycken, H.F. van de Rijdt
and Nan Hoover.[12]

Several articles devoted to video appeared in the film magazine *Skrien* in the late 1970s. These were initially accompanied
by a small announcement in September 1978 that some 40,000
video recorders had been sold in the Netherlands. In October of
that same year an extended article gave a review of the various
forms of video use, including artistic expression. From the
writer's viewpoint not very much was happening in this field:
'In the Netherlands video art is still only carried out to a limited
extent. Occasionally museums give it some attention. Galerie De
Appel in Amsterdam sometimes has video art within its walls'.[13]
Compared to Reedijk's review, Van Steegeren's was quite
concise. Can you expect a journalist writing for a film magazine to
be better informed? Apparently the editorial staff thought so,
because in April 1979 an article appeared that went much
deeper into video art.[14] Nevertheless this writer also only bases
her article on Amsterdam venues like Montevideo and De Appel.
She interviewed René Coëlho and his artists Livinus and Jeep
van de Bundt as well as Joshua Janssen. In De Appel she spoke
to Liesbeth Brandt Corstius and Wies Smals. The conversations
with these people give a good idea of video at the time. However,
from simple misspellings of the names of various video artists in
the introductory article it is clear that the writer has not dug
further into the medium than was strictly necessary for the
interviews.

The 1980s

What *Studio International* did on an international level in 1976,
the Openbaar Kunstbezit Foundation did for the Netherlands in
1984 via a theme issue of the magazine *Kunstschrift* on video.
This included articles by Hein Reedijk again, Dorine Mignot,
Rob Perrée and Ernie Tee. The magazine wanted to give a
complete overview of video in the Netherlands, from the first
video users to video art after 1975. Also highlighted was the
work of the artists Wim T. Schippers, Bruce Nauman, Ulrike
Rosenbach and Dara Birnbaum. An editorial gave background
information about the choice of subject matter and for the first
time video was referred to as a 'new medium'.[15]

[12] H. Reedijk, M. Bijvoet, article for *Openbaar Kunstbezit*, 1978.
[13] Van Steegeren 1978.
[14] Linders 1979.
[15] Van Ginneken 1984.

Over at the Stedelijk Museum Dorine Mignot was drawing attention to the medium and in 1984 organized an exhibition about feminism and video. The accompanying text to the mini show emphasized the freedom and controllability of video as well as the power of transference via the monitor screen, although she does not explain exactly what she means by that. This can also be gleaned from her article 'Video Art in Rembrandt's Country' which appeared that same year in the magazine *Dutch Art and Architecture Today.*[16] In this Mignot distinguishes three generations of international artists working with video from the 1960s to the 1980s. This distinction does not easily translate to the Dutch situation, as is apparent from the follow-on list of Dutch artists. Some have not worked with video but with film, while others are not even Dutch. Mignot then provides a summary of organizations showing video, like the Lijnbaancentrum, Meatball and the Agora Gallery, but she does not make a real point. The article remains caught up in dividing up video into different movements and periods.

A more ambitious approach than a selection of feminist video tapes was the 1984 Stedelijk Museum exhibition 'The Luminous Image' – an overview of various installations, including work by Dara Birnbaum, Michel Cardena, Nam June Paik and Lydia Schouten. The exhibition received a positive review in the magazine *Metropolis M*, which ended with the remark 'video when used in installations is a powerful artistic force with more artistic possibilities than the single videotape'.[17] The author preferred the artistic quality of an installation to the single-channel work and backs up this in the article with the argument that single-channel work is too similar to television which has corrupted the way the observer looks. Television returned again to the debate on video, in the same way it functioned in the 1970s as an example of an accessible medium for bringing art into the living rooms of the masses (see Reedijk's remarks about television in the 1970s). However, Bouma in his *Metropolis M* article in the 1980s claiming that through this same accessibility television was no longer a 'good' but a 'dubious' medium turned the argument around. This is evident from the sentence: 'The exhibition clearly shows that video is more than another kind of television, but an art form which has real possibilities and a visual language'.

In 1987 the Amsterdam Stedelijk Museum organized a symposium 'The Arts for Television' and for *Mediamatic* that was reason enough to devote several articles to the topic. Of course video art came up – seeing that television is one of the roots of the medium, especially in the work of Fluxus artists like Nam June Paik and Wolf Vostell. This was elaborated upon in the article 'Fluxus + Video' in which Wim T. Schippers acted as the Dutch Fluxus 'representative'.

109

16
Mignot 1984.
17
Bouma 1984.

However, it was unclear what Schippers had to do with video seeing that, apart from his television work, he chiefly made sculptures, collages, performances and installations.[18] Not one video of Schippers was mentioned. In a report of the symposium video was discussed as an extension of television and not as an independent medium.

In the early 1980s, magazines not devoted to the arts began to write about video. For the *Haagse Post* journalist Hansmaarten Tromp wrote a piece on video art in which he describes the hesitation of the television world to give artists access to studios and facilities so that video would remain in isolation. He stressed that video was a logical step in the development of television and, according to him, video artists should thus have more access to this mass medium.[19]

Video policy

Gallery owner and ex-VARA television assistant, René Coëlho, from Montevideo, did not reach for the metaphor of television but of painting in relation to video. In a 1982 interview with *Elsevier* he did not mince words: 'in the same way you use paint to make art, you can use video'. Video is there and art is made with it. He was annoyed by the fact the Montevideo had not as yet received any funding for its activities. Despite the fact that video had been around for a decade, the government, apparently, still did not take it seriously. While Coëlho showed his ill-feelings towards the government in the interview, it had in fact begun to take action, even though according to a 1981 Arts Council information bulletin, a string of funding requests had been necessary.[20] After a public hearing which drew attention in the media to video artists' situation, the Council decided to bring requests for funding under the budget category 'short artistic and cultural films'. It also regarded the distribution of video an important issue and commissioned a white paper to be written. As a result of the hearing, art critic Lily van Ginneken aired her views on video art policy in the daily *de Volkskrant*.[21] She described the situation in which video artists found themselves and mentioned several organizations where they could go to translate their ideas into work. She was not terrible clear about what should happen next, but concluded that video was not really alive and well in the Netherlands.

In the monthly arts magazine *Kunstbeeld* Rob Perrée argued that video art was dying a death and that it should be allowed more time. He touched on the irresponsible attitude of the networks whereby artists often had hardly any facilities with which to make their work.[22] He went further into this in a follow-

---

[18]
Rajandream 1987.
[19]
Tromp 1979.
[20]
Beleid 1981.
[21]
L. van Ginneken, 'Video-beleid', de Volkskrant, 27 November 1981.
[22]
Perrée 1983b.

up article in the October 1983 issue of the same magazine.[23] He was specifically concerned by the fact that funding for video, as was apparent from the Arts Council's second policy advisory report, was still not well regulated. The Council recommended that video art should fall under visual arts policy, while its recommendation concerning requests for funding should be maintained.[24]

Meanwhile, in 1983 the Vereniging van Mediakunstenaars [Association of Media Artists] set-up the foundation Time Based Arts, with Rob Perrée as the chairperson. It is apparent from a series of articles that appeared in *Kunstbeeld* that Perrée instantly launched a media offensive – and with success: in October 1983 the magazine *Nieuwe Revu* visited TBA and gave it a write up.[25]

The newspapers chiefly published reviews of exhibitions of video artists, including the World Wide Video Festival held for the first time in 1982. Artists like Livinus van de Bundt, Lydia Schouten, Stansfield/Hooykaas and Servaas received wider attention in separate interviews. By and large, however, video did not receive more attention than other visual art forms. Likewise in the press there was not a special correspondent for video art; generally this was also assigned to the art critics. Both *de Volkskrant* and the *NRC Handelsblad* regularly reported on video developments, the Amsterdam newspaper *Het Parool* somewhat less, even though most exhibitions were held in the city in the 1980s.

When the critics did write a review they were often doubtful or negative and their opinion changed little over time. In 1977 G. Waller wrote in the *NRC Handelsblad*: 'Video allows scope for many tricks. Art has still got to be given a chance'.[26]

In response to an exhibition in Museum Boymans-van Beuningen in Rotterdam in 1981, *de Volkskrant* wrote that 'video was too pretentious'.[27] A few months later Lily van Ginneken concluded that 'video did not really live'.[28] However, with journalist Pauline Terreehorst *de Volkskrant* gradually acquired a regular video reviewer for its large features. In her review of the exhibition 'The Luminous Image' (Stedelijk Museum Amsterdam, 1984) she is not unreservedly positive, rather it appears as if video art has lost its special status. Not for nothing does she ask the duo Stansfield/Hooykaas whether video has come of age. She ends the article with a positive quote from Dorine Mignot: 'As an artist you can't change the entire world, but you can show your own world.

23
R Perrée 1983a.

24
Tweede 1984. Members of the Video workgroup which advised the Council included René Coëlho, Rien Hagen (Meatball) and Dorine Mignot.

25
Schoondergang 1983.

26
G. Waller, 'Video nog op zoek naar zijn eigen beeldspraak', *NRC Handelsblad*, 22 December 1977.

27
P. Heynen, untitled, *de Volkskrant*, 22 May 1981.

28
L. van Ginneken, 'Video-beleid', *de Volkskrant*, 27 November 1981.

Video is simply a means to express something, without the euphoria at the beginning about all the technical possibilities. It is about ideas'.[29]

Recognition

With her remark that it was all about ideas, Mignot gave video the artistic recognition it deserved and in this she was not alone. Nevertheless, not everyone held the same view as the writers quoted here. In 1974, Rudi Fuchs, for instance, was scornful about 'Saint Video'.[30] The immense potential that, according to media theorists, video contain had not been fulfilled. It was not regarded as 'new', despite the fact that in art magazines the medium was usually introduced to readers with a brief history. Publications show that over the years video art became more interesting to write about simply because more was happening. The immense ideologies which were attached to video in the early 1970s had somewhat eroded and thanks to the efforts of institutes like Montevideo the technical possibilities were greater.

The authors of the articles at the time were not lacking in knowledge of the medium. The writers as art historians were well, or even very well, informed since they often wrote from their experience in the field, like Hein Reedijk and Rob Perrée. In an attempt to make video accessible to a wider public, Perrée even published a reader.[31] Nevertheless, he paid relatively little attention to Dutch video art. Compared to the attention video now receives, it was quite different in the 1970s and 1980s. Ultimately the press did not pay less attention than usual to the subject, but neither did they pay more. The book Perrée wrote on video was unable to do anything to change the situation.

Hinke Kappert studied the history of art at the Free University in Amsterdam and graduated with her dissertation on the videos of the former Lijnbaancentrum (1970–1984) in Rotterdam. She has also worked on a number of catalogues and was editor-in-chief of the art history periodical, *Kunstlicht*, until 2002.

[29]
P. Terreehorst, 'Stedelijk Amsterdam brengt video als beeldende kunst', *de Volkskrant*, 8 September 1984.
[30]
Perrée 1988.
[31]
Perrée 1988.

Sebastián López

Video exposures
Between television and the exhibition space

The primary scene

History always asks for a primary scene. And the history of
Dutch video art is not strange to this dictum. It looks like this:
one evening in 1963, a national television network broadcasts
Signalement,[1] in which Wim T. Schippers performs a Fluxus
action by emptying a bottle of lemonade into the sea. For many
years almost all accounts of video art have used this reference,
so that a television programme with information on the
developments in the visual arts has come to take the place of
the historical appearance of the new medium video. In this
television programme, Schippers is interviewed after his
performance about the new art (Fluxus, Pop Art, Nouveau
Realism and Zero were discussed), statements are made about
his piece, and the report – not a video work – is over. This
primary scene is also interesting because it reveals the way in
Dutch television and its own history have come to replace the
use of the new challenging medium by artists. Playing on the
fact that new works of the 1960s could only be 'documented' –
indeed, many of the first videos arose from this fact of life – a
television programme has come to establish the rule. There is a
similarity in the way Gerry Schum entered Dutch video history

---

[1]
The broadcasting was by VARA Television on 19 December, 1963.

through his 1970 *Identifications*, broadcast at the Sudwestfunk Baden-Baden.[2] This television programme included works by Jan Dibbets and Marinus Boezem, but they were originally made on film, and were later translated to video to fit the medium that Schum had chosen to spread and make known the new works in the visual arts and to serve educational purposes.[3] Schum called what he did 'television exhibitions', and this name helped to describe one of the ways the new works could be displayed.

These references even become ironic if one remembers the second dictum of the tale: video art was started and developed against television. Dibbets, again, an artist who is not known for an active practice of video, produced a telling television tour de force, but once again, as a film: his *TV as a Fire Place* (1969) established the relation of works made by artists and television in a new way, during the cold winter evenings of December, starting on Christmas Eve and ending on New Year's Eve.

At the end of the broadcast, short three-minute fragments were broadcast showing the lighting, flaring up and burning down of a fire, ending in ashes on the eighth day. It was a literal translation of what television had become, replacing the fireplace as a centre around which people gathered, not the family – an institution which was under heavy fire in those days – around the 'box'.[4]

These works have been declared part of Dutch video history by a generation of writers and curators who witnessed two parallel phenomena in the late 1970s: the increasing reference to television in exhibitions and international symposia (following the interest of one section of video practitioners in occupying, criticizing or using television language) and the way video practice was seen as an alternative to television at the time; and the way documentation became the standard way to describe images related to some practices of conceptual art. In the field that ranges from art criticism to curatorial initiatives, the plurality of video practice is placed between television and the exhibition space. Outside this field, but including it, another rich history was to be developed. Issues such as the personal, the political and the social, the exploration of the medium within new 'performative' parameters (in which 'performative' should be understood in terms not only of 'performances', but also of dance, ethnology and the archaeology of everyday practice), and a new exploration of nature, could all count on many practitioners. In this way the history of video art in the Netherlands has been the result of conflicting interests: a new medium that tried to establish itself by opening its practice in numerous ways, at a time when such a history had become difficult to establish, reclaiming an autonomy for works that

Gerry Schum, *Identifications*, 1970, film for tv, b/w, sound, 35'00"

Jan Dibbets, *TV as a Fire Place*, 1969, film for tv, colour, sound, 8 x 3'

<hr>

2
The broadcast was on November 30, 1970.

3
'To confront as wide a public as possible with present-day trends in international art', in Amsterdam 1979, pp. 12-71.

4
Dibbets' work was a series of eight three-minute fragments. It was based on an early work made in 1968–1969 called *Fire*, and shown at the opening of an exhibition in Haus Lange in Krefeld. The film showed the slow burning of a film screen, two minutes.

were no longer able – and some of which did not even want –
to have this autonomy. It was a time in which the numerous
transfers that started in the 1950s (from the pictorial to the
photographic, from the performative to the theatrical, from the
artistic to the mediatic) led to an artistic practice bent on
disrupting categories that put an end to the search for
essentialisms. Martha Rossler has eloquently said: 'Video's
history is not to be a social history but an art history, one related
to, but separated from, that of other forms of art. Video, in
addition', she adds, 'wants to be a major, not a minor art'.[5]

Placed between television and film, video was to encounter
this destiny of mixed classifications from the start. On the other
hand, as John G. Hanhardt has stated, when video has been put
to work as an aesthetic tool, it has 'played a role in a variety of
art movements that have defined the period, including Fluxus,
Happenings, Conceptual, Body and Performance art. In addition, the video medium has expanded beyond the single-channel
discourse [...] to add a new dimension to sculpture and
multimedia installations. The history of videotapes is composed
of a variety of genres and styles, including documentary,
narratives, image processing, dance and performance tapes, as
well as a variety of running times, subjects, and formal
concerns, from the straight recording of what is before the
camera to the development of abstract imaginary '.[6] The summary Hanhardt gives is relevant in as much as every single
movement had a different exhibition (or display) space in mind.
At the same time videos, which are based on recording, can be
later shown in regular exhibitions.

The exhibition of video art as a medium made its appearance
in the Netherlands in two places: the galleries run by artists, and
the art colleges. In the first category, the In-Out Center, an
alternative gallery in which artists from diverse cultural
background introduced videos, performances, films and textual
pieces to the Dutch art world, established video as a recurrent
presence in 1972, and Michel Cardena was the one who
persistently managed to put the medium to difference uses:
the direct recording of an event or performance, independent
works, and (later on) the use of dance and movement. In his
1972 *Cardena réchauffe en vain la famille B. à Hilversum* and
Two hands warm a cube into a circle no. 1 the almost
anthropological way of analyzing Dutch society (and its art
history) looks forward to works like those of Rirkrit Tiravanija,
while erotic undertones are often present in his other works.
With Cardena, artists like Gudmundsson, Fridfinnson,
Marroquin, Carrión and Gibbs represented the introduction of
'many new elements to artistic life in the mother country', in the
words of Harry Ruhé.[7] Foreigners with a foreign medium, both

115

Michel Cardena, *Cardena
réchauffe en vain la famille B. à
Hilversum*, April 1972, video, b/w,
sound, 19'40"

5
Rossler 1990.
6
Hanhardt 1995.
7
Ruhé 1982.

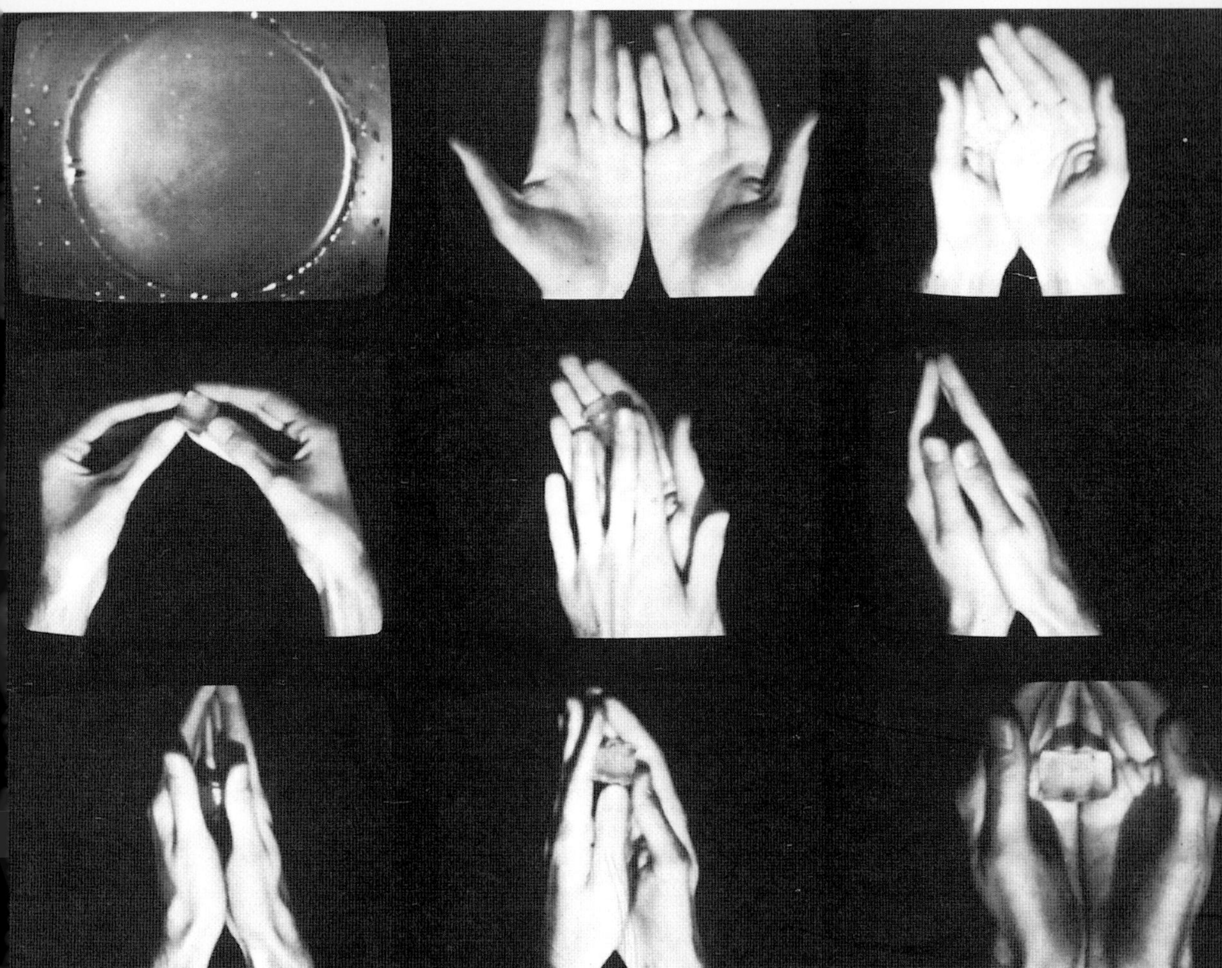

116   Michel Cardena, *Two hands warm a cube into a circle no. 1*, video, b/w, no sound, 20'35"

estranged in place and time, contributed in a fundamental way
to visual art in the Netherlands.

The role of the art colleges has not been properly highlighted:
as places for production and presentation, they provided the
expensive hardware necessary for working in the new medium.[8]
If the myth of the Portapak has grown to vast proportions, and
the extremely limited or unedited works have set the tone, this is
mainly because, in the final analysis, complex and even simple
editing procedures were difficult without the technical facilities
that were only available at first in the art colleges. The AKI in
Enschede and the Jan van Eyck Academy in Maastricht
therefore played an important role in the history of video in The
Netherlands. Training proceeded hand in hand with presentation, and in this way several video artists were introduced to
students and a new public. Tapes by video artists could be
borrowed, which soon became a regular practice.

Facilities for production and presentation already featured in
an exhibition in 1971. During 'Sonsbeek buiten de perken'

8
David Hall has highlighted this situation in relation to the USA and the UK in 'Some thoughts on
Video Art Education', in Amsterdam 1984. pp, 48-53.

[Sonsbeek beyond the pale] a tent was installed where artists
and the public could make videos, though only Stanley Brouwn,
Tajiri and Jack Moore used it, and the public stayed away.
Trapped in an event that established the massive and
unavoidable presence of minimalism and land art, the one-
dimensional approach at a time calling for a plurality of voices,
video came to fulfil a democratic role on the side – not that
video itself as a medium was uncomfortable with that. The new,
expanded way it could be used, and in fact was used, included
the social. The open tent during Sonsbeek was somewhere
between educational purpose and playful participation.

It was the Lijnbaancentrum in Rotterdam which took the
initiative in 1973 of putting together an exhibition to show the
ways video could be used in a larger way. Examples for art
education, the use of video in Rotterdam in particular, and in the
Netherlands in general, were shown together with the use of
cable television, a medium that later in the 1980s would
become fundamental to develop works in a different way by
artists and different communities, and recordings of performances by artists introducing one of the early uses of video.
Equally important, however, was the way different agencies,
from local and provincial authorities to the Ministry of Culture,
Recreation and Social Work, made the effort to spread and use
video not only for artistic purposes, but also for educational,
community and other purposes. Each and every one of them
made a place for video art. In 1978 the Nederlandse Kunststichting and the Ministry produced the special programme
'625 lines' as a documentary, showing firstly videos from abroad
and secondly works by Livinus, Cardena, Hoover and Struycken.
This period and this process have been given the label of
'democratization' in Dutch historiography. The process and
name applied to a complex fabric in which not only a new civil
participation entered the strictly controlled Dutch political and
cultural arena, but also the collective process of individualiza-
tion, centring on the I and on liberation from constrictive social,
political and cultural norms. Certainly not every part of the
process can be mentioned here, but it was accompanied by a
phenomenon that is seldom mentioned as a pendant: the
massive influx of cheap labour through the selective import of
labourers from Turkey and Morocco, and the migration of
Spaniards and Italians, among others, to escape the miseries of
poverty in their own countries. This, and the gradual entrance of
people from the colonies, in different decades, are what have
given the country the rich variety that it has today.

Mass media

The idea of *dematerialization* promulgated by Lucy Lippard, that
by way of conceptual art has become the most recurrent
definition of the whole period, was earlier developed in Latin
America. Already in 1966 the Argentinean art critic and media
theoretician Oscar Masotta established the concept of dema-

terialization as a main tool to describe the artistic phenomena in Argentina and beyond, particularly in *Después del pop: nosotros desmaterializamos* [After Pop: we dematerialize][9]. Lippard travelled to Buenos Aires in 1968 and met Masotta, publishing the same year her text 'The dematerialization of art' in *Art International*.[10] Lippard encountered one of the most lively scenes in the Americas. She was, as she put it, 'politicized by my trip to Argentina', mostly when she talked to Argentinean artists 'who felt that is was immoral to make their art in the society that existed there. It becomes clear that today everything, even art, exists in a political situation'.[11] Later, in her book of 1973, she introduced references to *Tucumán Arde*, a complex socio-political work developed by the Rosario Group, the only reference to a work from the South outside the typical North Atlantic line that governs the accounts of those years.[12]

Masotta's text is anchored in the Argentinean situation and beyond, emphasizing the way art and the media were penetrating each other, in contrast to Lippard's strictly artistic concerns of establishing the new. He opens his text with a direct reference to El Lissitzky when he established in *The Future of Books* that continuous changes in media to convey messages bring with them an increasing dematerialization in relation to the diminution of material. In other words, the ideas of McLuhan had been established by El Lissitzky already thirty years earlier.[13] Masotta concludes that the 'questions of art today can be found less in the search for new content than in research on the 'media' to convey this content'. His idea of dematerialization is this research on media, understanding by 'media' the mass media of 'television, film, magazines and newspapers'. 'What has happened today', he stresses, 'is that in the best works the content is welded to the media used'.[14] Masotta then establishes that what is definitive in this new situation is to define the work as a 'hybrid', since in the work of art 'tactics' and 'media' are mixed, and the definition of the work based on the medium used is irrelevant.

Masotta's way of defining dematerialization is more useful than Lippard's when it comes to understanding the constant search by Dutch artists to find a place for their hybrid works at a time in which media-based definitions were relevant. The artists excluded from television because they could not offer what the broadcasting companies in Hilversum were asking for went in

118

9
Masotta first developed this idea in a lecture in 1966 published later as a chapter of his *Conciencia y estructura*, Masotta 1968, pp. 218-244. The lecture was one of the three parts of work developed by Masotta at the Di Tella Institute in Buenos Aires consisting of a happening called *El Helicoptero*, a 'communicational' work or 'anti-happening' called *'El mensaje fantasma'*, and finally a lecture 'explaining' the work called *Nosotros desmaterializamos*, see *Conciencia y estructura*, p. 227.

10
Lippard wrotte this text together with John Chandler: Lippard/Chandler 1968, pp. 31-36; reprinted in A. Alberro and B. Stimson (eds), *Conceptual Art: A Critical Anthology*, MIT Press, Cambridge 1999, pp. 46-50, where it is stated that the text was written in late 1967.

11
Lippard 1973, p. 8

12
Lippard 1973, p. 59.

13
Masotta 1968, note 9, p. 242.

14
Masotta 1968, p.222.

for plainer narratives against the grain of the established standards of the art world of the time.

David Ross stated in 1973: 'Many critics have confused video art with the liberal political movement to decentralize the television industry'.[15] Video artists shared the medium with television, just as in the avant-garde era artists had used newspapers, posters and architecture to stress how they conceived the modern way of working in the visual arts. Setting out to produce in a different way and to implement different ideas, video art was engaged from the start with the confrontation with, and later direct opposition to, the content of television in its poetics. The question was not whether video produced by artists could supplant television. That was never at stake. Television has always been more powerful in terms of presence and the promotion of its products, and artists themselves have always known that nothing could be done to replace it. Art and television each has its own economy, rules and mechanisms. Those of television, and the particular situation in the Netherlands, were responsible for two consequent phenomena in Dutch video history: The television programmes by Wim T. Schippers, *Hoepla* and *Waldolala*, and the applied arts in television format made by Peter Struycken, on the one hand; and the pirate programmes on Amsterdam cable television made by artists such as PKP-TV, on the other. Schippers and Struycken both worked with national broadcasting stations, one in comedy and the other in 'scientific' programmes. While Schippers entered television comedy making use of the psychological tricks already present in Dutch comedy, with its surreal and unexpected situations, Struycken formed his serious and geometrical counterpart by working on commissions for corporate identity and television graphics for Hilversum. The history of video art in the Netherlands has also been conditioned by these negotiations. To interrogate and understand them is to answer the way institutions and artists are constituted as such.

During the 1970s and 1980s, video was strongly criticized because of the long duration of the pieces, or simply because the public and the specialists needed to spend time in extracting a meaning from a work. The artists, in turn, often responded by adjusting their works to produce short pieces to match the expectations of both audiences. This also enabled television, in particular the VPRO station, to produce programmes like BGTV and Tape TV with the broadcasting of videos.

15
Ross 1973, p. 5.

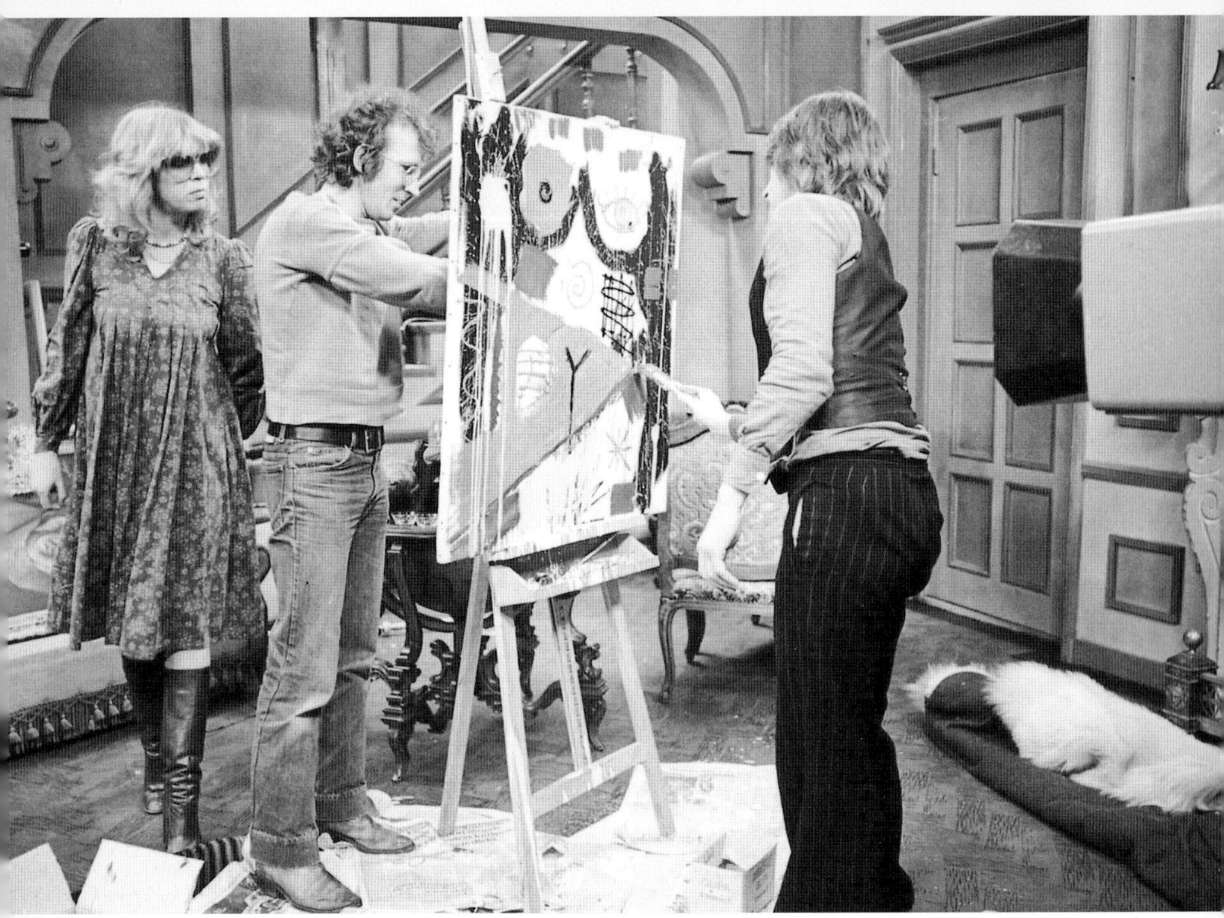

Wim T. Schippers, *Hoepla* (part 3), VPRO, 10 November 1967

120 Video frames

Video artists met with resistance from museums and galleries in
the 1970s. In spite of the increasing introduction of minimalism
and the selective entrance of conceptual art, what was exhibited in most places was painting.[16] From the students of Ateliers
63 to the exhibition 'Fundamental Painting' at the Stedelijk
Museum, the re-establishment of the value of the object was
central. The 'experimental' group was small, even if we include
in it not only video practitioners but also performance artists and
film.

In this panorama it is not surprising that traditional categories
were used to discuss video in criticism and in galleries and
museums. 'Video sculptures' was the name given to works in
which the monitor was combined with three-dimensional forms,
a simplistic way of reducing a work to its material appearance.
This happened at a time when artists like Richard Serra were
developing film sculptures, a post-surreal arbitrary juxtaposition
of heterogeneous situations. And in *25 Caramboles and
variations*, a multiple-monitor work, Michel Cardena explored
the new space and time-based dimension video could have in a
complex installation. The way video was simply ascribed to the

16
Gribling 1982.

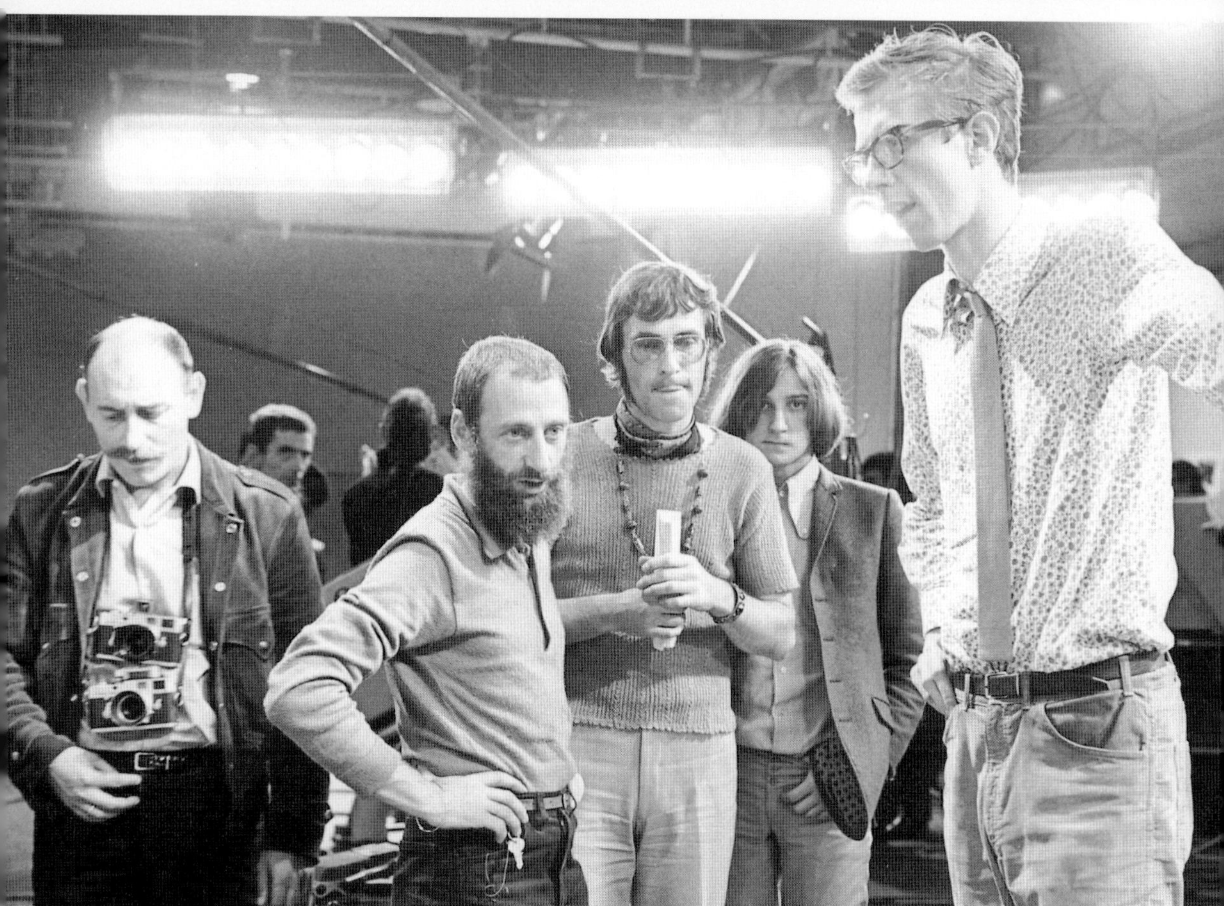

Wim T. Schippers, *Hoepla* (part 2), VPRO, 22 September 1967

category of film in national and international exhibitions, by
virtue of the moving image, was not very different. But it also
needs to be remembered that artists themselves, lacking
distribution facilities for their work, found the way to make their
tapes available in experimental film distribution companies.
The presentation of Dutch video artists at the Centre Pompidou
in Paris in 1978 was called 'Cinéma experimental hollandaise'
and was organized in cooperation with the Holland Experimental Film.[17] In the same year the Venice Biennale mixed works
by Man Ray and Moholy-Nagy with works by Baldessari, Michel
Cardena, Bas Jan Ader and Peter Struycken, among others, in
a section called 'Art and Cinema'. Other exhibitions, however,
retreated from these reductive categories and produced a
larger view not so much of the medium but rather of the artistic
and social frame in which it developed. An example is 'Actie,
werkelijkheid en fictie in de kunst van de jaren '60 in Nederland',
an exhibition curated by the Museum Boymans-van Beuningen
in Rotterdam at the end of 1979.

Within Dutch video history, the Fluxus tendencies have been
highlighted together with the techno-electronic tendencies at
the expense of the group of more alternative tendencies that

17
This presentation took place from 15 to 26 November 1978.

were putting fundamental questions to the arts in the 1960s
and the 1970s. These other tendencies can still be seen in Raul
Marroquin's *HoekSteen*, first for local television and now on the
internet. The success of his endeavour is shown by the fact that
his work is no longer regarded as an art event, as alternative
tendencies in the 1970s wanted, but as television, having
disembodied its 'signature' in a collective discourse. There is
not enough space here to go more fully into the way Marroquin
has been operating, but mention should be made of his transition from video tapes and installations, in which the focus was
always on political issues, to alternative uses of local television,
the continuous raising of new questions in practice and on what
technology delivers, and his way of engaging in a dialogue on
art, culture and politics with the recipient. He puts the global
promise to work for the sake of the local.

A chain of events

There has not been, nor can there be a definitive turning-point in
the presentation of video, but between 1982 and 1984 a
succession of exhibitions and broadcasts shows the complexity,
the definitive assimilation within the museum culture, the
permanence of early protest activity, the marketing of the
medium video in a festival format, and the continuation of artists'
initiatives based on early beliefs. It marks, at the same time, the
end of an era and the beginning of a new one: Beatrix as Queen
of the Netherlands, the Christian Democratic policy of breaking
down the areas conquered in the battle of twenty years of
democratization, and the slow decline of the 'democratic
movement' to enter the wide field of new political and artistic
negotiations.[18] These are the years in which foreigners were
identified as a new target (later labelled 'allochtonen'), that is,
those who had broken artistic standards and contributed to the
birth and rise of a medium were now among the items being
negotiated on the new political agenda that would later use the
term 'multiculturalism'.[19] It was an art scene divided from the top,
categorized by ethnic background and race, where the first
generation of students trained in the Dutch art colleges were
beginning to make an appearance. They were the years in which
video was viewed with suspicion and discussions started up
within the national subsidy system on the need to close it down
now that the growing relevance of painting as a new marketable
exhibit was setting the standard for the new period. The reor-
ganization of this field was to be given definitive shape in the
creation of Montevideo/Time Based Arts as a National Dutch
Centre for Media Art. This history can be summed up in the
following chain of events:

– In 1982 Agora cooperated with the Bonnefantenmuseum in
  Maastricht on the International Media Meeting, at which
  twenty installations were shown;

[18]
Ligthart/Smithuijsen 1982.
[19]
López 2002, pp. 137-144.

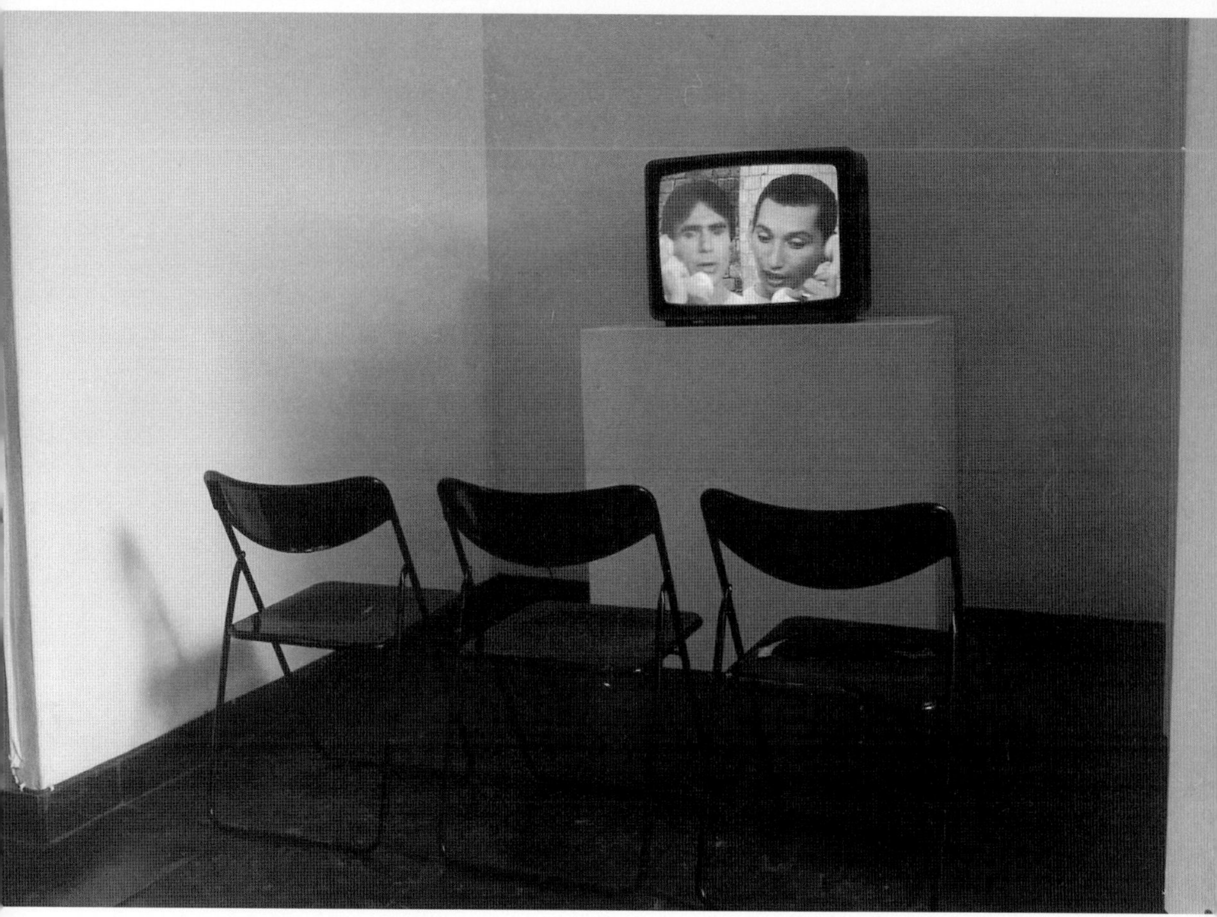

- The First World Wide Video Festival opened in The Hague (1982);
- The pirate station Rabotnik TV (a continuation of PKP-TV) started to broadcast (1982);
- The Stedelijk Museum Amsterdam opened its 'video staircase' to provide regular viewing of its video collection (1982);
- The Association of Media Artists, assisted in its foundation by the De Appel, gave birth to Time Based Arts (the transfer of the video collection belonging to De Appel brought a period to a close, restored what it had received from artists' initiatives, and drew a demarcation line with Montevideo);
- 'The Second Link. Viewpoints on Video in the Eighties' (1983) opened at the Stedelijk, an exhibition from the Canadian Walter Philips Gallery in Banff, to which the Stedelijk contributed with *City of Angels* by Abramovič and Ulay and Shift 31 by Peter Struycken. (It is worth noting that in the catalogue Mignot states that European video was separated from television while in America they were together, which is incorrect with regard to the history we are telling here);
- The TV programme *Golfbreker* (1984) was sponsored by the South Holland Cultural Council. Directed at artists in the

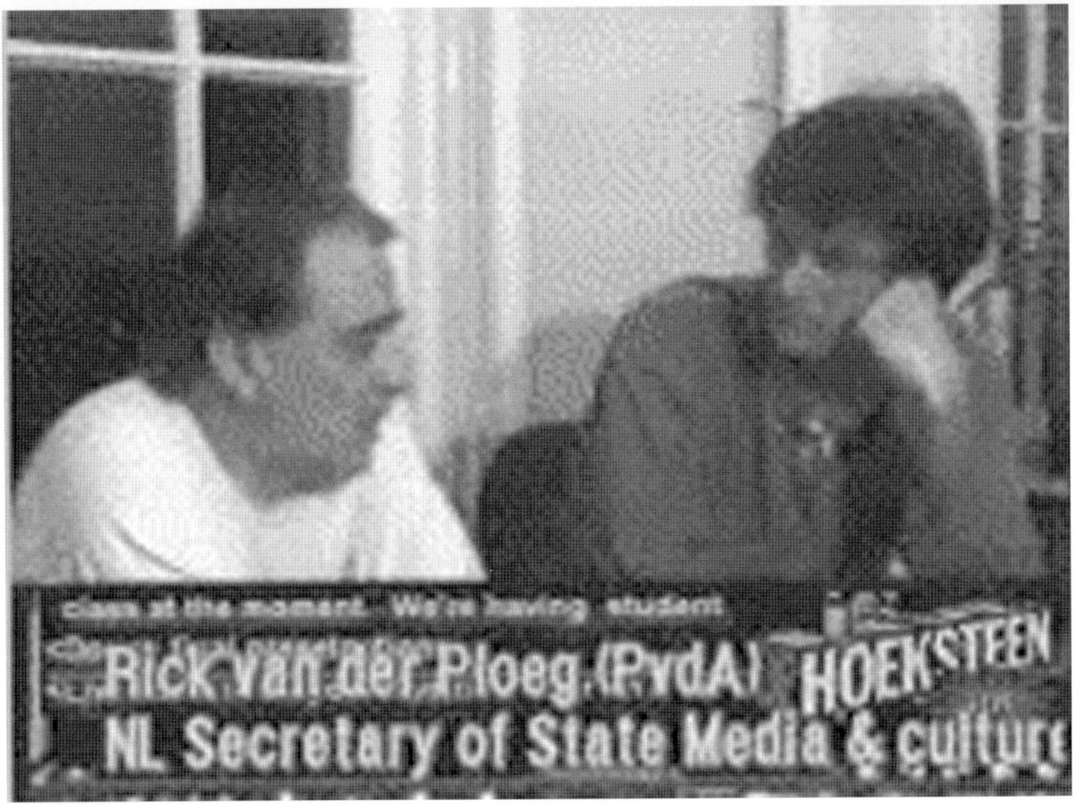

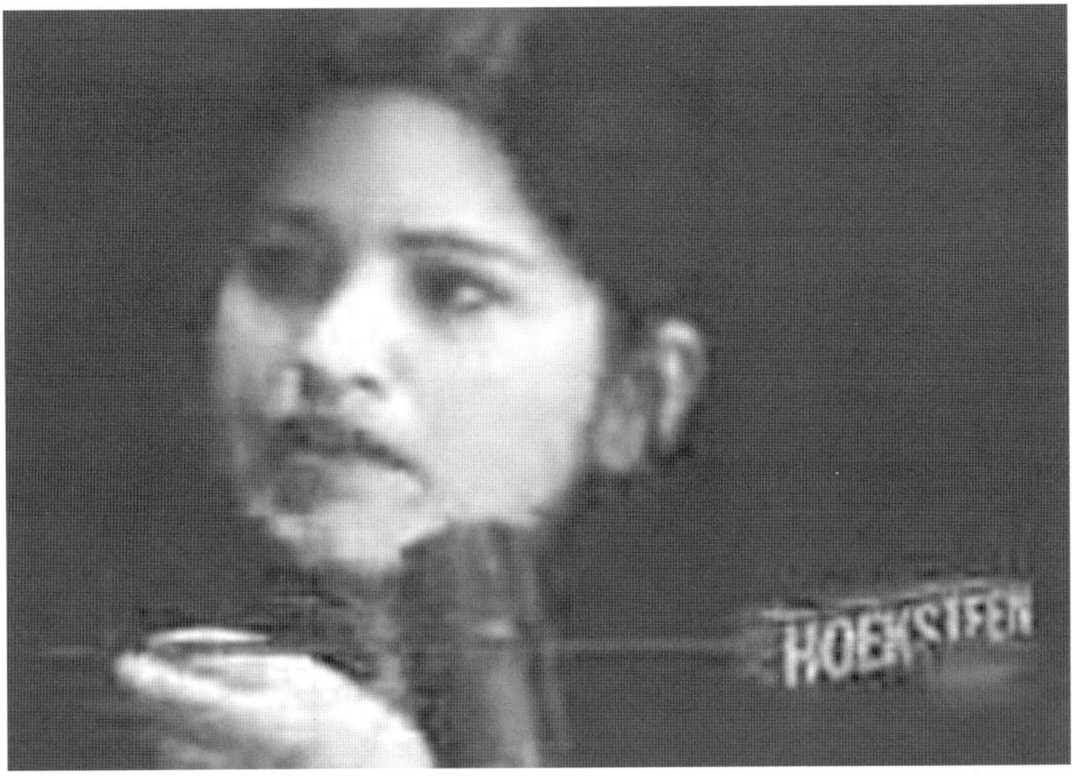

Raul Marroquin, transmission of *HoekSteen*

provinces, new productions were made for this programme;
– 'Talking Back to the Media', (1984) a fully multi-media event
  opened with production of works and an exhibition, relating
  video to wider phenomena in other media;
– 'The Luminous Image' (1984), the official presentation of
  video in a large exhibition to a wide audience.
All the tendencies of the previous decades came together, each
modified or stubbornly continuing its ideas and ideals from the
past.

'Talking Back to the Media', a large event highlighting the
relationship between mass media and visual arts, was a
complex exercise intended to reflect the works, the politics,
the issues, the language and the system of the visual arts in the
1980s with reference to the previous decade. The complexity
started with the intention not to talk from outside, that is not to
organize a regular exhibition, but to let the visual arts appear
inside and outside the media and the art system. Starting out
from the discussions and concerns of video art(ists), and taking
into consideration the way video and other related media had
acquired a raison d'être experienced in the previous decade, it
was less of an 'exhibition' than a rhizomatic series of events:
four television programmes with specially commissioned works,
four radio programmes with live 'performances' of audio works,
posters in the street, a video festival in a theatre, talks and
discussions by artists, and a photographic exhibition in a
gallery. The publication was planned as a magazine with works
commissioned in magazine format that would be sold at kiosks.
Lectures and talks with artists brought together young and old
practitioners not so much on the medium of video but on the
questions that had been discussed extensively for more than ten
years and the state of play in the early 1980s. Seldom had the
concerns of media and the visual arts and the new practices of
the early 1980s been highlighted to this extent in the country.[20]

In retrospect, 'Talking Back to the Media' closes a cycle of
concerns and engagement with taking the media and the art
system as a space of operations. From this moment on video
was to be included in museum exhibitions like 'Kunst voor
televisie' at the Stedelijk Museum in 1987 and was to enter new
negotiations of selective acceptance for exhibition purposes.

The same year 'Talking Back to the Media' took place, the
first large exhibition of video installations, 'The Luminous Image',
was displayed at the Stedelijk Museum for the enlightenment of
a larger audience. The exhibition had a wide scope in which not
only artists who had been consistently engaged with video were
included, like Bill Viola, Francesco Torres, or Dara Birnbaum,
but also theatre makers like Bob Wilson and musicians like
Brian Eno. Artists working in the Netherlands (Cardena,
Stansfield/Hooykaas, Nan Hoover, Lydia Schouten) were
presented together with a massive presence of Americans.

125

20
The event was initiated by David Garcia and Raul Marroquin, and developed with the participation of
Ulises Carrión, Aart van Barneveld, Rob Perrée, Sabrina Kamstra and Sebastián López.

The catalogue speaks volumes. First the director of the
museum, Edy de Wilde, introduced the exhibition 'The Luminous
Image' as follows: 'The Stedelijk has paid regular attention to
the medium video not because the medium as such is of any
artistic interest, but because a number of important artists have
made use of it'.[21] As the guardian at the gate, De Wilde rejected,
as the selection had also done, any other form that artists had
given to the medium, and how the medium as such had been
developed. His words also stressed that this was an exhibition
about art, not about a medium. His determined statement
sounds very close to the dictum of Castelli-Sonnabend Tapes
and Film Inc., the New York firm that started to market video
based on artists who already had a reputation in other media.
Castelli-Sonnabend, as Gigliotti has stated, 'refer to their
product as "artist's video tapes" rather than video art, the
implication being that these artists were mostly busy making art,
and sometimes had the time to make the odd video tape or two,
which might be of interest to collectors'.[22] Tellingly, the biblio-
graphy of the exhibition catalogue includes a reference to the
Castelli-Sonnabend Catalogue.

126

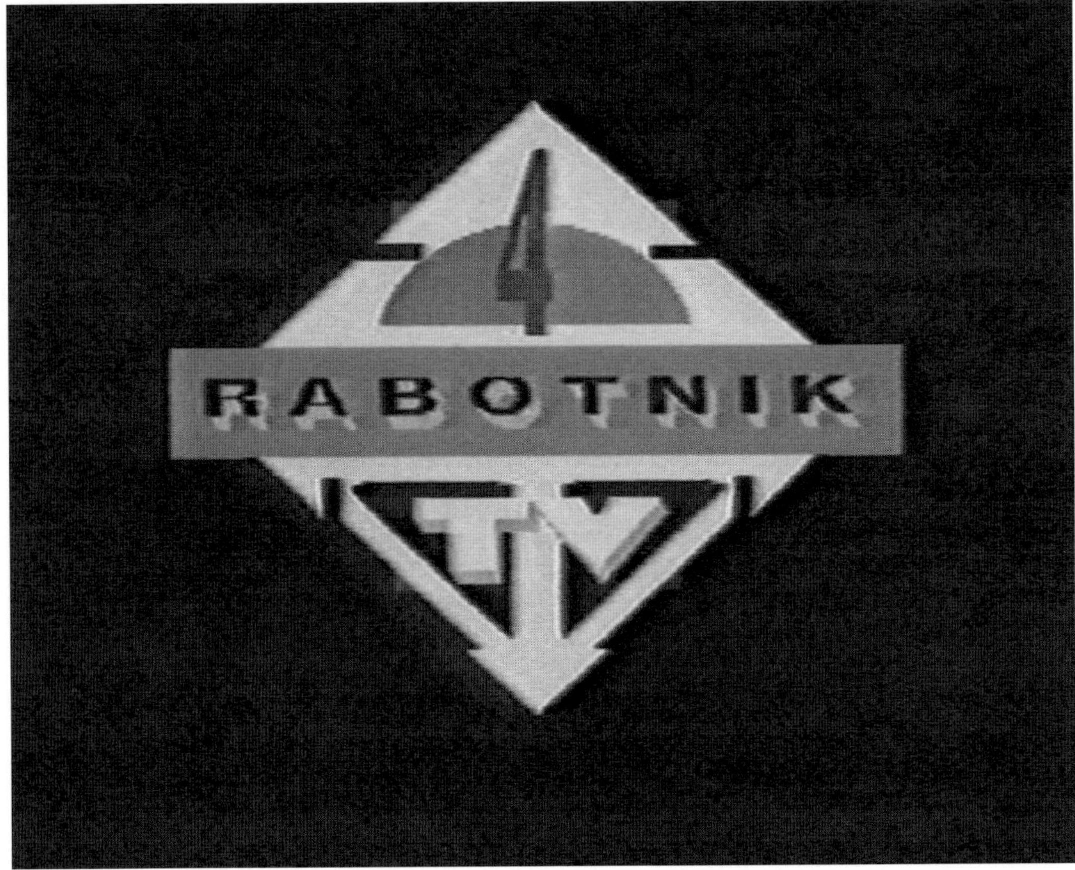

Logo Rabotnik TV

21
Amsterdam 1984, p. 5
22
Gigliotti s.a.

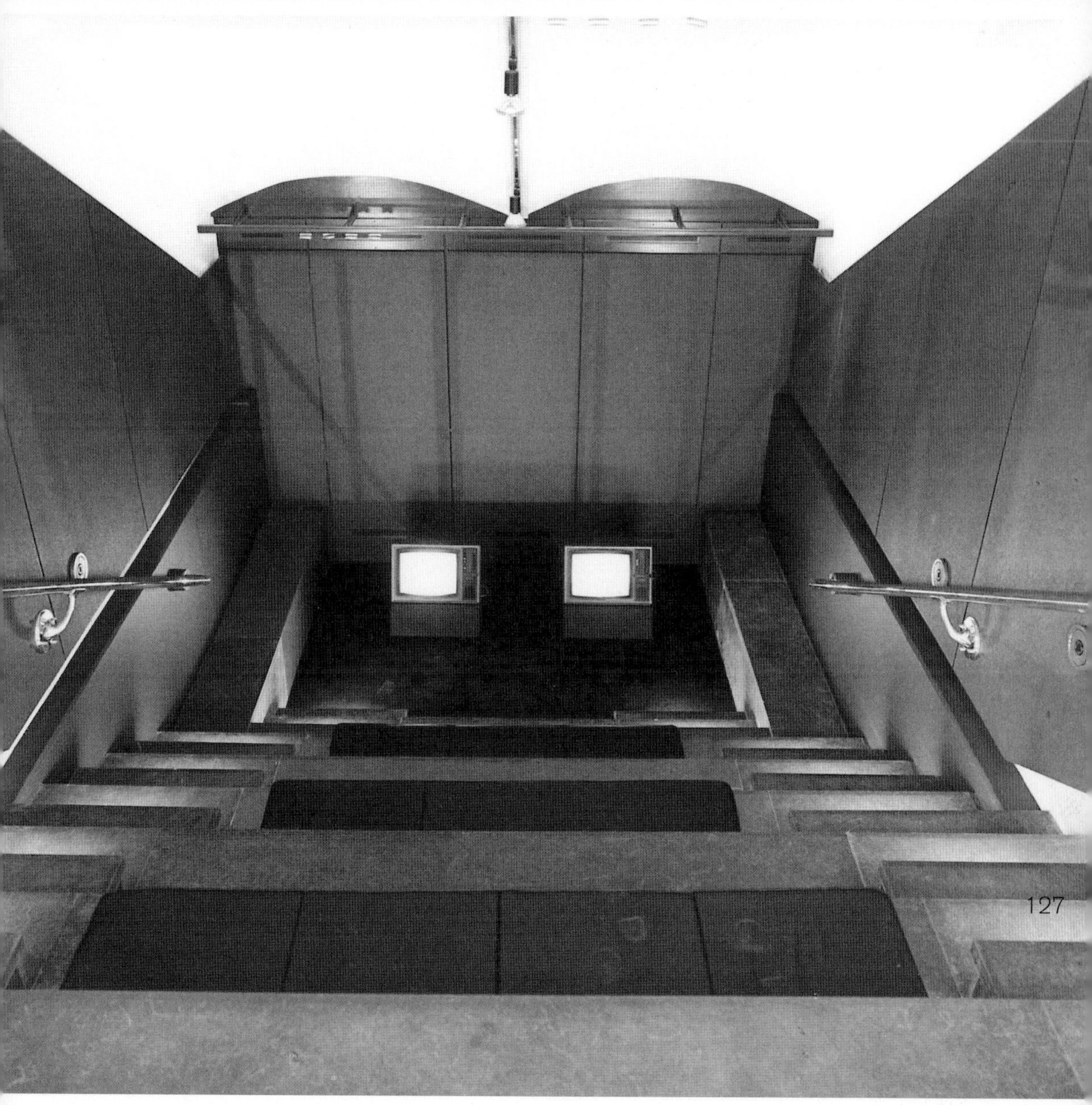

Videos by Stansfield/Hooykaas, video stairs, Stedelijk Museum Amsterdam, 1981

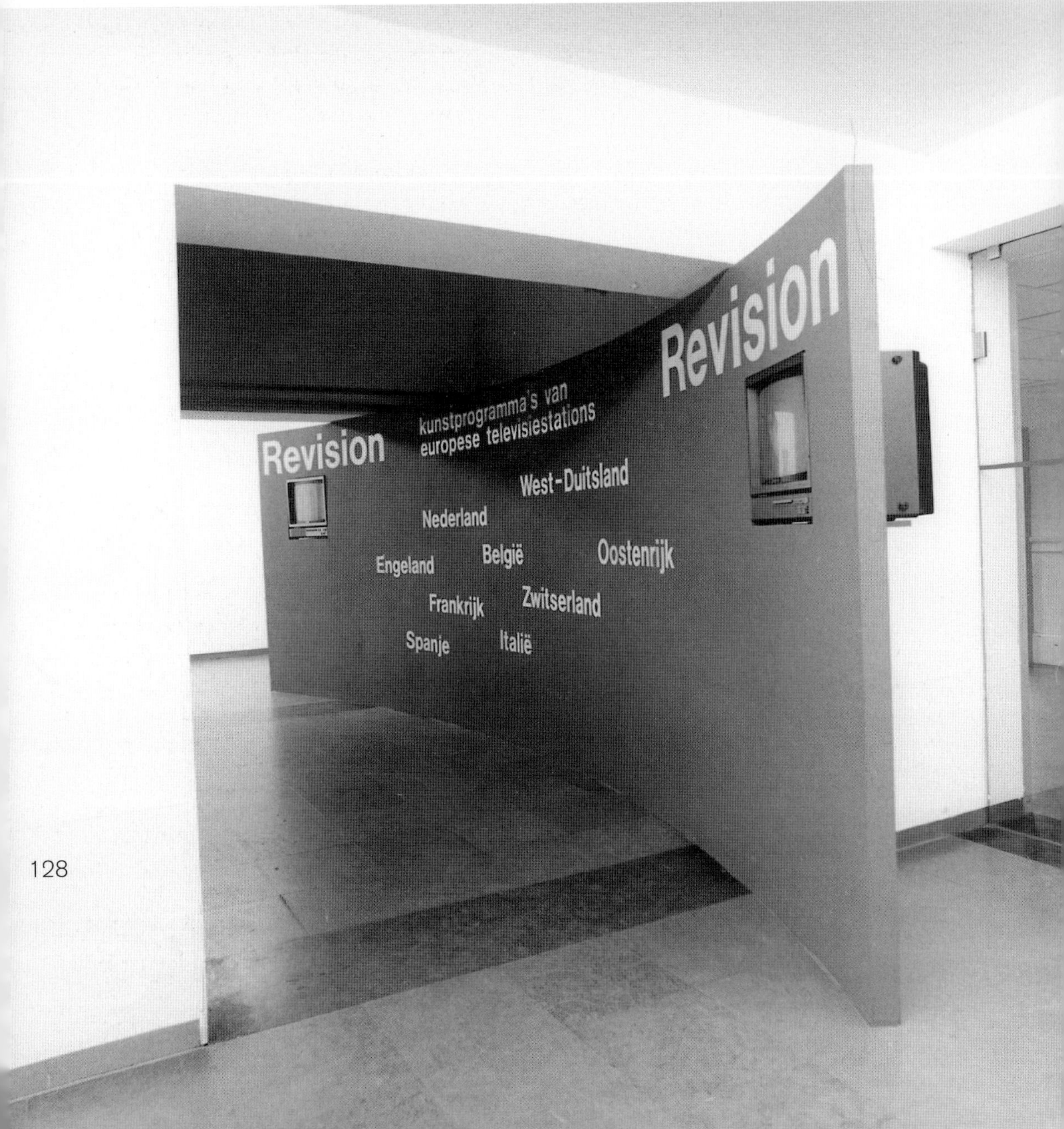

128

'Art for television', Stedelijk Museum Amsterdam, 4 September–18 October 1987

No less revealing is the way Wim Beeren established a formalist travesty of art history with the aim of constructing a relevant artistic past to validate the introduction of video to the museum. 'I am prepared to regard video as an art when like art, i.e. as a unit, it concentrates on aspects of colour, line, three-dimensional form and their possible relationships'.[23] The text is an incredible summary of all the formal elements of the arts and the way video uses them: light, movement, animals, colours, lines, traces from the Renaissance down to Abstract Expressionism, from Cubism to Futurism. Perhaps this is why issues already present among video and other practitioners, including painters, such as gender, race or politics, were not present. The text focuses on paintings, drawings, sculptures, and graphics, stressing that they all have a relation with video, but it also includes applied arts and their use of materials, gold and silver in churches, etc. Beeren summarizes: 'I see something similar in video'.[24] Seldom has video been so wrongly framed, and seldom, even by formalist standards, has formalism been so bad.

Away from the framing devices of the museums, and aware of the still fragile status of the medium, Servaas staged in the same year his installation *Are you afraid of video?* A monitor was attached to a turning platform in the middle of the room. Fixed to it, a long whip continuously turned dangerously in all directions, prohibiting anyone from entering.

[23]
Beeren 1984., p. 27.
[24]
Beeren 1984, p. 31.

Sebastián López is Artistic Director of the Gate Foundation, Amsterdam, and Guest Lecturer at the Art History Institute of Leiden University. He was the editor of *Talking Back to the Media* (1984), and *Van het Post Modernisme* (1985) and contributor of *Third Text* (London) and *KunstForum*, a.o. He has curated several exhibitions on media, a.o.: 'In de Ban van de Band' (1984), Stedelijk Museum Amsterdam and 'On(e) Line' (1999), Gate Foundation, a virtual presentation and live webcast from four continents.

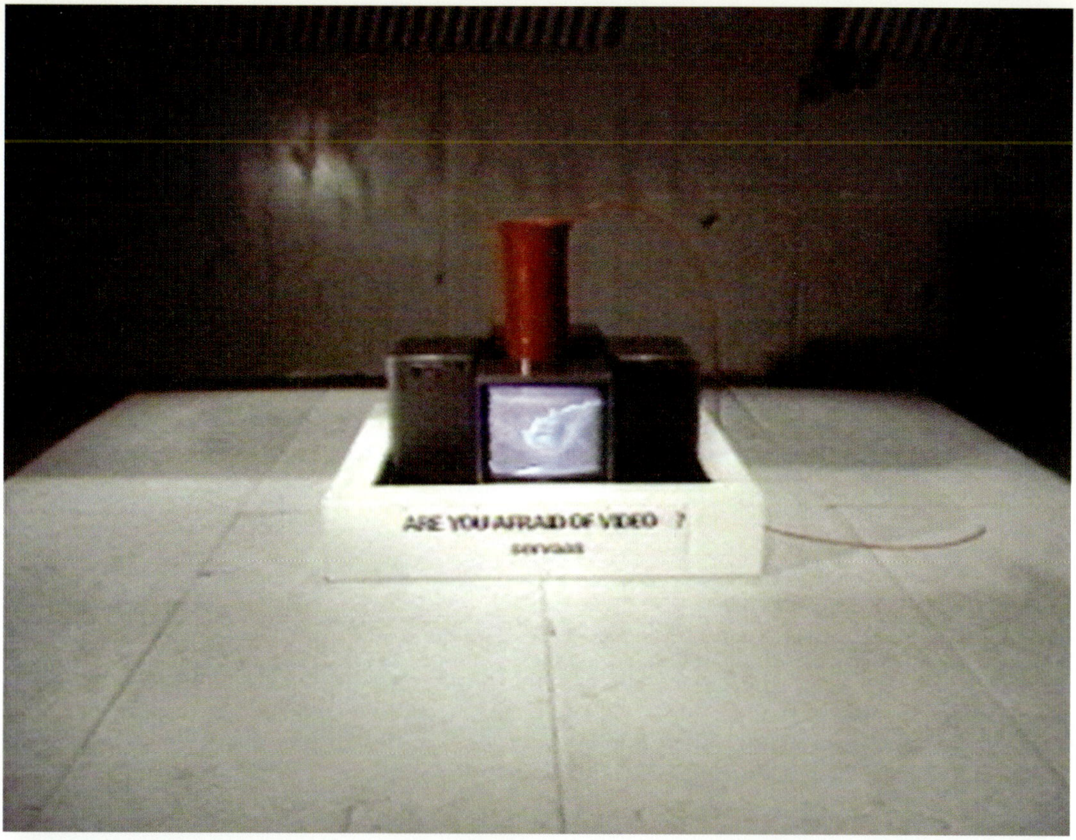

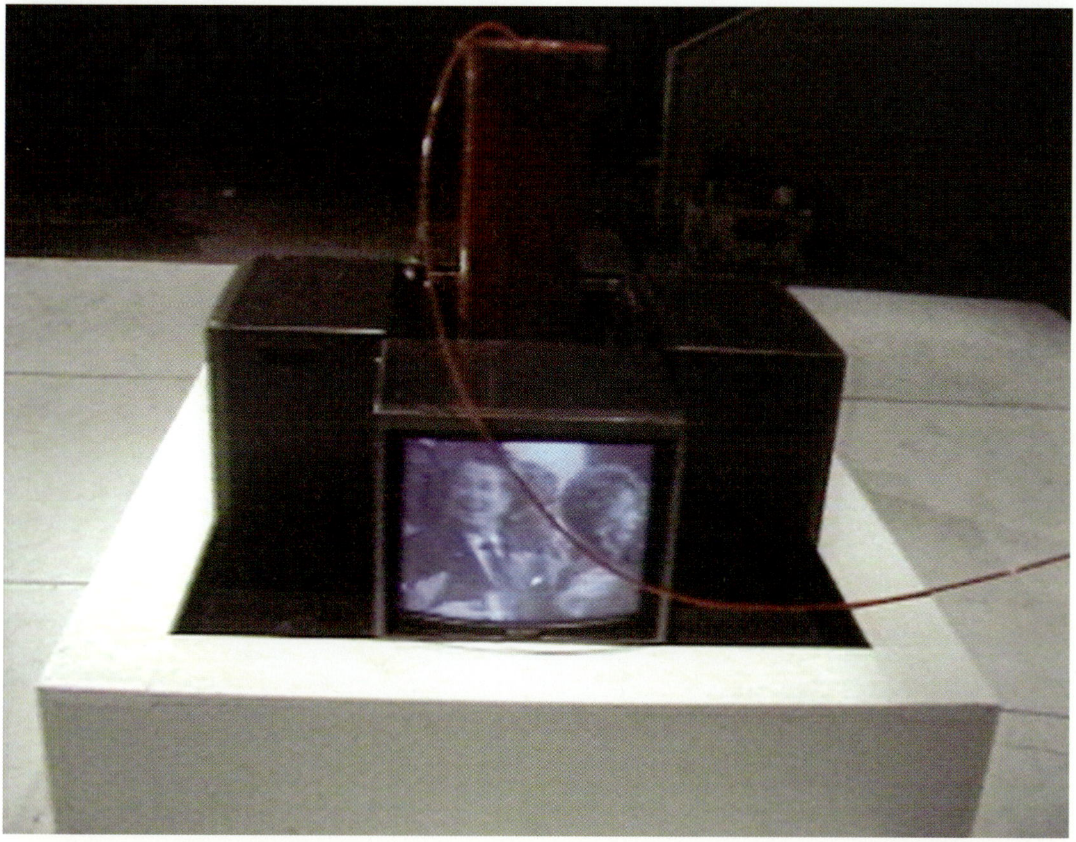

Servaas, *Are you afraid of video?*, 1984, video sculpture

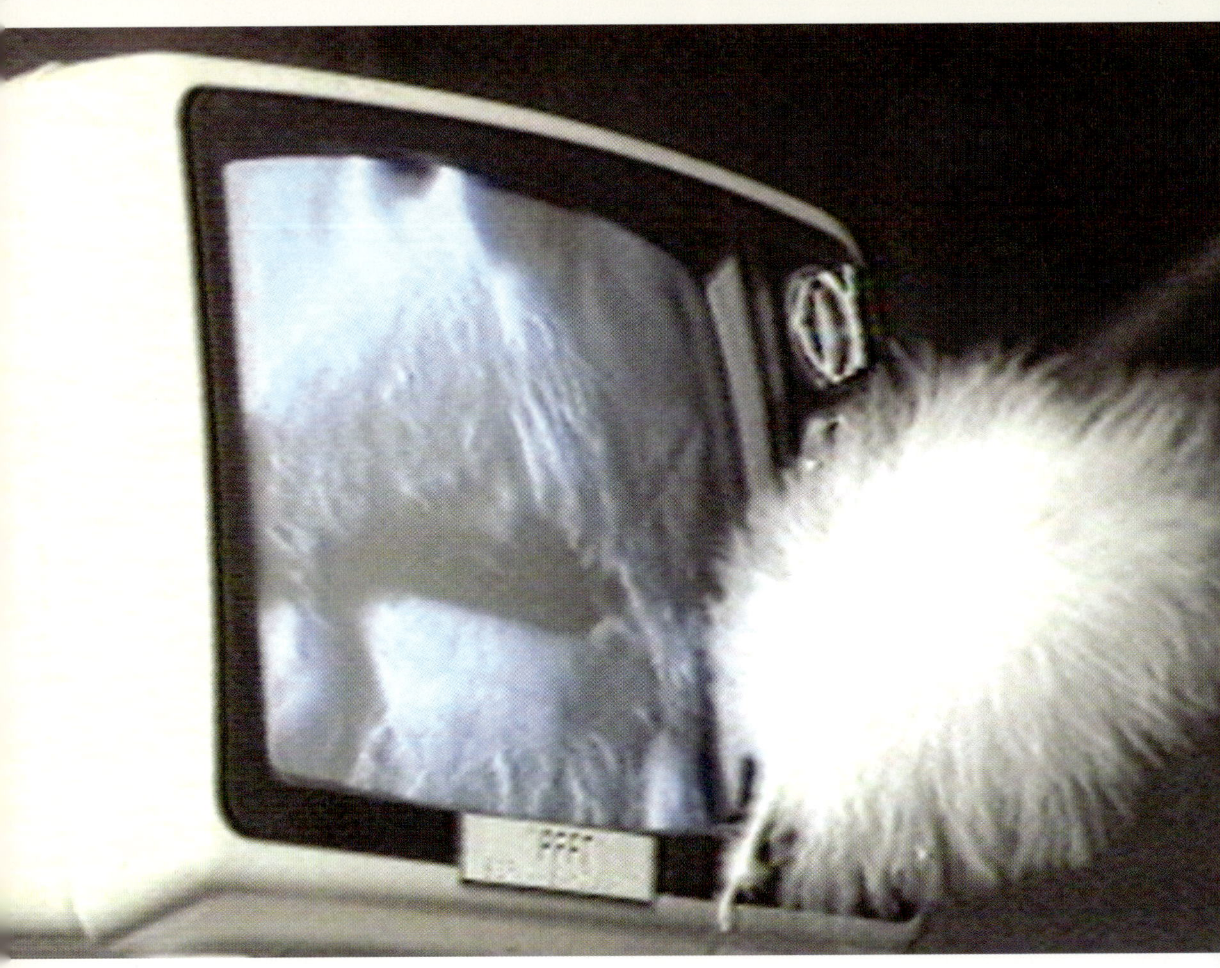

Servaas, *Pffft*, 1982, video sculpture

132

Anne van Driel

The entertainment years

In retrospect it was a turning point, the last straw. After the Venice Biennale a lot of people had had enough. Of course, international media festivals, prior to the biennial presentation of international art, had already set the mood. Group exhibitions and graduation exhibitions in previous years had sometimes prompted fears for the worst. But the lament heard at the Biennale in 2001 was louder than it had ever been before: video art is in the doldrums.

'Oh, I'm so *bored* with video art', the authoritative New York gallery owner Barbara Gladstone sighed – before she had even seen a fraction of the video works that the director, Harald Szeemann, was presenting to the public in Venice. And although that cry from the heart sounded rather general and premature, many were to echo it later: the lack of quality of the works at the Biennale was not an isolated phenomenon, but it was typical of the malaise in which video art found itself. Too long, too long-winded, too inaccessible or all too literal – since the 1990s, the shared opinion suddenly seemed to be, video art had produced little of any value.

How have matters come to such a pass? That was the question Lucette ter Borg and Sacha Bronwasser asked themselves in a polemical article in *de Volkskrant*.[1] How has

1
Lucette ter Borg and Sacha Bronwasser, 'Ziende blind', *de Volkskrant*, 18 October 2001.

video art managed to end up as works with an 'unremittingly coarse image' and 'unstable camera work', or tapes in which the ego is uncritically celebrated and everything that crosses the lens of the digicam – 'no matter how stupid or unoriginal' – is labelled art? How is it that the artist Anri Sala, to take just one example, can simply record how a tramp falls asleep on the pews in the cathedral in Milan without giving any original twist to the 'story' – and that exhibition curators still show it (and even give it awards)?[2] The answer, they claim, lies in the history of how this branch of art emerged: video art is still struggling with its image of a counterculture from the 1960s – the era when the young medium explicitly presented itself as low art and tried to shake off the Modernist ideals that dominated more elevated art. Video, the pioneers discovered, for example, can make time visible, a property that makes it pre-eminently suitable for performance and process artists. So we can still see Bruce Nauman walking round for hours in his studio, follow Marina Abramovič and Ulay in tireless confrontation with one another, or watch a block of ice melt in twenty-two minutes (Miguel-Ángel Cardenas).

'It was of no account whether those activities in themselves also yielded interesting images', Ter Borg and Bronwasser write, 'the excitement of the new was too great for that'. Nevertheless, they note, most video artists still model themselves on those heroes of the first hour. As a consequence, in spite of all the technological developments of the past thirty years, contemporary video art is still characterized by its indigestibility. Indeed, anyone who remembers the ego-documents and home video art that flooded the exhibitions of the 1990s – from the interminable recording of being drunk (Noa Sadka) to the artist's combing her hair until the scalp bleeds (Hester Scheurwater) – will be bound to agree with Ter Borg and Bronwasser: many videos from the 1960s and 1970s (no montage, no editing, no narrative structure or special recording technology) still exert an influence today.

All the same, the picture they present is only a part of the story. After all, the quest for 'authenticity' that characterizes many of the videos of the past ten years is not *accounted* for by referring to the 1960s and 1970s. Nor does falling back on that initial period help to explain another – opposite – tendency of the 1990s: the striking increase – from Aernout Mik to Gillian Wearing, from Saskia Olde Wolbers to Pipilotti Rist – in *narrative* video art.

Both of these tendencies have their roots in the 1980s, so if we are to understand them we have to go back to then and to the video art produced in that decade.

2
Sala's *Uomodomo* was acclaimed by an international jury of professionals during the opening days of the Biennale.

Forgotten bloom

The video art of the 1980s has always been neglected, over-shadowed by the two decades between which it is sandwiched. In the literature it is discussed less often and less extensively than the precursors from the 1960s and 1970s, and it has rarely been shown in later exhibitions. Yet it was an era when video art was experiencing a genuine bloom, especially in the Netherlands.[3] The technical possibilities and knowledge of the medium took off[4], the production and distribution facilities expanded, and so did the number of places where video art was shown.[5] The number of video artists kept on rising too; moreover, an increasing proportion of the second- and third-generation video artists had taken courses specifically devoted to video and media art.[6] Even more important was the fact that Dutch video art of that decade could count on a warm welcome abroad. Artists like Dedo (pseudonym of Harry Heyink) or Kees de Groot showed abroad more than in their own country, and the work of Servaas was included in international retrospectives alongside classics by Nauman or Nam June Paik. Looking back today, the art of that era can be regarded as successful.

Success – that was precisely what most of the video artists of the 1980s were aiming for, more purposely and deliberately than their predecessors had done. A process that got under way abroad around 1975 began to emerge in the Netherlands in the 1980s: video art became more commercial.[7] Artists deliberately began to shape their ideas in such a way that their videos could be sold and shown in museums and galleries. While the pioneers of the 1960s and 1970s had tried to rescue art from the constraints of those institutions, in the 1980s the status of video art was derived precisely from a place inside them. Video art still had a world to win and a battle to fight. After all, video artists of the early 1980s were confronted with the legacy of their predecessors: all the elevated properties that the pioneers had attributed to the new medium (anti-élitist and democratic), all the lofty ideals to which these believers had been 'converted' (art for the people, pure and honest), had mainly resulted in the opposite. Video art, which owed its existence since the 1960s among other things to its function as a critique of television (a critique of passive viewing behaviour, of the manipulation of the viewer by the objectionable montage of images), had not managed to engage the viewer's

135

[3]
Perrée 1988, p. 10.
[4]
This was partly due to the electronics company Sony, which supplied the Dutch video scene with free know-how and equipment until 1987.
[5]
The Vereniging van Videokunstenaars [Association of Video Artists] was set up in 1980, from which Time Based Arts was created in 1983. Montevideo was founded in 1978. The first World Wide Video Festival was held in 1982, and the Stedelijk Museum in Amsterdam, the (then) Gemeentemuseum in Arnhem and the Bonnefantenmuseum in Maastricht increasingly organized video presentations.
[6]
In 1980 the Jan van Eyck Academy in Maastricht set up a postgraduate course in video art, the AKI in Enschede trained its first batch of video artists, and a number of art academies had recently introduced 'audiovisual' as a graduation subject.
[7]
Perrée 1988, p. 7.

participation. On the contrary, it had alienated the viewer.[8]

The general public turned its back en masse on the real-time recordings of reality, which it did not consider worthy of the name of art. Many exhibition organizers and museum curators were by no means convinced that video was one of the arts either. Video did not play a role of any importance at major exhibitions like 'Westkunst' (Cologne, 1981), 'Zeitgeist' (Berlin, 1982), 'Von hier aus' (Düsseldorf, 1984), or the Kassel Documenta curated by Rudi Fuchs in 1982. It was the new wave of painting that was celebrated there – there was hardly any room for the medium that had traditionally rejected 'art as illusion' at the beginning of the Postmodernist 1980s.

Accessibility was the buzz word that Dutch video artists opposed to it in the 1980s. Their videos had to be made more user-friendly – less archaic, more accessible to the public. This did not mean that all the vetoes of the 1960s and 1970s were immediately thrown overboard, that there was no aftermath of performance art, or that all forms of television critique vanished. Nan Hoover, the grand old lady of video art in the Netherlands, still clung to the slow-motion, almost timeless recordings, avoiding any form of montage, that she had practised in her silent videos of the 1970s. The legendary duo Abramovič and Ulay still continued to use video as a direct medium for a long time, even when their tapes were no longer a recording of the performances in which they went to the limits of their physical and emotional endurance: they did not allow themselves any rehearsals, any retakes, or any interventions as long as the camera was shooting, nor any corrections or complicated montage afterwards.

But although those video artists of the first hour remained faithful to the principles of conceptual art, at the same time they were also looking for new forms. Take Servaas. Although his generation had grown up with television as an essential part of everyday life, and hardly felt any need to criticize it, Servaas was a violent opponent of the 'illusory medium'.[9] He also absolutely refused to use montage: his videos, he argued, must be a faithful reproduction in duration and time of the action that was filmed. That in his case this did not lead to indigestible conceptual art was thanks to a discovery that he made in the early 1980s.

[8]
Nairne 1983, p. 22; Perrée 1988, p. 7.

[9]
In the Netherlands video art as a critique of television had always played a marginal role, perhaps because Dutch television itself, especially the VPRO (in programmes by Wim T. Schippers and others) already made fun of the conventions of television. See: Perrée, 1985, p. 8.

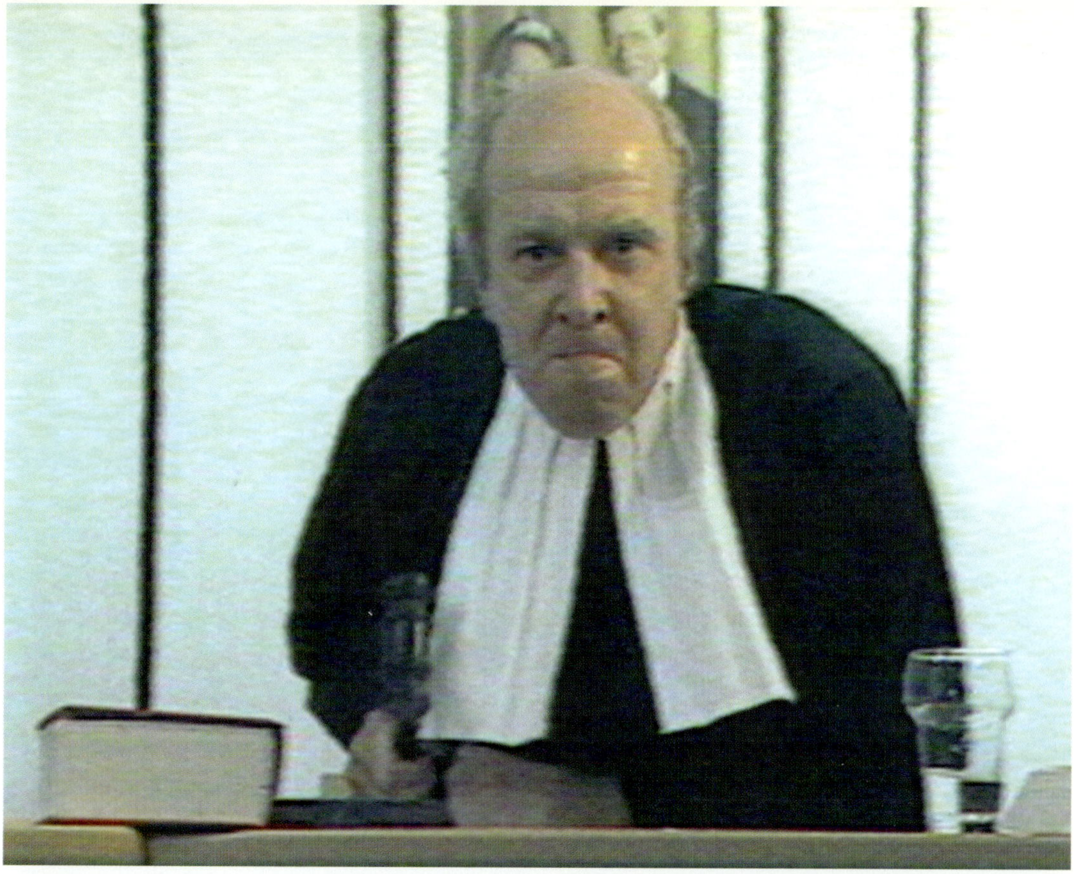

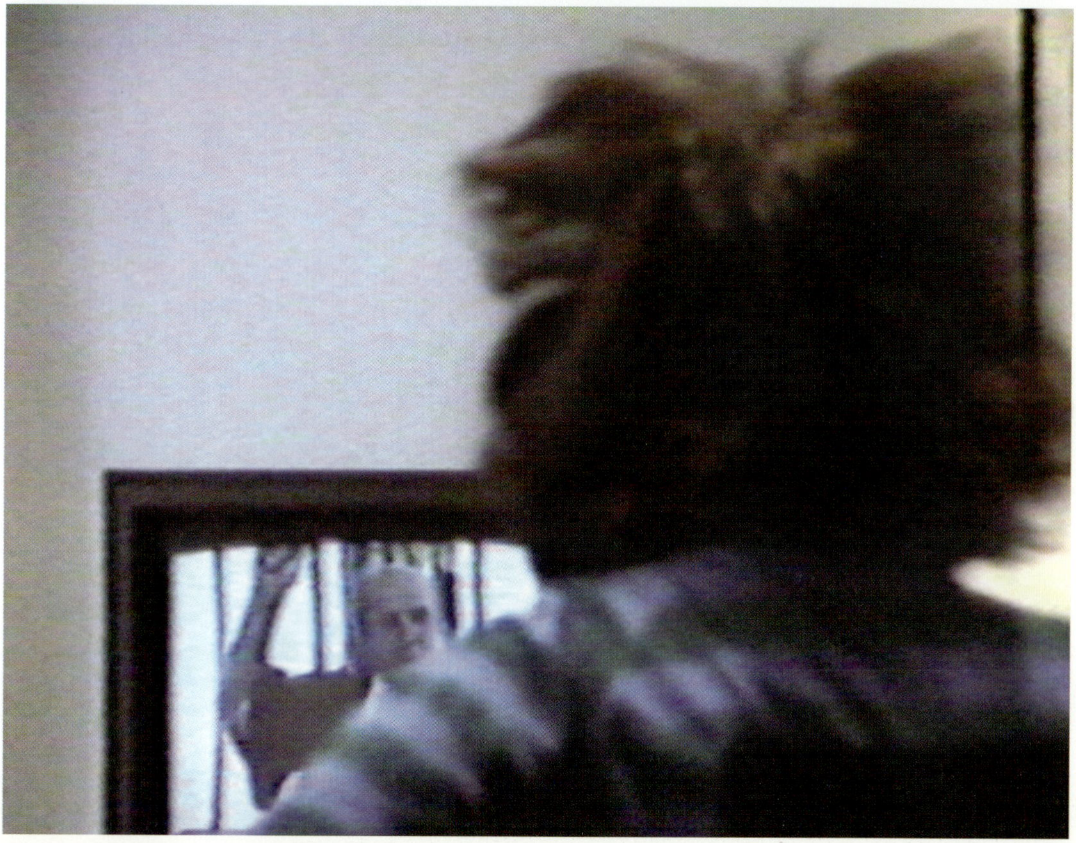

137

Servaas, *Court of Justice*, 1986, installation

Take *Pffft* (1983), an installation that made the self-taught artist Servaas (who had been a radio and television engineer) world-famous and created a classic of Dutch video art. A man on the monitor blows a feather that has been set in front of the screen, and (to the total amazement of the audience at the Holland Festival)[10] it actually vibrates. Or take *New Resonances* (1982), one of the first video tapes in which Servaas criticizes the lack of involvement of the television viewer. While a newsreader runs through the wars of the day on a sound tape, a listener on a video monitor appears literally shocked by the news. At every sound the radio makes, his image bounces at a hilarious tempo over the screen, and only calms down again when the newsreader pauses for breath.

Servaas achieved the alienating effect of both tapes by a simple application of pneumatics: sound was turned into air pressure (vibrations) that set the video images (or objects) in motion. At first it produced innocent, almost poetic works. Later Servaas resorted to more aggressive methods. In *Are you afraid of video* (1984), the viewer was pitilessly punished for his nonchalant zapping, in which fragments of reality are just as carelessly switched off as fictional images. While four monitors alternated between newsreels (of wars, Thatcher, Reagan or Gorbachov) and fragments from films (soaps and martial arts films), a long whip cracked through the space to the rising volume of the television. And in *Court of Justice* (1986) Servaas went even further with his reign of terror: whoever sat in front of a monitor on which the judge sentences the viewer for 'passive viewing behaviour' was given a vigorous shaking in his armchair in time to the beats of the gavel with which the magistrate added force to his words.

Servaas eschewed neither the spectacular nor the theatrical in his attempt to strip television and video of their illusory aspect.[11] Within a short space of time his work grew from tapes shown on small monitors to room-sized installations in which the viewer was forced to take part in a drama in which the role of the other actor was played by the video. Servaas was not the only one to do so. Other video artists went in search of space too from the first half of the 1980s on. The video tape prised itself loose from the mother screen, repeated and multiplied itself on a number of monitors. They were stacked to form a 'video sculpture', decorated with parasols (Abramovič), surrounded by a mural (Dedo), or embedded in a decadent Greek temple (Lydia Schouten). While in some cases that expansion in space was a logical extension of the work

---

10
Pffft was first shown here.

11
'At first Servaas only used video, but the *remote coolness* of the screen could not satisfy him. A screen on which fiction and reality overlap to convey the message is not suitable if the aim is to make people aware of reality.' See: Lyon 1988. Besides, both television and video were 'an illusion' in the eyes of Servaas. 'You see people lying dead in *Miami Vice* and you see the same people lying dead in Nicaragua in the news. You have no control of the image any more. What is real? TV is nothing, it is not real, it is a picture.' In order to bridge the gap between illusion and reality, Servaas wanted 'to set things outside the image in motion', to 'shake the hands of the people outside the image'. See: Servaas/St. Metropool (broadcast by the Stichting Culturele Hoofdstad Zender/Amsterdam C), 1988.

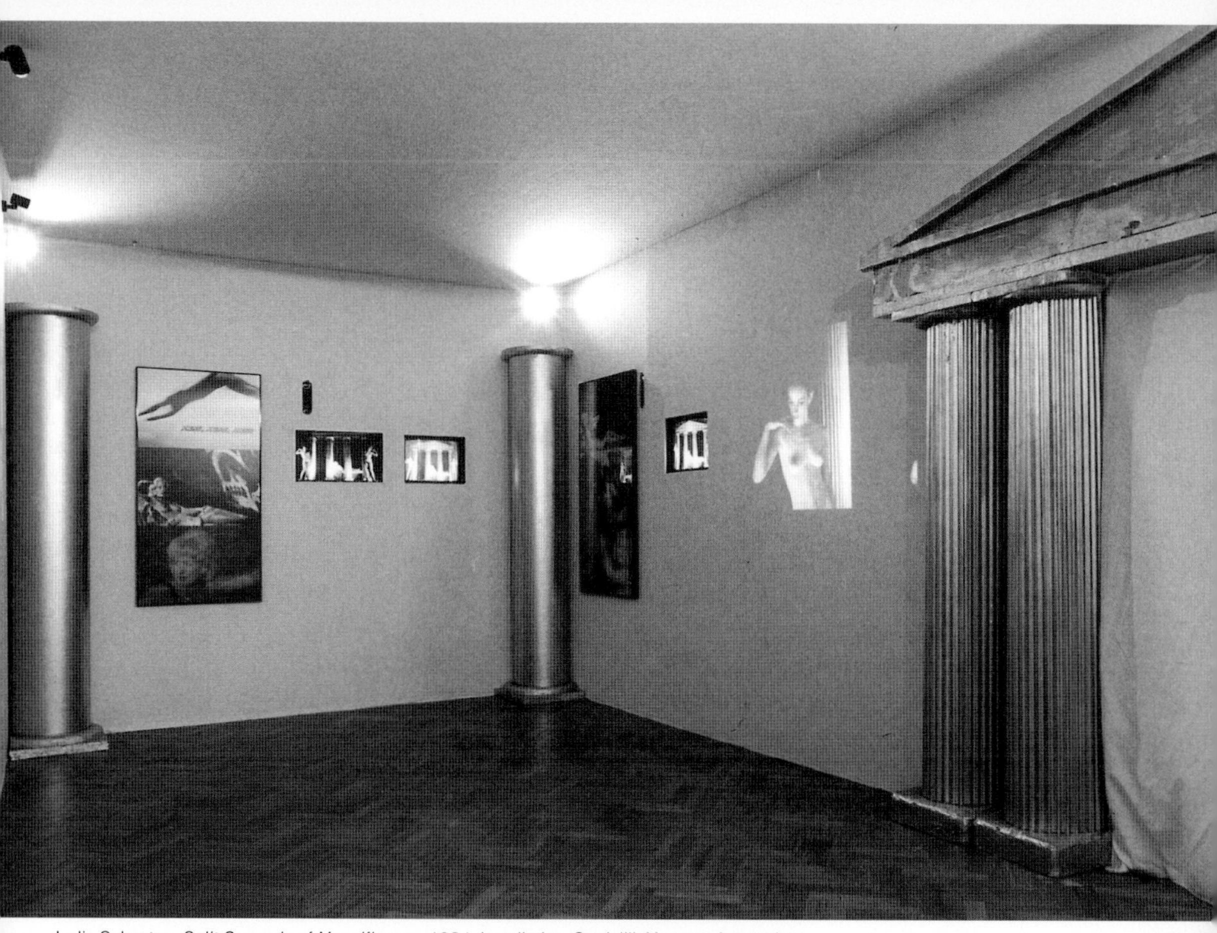

Lydia Schouten, *Split Seconds of Magnificence*, 1984, installation, Stedelijk Museum Amsterdam

(intended to involve the audience in the video, or at least to prepare them for the mood of the work), the architectural, sculptural or painterly attributes often served a sole purpose: to emphasize that video was just as much a higher art as the traditional disciplines. And it was above all intended to make it clear that video has nothing to do with 'bad television', which is what the average audience only too often took the medium to be.[12]

Video art did not just expand in space; the thematic horizon was broadened as well. Video art developed from an introspective medium that wallowed in self-investigation – aimed at the basic conditions of video, or at the limits of the body – to become a discipline that looked more and more at the world around it. Even the 'Conceptuals' followed suit. Thus while the duo Stansfield/Hooykaas targeted the formal similarities between video technology and nature in the 1970s, in their later work they exchanged the investigation of the basic conditions of video for a search for the metaphorical implications of the medium: the recycling of images on television and in video was compared with recycling in nature or with the endless return of fragments in archives and in memory.

12
L. Falke, 'The Second Link & the Habit of TV', in: Falke 1983, p. 5. ('The average public still regards video art as bad TV or, at best, as popular culture'). Art critic Beatrijs Ritsema could still write in 1987 that she could see no reason 'to go out and watch television with twenty other people'. See: *NRC Handelsblad*, 10 September 1987.

Lydia Schouten, whose first video tapes were recordings of 'old-style performances' in which her own inalienable body was deployed to explore her own female identity, abandoned that 'narcissistic' vantage point around 1982 to tackle wider social themes in her videos.[13] And from 1983 Abramovič and Ulay did not even appear physically in their own work. *City of Angels* (1983), the first work that they made specially for video, sought a higher awareness outside oneself – in oriental spirituality, particularly Buddhism. In content that work still displayed some similarities with their performance past, but formally it came close to painting. From a fixed position the camera showed static shots of a Thai garden, *tableaux vivants* of almost motionless people resting in the grass. It was hazy, like a painting, in the electronic colours of the video screen.[14]

Abramovič /Ulay, *City of Angels*, 1983, video, colour, sound, 20'00"

Narrative video

Video art came of age. After abandoning the old benchmarks, it became emancipated from a purely recording or documentary medium or a critique of television to become an autonomous medium, a medium in search of its own visual language. In conceptual video art that visual language was still dictated by reality: with an unshakeable belief in the fidelity of video, the conceptual artists adhered to a one-to-one reproduction of the events that had taken place in real life. In the Postmodernist 1980s, however, that point of view was no longer defensible. After all, any representation of reality was subjective, removed from its context, and thus inherently 'not to be trusted'. Every reality was a construct. And precisely video art was capable of generating all those models of reality, of manipulating reality.

Technology provided the tools. Using a video synthesizer, the chromakey or wipe technology, artists could accelerate and decelerate their images to their heart's content, overlap them, distort them, or change their colour. Sometimes they went so far that reality became unrecognizable, as in the videos by Roos Theuws, in which abstract forms that change colour, reminiscent of the paintings of Mondrian or Malevich, alternate in an almost musical rhythm.[15] Or they went so far that they completely negated reality: the graphic, fluid video images of Peter Struycken were all generated on the computer. There was no camera involved.

13
'A world opened up before me, because those performances had always been very much about myself, about my ego. As a performance artist you did not really have to play something, but you always had to do things very much from inside yourself. When I discovered that I could actually start involving everything in my work, it was such a relief.' Lydia Schouten cited in: Wolfs 1987, p. 37.

14
The video performances of Nan Hoover (1931) also took on more of a painterly character in the 1980s. In the recording of the performance *Walking in any direction* (1984), moreover, the play of light and shadow is not just caused by Hoover's own body intersecting the coloured bundles of light; the visitors who walk through the space are also a part of the performance, and their bodies too are a part of the work. See: Amsterdam 1984, pp. 118-121.

15
Roos Theuws (1957) started as a painter. In her early work a realistic, recognizable visual idiom surfaces among the abstract forms. In her later work, the video tapes are reduced to abstract, silent compositions in which the mutual coherence and alternation of intense colours and forms become more and more important. The video images she uses and manipulates are often derived from television.

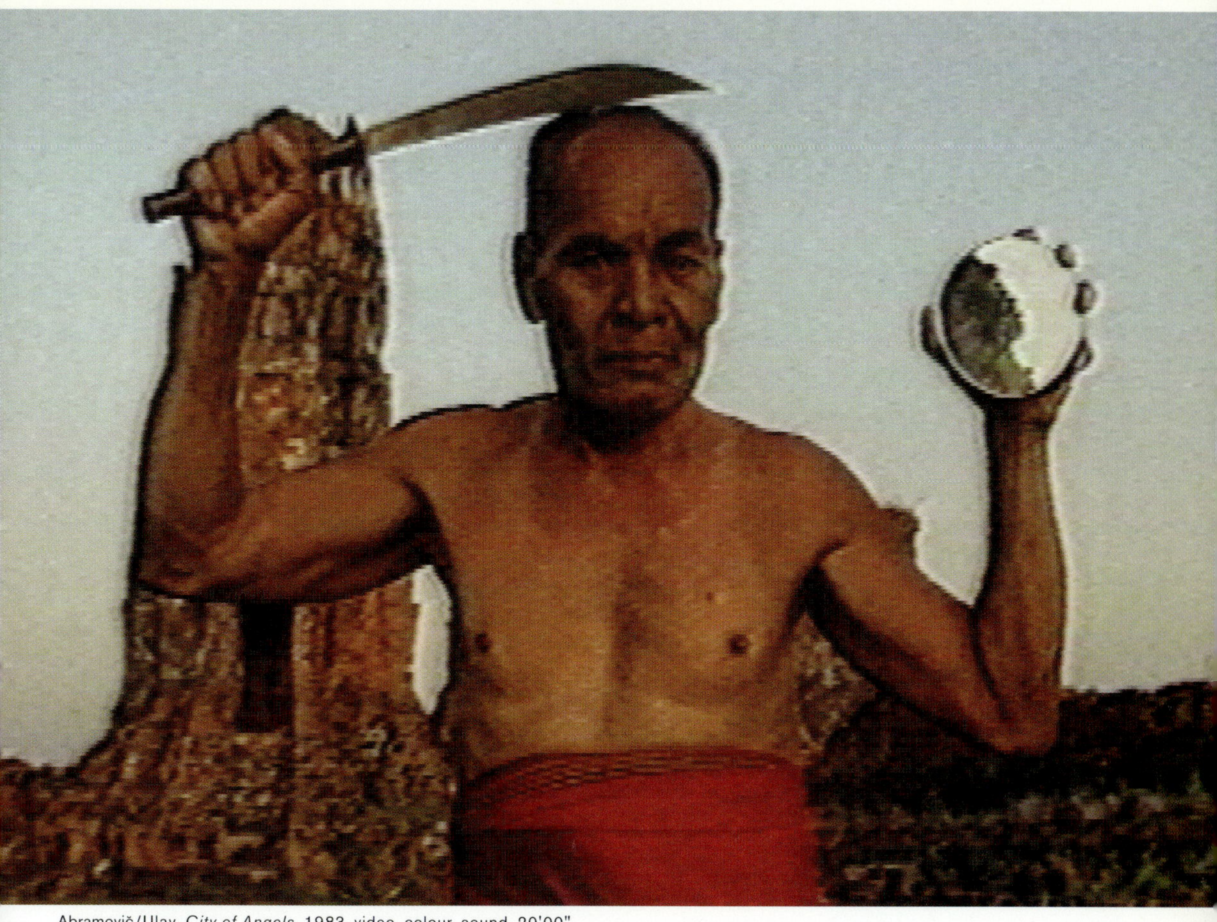

Abramovič/Ulay, *City of Angels*, 1983, video, colour, sound, 20'00"

But television and the rise of the video clip also contributed
to manipulation in video art. The third generation of Dutch video
artists in particular – the first batch to have become skilled
through training in the technological potential of the medium –
drew their inspiration for rapid alternation and controlled build-
up of tension of images from strategies used on television.
And during the wave of Neo-Expressionism that swept through
Dutch art in the 1980s, the video clip served primarily those
artists who not only engaged in video art, painting and sculpture
but also formed bands, as the ultimate model for achieving
harmony between image and sound.

It was during that Postmodernist period that the foundation
was laid for the video art of the later period, for the narrative
videos of artists like Saskia Olde Wolbers and Aernout Mik. The
1980s had no time for the taboo that had rested on everything
with a whiff of anecdote about it during the age of High
Modernism. Just as painters and sculptors were poking fun at
their conceptual predecessors by flirting with figuration,
allegory, irony and narrative elements, video art openly flirted
with narrative structure – even though it was much more
fragmentary and less linear than in the narrative video art that
was to emerge in the 1990s. Still, the rupture with the past is

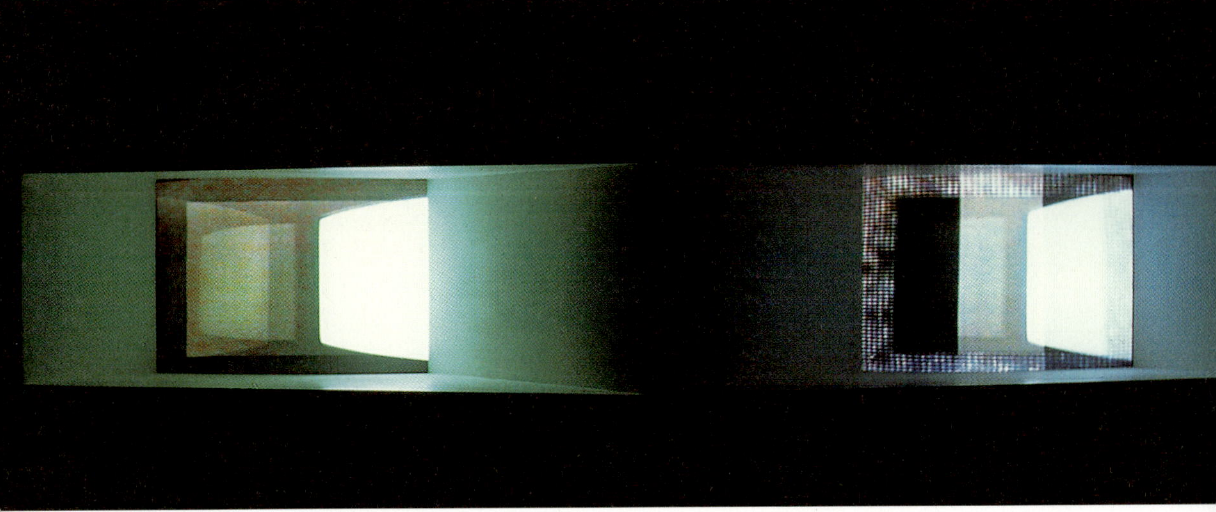

Roos Theuws, *Forma Lucis III*, 1986, installation

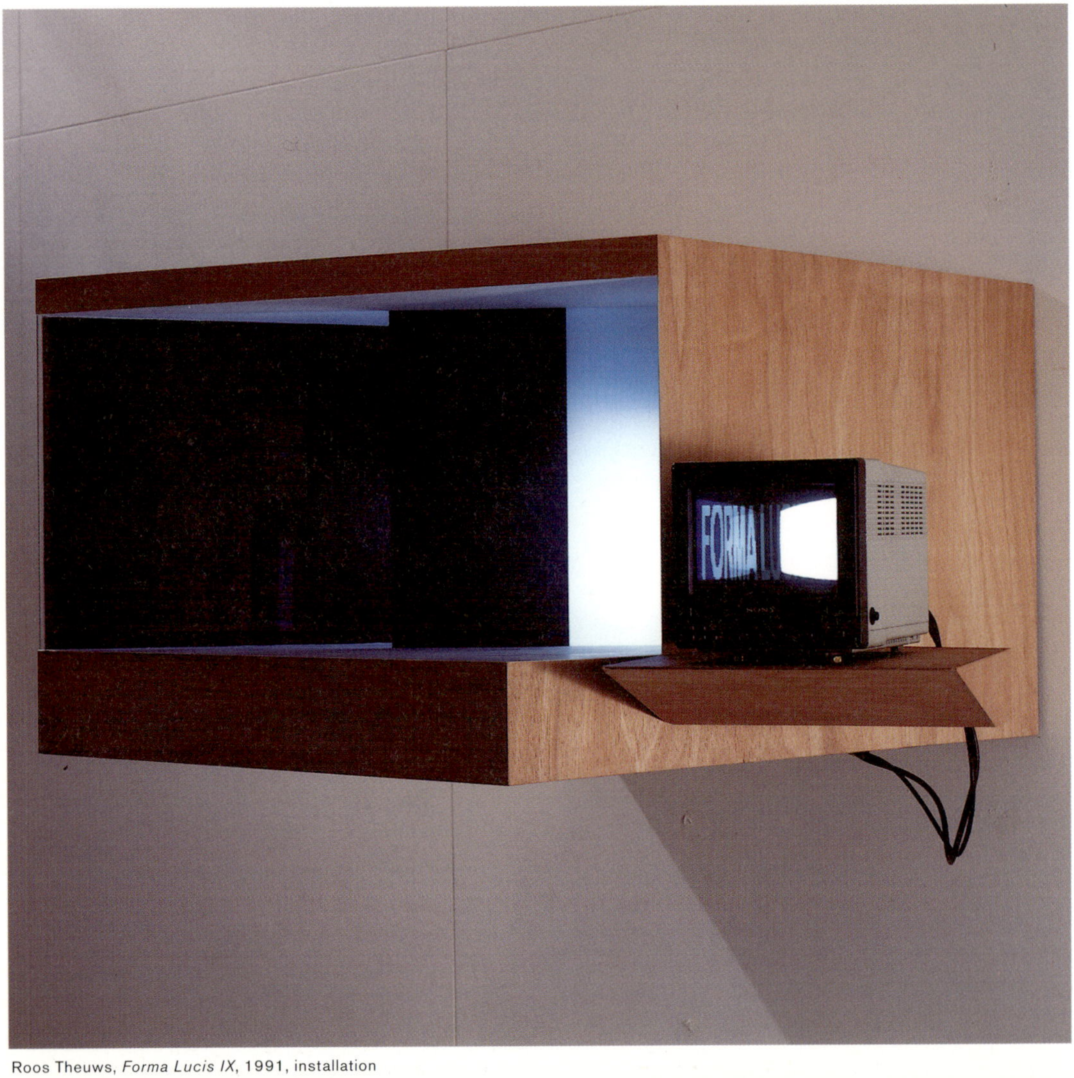

Roos Theuws, *Forma Lucis IX*, 1991, installation

evident: recording is replaced by directing. Real time is reduced to artificial time.

That tendency falls roughly into two camps in Dutch video art of the 1980s. One group of artists took as its starting point not so much reality itself as already existing images of reality, and mixed images from television or film to form a collage of second-hand and original images. The second group resorted to the resources of the theatre and imitated reality (often in décors that they made themselves), thereby trying to deconstruct or to make fun of the reality that was reflected particularly in the mass media. Both tendencies shared the Postmodernist notion that originality (the ability of the artist to create authentic images) no longer holds in a media society dominated by reproducibility.

The frst group included artists like Ron Sluik and Reinier Kurpershoek, who had been collaborating since 1982 under the name Sluik/Kurpershoek. It was no accident that they had both studied at the AKI in Enschede. The generation of video artists that this academy produced in the early 1980s stood out by not referring to theatre, television or cinema, but trying to make contact with the new painting and sculpture. They were sometimes called the Postpunk artists, the AKI generation which also included Dedo and Kees de Groot: their videos were intensely expressive – almost aggressive – when it came to the handling of both image and sound. And like their painterly counterparts, the Neue Wilden, the Neo-Expressionist video artists drew on a heavy symbolism.

In the case of Sluik/Kurpershoek, this was at first expressed in video works in which recordings of their own wild painting actions were mixed with a fairly arbitrary sequence of images with dancers, skulls and musicians drumming on oil drums, accompanied by an abstract electronic sound. The later, more structured works relegated those fragments of painting performances to the background as Sluik and Kurpershoek sought emotion more in the processing of images derived from television, in dramatic repetition and in the frenzied rhythm.[16] Typical in this respect is *The March Konkret* (1984), a 'video clip' in which, to the dramatic music of Mahler, images of the police operations during the notorious squatters' riots of the 1980s (tanks and helicopters storming the barricades) alternated and were equated with historical recordings of Hitler and marching Nazis.

In *The March Enkor* (1984), a follow-up to *The March Konkret*, the violence and show of strength is even more emphatically present, while in the background four pensioners lean over a Risk board. For twenty minutes the viewer is exposed to the carefully built-up series of explosions of violence. Literally and metaphorically, airplane raids, creaking ice and marching soldiers change places at lightning speed.

143

Sluik/Kurpershoek, *The March Enkor*, 1984, video, colour, sound, 23'00"

16
The image is adapted to the sound 'more or less as it is done in video clips'. Sluik/Kurpershoek in: Aemelia de Koningh, 'Risk en oorlog in videokunst over Nederlandse televisie', *De Waarheid*, 30 August 1985.

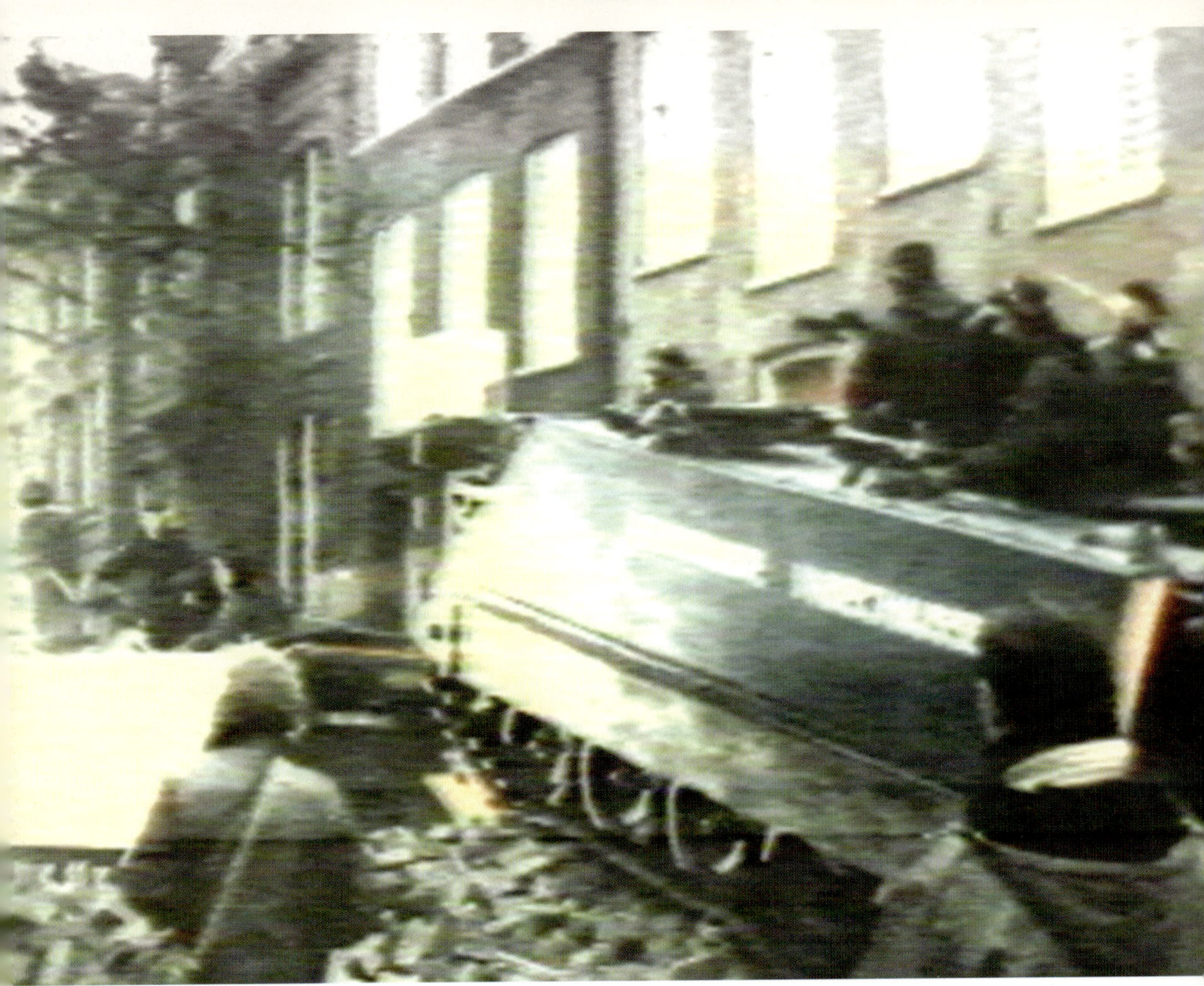

144   Sluik/Kurpershoek, *The March Konkret*, 1984, video, colour, sound, 12'24"

On two occasions that rain of fire of staccato images is
interrupted by a series of fragments of children playing and
people dancing in different times and countries – both series of
images conclude with shots of the pensioners bent over their
game of Risk. But in between and afterwards it continues: a
flood of images (a papal assembly with the sound of repeated
phrases from a speech, demon-strations against Khomeiny
accompanied by the commentary to a tennis match) that
reaches its climax in an inferno of exploding nuclear bombs and
collapsing buildings. *The March Konkret* ends in a vision of the
world as a roundabout, once again literally in a cacophony of
sound and a whirling big wheel.

    The lesson that Sluik/Kurpershoek want to drive home in *The
March Konkret* is that history has no logical, linear course – that
is a Modernist falsification. 'Historical reality' can only be known
in fragments, in arbitrary shards that, glued together, display at
most affinities or parallels.[17] If history has a pattern at all, it is
one of repetition without progress, of endless recycling, in
which permanent values shift, become ambiguous, and can turn

17
Sluik/Kurpershoek 1984.

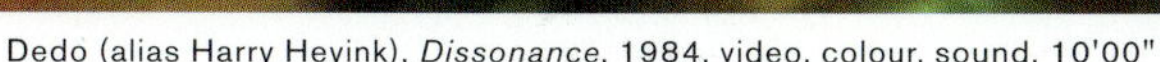

Dedo (alias Harry Heyink), *Dissonance*, 1984, video, colour, sound, 10'00"

into their opposite.[18] Guilt can turn into innocence, repugnance into fascination.[19]

Dedo too based his videos on the idea of history as a series of repeated moves, but he reacted to events of his time more than Sluik/Kurpershoek did. In *Dissonance* (1984) a flood of archive images from the period 1940-1945 pass in review, some of them distorted by the video synthesizer. They are part of a newsreel-style item entitled *The colour of 1983*, accompanied by the dry comments of a newsreader written by Dedo. The situation of 1983 is literally 'coloured' by television and other mass media – the images are intensified with bright television screen colours. A succession of electrical devices seems to propagate (technological) progress, but 'the situation is still

[18] In *The March Enkor* history as 'repetition without progress' is given shape not just by the recycling of existing TV footage (including documentaries over the Second World War and the Vietnam War), by the repetition of 'interchangeable' images, and the symbolism of the big wheel, for instance. That repetition is also embodied in the detailed processing and composition by Sluik/Kurpershoek of sounds that are not related to one another: the succession of fragments of radio transmitters and interference (like what you hear when you search the different frequencies on a transistor radio), the 'sticking' of a sound fragment (like a needle sticking in the groove of a record), and the endless repetition of phrases from a speech.

[19] The accumulation of violence in *The March Enkor* is deployed ambiguously by Sluik/Kurpershoek: on the one hand, the irreversible spiral of violence is intended to evoke a feeling of oppression and shock, while on the other hand it is also clearly utilized for the aestheticism of the repeated explosions of violence.

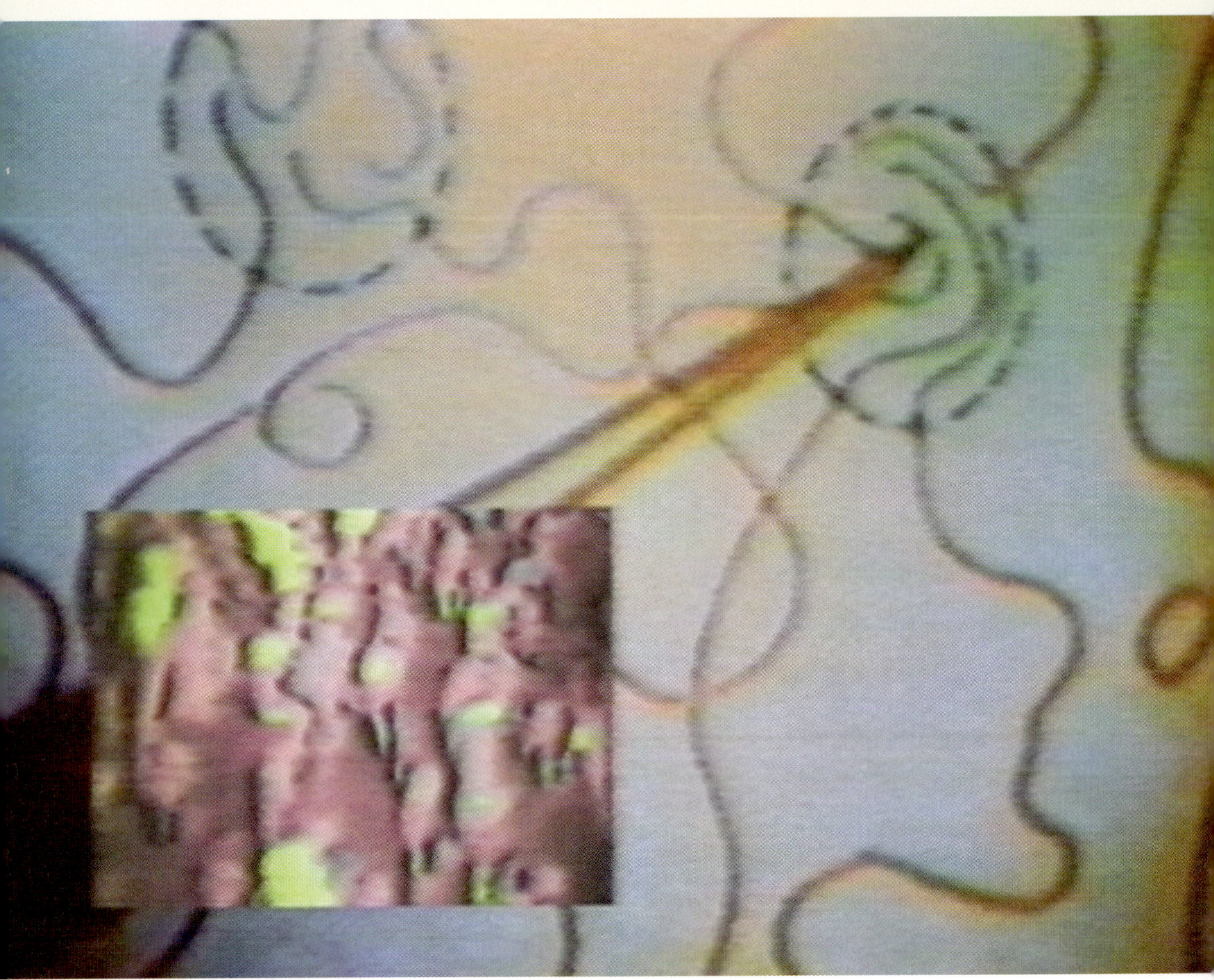

146 Dedo (alias Harry Heyink), *Dissonance*, 1983, video, colour, sound, 10'00"

troubled' is Dedo's comment on the 'newsreel' from the Second
World War. The past is still topical, it is repeated in the present,
in the Cold War.[20]

Postmodernist images

Although the Postmodernist view of history could lead to works
of social criticism, it resulted just as often in an 'anything goes'
mentality. Kees de Groot, who started making videos in 1981
under the name Auto Awac (a 'post-punk collective' to which
Ron Sluik, Emile Toorop and Frank Morssinkhof also belonged
in shifting constellations, and that consisted of De Groot alone
from 1983 on) seemed to accept the standpoint that was in
vogue at the time that (art) history is a jumble of fragments that
are meaningless in themselves and only gain significance from
the context in which they are placed. In his video installations

[20]
In *Our Flag is Going Forward Too* (1983) Dedo's criticism of the notion of progress in history is even
stronger. In an intensely blue, formless space a procession appears which seems to be being led by
a flag-bearer towards the end of the world. The procession is watched by silhouettes wearing
pointed hats like those of the Ku Klux Klan and by people in leather uniforms, who determine the
direction of the route. The figures are in sharp contrast to the bright colours of their surroundings.
These shots are occasionally interrupted by fragments in which we see the boots of marching
soldiers. The procession suddenly turns right at the end of the video, where the text 'some things
just happen' appears on screen. This turn seems to refer to the general right-wing shift of society in
the 1980s and a far-reaching form of patriotism in the form of right-wing extremism in particular.

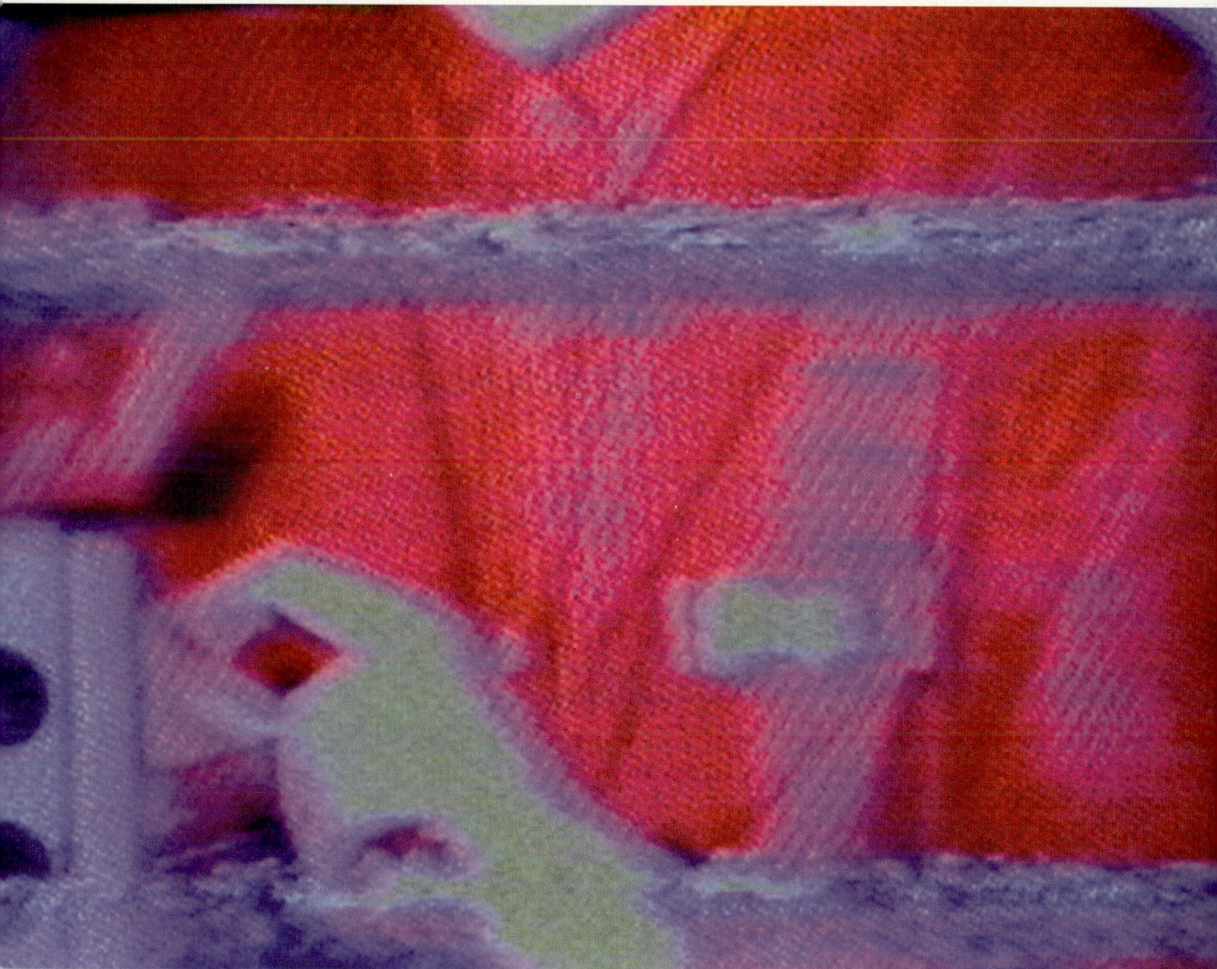

Kees de Groot/Auto Awac, *Audio Mutant*, 1983, 18'00"

Kees de Groot/Auto Awac, *Audio*
Mutant, 1983, 18'00"

consisting of a number of monitors that formed mini-theatres,
De Groot wove symbols from antiquity, the classics, the bible
and the Middle Ages to form associative visual stories that
loosely referred to rituals of death and birth, violence and sex.
A video work like *Audio Mutant* (1983) consists of a collage of
images of calculators, digital watches and multinationals like
Shell and Esso – but De Groot was ambiguous on whether this
sequence of images was intended as an ode to the benefits of
the welfare state or as a rejection of them.

Theatrical video art also moved in a diffuse area between
celebration and irony, although it tended towards the latter.
Instead of using existing television material, these videos
applied different television formats, often making use of
deliberately naive décors in line with the comic strip tradition
and the new painting. For instance, Michiel Vijselaar and Tjarda
Sixma took the cloying romanticism of *Heimat* films like *Sissi* to
extremes in their very short video tapes. Using artificial décors,
made of polystyrene and decorated with kitsch attributes, they
presented fairy-tales about pining girls in the Alps (*Gretel*,
1984) or a wedding that almost goes wrong (*Hochzeit im*
Schnee, 1986). Their acting was always laid on thick, and the

Vijselaar/Sixma, *Hochzeit im*
Schnee, 1986, video, colour,
sound, 4'40"

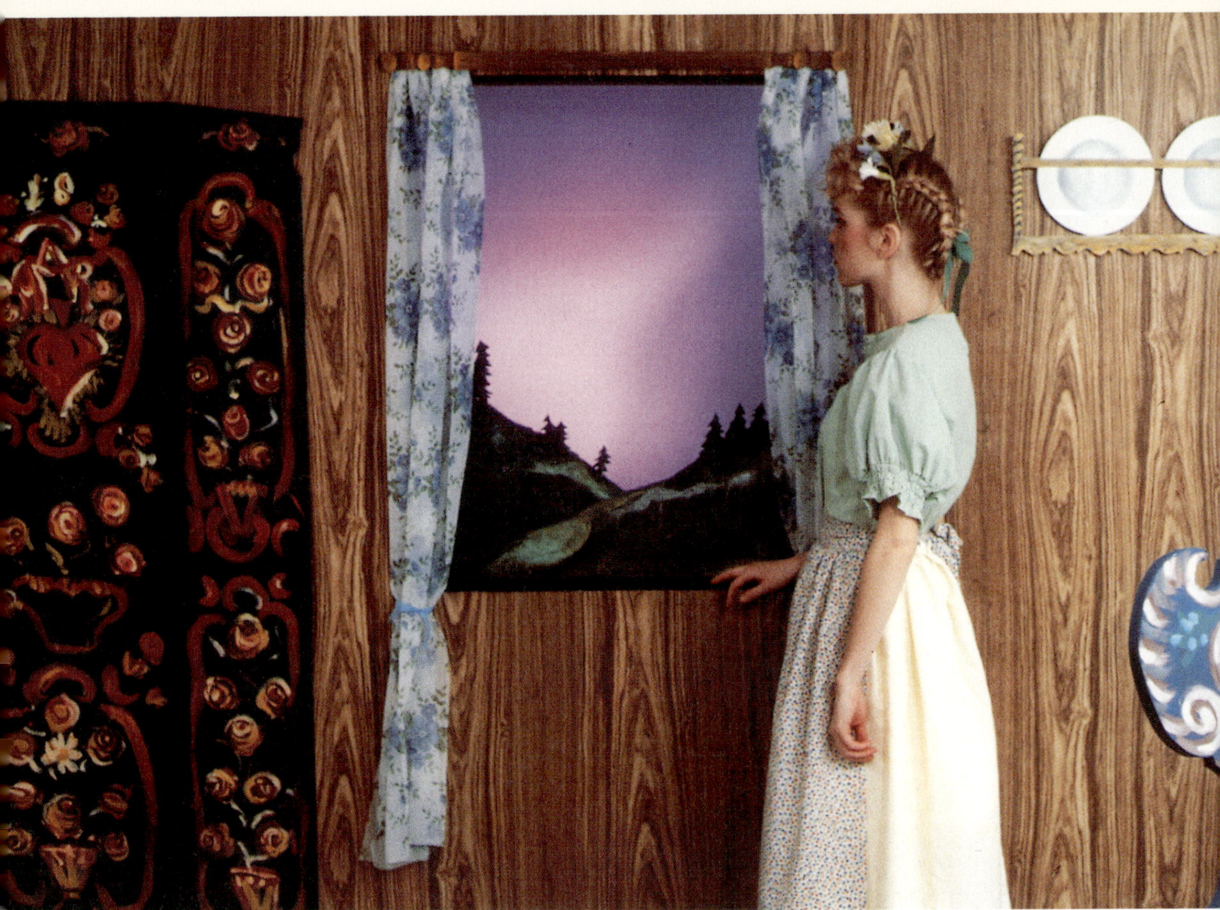

Vijselaar/Sixma, *Gretel*, 1985, video, colour, sound, 3'84"

148

moral was always derived from dime novels and calendar
proverbs. For instance, SKET (Stichting Kunst en Tijdwinst:
Foundation for Art and Gaining Time), in which Rob Dieleman,
Wim Liebrand and René Reitzema collaborated, made fun of
former porno broadcasts by TV pirates in *Edelweiss* (1984):
after an amateurish announcement – complete with interference
and shaky images – the camera zooms in on the throbbing flesh
of two copulating deep-freeze chickens. And while David Garcia
and Annie Wright parodied news programmes and TV quizzes in
their videos, Moniek Toebosch tackled the 'in-depth interview'.
In *Verzamelde beelden en Toevallen* [Collected images and
coincidences], made for VPRO television, she plays a woman
who is in a state of total uncertainty, who makes a hilarious
confession on TV about how she discovered 'it' – without ever
making it clear to the viewer exactly what 'it' was.

Humour – sometimes corny, sometimes razor-sharp – and
above all exaggeration. The strategy of theatrical video art was
that of the hyperbole. It was exactly for that reason that Lydia
Schouten stopped doing deadly serious performances to
concentrate entirely on video from the start of the 1980s.[21]

SKET, *Edelweiss*, 1984, video,
colour, sound, 4'00"

21
See: Paul Depondt, 'Het onechte is echter dan het echte', *de Volkskrant,* 15 January 1988.
And: Wolfs 1987, p. 37.

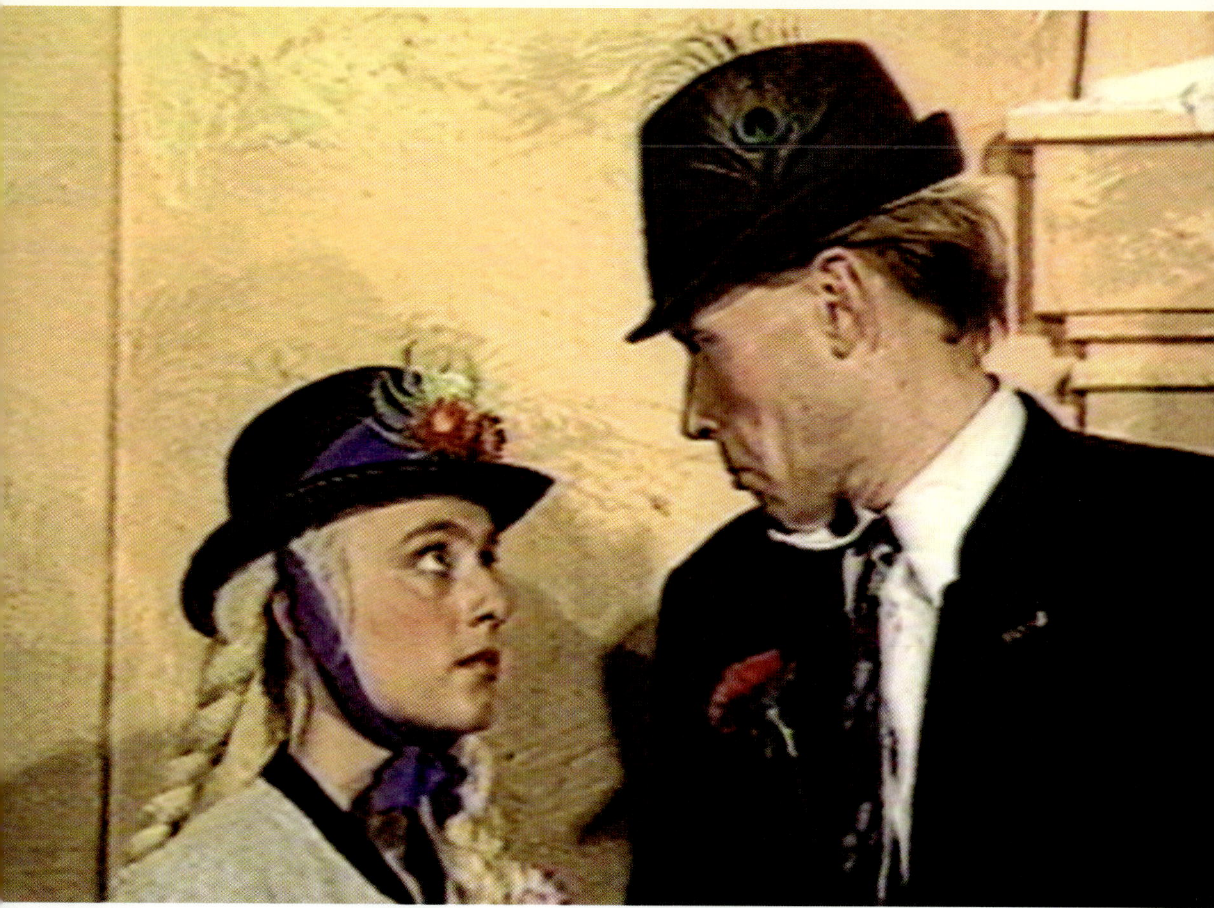

Vijselaar/Sixma, *Hochzeit im Schnee*, 1986, video, colour, sound, 4'40"

Lydia Schouten, *Romeo is Bleeding*, 1982, video, colour, sound, 11'26"

Her earliest works are peopled primarily by cartoon figures and actors from B-films in a cardboard fantasy world. Within that world, sustained as it is by the mass media, Schouten herself plays the role of femme fatale, and models her behaviour (like Cindy Sherman in her early photographic works) in different guises on the characters offered by film and television. An example is *Romeo is Bleeding* (1982), a journey through different continents, in which the Western cliché images of those worlds are exaggerated (the savage Black, the warm-blooded Latino, the American gangster) and Schouten makes love to a polystyrene Tarzan.

At first Schouten appropriated the archetypes from the media to unmask them in her dream world as unambiguous fictions, but in later videos she toys with the theory that the artificial, postmodern world and the constructed codes from which advertising and the mass media are constructed are 'more real than reality' (Jean Baudrillard).[22] *Split Seconds of Magnificence* (1984) is in this respect a turning-point in Schouten's oeuvre. From now on, she derives her material not just from cartoons and films, but above all from adverts in glossy magazines. Some

22
Paul Depondt, 'Het onechte is echter dan het echte', *de Volkskrant*, 15 January 1988.

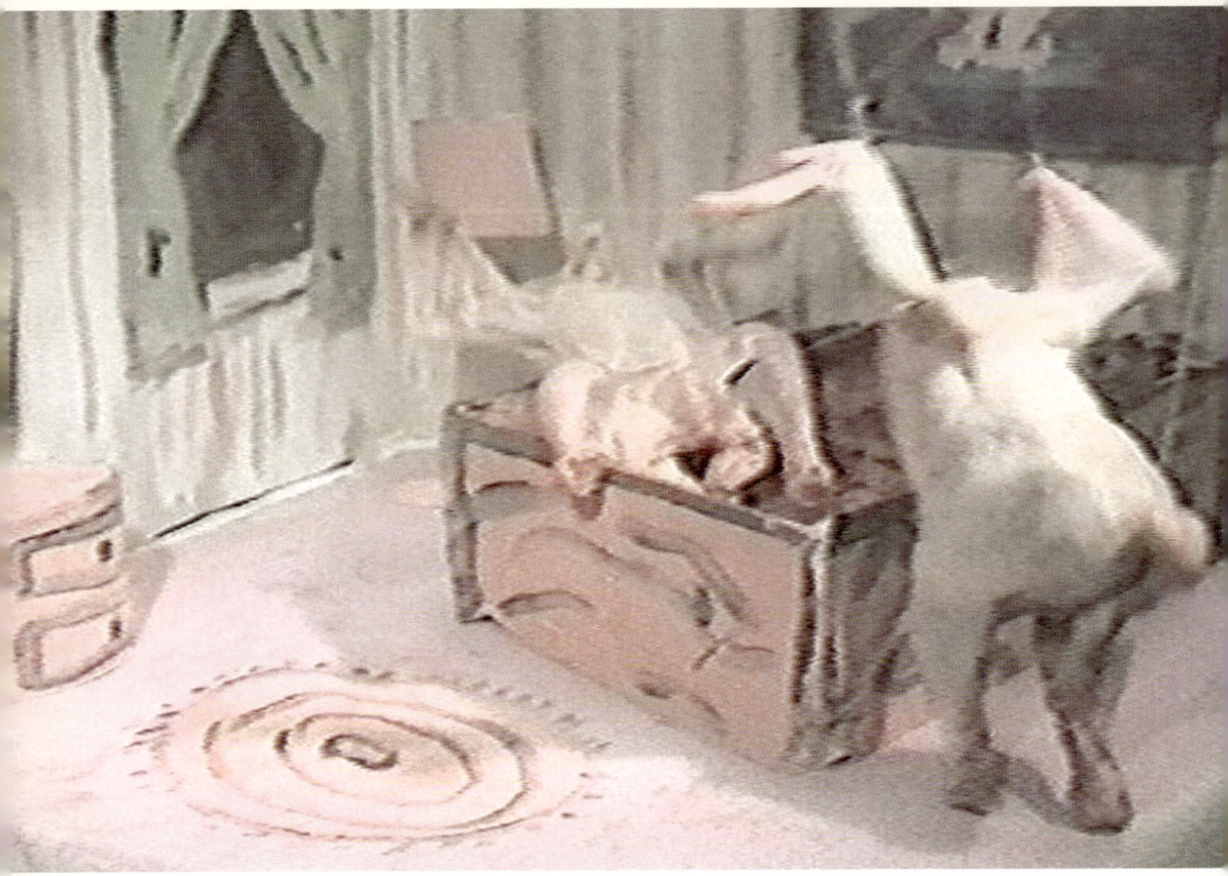

SKET, *Edelweiss*, 1984, video, colour, sound, 4'00"

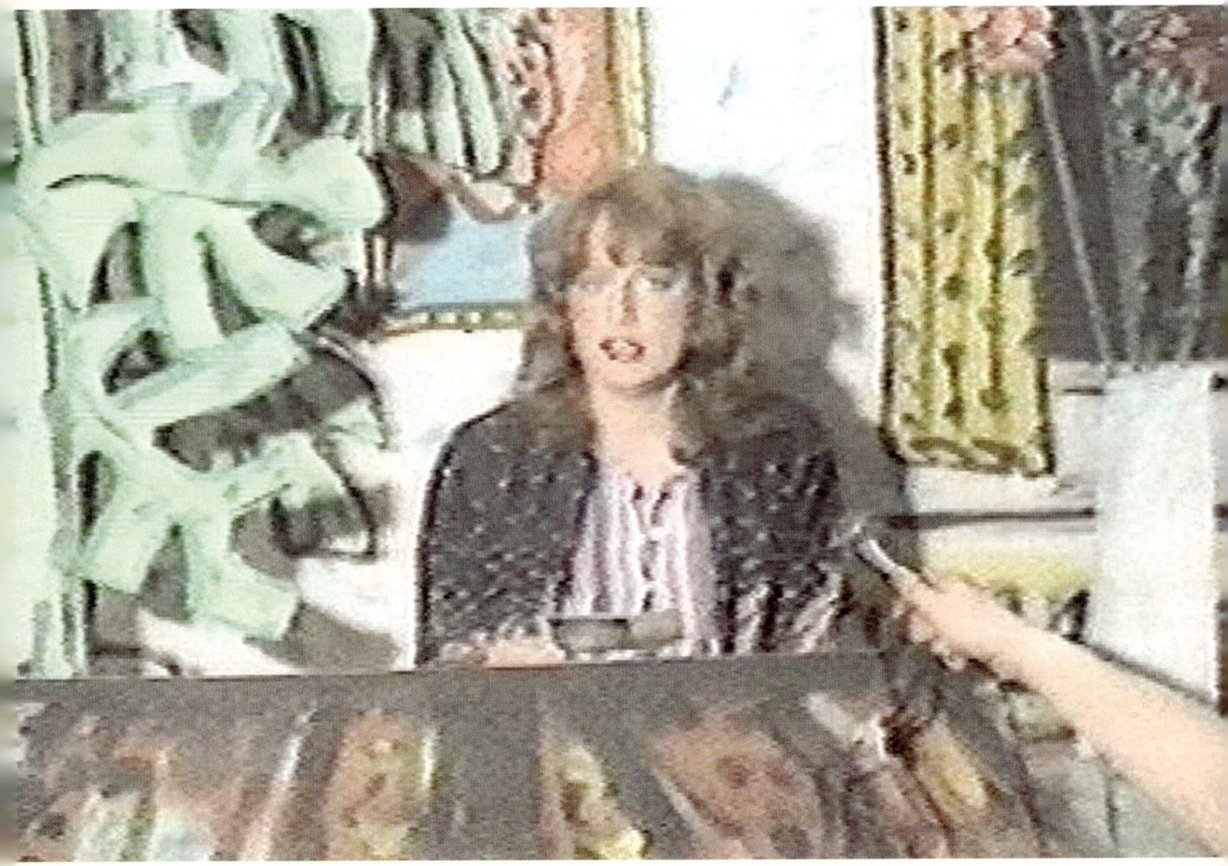

SKET, *Edelweiss*, 1984, video, colour, sound, 4'00"

video images are exact copies of adverts (a stiletto heel pierces
the ground precisely between the fingers of a man's hand;
a woman wriggles around the muscular naked back of a male
torso), and the one-liners recorded between the images are also
taken directly from advertising slogans. Together they form a
video that unfolds as a fragmentary photographic novel – each
aspect is shown with a brief shot, with the perfect styling of the
commercial photograph.

The imaginary world served up to us by the media, Schouten
claims, has gained increasing control over the world that we
take to be reality. The world of semblances is so seductive and
the emotions reflected in it are so refined that our world is in
stark contrast to it. So we long to exchange reality for the world
of illusion, we strive and live for the codes and norms that are
presented in the mass media. What is unreal looks more real
than reality to us, the distinction between reality and the illusion
of reality has disappeared. The subject has no active role in it at
all: it is temptation, not desire, that governs us.

In *Split Seconds* Schouten subtly allows the ups and downs
of that situation to trade places. In the love story she imperson-
ates various characters and displays an unstable identity:
femme fatale in one fragment, victim in another. The freedom of
the individual to assume any conceivable identity seems to be
presented as a gain, but at the same time Schouten also points
out how it can lead to an extreme state of alienation from
oneself.[23] Some appreciated that ambiguity, while others
accused her of an uncritical attitude and cold-blooded
nihilism.[24] If we view her early videos as attempts to deconstruct
the codes of the mass media, then her later work seems
increasingly to confirm those codes. They are fairy-tales, played
by someone who surrenders to 'romantic escapism', who
'institutionalizes uncertainty and relativism', and is prepared 'to
switch to a different world tomorrow and to exchange the order
of the day for a new one'.[25]

Lydia Schouten, *Split Seconds of Magnificence*, 1984, installatie, Stedelijk Museum Amsterdam

151

[23]
Jorinde Seijdel, 'Nieuwe uitdagingen voor Montevideo/TBA', *Het Financieele Dagblad*, 12/14 July
1997.
[24]
Velthoven 1987, p. 4.
[25]
Wolfs 1987, p. 39; Velthoven 1987, p. 180.

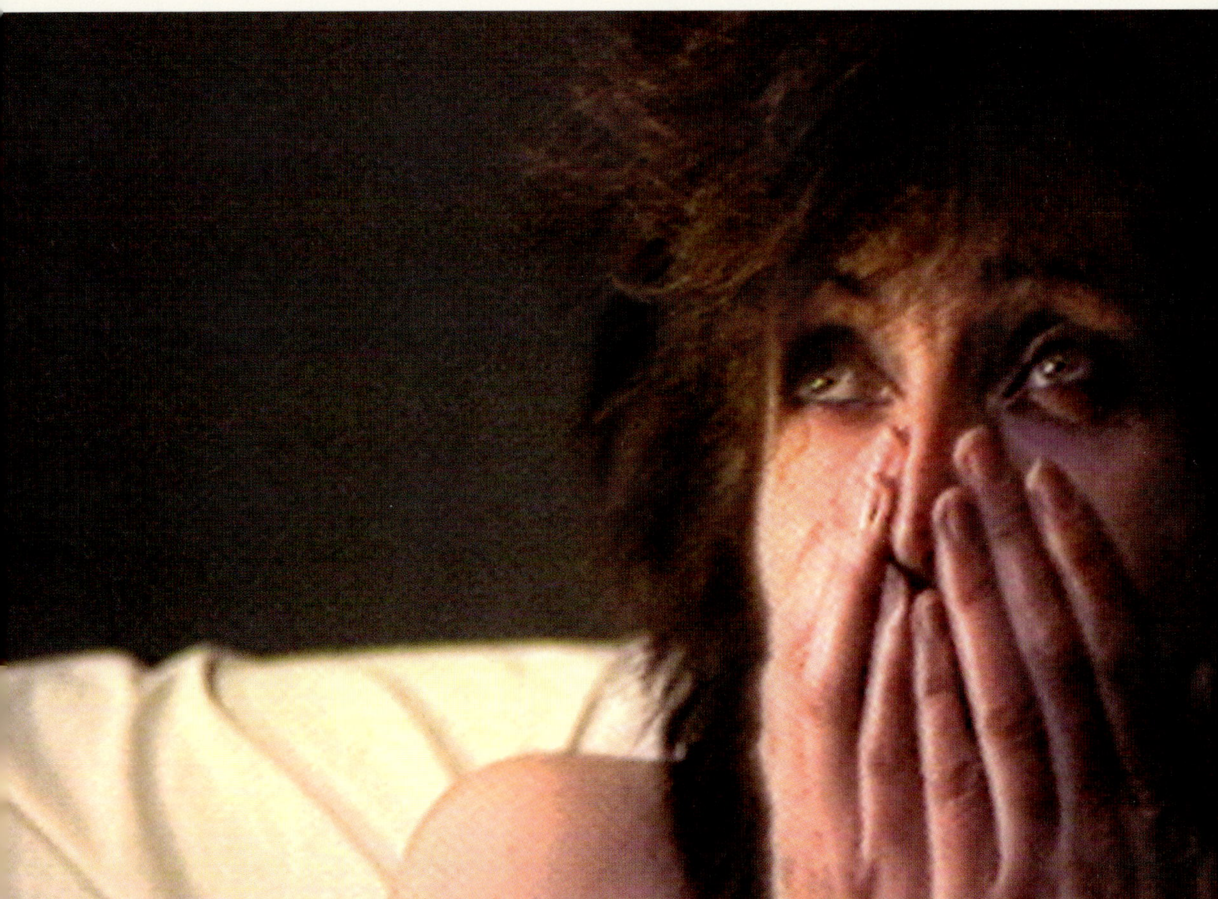

Moniek Toebosch, *Collected images and coincidences*, 1983, video, colour, 33'25"

Lack of attention

Although Schouten regularly showed abroad (including the United States, where appropriation artists like Jenny Holzer were also trying to deconstruct the codes of the media and Dara Birnbaum – the artist who inspired Schouten – was also making videos in which the image of women presented by the media was criticized), she had more difficulty in establishing a place for herself in Dutch museums. For many curators, exhibition organizers and funding bodies, the discussion about the position that video art ought to assume – was it art, was it film, or did it belong to a popular medium like television? – had still not died out in the late 1980s.[26]

The exhibition 'The Luminous Image', that the Stedelijk Museum in Amsterdam devoted entirely to video installations in 1984, brought about a change in thinking about video art, but although afterwards other museums, like the Gemeentemuseum in Arnhem, did allow a trickle of videos inside, video artists remained largely dependent for the showing of their work on video institutes and festivals. However, that video circuit began

26
On the unpredictable policy of the then Ministry of Welfare, Health and Cultural Affairs see: Terreehorst 1985, pp. 15-65. For the discussion of Dutch museums see: Perrée 1988, p. 7.

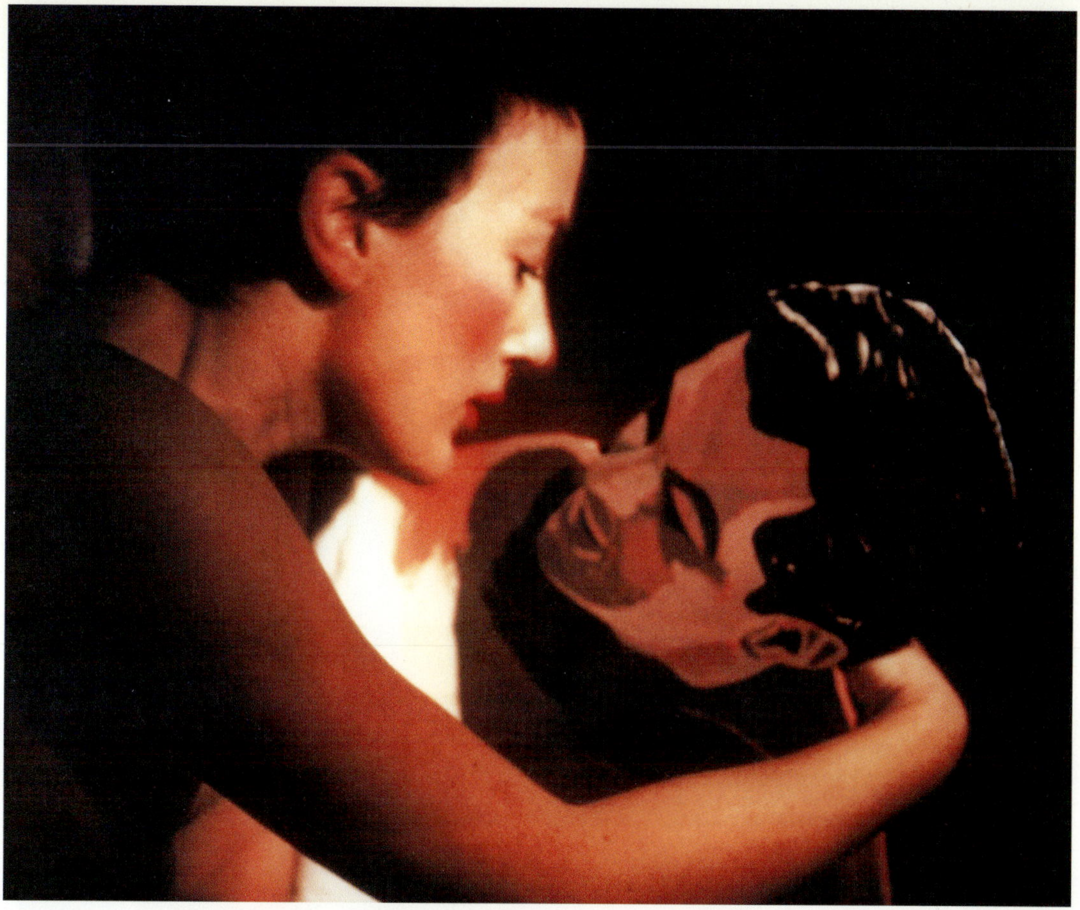

Lydia Schouten, *Romeo is Bleeding*, 1982, video, colour, sound, 11'26"

'more and more to resemble an inaccessible sect with an incestuous character': too much was shown (in dark, small rooms); there was not enough attention paid to the diversity of video (the emphasis was on video tapes, not on installations); and the selection was not critical enough. The result was that the broader public avoided the institutes and festivals, and the video circuit became nothing but an in-crowd.[27] That lack of public and artistic interest (followed in 1986 by the cessation of subsidies to Montevideo and Het Kijkhuis) meant the end for many video artists.[28] Lydia Schouten – disappointed by her isolation in the video circuit – stopped abruptly, and was hardly prepared to do anything with video for ten years. René Reitzema from SKET also pulled out. And Gerald van der Kaap, who mixed diverse images together in his video tapes, switched to working as a VJ in the Amsterdam disco RoXY. Ironically enough, it was precisely that genre of video – the music video – that was to be the subject of a successful museum presentation. But by then the 1980s were over. Frans Haks' 'What a wonderful world' (1990) in the Groninger Museum, a massive

[27] **Perrée 1988, p. 66.**
[28] **Terreehorst 1991, pp. 36-37.**

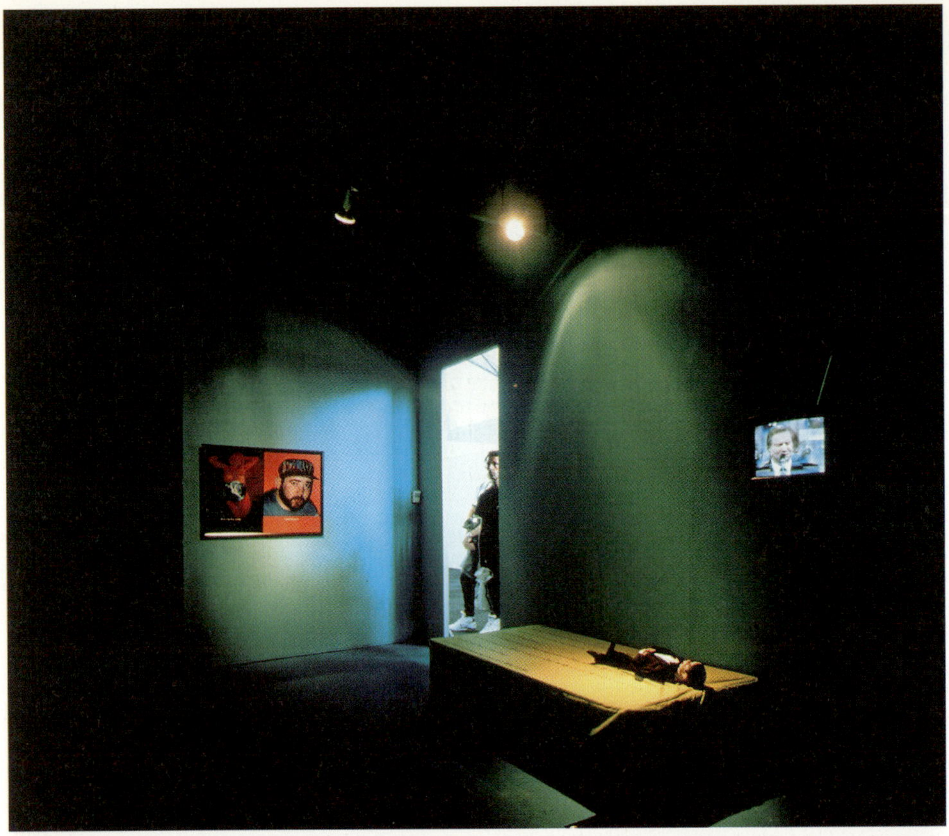

Lydia Schouten, *A Virus of Sadness*, 1990, installation

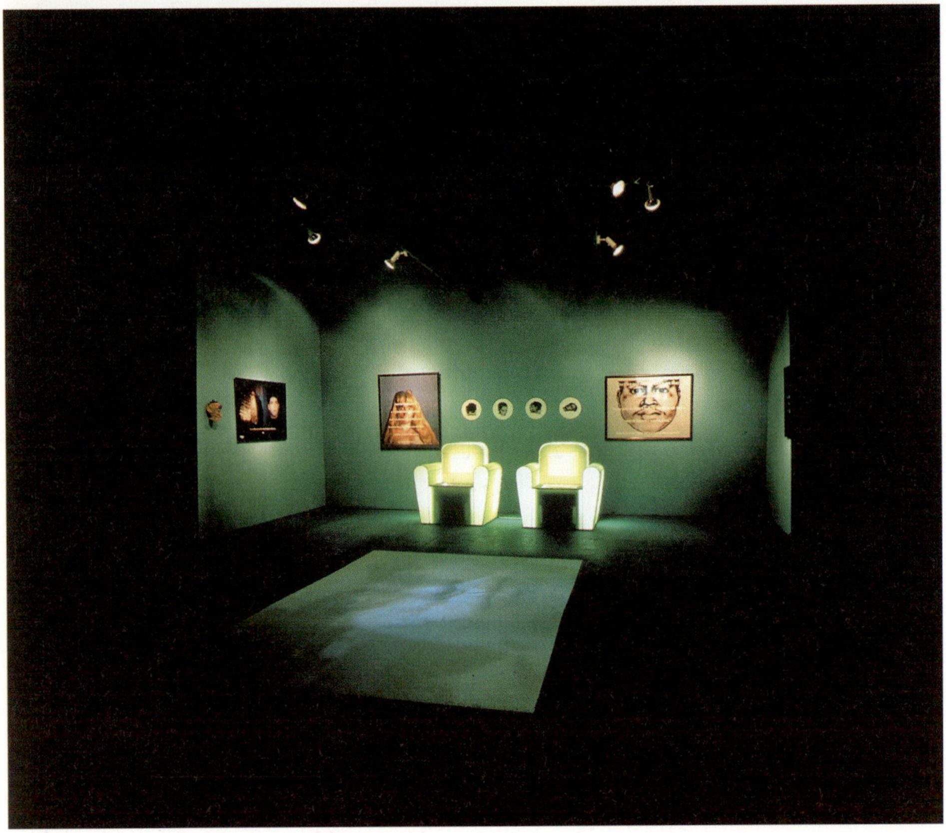

154

Lydia Schouten, *A Virus of Sadness*, 1990, installation

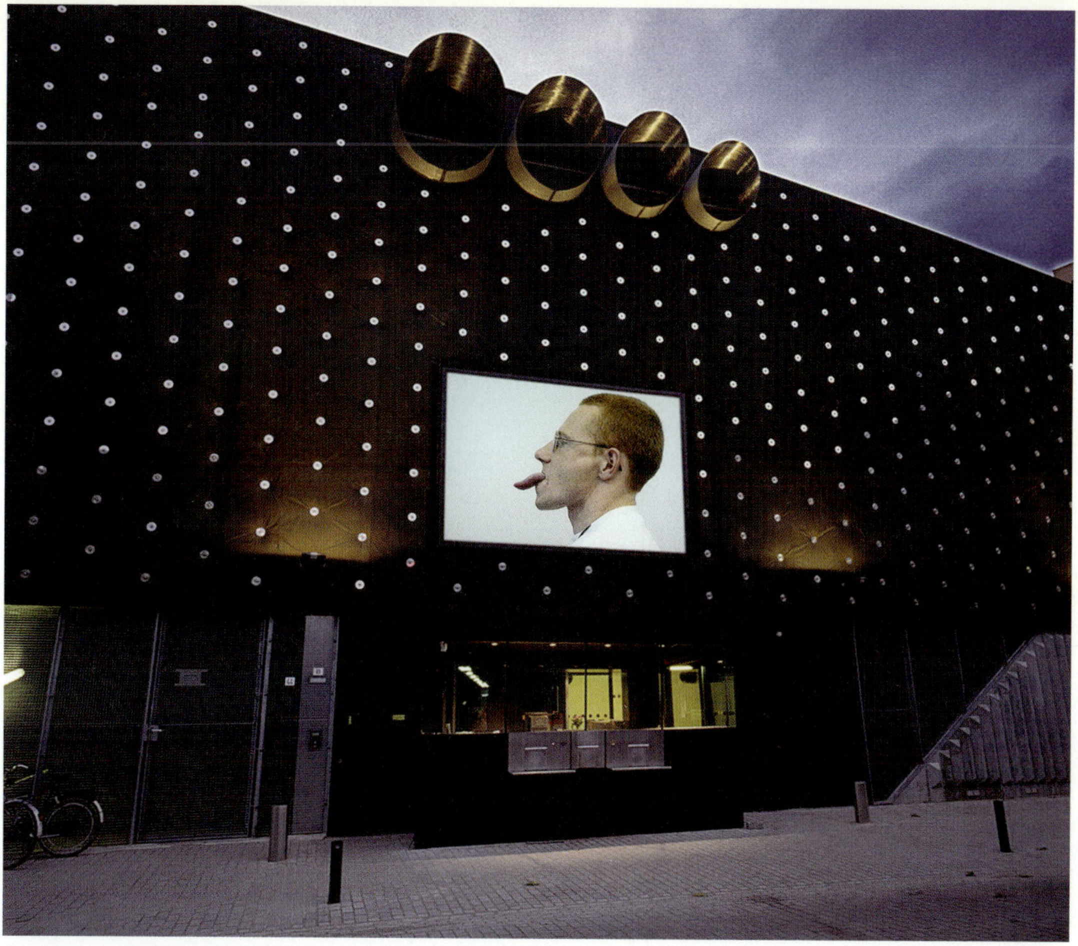

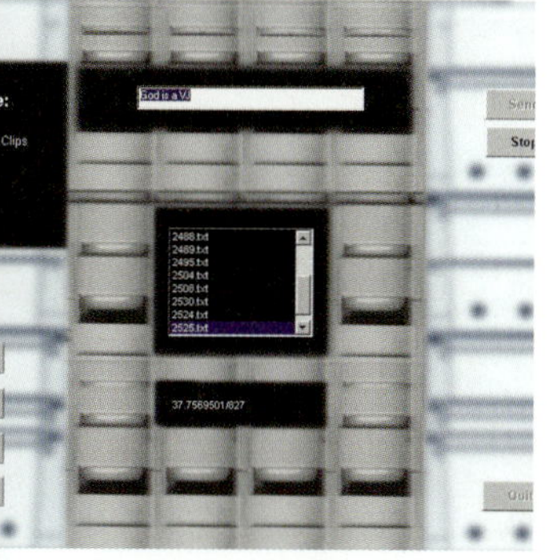

Gerald van der Kaap, Automatic VJ Machine, Pop Centre 013, Tilburg

Gerald van der Kaap,
Automatic VJ Machine

video clip exhibition, heralded the dawn of a new era in Dutch video art.

In the 1990s video artists began to realize that they were no match for the explosively growing and increasingly commercial music industry, which had masses of money and resources to produce the most advanced, streamlined and slick video clips. They turned to the other extreme: the simplicity of rough, coarse-grained home video art. The artists of the 1990s had little time for the video art of the previous decade either, which had maintained an ambivalent attitude towards the constantly increasing flood of images that bombarded people on a daily basis. The theories of the 1980s (everything is illusion, everything is a construct) had in their view only led to fragmentation, superficiality and a non-committal nihilism. In reaction to that, many of them tried to find the last trace of inalienable authenticity, the last fragment of intact reality, in themselves and their own surroundings. Their emphasis on reality, their narcissistic self-preoccupation, their preference for low-key technology rang a bell with many video artists of the 1960s and 1970s, the pioneers who had started it all. Video was no longer 'cutting and pasting' in the filmed material. Video was no longer, as Livinus van de Bundt had ecstatically exclaimed, 'painting with light'.

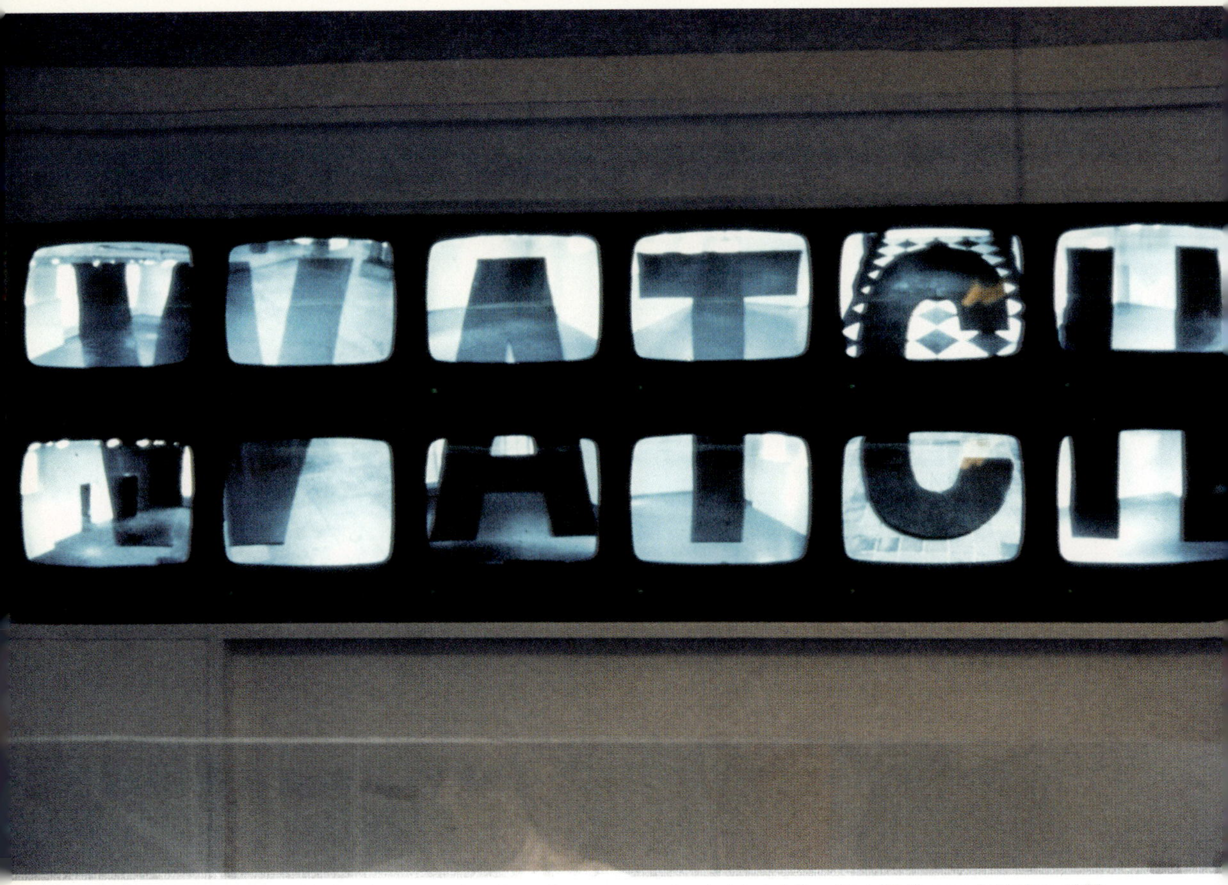

Giny Vos, *12 sculptures with security personnel, an image for a museum attendant*, installation, Stedelijk Museum Schiedam, 1988

156   Video was no brush, but a never-blinking eye. The 1980s could be forgotten, the video synthesizer could be dumped in the attic. And the box of tricks that the digitization of video had introduced was banged shut with a resounding crash.

Anne van Driel studied the history of art at the University of Amsterdam. She works as an editor on the arts desk of the Dutch national daily *de Volkskrant*.

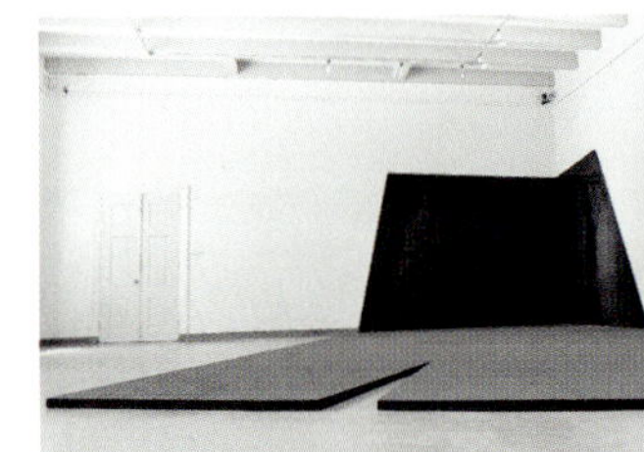

Giny Vos, *12 sculptures with security personnel, an image for a museum attendant*, installation, Stedelijk Museum Schiedam, 1988

Jorinde Seijdel

The digital vanishing point

From 'I see' to 'do I see?'

Every art has a physical component that can no longer be regarded and treated as until recently, and can no longer be safeguarded from the intrusions of modern science and modern technical advances. Neither material nor space nor time, in the last twenty years, have remained what they were since time immemorial. It can be predicted that such great innovations will change the whole technique of the arts, thereby influencing artistic creation itself and perhaps even changing the concept of art in an astonishing way. (**Paul Valéry**)

Just what is 'medium'? I would suggest that the only plausible answer to this question would be: language. Behind the media image lies concealed nothing other than language, and this in two respects. First, it is the language of the technical instructions according to which the technical devices that produce media images are constructed. Second, it is the discourses on the media that focuses on the non-evidence of medium in the image – a radical absence of the medium, a radical impossibility to represent the medium of the image in this image itself. (**Boris Groys**)

0.

The literal (Latin) meaning of *video* is 'I see'; regarding the implications of the digitalization of culture for video, we cannot avoid wondering what the 'I see' means now. What is it that I 'see'? Who is the 'I' who sees? Aren't the autonomy, authenticity and individualism expressed by the phrase 'I see' diminished in today's digital culture? The media, which used to be individually associated with specific forms of perception and representation, may well lose their separateness in the digital realm. The digital coding of binary numbers, the reduction and translation of image, sound and text into bits, to ones and zeroes, converts the formerly distinct media into standardized formats which can be seamlessly mixed. 'Numbers make anything possible. Modulation, transformation, synchronization; delay, storage, displacement, distortion, scanning, design – total media compatibility on a digital basis will eliminate the very concept of "medium"', wrote the German media archaeologist Friedrich Kittler.[1] The question is thus what remains of *video*, of 'I see', in a culture where reality can be translated into mutually mergeable arrays of numbers. Some people believe that the digitalization of culture will lead to a fundamental transformation of our world view, to a new constitution of our experience of the world. What is certain is that something substantive is changing: technical images, photographs and videos, are no longer valid as evidence of social and political realities. They have indeed become co-producers of those realities, but at the same time they are immediately open to doubt because of their inherent manipulability – because it is now possible to create such images without needing to record some external reality.

In art, the possible disappearance of the concept of medium and the questionable validity of 'I see' both carry specific implications. This is not only because a media-based typology long vouched for order and clarity in art, but also because of the modernist preoccupation with issues of representation, authenticity and individuality. The authentic, which in the canon of modern art is representative and productive, both in material and symbolic senses, must be redefined in the digital visual culture. The subjective viewing instrument of the video camera, treated by artists until well into the 1980s as a counterweight to the deemed obscenity of the mass media, or as an artistic technique to replace the paintbrush, must be reconsidered in the light of a universally digital society. The media no longer make up a separate culture from which art can afford to keep its distance. Perception of the world, which first took place through the eye and then through the lens, now happens through the screen in every cultural domain.[2] If nothing else, this makes reflection on the digital dimension, on what is going on behind today's computer and TV screens, imperative.

---

[1]
Kittler 1999, p. 2.

[2]
In the case of video, if only because a typical video filmmaker today no longer views reality through the lens but through the LCD viewfinder of a digital camera.

```c
void	VWB_DrawTile8	(int x, int y, int tile);
void	VWB_DrawTile8M	(int x, int y, int tile);
void	VWB_DrawTile16	(int x, int y, int tile);
void	VWB_DrawTile16M	(int x, int y, int tile);
void	VWB_DrawPic	(int x, int y, int chunknum);
void	VWB_DrawMPic(int x, int y, int chunknum);
void	VWB_Bar	(int x, int y, int width, int height, int color);

void	VH_SetDefaultColors	(void);

#define	VW_Startup		VL_Startup
#define	VW_Shutdown		VL_Shutdown
#define	VW_SetCRTC		VL_SetCRTC
#define	VW_Setscreen		VL_Setscreen
#define	VW_Bar		VL_Bar
#define	VW_Plot		VL_Plot
#define	VW_Hlin(x,z,y,c)	VL_Hlin(x,y,(z)-(x)+1,c)
#define	VW_Vlin(y,z,x,c)	VL_Vlin(x,y,(z)-(y)+1,c)
#define	VW_DrawPic		VH_DrawPic
#define	VW_SetSplitscreen	VL_SetSplitscreen
#define	VW_SetLineWidth	VL_SetLineWidth
#define	VW_ColorBorder	VL_ColorBorder
#define	VW_WaitVBL		VL_WaitVBL
#define	VW_FadeIn()		VL_FadeIn(0,255,&gamepal,30);
#define	VW_FadeOut()	VL_FadeOut(0,255,0,0,0,30);
#define	VW_screenToscreen	VL_screenToscreen
#define	VW_SetDefaultColors	VH_SetDefaultColors
void		VW_MeasurePropString (char far *string, word *width, word
#define	EGAMAPMASK(x)	VGAMAPMASK(x)
#define	EGAWRITEMode(x)	VGAWRITEMode(x)

//#define	VW_MemToscreen		VL_MemToLatch

#define	MS_Quit		Quit
#define	LatchDrawChar(x,y,p)	VL_LatchToscreen(latchpics[0]+(p)*16,
#define	LatchDrawTile(x,y,p)	VL_LatchToscreen(latchpics[1]+(p)*64,

void	LatchDrawPic (unsigned x, unsigned y, unsigned picnum);
void		LoadLatchMem (void);
boolean		FizzleFade (unsigned source, unsigned dest,
	unsigned width,unsigned height, unsigned frames,boolean ab

#define	NUMLATCHPICS	100
extern	unsigned		latchpics[NUMLATCHPICS];
extern	unsigned	freelatch;
```

JODI, *SOD.C CO.ASM – start Up Code Turbo C++ Run Time Library*, website

1.

Media art, multimedia art, techno art, installation art, interactive art, Net art, cyber art, e-art... It has become increasingly problematic to adhere to a media-based typology for art in recent decades, a fundamental typology such as that adopted by modernist theory and practice to structure and legitimize cultural arguments and institutions. The emergence of ill-defined new generic terms such as 'media art' and 'installation art' is in itself enough to demonstrate this. These terms are equivocal about the actual medium, and indeed are almost tautological. All art forms – video art, photography, painting, sculpture, graphic art etc. – use media and are thus 'media art', just as all visual art forms have to be installed somewhere to be exhibited.

Of course it is widely accepted that 'media art' refers to art made with technological media, and that 'installation art' refers to spatial combinations of differing media or materials, but this does nothing to dispel the terminological vagueness. The medium in its role of a determinative and analogue concept seems, in modern art, to have evaporated into the hazy mixture of the 're-medial', multimedial or intermedial, into the instability

and non-physicality of the techno-digital. American critic
Clement Greenberg, the ultimate modernist, could still claim the
mutual autonomy of media and could accord every medium its
own aesthetics and visual idiom, but in the digital, pure-
autonomous-medium-absorbing culture, this looks hard to
maintain. Greenberg's insistence that art should conduct
research into the inherent reality of the medium it uses becomes
similarly untenable, or at least complicated, once the medium
has become indistinct and can no longer be reduced to a
transparent, fundamental identity.

The constitution of the artistic medium has been undermined
at other levels too. For example, contemporary art can not only
utilize countless ready-made objects and images of everyday
life, but the technical media it uses are not peculiar to the
artistic domain: computers, cameras and TV screens are
present in abundance in practically every Western household.
Traditional media like painting and sculpture still possessed a
certain exclusiveness and cachet, but the so-called new media
are used and experienced by everybody. The new social
economy of the medium is one reason that art is becoming less
and less a separate, easily recognizable ideological, material or
visual category which is detached from the mass media and
from commercial or popular culture. This greater indefiniteness
of art is matched by the progressive haziness of its media.

0.

The time when video enjoyed a special status as part of art,
reflected in special video art festivals, exhibitions and theorists,
seems finally to have ended in the digital, media-saturated
culture. The established general art circuit has long been
permeated by the medium of video, which now no longer needs
to prove itself as to content and form compared to the traditional media of art. The digital video camera and the computer
increasingly form part of the artist's standard equipment, as
once did pencil and paper, or canvas and paintbrush. Art made
using video no longer appears only on monitors or projection
screens in physical exhibitions, but is also disseminated through
the Internet, on CD-ROMS, in art cinemas and by VJs at parties
and in clubs. The increased options for showing and distribution
have been made possible, not in the last instance, by digital
technologies. In a digital form, image, text and sound are not
only mutually convertible, but can also be presented and
preserved independently of their original storage and/or transmission medium.

Ironically, digitalization thus not only contributes to the
acculturation of video art, but also to its disappearance as a
specific manifestation: the integration of video art into the
digital also implies its standardization and growing uniformity,
the loss of its primary characteristics. If photography, film, video
and television can henceforth all be recorded with the same
apparatus and on the same physical recording medium, this not

only results in compatible images and sounds, and not only puts the uniqueness of the image at stake, but also undermines the uniqueness of the media.

The 'monomedia' of the past either merge into the digital multimedium or are consigned to the museum – a place, according to the German theorist Boris Groys, where it becomes singularly obvious that the technical medium is no longer legible in the actual image, but is evident solely through the institutional discourse. As Groys puts it, 'The medium is nothing else than the language. One can only speak about the medium, one cannot show it.'[3] Groys notes that the digital media, like a perfect crime, leave no trace of themselves in the images they form – as opposed to a painting, for example, in which the physical gestures of the artist are often visible.

If the medium is no longer perceptible in the digital image, what does that image show? Reality? Media essayist Arjen Mulder holds that video represents reality at a 'medial' level; i.e. the video image is not a representation of a real world, but of other visual media. 'If video does have an archetype, then that is the media, all old media, including itself and whatever new medium may appear after the camcorder.'[4] Video represents how other media represent reality. This makes the video image as such irreducible, uninterpretable, meaningless and incapable of representing anything.

This is only true, however, when we try to interpret digital video in the same terms as the traditional art canons, brimful as they are of meaning. These canons admittedly won't work for the digital image, but they still serve widely as standards of comparison. One might as easily argue that the digital image represents a reality or meaning which people do not recognize yet, for it is a hitherto unconscious or invisible reality that earlier media were incapable of representing. In other words, it is a reality or meaning which did not exist before, and is generated by the digital domain itself. Be that as it may, the fact that we relate digital images to reality despite their 'unreality' is partly due to the extent to which older media still set their seal on them. We seem to be able to relate to those images only by largely ignoring the essential newness of their medium and concentrating on the features they bear of the older media.

161

3
Groys s.a.
4
Mulder 2000, p. 100.

1.

Digital images are in fact binary-based simulations: the ones and zeroes are completely neutral and, in themselves, do not refer to any extramedial reality. It is not reality but the digital dimension that generates the images – and the digital is beyond reality. But a question that crops up time and again in the assessment of the media is their degree of veracity. Both life and reality have actually become illusory effects of the media, yet it is authenticity, of all things, that seems to have become an obsession of the digital culture. New media claim to be ever more direct, real, realistic or communicative than their predecessors.

Are these claims defensible? Marshall McLuhan noted that older media ultimately become the content of new ones. McLuhan, writing in the 1950s and 60s when television ownership was becoming almost universal, stated for example that '... the new TV environment is an electronic circuit whose content is a former environment, notably photography and film'.[5] In other words, older media dominate functioning of the new for a considerable period. Jay David Bolter and Richard Grusin launched the term 'remediation' to refer to this process in a contemporary context.[6] The 'dual logic of remediation' instigates a two-way process of influence between the old and new media. The World Wide Web, for instance, is influenced in its content and form by radio, film and television; but its specific characteristics and aesthetics are conversely visible in the contemporary formal and social structures of these older media. The process of remediation makes new media manageable and comprehensible for the user/spectator/consumer, while the older media, updated by inspirations from the new, gain an extended lease of life.

Remediation thus presupposes an interdependence of representational forms, so breaking with the modernist myth of the new which all too often still prevails both in technology and art. All media form part of a network of technological, social and economic contexts and distinguish themselves through specific combinations of those contexts, instead of through exclusive, essentialistic properties. The reality experience of a medium is thus partly determined by other, older media – just as images originally produced in analogue media are now viewed digitally.

Yet every new medium aims to be experienced as unique and real. This is true for 'hypermedia', which stress their own mediating function and which are 'full' of themselves, in the way that web pages are full of buttons and links. It is equally true for 'transparent media', such as virtual reality and webcams, which instead try to be invisible as media and minimize the presence of interfaces.[7] Both hypermedia and transparent media strive to go

162

---

[5]
McLuhan 1964, p. 63.

[6]
Bolter/Grusin 1999.

[7]
Terms from Bolter/Grusin 1999.

beyond the frontiers of representation and be as realistic as possible in the experience of the viewer: to become transparent as media by denying the fact of mediation, and hypermedia by creating a sense of fullness, an oversaturation of experience which can be taken for reality. In either case, the experience of reality is engendered by an interplay of old and new media.

The representational interdependence involved here takes place at first sight primarily within the digital realm, in which media engage in a constant dialectic with one another. At the same time, however, this is the location of the vanishing point of representation and media: that is to say, the point of uniform digital code. Every image in a digitized form can undergo unlimited algorithmic transformations; the uniformity of the digital code can hence enable a mutual communication of characteristics between images of different origins. Within the digital domain, thus, there occurs both a hybridization or remediation, which discloses itself at the surface, and a levelling out, which takes place at an internal level.

McLuhan believed that the hybridization of media would open up new formal possibilities: 'The hybrid or the meeting of two media is a moment of truth and revelation from which new form is born. (...) The moment of the meeting of media is a moment of freedom and release from the ordinary trance and numbness imposed by them on our senses.'[8] The newness he thought would result from the cross-fertilization of media is less evident within the digital culture (whose development McLuhan could hardly have foreseen in his time), for the digital realm has the capacity to erase visible traces of media. It is virtually imposs-ible to establish the prime origin of an image in digital form; sometimes no such origin even exists outside the digital domain despite the traditional 'media format' (photo, film), a traditional style (e.g. realistic, cinematographic, photographic, painterly, cartoon-like) and a correspondence in representational respects with an extra-medial reality. The image originated from within the digital domain and is in fact a media surface-effect.

Within the digital domain, however, media images go beyond simulation, or the *simulacrum* à la Jean Baudrillard. Baudrillard considered images as simulacra because they no longer bear any relation to some underlying reality. If, however, that underlying reality has now been absorbed by the prevailing digital culture, and has thus become reality '*in optima forma*', the simulacrum concept becomes redundant. A term which perhaps conveys more about the status of the image in the digital culture is 'emulation'. In the context of art history, this term formed part of the Renaissance doctrine of 'translatio-imitatio-aemulatio' (i.e. translation-imitation-rivalling/emulation). To become a 'creator', an artist had to proceed through these stages one by one with regard to the great Classical models. In computer terms, an emulator is software you can run on one

163

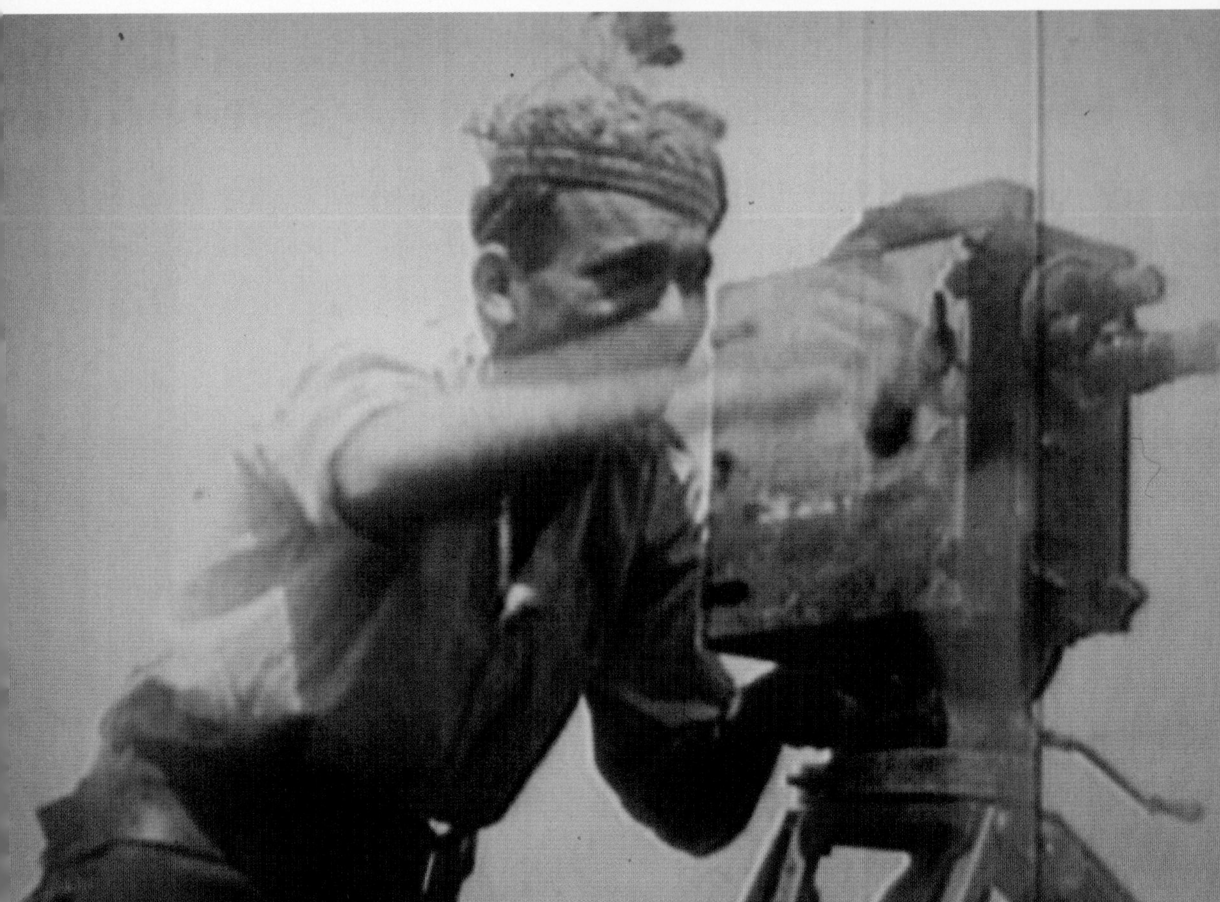

Fiona Tan, *Facing Forward*, 1999, video projection

164

computer to mimic another computer – for example so that you
can run Windows software on a Macintosh or old Atari games
on a modern system. It thus refers to the use of models or
programs, by means of translation and imitation, within a system
or medium for which these were not originally designed.
As a theoretical mental figure, emulation thus expresses the
capacity of the visual culture to 'store' all kinds of reality
principles, belief systems and media programmes, both in the
sense of 'clearing up' and 'reproducing' – making these things
vanish and reappear. Coding and decoding take place simultaneously in this process; the digital domain, the computer,
writes media history just as much as it erases it. Emulation and
remediation are connected, but the principle of emulation,
which operates more behind the scenes, demonstrates that in
the digital culture the media become instantly Arcadian, in the
sense that the post-media era has begun.

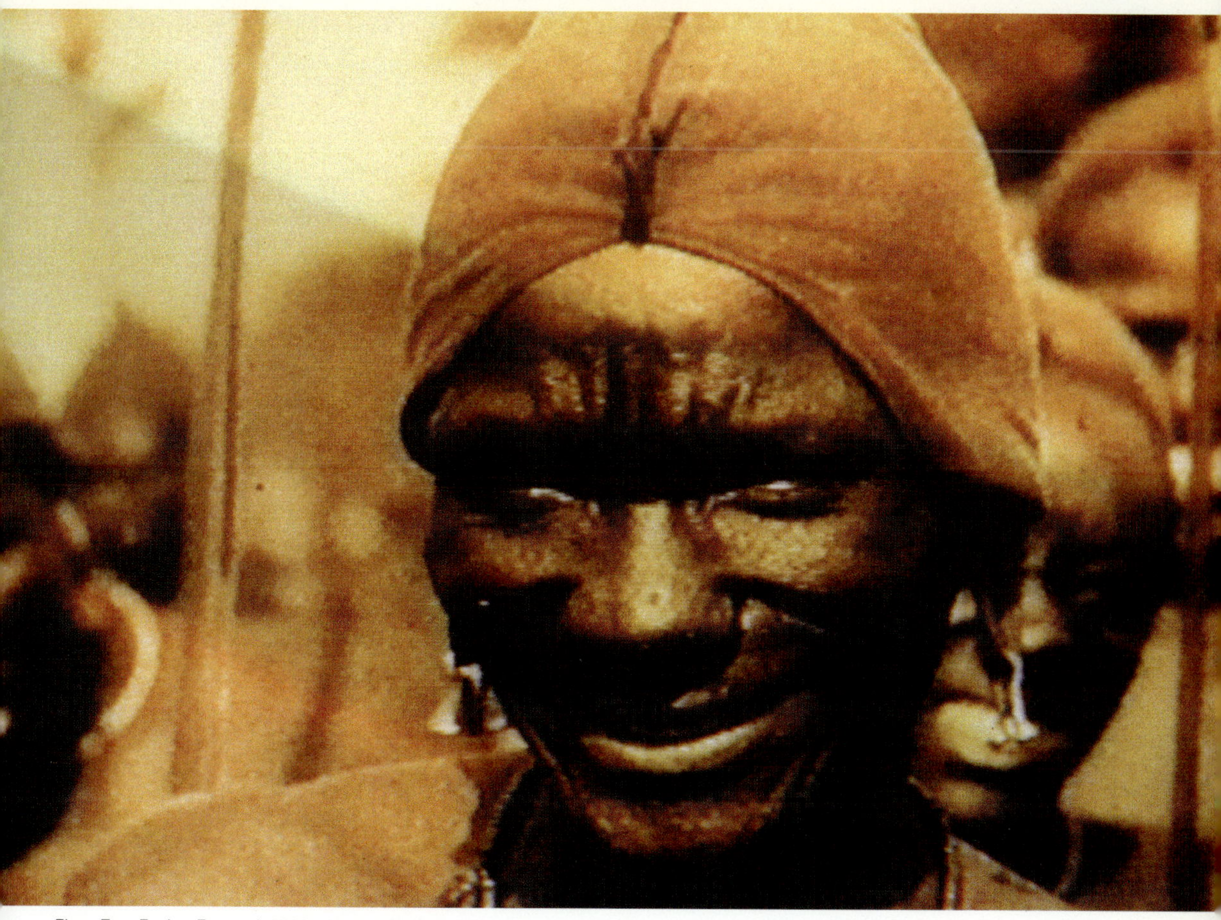

Fiona Tan, *Facing Forward*, 1999, video projection

0.

The digital imperative is the perfect embodiment of the idea, stemming from the Enlightenment, of the makeability of reality. At the same time, it goes even further by shifting the stress from makeability to kneadability, the capability of coding and decoding reality. It is the code that provides access, or alternatively conceals secrets. It is the code that has to be deciphered or cracked, or in which information is stored. It is nowadays the code that lies at the root of everything, that forms the internal architecture of life, of the images.

The possibility of manipulating and mixing the codes opens the way to a new compatibility and exchangeability of cultural protocols. The effect of the order of the code is both transparency and a new opaqueness: euphoria about the visibility of everything lies behind the widespread fascination for the hidden, for the superiority and strangeness of the code.

Digital code is a text consisting of alphanumeric symbols, a text which is invisible in the final product, in the image. It involves an algorithmic game that generates perfectly artificial images – artificial, at least, from the point of view of beliefs about authenticity and reality. The traditional concept of a medium, based on the physical properties and representational capability of a given medium, i.e. on the relationship between the signifier and the signified, falls down here.

In the digital culture, old models and media are easily emulated within new systems, and easily incorporated into old forms. Art, daily life, fashion, commerce, entertainment, advertising, television and information, among other things, are forever popping up in new combinations and swapping codes among themselves. In the ostensibly open and transparent digital society, the control mechanisms (such as surveillance cameras, PIN codes, satellites, DNA banks etc.) are relatively invisible and hard to localize. Gilles Deleuze, in *Postscriptum sur les sociétés de contrôle*, holds that the mechanisms of the control society are not typically non-physical, dynamic, intangible and subject to continual change.[9] It is no longer the shibboleth, demanded by the sentinel initially to deny you passage, that matters in the control society, but a numeric language of control, the code and the password, which is gauged to the illusion of passage.

The hybrid, digital reality is gauged to a new outlook and new behaviour patterns. The contemporary member of the public is an all-rounder in respect of perceiving and communicating: as a film and TV viewer, as a filmmaker and photographer, as a computer and Internet user, as a mobile telephonist and SMS adept... He or she mobilizes, with the greatest of ease, different manners, techniques and media of perception, which continually intersect and infect one another. Attitudes and outlooks are less exclusive to a specific cultural or social domain than they used to be. Zapping, scanning, scrolling and browsing are the latest ways of perceiving: on the one hand they are volatile, fluid, equivocating and levelling, on the other hand scrutinizing and penetrating and they seek 'connection'. As a shopping addicts and as consumers of entertainment, as partygoers, the public have also learned to associate and combine perception with consuming and using.

The analogue, continuous and ordering manner of perception has been ousted by the digital or interactive gaze, which flourishes in the network society. The digital gaze is moreover the outcome of the 'interactive ideal' propagated by the technology of consumption. By means of short-lived connections, the interactive gaze is in constant search of change and novel experience; it aspires to a permanent interplay with its surroundings. The interactive gaze strives to get inside things, incessantly seeks points of contact and of entry, and seeks immediacy. From the old perspective, the digital gaze is repeatedly frustrated, for it is by definition insatiable. The act of looking can never be completed: it is not concerned with the content or meaning, but with the euphoria of constant change. Within the digital domain, it is the interactive gaze that determines the act of seeing.

[9] **Deleuze 1990.**

1.

Returning to *video*, to 'I see'. We lost sight of video in the course of this argument amid the vagueness and the profusion of the digital: the digital not as a medium, but as a modality, as a contemporary paradigm. As stated, video has become part of the digital, i.e. the autonomous medium of video has dissolved into the digital, synthetic mix of post-medial reality. 'The mix indicates that we must travel through a huge emptiness before arriving at a new meaning', Bilwet argues in *Theorie van het mixen*.[10] It is this emptiness where the medium of video, the 'I see', is now located. The emptiness is both a liberating one, a zero-point that entails the freeing of traditional meaning, and a space, a black hole, in which 'I see' is reformulated as 'do I see?'.

The digital domain has the power to increase the presence of video more than ever, but it also functions as a vanishing point. On the one hand, this discloses a new metaphysics of the video image, which can present itself as uncompromisingly mysterious and mystical; on the other hand, it transforms video into a superficial effect. The latter implies the emergence of videographics, which is an emulation of the medium of video. Just as video is capable of generating the photographic, filmic, cartoon-like, realistic, painterly or realistic, so is the video-graphic, within the digital, generated or shaped by other media.

If there no longer exists any valid, media-based typology to shore up art, it becomes problematic to expect art to give expression to the material of the medium itself – an expectation considered characteristic of the artistic use of a medium. A more current, challenging or effective goal for art in the digital culture could be to cut through the surface phenomena, reality constructions and interfaces, and to give voice to the digital dimension itself; to crack the codes, to tinker with the source. The artist would become an alternative 'programmer' – not just in a technical sense but in a cultural one. Inevitably, art will thereby put its own foundations, visibility and legitimation at stake...

10
Bilwet 1992, p. 176.

168   **Jorinde Seijdel** is an art historian and author. She lectures in media theory at the Arnhem Institute for the Arts, Arnhem, and regularly publishes essays in books and periodicals.

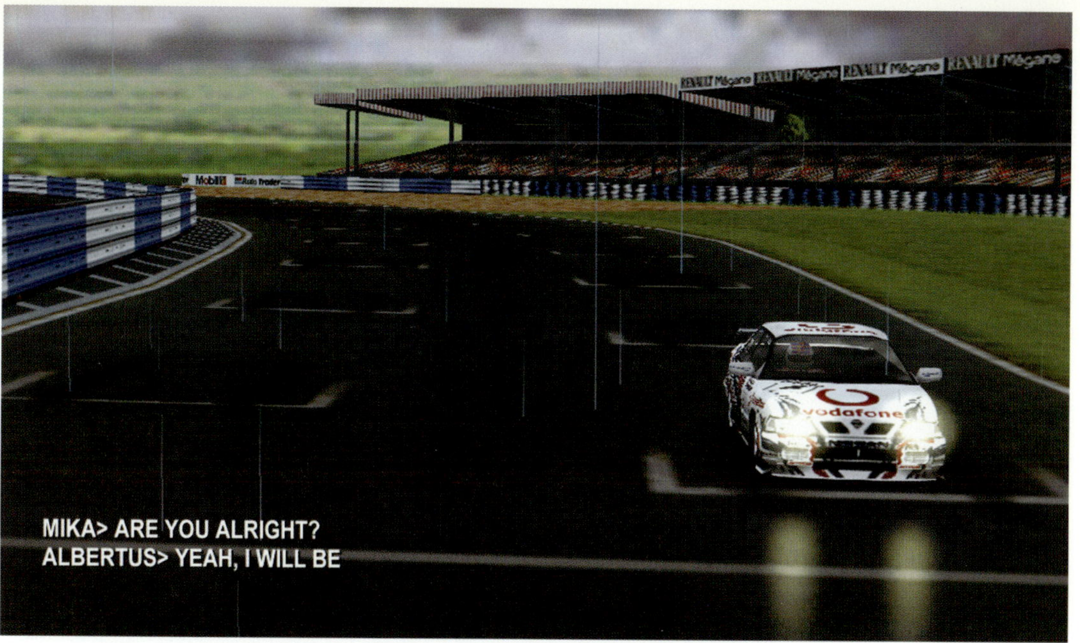

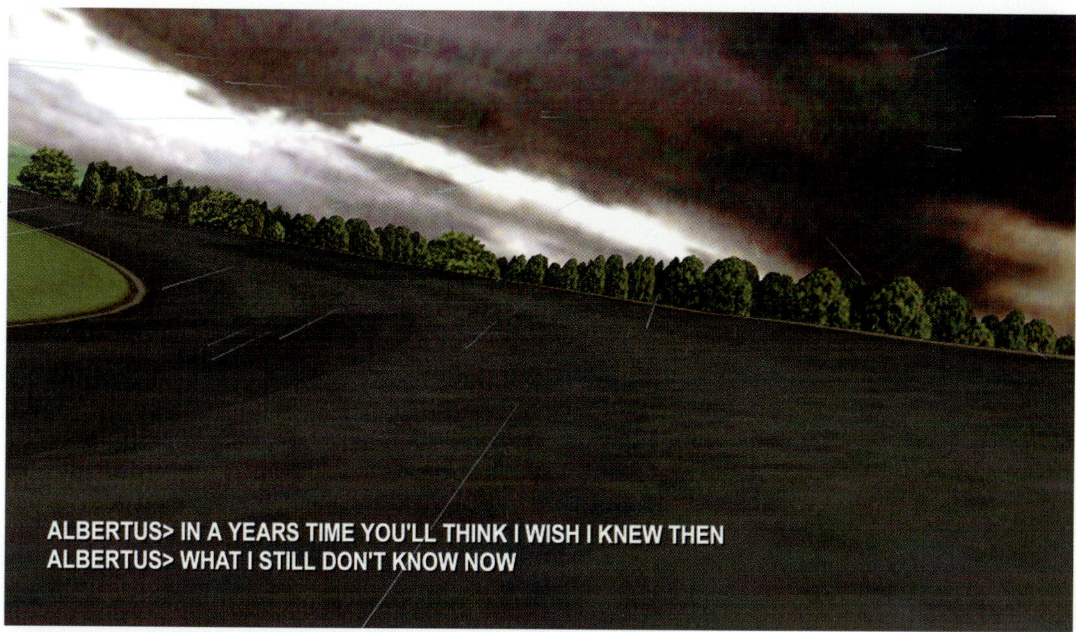

A.P. Komen/Karen Murphy, *What's another year (waiting for Mika)*, 2000, installation

This list includes work by Dutch artists, or artists living in the Netherlands between 1970 and 1985, whose work is represented in museum collections or in the Netherlands Media Art Institute. Artists have not been included for whom there is no current biographical information. These are Beeldend Theater, Mieke Caris, Pieter Cornelissen, Michael Druks, Geert Duintjer, Renate and René Eiseninger, Hannes van Es, Ap Esembrink, Peter Hessendahl, Ronald in 't Hout, Carel Kuitenbrouwer, Marc Kurkett Bob Lens, Johan Oskam, Viduo, Harm van der Wal and Jeroen Wilhelmus.

Abramovič, Marina (Belgrade, Yugoslavia, 1946) trained at the Academy of Fine Arts in her native town. From 1975–1986 she worked closely with Ulay (F. Uwe Laysiepen), also in Amsterdam on a series of provocative and ritual performances entitled *Relation work* in which the human form was the medium and subject matter. From 1981–1986 she worked with Ulay on *Night Sea Crossing* and later on the 'continental video series', including *City of Angels* (1983). In 1986 their collaboration ended with the works *China Ring* and *The Great Walk*. Since 1976 Abramovič has videotaped her performances and continues to make video installations. She lives and works in Amsterdam.

Ader, Bas Jan (Winschoten, 1942). In 1963 Ader crossed the Atlantic in a yacht and settled in Los Angeles where he studied art and philosophy. Well-known performances he captured on film are *Fall I, Los Angeles* (1970), *Fall II, Amsterdam* (1970), *Broken Fall* (organic) (1971) and *I'm Too Sad to Tell You* (1971). Ader's most well-known video work is *Picnic*; his video performances are less well-known. Ader went missing in 1975 when attempting to cross the Atlantic Ocean.

Amen, Woody van (Eindhoven, 1936). Studied for a short time at the Rotterdam Academy of Art, then lived in New York from 1961–1963 and attended the Cooper Union. During this time he made assemblages and came into contact with Pop Art. In 1976 he made the video *Money Just Wait*. From 1969-2001 Amen taught at his former Rotterdam art school, now the Willem de Kooning Academy.

America, Lous (Wassenaar, 1954). Attended Tilburg's Academy of Art and then studied multimedia at the Jan van Eyck Academy in Maastricht. Her videos and performances focus on depicting physical expression and she has made a work with 165 photographs depicting various facial expressions. America has made several videos, including *Labyrinth* (1981).

D'Armagnac, Ben (Amsterdam, 1940–1978). Studied painting from 1959–1963 at Antwerp's Academy of Art. Began making performances in 1973. It is chiefly D'Armagnac's performance in Maastricht (1976) that earned him recognition and this is also one of the few works he made specifically and directly for video. Before this he worked together with Gerrit Dekker on several land art projects in Zeeland, including *Huisjes* (1968) and *Ruiterstokken* (1969). D'Armagnac died in 1978.

Arts, Arno (Boxmeer, 1947). Studied at the Academy of Art in Arnhem. He made one or two videos around his own name – *Every Picture Tells a Story* (1981), *Remember My Name* (1982), *Representing the Arts* (1983) and *Self-historification* (1984).

Auto Awac, Kees de Groot (Marum, 1956). Followed a video course at the AKI in Enschede and here in 1981, along with three other artists, founded Auto Awac (first part of the name means 'self'; second part is an abbreviation of Airborne Warning and Control System). He was also one of the promising young artists in 'The Luminous Image' exhibition at Amsterdam's Stedelijk Museum (1980). Two years later his *Auto-Mutant* appeared and in 1983 he made two video installations: *Dialogue-select* and *Buro-Ridders*. Since 1984 he has worked with Frank Morssinkhof (Hengelo, 1959) on several videos and is currently the driving force behind 'Planet'.

Babeth (van Loo) (Heerlen, 1948). First studied architecture and then painting and performance art with Joseph Beuys in Germany. She arrived in San Francisco on a grant, gained a Masters in film and art in 1977 and then began teaching. She is currently a documentary film and video maker. A well-known video is *Videya I, II, III* (1984).

Baren, Peter (Haarlem, 1951). Studied at the State Academy in Amsterdam from 1972–1977. Since 1980 he has referred to his creative enterprises as *Exploitation Performances*. Among his video works are *Westerse Mantra* (1980), *Oosterse Mantra* (1981) and *Panorama Faulhorn* (1983).

Bastiaans, Christiaan (Amsterdam, 1957). Studied at the Amsterdam Rietveld Academy of Art from 1971–1976, New York's Pratt Graphic Center (1982) and Kyoto University of Art from 1976–1978. He began working with video in the mid-1970s and is mainly interested in non-western cultures. Two of his well-known works are *Jukai* (1983) and *The Nara Tape Factor* (1985). He lives and works in Amsterdam, Osaka and Tokyo.

Beckmans, Fredy (Berlin, 1956). Worked with Yntse Vugts under the name Artis Facit Saltus on several multimedia productions, including *Legato*, *Cantus Firmus* and *Tempo di Valse* (1987). These were sound projects for video monitors and cellos.

Berkhoff, Arthur (Apeldoorn, 1959). Has made various videos, including *Experimental Psychology* (1982), *Qybmoraf* (1982), *Prose must be Poetry* (1983), *Recorded Viaduct* (1983), *Spectrum analysis at space 9B* (1983) en *The Power of Neonism/Anti-Neonism/Pregroperativisme* (1986).

Bien, Waldo (The Hague, 1949). After studying political science for a short time in Heidelberg, in 1970 he attended the Staatliche Hochschule für bildende Kunst, Düsseldorf, studying with Joseph Beuys.

From 1976–1980 he also studied anthropology. Bien, whose works include *Regal Star* (1983), lives and works in Amsterdam.

Bierman, Han (Purmerend, 1944). A conceptual artist who works with various media, he has worked with film and video since 1979. His most well-known work is *Nothing* (1979). Other works include *Untitled/Untitled II* (1981), *Marktkraam* (1982) and *Verbeeldingskracht* (1989). In *Avondvullend TV* he enters into a relationship with television culture. Bierman is presently making large mixed media installations and lives and works in Amsterdam.

Boegel, Klaus (Mühlheim, Germany, 1948). Studied from 1969–1975 at Düsseldorf's Academy of Art and lived in the Netherlands from 1975–1977 on a DAAD grant. Made *Auto totems, Helden, Porträt* in 1979 and then worked with Heiner Holtappels on *Stille* (1977), *Atmung 1, 2, 3, 4* (1979), *Monotonie* (1978), *Relationen* (1978) and *The boomerang rings twice* (1982).

Boezem, Marinus (Leerdam, 1934). In the second half of the 1960s, along with Jan Dibbets and Ger van Elk, he belonged to the leading exponents of Conceptual Art and Arte Povera in the Netherlands. Two works *Een briesje in mei* (1974) and *Het beademen van de beeldbuis* (1971) were recorded on video. Boezem also makes 16 mm films and three dimensional works.

Bogers, Peter (Dordrecht, 1956). Graduated from the Academy St Joost of Art, Breda, in 1982, and is regarded as one of the pre-eminent video artists in the Netherlands. A few of his videos are *Opname 17* (1982), *Opname 18* (1983), *Getting Involved* (1984), *Nature I* (1986) and *Life by life* (1988). He made a breakthrough in the 1990s with his video-installations *Breathing World* (1989) and *Nóóó, You Don't Understand!* (1991). Bogers lives and works in Amsterdam.

Brouwn, Stanley (Paramaribo, Surinam, 1935). Settled in Amsterdam as a painter in 1957, where in 1961 he began working on an on-going series of works entitled *This Way Brouwn*. Around 1970 he started using his own footstep as a starting point to his work. Brouwn is one of the most influential conceptual artists in the Netherlands. He participated in *Identifications* (1970) by Gerry Schum and made *Een stap* (1971) for Dutch television. Brouwn divides his time between Amsterdam and Hamburg, where he teaches at the Academy of Art.

Brun, Daniel (Paris, 1944–1994). Self-taught artist who had lived in Amsterdam since 1978. His installations and videos were mainly based on performances and happenings in which his own presence could always be counted upon. His first video was *Walk Off* (1978), later followed by *L'Orphee* (1983), a mini, six-part opera. From 1986–1988 he was director of the Netherlands Association of Video Artists and a TBA board member.

Bundt, Livinus van de (Zeist, 1909–1979). Following a period of painting, doing graphic design and photography, he came into contact with video in the late 1960s thanks to Nam June Paik. Bundt felt the medium was eminently suited for capturing light and he was the first Dutch artist to create abstract images using video. He worked alongside his son, Jeep van de Bundt (The Hague 1951), who provided the sound for his video productions. Among his works are *Percussion* (1975) and *Fifty out of two* (1975).

Capelle, Herbert (Hengelo, 1962). Studied first at the AKI, Enschede, from 1980–1985, and then at the Rijksacademie, Amsterdam (1986). As an 18-year-old painter he began experimenting with video, incorporating painterly techniques into it. Together with Frits Maats, Capella made *Autumn* (1983) and *Ambrosia* (1984–1985) and chiefly used the medium in the 1980s.

Cardena, Michel (currently Miguel-Ángel Cardenas; Espinal, Columbia, 1943). Began his career painting and making drawings. He has lived in the Netherlands since 1962 and has been using video, audiovisual installations, performance and photography since 1968. Cardena's immense body of work has had a huge impact on the first generation of video artists. He teaches at various art schools in the Netherlands. His *Somos Libres!?* (1981) was the first Dutch tape to be purchased by a museum (Boymans-van Beuningen).

Carrión, Ulises (St Andres Tuxtla, Mexico 1941–1989). Studied philosophy and literature in Mexico City, Paris and Leeds and wrote several books. Carrión, who lived in Amsterdam from 1970 on, was an artist/arranger and founder of Other Books And So. He also devoted his time to mail art whereby he came into contact with performance, film and video. His work includes *Gossip, Scandal and Good Manners* (1981). During the 1980s he concentrated on media happenings.

Chiffrun, Christine (Paramaribo, Surinam, 1942). From 1963–1976 studied art in Paramaribo, Amsterdam (Rietveld Academy) and Groningen (Minerva Academy). From 1976–1979 she did experimental work at the Jan van Eyck Academy, Maastricht. Her works include *Line Structure Environment* (1981), *Between Questions and Statements* (1982), *Line Structure Environment* (1982) and *Pandora's Box* (1983). Chiffrun lives and works in Veendam.

Coëlho, René (The Hague, 1936). From 1958–1978 he worked for VARA television as cameraman, documentary film director and producer. He is the founder and former director of Montevideo/TBA, Netherlands Media Art Institute and has taught at the Enschede AKI and the Amsterdam Rietveld Academy. He has made several monitor installations, including *Het Van Onderen Project* (1979).

Dedo (Harry Heyink; Lochem, 1957). Attended the AKI in Enschede and belongs to that first generation of artists to have formally trained in the medium of video. He is involved in performances, painting and audiovisual work, uses sampling and collage techniques and is part of the New Wave movement. From being an artist, he now spends more time organizing large and small scale projects, including 'Park of the Future'. He has made *Our Flag is Going Forward Too* (1984), *Nationaal* (1984) and the video installations *Ahorcado Nudo* (1984), *marefonie* (1983), *Wir machen das schon* (1983) and *Made* (1983).

Dekker, Gerrit (Hilversum, 1943). Chiefly makes minimal interventions and performances. Has worked closely with Ben d'Armagnac for 15 years. Dekker presented his last performance after his death in 1978, but this was never recorded on video. His works include *4 maart Bonnefanten museum 1977* (1977).

Dibbets, Jan (Weert, 1941). In 1967 he received a grant to study at St Martin's School of Art in London. Dibbets initially focused on Land Art and later on perspective correction, which was to form the core of his body of work. He makes use of photography to explore his ideas. In the early 1970s he made several films and videos, including *4 Diagonals* (1970–1971) before continuing with his photographic perspective correction work.

Dijkman, Bart (Naarden, 1959). Trained at Arnhem Academy of Art and has been working with video since the 1980s, exploring various genres within this. His works include *Stefan zal straks stil zijn* (1984), *Oog* (1985), *Miranda* (1987) and *Billy* (1990).

Drupsteen, Jaap (Hasselt, 1942). Studied graphic design at the AKI in Enschede. Worked as a graphic designer for NOS and VPRO, specializing in the making of leaders, music videos and video-graphic productions. In recent years he has broadened his field by designing websites and interactive TV and video productions. A well-known video is *Hyster Pulsatu* (1984) and he has made and produced *The Flood* (1985) for television.

Elk, Ger van (Amsterdam, 1941). Studied art history and later made use of it in his work. He makes sculptures, painted photographs, installations, slides and films. Along with Jan Dibbets and Marinus Boezem he is seen as the leading exponent of conceptual art in the Netherlands. In 1970 he participated in *Identifications* by Gerry Schum and in 1971 *Beeldende Kunstenaars maken TV, en Schilderkunst Fase 1, Fase 2*.

Engels, Pieter (Rosmalen, 1938). Studied for a short time at Den Bosch Academy of Art and at the State Academy of Fine Arts, Amsterdam, where he specialized in sculpture and architecture. Until 1962 he painted monochrome canvases. As well as painting, his work also comprises words and actions. He is regarded as a Dutch conceptual artist. He made *Expressionistic Spoken* (1972), *Oral Signature* (1972) and *Para Marche* (1972). Engels lives and works in Amsterdam

Ex, Titia (Terwinselen, 1959). Studied from 1985–1988 at the State Academy of Fine Arts in Amsterdam. Her work includes *Jane* (1984) and, in collaboration with Elly Goede, the videos *Landval* (1986) and *Appel* (1987).

Faassen, Roel (Schoonebeek, 1958). Studied from 1978–1983 at the AKI in Enschede, where he still lives and works. He is chiefly engaged in sculpture, film and video as well as installations and performances. His work is distinguished by a fascination for prehistoric cultures like the Celtic druids. Between 1983 and 1985 he made his six-part *Videosculpture*.

Flipse, David (Rotterdam, 1948). In the early 1970s he studied drawing and graphic design at the San Francisco Academy of Art and then performing sculpture at the San Francisco Art Institute. He returned to the Netherlands in 1976. His work includes *Strings/The Basics of Drawing* (1978), which are experimental video shorts.

Fortuyn, Irene (Geldrop, 1959). Worked for many years with **Robert O'Brien** (1951–1988). Their artistic collaboration produced a few videos in the 1980s, including *Much ado about nothing* (1984) and *The Reflex* (1984), but they are chiefly known for their sculptures. Following O'Brien's death, Irene Fortuyn continued to work under the name Fortuyn/O'Brien. She now makes three-dimensional objects and teaches at the KABK in The Hague, while living and working in Amsterdam.

Füglistahler, Ricardo (Hengelo, 1960). Studied graphic and video art at the AKI, Enschede, from 1979–1985. In the following years he made diverse installations and registrations of his paintings. In his performance-like videos using paint, the soundtrack plays a major role. Among his works are *Loops* (1985), *Nightsoil* (1985), *Und die Seele erwerben im Geduld* (1985), *Ritual III* (1986) and *Panta Rhei* (1988).

Gadiot, Marion (Maastricht, 1955) In the 1980s was chiefly involved with feminist performances like *Flying Objects* (1980), *How do you feel today, let me have a feeling, how do you have a feeling tomorrow* (1981), *Parallel Paperpasting or Who's the Murderer* (1981) and *Throwing darts at somebody's breast, prick and eyes* (1981).

Gajewski, Henryk (Bialystok, Poland, 1948). First studied mathematics, film, art and photography, then computer electronics at Warsaw Polytechnic. While living for a few years in Amsterdam, he drew up a plan to produce a film about mail art. He made the thought-provoking *Punk in Poland* (1984) and the autobiographical video *Identity* (1985).

Garcia, David (London, 1952). Studied from 1969–1973 at the Byam Shaw School of Art and from 1973–1976 at the Royal Academy Schools. **Annie Wright** (Winchester, 1952)

studied from 1975–1976 at Winchester School of Art and from 1976–1979 at the Byam Shaw School of Art. In 1979 both artists moved to Maastricht to study at the Jan van Eyck Academy, where their collaboration began. Their most ambitious project was *The Underpass* (1983) and in the 1980s they gained wide recognition with *Callisto* (1984). Garcia has also made *A House Without a ghost is not a home* (1984) and *Terra Incognita* (1985).

Geerlings, Bram Makes small restrained performances in his own studio, like *Famous Impersonation of a Blind Snail* (1978).

General Idea. Artist's collective from Toronto, Canada, founded in 1969 by **AA Bronson** (1946), **Felix Partz** (1945–1994) and **Jorge Zontal** (1944–1994). Was abandoned in 1994 following the death of Zontal and Partz. General Idea made use of film, video, performance, photography, painting and sculpture to explore popular culture, mass media and the artist's role. They made *Test Tube* (1979) at De Appel and during the manifestation 'Talking Back to the Media' produced *Shut the Fuck Up* (1985). General Idea was frequently in the Netherlands.

Gerrets, Boris (Amsterdam, 1948). Studied art history at Bonn University, then painting and sculpture at the Düsseldorf Academy before moving to Paris to study dance at the Atelier International de Théâtre and theatre with John Strasberg. Since 1979 he has explored the various forms of interaction between dance and the visual

arts. This has led to the installations *Pompeii* (1987) and *Timepiece* (1994). In 1983 he settled in Amsterdam again. Gerrets is currently much involved in working with dance groups.

Giezen, Krijn (Noordwijk, 1939). Attended the Royal Academy of Fine Arts in The Hague. In 1969 he received the Association Internatonale des Critiques d'Art award. His works *Eend in de klei* (1979–1980) and *Krijn Giezen* (1985) belong to the first art videos in the Netherlands. Giezen lives and works in Normandy, France.

Gijzen, Wim (Rotterdam, 1941). His conceptual art projects drew much attention in the 1970s. Gijzen paints, draws and makes photomontages. His works include *7 werken van Wim Gijzen* (1970), *Mistakes* (1971), *Beursplein Rotterdam* (1971), *Coolsingel* (1973) and *Serie Vergissingen* (1973). Lives and works in Rotterdam.

Goulart, Claudio (Porte Allegre, Brazil, 1954). Graduated as a civil engineer and architect from Rio de Janeiro Federal University and now lives and works in Amsterdam. His work consists of installations, performances, photography, video and television. Identity and recollection are major themes in his work, which includes *Portraits* (1978), *Dialogs* (1980), *The Image Maker* (1983) and *Reclame* (1984). His collaboration with **Flavio Pons** (Don Pedrito, Brazil, 1947) produced, among others, *Concerto* (1980) and *Lovers* (1980). Pons has lived and worked in the Netherlands since 1975.

Grinberg, Buky (Israel). In the 1970s made diverse performances, including some for De Appel and the Amsterdam Stedelijk Museum. In his recorded performances Grinberg's limits certain of the spectator's choices, such as the route that can be taken in the exhibition space. Among others has made *With and without People* (1977).

Harding, Noel (London, 1945). A media artist, sculptor and artist, Harding began using video in 1971. Later he chiefly made installations and theatre pieces. He taught at Enschede's AKI and left a huge body of work behind. His work includes *Houses Belong to Those Who Live in Them* (1983). Lives and works in Toronto en Amsterdam.

Heebink, Loes (Utrecht, 1955). She attended the Academy of Visual Education in Amersfoort and along with video installations makes neon photographic works and monumental assignments. Made *Crossing Square* (1986) and three parts of *Moving Square No 31* (1986).

Hefti, Richard (Enschede, 1936–1993). Studied interior design from 1953–1957 at the AKI in Enschede. After graduating, he lived in Germany for a few years before returning to the Netherlands to settle in Amsterdam in 1965. A year later he began working as an artist. He made among others *Space Time/Imagination* (1984), *De Muur* (1987) and *Alisma Statica* (1989).

Hegedüs, Agnès (Budapest, 1904). Studied at the Hungarian Academy for Applied Art, Budapest, then video art for one year at the Minerva Academy, Groningen, the AKI, Enschede, and the Institut für Neue Medien, Frankfurt, Germany. Works include *Plain/Plane/Playing* (1989), *And Grind Hard Stones to Meal* (1989), *Image to Paul Klee* (1989) and *Ise d'Oil* (1990). In her work Hegedüs attempts to create an interaction between video and computer with the idea of visualizing the interchange. She also experiments with diverse montage techniques. The artist lives and works in Karlsruhe.

Heideveld, Henk (Winterswijk, 1950). His involvement with video stems from 1978, having first made paintings and drawings. In *Making Visible I* (1980) he continues exploring the process of drawing. He also made *Vierkant onderschrift* (1978).

Hermans, Marcel (Brunssum, 1961). During his training at the Maastricht Jan van Eyck Academy, he specialized in working with video. Made *On the Border* (1986), *Outside Interference* (1987), *Den Weg Entlang* (1987) and *Die Gleichzeitigkeit des Anderen* (1989).

Hocks, Teun (Leiden, 1947). Trained at the Academy St Joost, Breda. He is a deviser of photograph situations, a set designer, photographer, director, painter and the main character in his depictions. In his often coloured-in black and white photographs he appears as a man doing business. His *Eeuwig zingen de zagen* (1985) is a recording of one of his perfomances.

Holtappels, Heiner (Krefeld, Germany, 1951). Studied in Düsseldorf and from 1975–1980 collaborated with Klaus Boegel on *Atmung 1, 2, 3, 4* (1976), *Reminiszenz, Stille* (1977), *Monotonie* (1978), *Relationen* (1978) and *The boomerang rings twice* (1982) – all video recordings of performances. Without Boegel he then made the videos *A Lay-out For Desire* (1985) and *TV World* (1988). He is currently director of the Montevideo/TBA, Netherlands Media Art Institute and teaches at the Arnhem Institute for the Arts.

Hoover, Nan (New York, 1931). Studied from 1949–1954 at the Corcoran Gallery Art School and moved to Amsterdam in 1969. After painting and drawing for a time she began working with video, performance and photography in 1974. Her video work arose out of her small performances and simple experiments with light and paper. Her works include *Impressions* (1978), *Selected Works I*, (1978–1982), *Selected Works II* (1983–1985) *Flora, Watching Out – A Trilogy* (1985–1986), *Wigry, Poland/ Blue Mountains, Australia* (1988–1989) and *Desert* (1985). She has taught on various distinguished international courses.

Hooykaas, Madelon (Maartensdijk, 1942) and **Elsa Stansfield** (Glasgow, Scotland, 1945) belong to the first generation of video artists. They began their artistic collaboration in 1972 after graduating from the Ealing School of Art and Design in London. Their work chiefly combines the use of video with natural materials and objects. In 1975 they made their first video environment. Since 1980 both artists have lived and worked in Amsterdam.

Horvers, Toine (Tilburg, 1947) After training as a teacher of handicrafts and drawing in Tilburg, as an Horvers has focused on works related to movement, time and space. He also gave performances in which the audience participated. The type of medium he uses to achieve his ideas varies each time. He uses light, sound, performance, theatre and drawing. Coincidence also plays an important role. Works include *Buitenvertoningen* (1980) and *Bewegingen* (1981).

Janssen, Joshua played a significant role in the video activities of others and was often involved with De Appel's manifestations. He made one video work: *Portret van Robbie* (date unknown).

Janssen, Servie (Eindhoven, 1949). Makes installations, performances and drawings. From 1971 he only concentrated on performances, but stopped with these in 1981 to return to painting again. Janssen has made 24 performances in total, including *I.A.M., Warszawa, Poland* (1978), *Ingehouden wil, feiten en vooruitgang* (1978) and *Z.T.* (1978).

Jepkes, Fransje (Amsterdam, 1950). Studied from 1980–1981 at the Amsterdam State Academy of Fine Arts, from 1981–1983 at the Psychopolis Free Academy, The Hague, and from 1984–1987 at the Amsterdam Rietveld Academy. Mainly uses video and computers to create sound and image compositions and is also in-volved with performances. Lives and works in Amsterdam. Works include *Bike* (1984) and *Poem* (1987).

Jochems, Frederieke (Schiedam, 1961). Studied from 1979–1980 at the Cinema Department, New York State University, Binghamton, US, from 1981–1982 at the Cineworkshop Free Academy, The Hague, and from 1982–1986 visual communication at the State Academy of Fine Arts, Amsterdam. Is a member of Franjo Film Foto Video. Work includes *Tele Visit* (1986), *Treppenwitz* (1996) and *Co & Jak* (1996).

Jonge, Jaap de (Amsterdam, 1956). Studied from 1977–1983 at the Academy St Joost in Breda and in 1983 at the Jan van Eyck Academy in Maastricht. In the 1980s he chiefly made videos and in the 1990s increasingly focused on large projects involving video and internet installations. He taught at the Amsterdam Riet-veld Academy from 1991–1995 and taught videographics at the Academy St Joost from 1990–1992. His work includes *Tanks* (1984), *Crystal Ball* (1996) and *Beperkt Houdbaar* (1996).

Kempen, Wink van (Balikpapan, Indonesia, 1948). Self-taught, he has worked as a performer and photographer. He is currently an internet entre-preneur. In 1975 he made four narrative works for the Lijnbaancentrum in Rotterdam. Works include *You are so beautiful* (1977) and *Save the last dance for me* (1977).

Kemps, Niek (Nijmegen, 1952). In 1972 he began studying publicity design at the Arnhem Academy of Art. He is now a sculptor and is mainly involved with objects and installations. *Een hors d'oeuvre* (1984) is his only video work.

Koenigs, Christine (Ede, 1952). Studied from 1969–1972 at the Arnhem Academy of Art. She paints, photographs and uses film and video. Koenigs is also a member of the Sea Level Association. Among other works she has made *Regen (rain)* (1978), *My line is rain* (1979), *i.i.i. industry, intelligence, integrity* (1984) and *Kill snoebel Kill* (1993).

Kolvenbach, Floris (1948). Operates on the fringes of diverse disciplines, including music, three-dimensional work, technology, computer graphics, video, dance and holography. Among his works are *Solar System* (1979) and *Colour Music A* and *Colour Music B* (1980).

Koning, Nol de (Amsterdam, 1944). Studied from 1967–1972 at the Amsterdam State Academy of Fine Arts. From 1973–1980 he was mainly engaged in painting and graphic art. In 1983 he began working more with installations and from 1986, using his painting as springboard, focused on the medium of video. His works included *Bulicame* (1987–1988), *Palinuro* (1989), *Miseno* (1990), *Vulcano Eolico* (1991/92) and *Het lied van Hylas* (1995). Lives and works in Amsterdam.

Kroon, Harrie de (Breda, 1948). Studied at the Academy St Joost in Breda. In the 1970s, along with photographic works, books and drawings, he also did performance work. Performance art is his preferred medium as he finds it the purist form of expression. De Kroon plays with the expectations of the specta-tor, for instance by breaking up natural causalities into staged processes. Several video recordings have been pre-served. He has made *Mother* (1978) and *Ourobouros* (1979).

Liebrand, Wim (Wisch, 1961). Studied from 1981–1985 at the AKI in Enschede. During this period he also founded SKET (Foundation for Art and Gaining Time), a joint venture with **René Reitzema** (Hoogezand-Sappemeer, 1959) and **Rob Dieleman**, (Arnhem, 1960). Together they made the video *Bos* (1985). In 1985 SKET was disbanded and Reitzema and Liebrand continued working as an artistic partnership. They performed together and also helped each other to produce individual tapes. Joint works are *Deadline* (1985) and *TEC performance* (1985). Liebrand's individual works include *Akker* (1985), *De Regent* (1985), *Paso Fino* (1987), *Luggar* (1988), *Abao* (1989), *Perro Caliente* (1991) and *Bare Hands* (1992). Now works with Axis Media.

Linaris-Coridou, Christina (Athens, Greece, 1946). Studied theatre and costume design at Athens Vakalo Academy from 1967–1971, and monumental art at Rotterdam Academy of Art from 1973–1976. Made *Textile Notebook*

(1978) and with **Robert Nollrol** (Wassenaar, 1952) *Zelfbeeld* (1978–1980), *Talisman* (1983-84), *Three Dreams* (1984–1987) and *Textual Revelations* (1983–1988).

Lupini, Saskia (Bandung, Indonesia, 1958). Works include *Landschap, Mensen, Stad, Cultuur* (1983–1984), *Pandemonium* (1984), *Innocence* (1987) and *Picasso's Balcony* (1988).

Maats, Frits (Dalfsen, 1949). Artist and co-founder of Mediamatic. Maats paints, makes installations and works with sound, photography and computer. Has been using video since the early 1980s. He explores the erasable aspects of video and painting, while searching for a synthesis between the two media. A few of his videos are *Blaze Abroad 1&2* (1983), *Hridaya* (1986), *Paracas Chimu* (1987) and *Die Universelen* (1988).

Marroquin, Raul (Bogota, Colombia, 1948). Studied visual arts at the National University of Colombia. Moved to the Netherlands in 1971 and studied at the Jan van Eyck Academy in Maastricht. He works mainly with audio/video installations. Since 1974 has lectured about telecommunications and alternative television productions at diverse European universities in Europe, the United States and Canada. Contributes regularly to the specialist press on these subjects. A few of his videos are *Andy Dandy works* (1974–1976), *Extra, Extra, read all about it* (1979), *Airport 1983* (1983), *Kiting* (1984),

Alienation (1985), *Castillo Fille* (1986) and *Discovery* (1988).

Maturana, Mariano (Santiago de Chile, 1955). Studied law at the University of Santiago before fleeing to the Netherlands. He currently works as media artist. Works include *Agua* (1987), *Paisaje* (1987) and *Muro* (1988).

Mirage, Merel (Amsterdam, 1960). Since the mid-1980s has lived in Nicaragua, Japan and Tibet. Her videos, films, installations and internet projects are about contact with other cultures. In the mid-1990s she attended the Media Academy in Cologne. She currently lives and works in Amsterdam and Cologne. Works include *Mirage I* (1988), *Natural Whispers in Japan* (1990) and *Blood in Blossom* (1995).

Mohr, Thomas (Mainz, Germany, 1954) Studied from 1974–1982 at the Johannes Gutenberg University in Mainz and from 1986–1989 at the Amsterdam Rietveld Academy. He makes abstract works and since the 1990s has been experimenting with the use of digital photography in video. Works include *Exercitium* (1988), *Composition met Strepen* (1989) and *Memento Vitae* (1991).

Müller, Pieter Baan (Zwolle, 1957). Studied at the AKI in Enschede from 1981–1986. As a video artist he began working with the computer ten years ago, using a conceptual approach to explore the boundaries of the medium. He lives and works in Enschede and teaches media art at the AKI.

Has made *Happy Hunting Grounds* (1984), *Sexuele Problemen* (1988) and *Maracaïbo, Ships that Pass in the Night* (1995).

Munster, Jan van (Gorinchem, 1939). Studied from 1955 to 1957 at the Rotterdam Academy of Art, then from 1957–1959 at the Amsterdam Institute of Art and Crafts. For a short time he experimented with film and video. Made among others *Pressed Light*, *Circles* and *Resistance* (1973). Lives and works in Renesse.

Nette, Adriaan (Sliedrecht, 1950). Chiefly known for his projects in public spaces, among them *Verblijfsruimte nr. 5A2, 5B2, 5C2* (1988).

New Electric Video Group comprised various technicians from Geldrop and Eindhoven who in 1968 began experimenting with video and television. Like the Lijnbaancentrum, this group was also socially engaged. They tried out the new media in youth and art centres and were especially interested in the anarchic use of video and allowed various activists to use their equipment. They made videos for the Van Abbemuseum, but little of their material has survived. Videos include *Geen* (1972) and *Kassel Documenta* (1972).

Nio, Maurice (Dapo (Singkep), Indonesia, 1959). Graduated from the Faculty of Architecture of Delft Technical University in 1988. Was co-founder of NOX, a media and architectural agency. From 1991–1996 also worked on large-scale architectural projects. He has taught at various art and architectural institutes, was editor of *Mediamatic*, designed books, made many video productions and published his own and other people's work. His videos include *Aucun Beaubourg* (1983), *Triompf van de Nacht* (1984), *The Spaceman* (1984), *De Belaagde Landen* (1989), *De Walvisspiegel* (1989) and *Day-Glo L.A.* (1995).

Oerlemans, Yvonne (Breda, 1945). Trained at the Free Academy in The Hague. In 1981 began using video intensively from a sculptural approach. The triangle is at the heart of her work. She has made *Vision* (1982), *Administration* (1983) and *7 werken* (1982).

Ogata, Atsushi (Kobe, Japan, 1962). Studied in Harvard from 1979–1983 and in Cambridge (US) at the Massachusetts Institute of Technology from 1986–1988. He makes single-channel works and collaborative installations. Has lived for some time in Amsterdam. Among his works are *Karan Koron* (1988) and *Kagen* (1988).

Oosten, Henny van (Stompwijk, 1934). Worked as developmental aid assistant in Africa. Attended the College of Fine Arts in Liberia, and completed her studies at the Free Academy in The Hague. Initially made gouaches and paintings but since 1981 has worked mainly with video. Works include *Love; a Triptych* (1983), *Dying on Wings of Light* (1983), *Beyond Reach, In Flore Vitae* and *Cathedral* (1985) and *Atropos, the Inescapable* (1986).

Oudendijk, Rob (Amsterdam) and **Monique van Kerkhof** (Maastricht) Both studied modern dance at the Merce Cunningham studio and Alvin Nikolais Dance School in New York. Have been making videos and performances together since 1985, including *Garbage* (1989). Since 1990 they have lived and worked in Japan.

Pagée, Pim van (Leiden, 1943). Made *Objects Tape A* and *Objects Tape B* (1979), a two-monitor installation. Lives and works in Deventer.

Päs, Gerard P. (Valkenswaard, 1955). A visual artist, maker of objects, painter, sculptor, performer and video, Päs divides his time between London, Canada and New York. Made among others *Art, Kunst, Diet* (1979).

Peeters, Sef (Venlo, 1947). From 1965–1973 attended various art schools in the Netherlands and Germany. Has taught at the Minerva Academy of Art, Groningen, since 1992. Peeters has lived and worked in Breda since 1973. Work includes *De poging* (1975) and *The 61 Hours in De Appel, Tape I* (1976).

Pink (Helen Scheerder; Haarlem, 1943). In 1966 attended the Conservatory of Dramatic Arts in Brussels and from 1968 tot 1972 worked as a theatre, film and television actress. In 1968 Pink began working as an artist and co-founded the Mass-Moving Collective. She has made various installations including *East West Home is Best* (1981) and *Sketching Book* (1983).

Plaat, Henry (Amsterdam, 1936). Began making short films in the late 1960s. These Surrealist associative works comprise montages of existing films and pictures (including his own) and the accompanying music helps create a distinctive atmosphere. Also makes travel documentaries, including *Spurs of a Tango* (1980), which received a Dutch Golden Calf award, *Fragments of Decay* (1983) and *Luz y Sombre* (1998). The video *9 werkstukken* (1968) is included in the Lijnbaancentrum collection.

Pollen, Rolf (The Hague, 1952). Mainly active in the 1980s, his video works include *Begeigerung; Solo für eine Grossstadt* (1984), *Interactions* (1985), *Junglefresh* (1984), *Futura Morgana* (1986).

Poppe, Ine (1960). In 1977 attended Artibus Institute of Visual Arts in Utrecht. She works as multimedia artist and documentary maker for VPRO, VARA, WWW, RTL5 and KRO and writes for the daily *NRC Handelsblad*. She made *Moedermelkkaas* (1983).

Raaymakers, Dick (Maastricht, 1930) Composer, theatre maker, artist and performer, Raaymakers teaches electronic music at The Hague Conservatory. He has independently composed 20 electronic compositions. *Grafische methode 2: fiets* (1979) was an experimental video.

Reitzema, René (Hoogezand-Sappemeer, 1959). Studied from 1980–1985 at the AKI in Enschede. During this period he also founded SKET (Foundation

for Art and Gaining Time),
a joint venture with **Wim
Liebrand** (Wisch, 1961) and
Rob Dieleman, (Arnhem,
1960). Together they made the
video *Bos* (1985). In 1985
SKET was disbanded and
Reitzema and Liebrand
continued working as an artistic
partnership. They performed
together and also helped each
other to produce individual
tapes. Joint works are *Deadline*
(1985) and *TEC optreden*
(1985). Reitzema's individual
works include *Reizen in twee*
(1985), *Zee* (1985), *Eiland*
(1985) and *De val* (1989).

Samson, Marja (Maya, alter-
ego Miss Kerr). Created a
female pseudonym for her work
and uses her own body to give
expression to 'Miss Kerr'.
Chiefly works with Super 8 film,
sometimes uses photography
and objects. Lives and works in
Amsterdam. Works include
Glovery (1975), *Marja Samson
Presenting Miss Kerr* and *Pink
Broom* (1976) and *Venetian
Blind* (1977).

Savert, Dorita (Rheden,
1962). Attended the Arnhem
Institute for the Arts from
1985–1989. Work includes
Sultan's Heart (1987), *Four
Roses* (1988) and *Watching*
(1989).

Schippers, Wim T. (Groningen,
1942). Studied graphic design
at the Amsterdam Institute of
Art and Crafts (later the
Rietveld Academy). Created a
furore when he sold several
study assignments to the
Amsterdam Stedelijk Museum
and had to leave the Institute
prematurely. Along with fellow
students Ger van Elk and Bob

Wesdorp, Schippers made 'a-
dynamic art'. A multitalented
and controversial artist, he
works in radio, television and
theatre as well as being a poet
and composer. His television
work is in diverse collections.

Schoeber, Rolf (Nijmegen,
1961). Studied from 1980–
1985 at the AKI in Enschede,
where he began working with
video. He has made *S.O.S. from
Outer Space* (1985), *Is is not is*
(1991), *Tantalus* (1992), *Chant
the Praises of Zero* (1995).

Schouten, Lydia (Leiden,
1948). First studied at the Free
Academy in The Hague, then
sculpture at the Rotterdam
Academy of Art. Began making
videos from 1978. Her subject
matter is the mass media and
she uses fantasy creatures –
eroticism is also an important
component of her work. After
graduating Schouten did
performance art all over the
world for four years, before
concentrating on narrative
videos and installations. Her
works include *Romeo is
Bleeding* (1982), *Split Seconds
of Magnificence* (1984), *Echoes
of Death/Forever Young* (1986)
and *A civilisation without
secrets* (1987). Schouten
teaches at diverse art schools.

Schutter, Bert (Assen, 1945).
Studied from 1965–1970 at the
Royal Academy of Art in Den
Bosch and from 1970–1971 at
Ateliers 63 in Haarlem. He made
several conceptual videos
before focusing on installations.
Lives and works in Antwerp.
Has made *Producing Lines*
(1978), *Related Forms* (1980),
Still Life/Still Alive (1981),
Woodsculpture (1981),

Mill/Molen (1982), *Escultura*
(1982) and *De Baadsters – Les
Baigneuses* (1996).

Servaas (Alkmaar, 1950–2001
Hoorn). In 1993 set-up the
Foundation for Art & Environment with the aim of stimulating
interaction between art, society
and the environment. He made
both single-channel videos and
installations, including *Vale of
tears* (1982), *Springtime again*
(1983), *Fish from Holland*
(1985), *Apartheid Is the devil*
(1986), *Video artists make us
drunk* (1986).

Shabtay, Michal (Haifa, Israel,
1952). Studied film at Haifa
University and in 1975 left her
country for political reasons and
came to the Netherlands. First
studied at the Free Academy in
The Hague from 1976–1977
and then at the Royal Academy
of Fine Arts in The Hague. Has
worked with Danniel Danniel.
Her videos include *Landscape*
(1983), *Elegy* (1987) and *The
Henny Penny Picture Book*
(1994). She lives and works in
Amsterdam.

Shaw, Jeffrey (Melbourne,
Australia, 1944). From 1962–
1964 studied architecture and
art history at Melbourne University, and from 1965–1966
sculpture at Milan's Brera
Academy and St Martin's
School of Art in London. Since
the mid-1960s Shaw has been
making interactive media
events, installations and
sculptures. He lived for many
years in Amsterdam and co-
founded the Eventstructure
Research Group (1967–1980).
He worked with Dirk Groeneveld
on *The Narrative of Landscape*
(1985), *Anamorphoses of*

Memory (1987) and *Legible City* (1989). He lives and works in Karlsruhe, Germany.

Sixma, Tjarda (Sittard, 1962). Until 1984 studied photography and video at the Arnhem Academy of Art; **Michiel Vijselaar** (Hoensbroek, 1959), studied graphic design at the Academy St Joost, Breda, and video (until 1988), also at Arnhem. Have been making films together since 1984, including *Gretel* (1984), *Vita Sott' Aqua* (1985), *Snöflinga* (1986), *Hochzeit im Schnee* (1986*)*, *La Rose Blanche* (1988).

SKET (Liebrand, Reitzema, Rob Dieleman) See entries Reitzema, René and Liebrand, Wim.

Sluik, Ron (in Enschede, 1961) and **Reinier Kurpershoek** (Amsterdam). Met at art school and have been working artistically together for 18 years. They began their careers in 1982 with the former Montevideo gallery. They chose film as their preferred medium in order to have 'beautiful images relate stories'. Their idea is to convey a message, to make videos that lie like 'a stone on the conscience'. Works include *The March Konkret* (1984), *The March Sirk V II III* (1986), *The March Matria* (1996).

Smits, Ineke (Rotterdam, 1960). Studied at the Rotterdam Academy of Art and the National Film and Television School in Beaconsfield, UK. She has made various short films and documentaries, including *Al het geluid van de wereld* (1985). Made her debut as a film director in 2001 with *Magonia*.

Spinhoven, Bill (Velsen, 1956). Worked as a photographer from 1976–1979 and then studied at Twente Technical University from 1979–1982 and the AKI, Enschede, from 1982–1987. Develops technically ingenious installations which explore how the media image is experienced. Has made *A shot across the nind* (1989) and *Time Stretcher* (1994).

Sprenger, Maarten (Amsterdam, 1958). Initially studied Dutch Language and Literature (1977–1979), then attended the Arnhem Academy of Art from 1979–1985 and the AKI in Enschede from 1985–1986. Works include *Beelden op een berg* (1985), *Gardenfull of Flowers* (1986) and *Luxe van het leven 1, 2, 3, and 4* (1987–1989).

Stiphout, Ivo van (Tilburg, 1960). From 1977–1981 attended the Graphic Arts School in Eindhoven, and from 1982–1987 the Amsterdam Rietveld Academy. He makes large sound and video installations, including *IC/You watch* (1989) and *Zoo+* (1989). Currently with the Amsterdam Sandberg Institute.

Struycken, Peter (The Hague, 1939). Has used the computer since 1968 for his own and commissioned work, first working in black and white and then, since 1972, in colour. Based on specially developed computer programmes, he has made photographic works, drawings, paintings, films, videos, sculptures and real-time computer-generated television and light works, ranging from small to monumental, including *Struycken in waves* (1977), *Kleur, ruimte en verandering* (1987).

Szulc-Krzyzanowski, Michel (Oosterhout, 1949). First studied photography at Academy St Joost, Breda, then photography and graphic art at the Royal Academy in Den Bosch. Began work as a freelance photographer at the age of 20, making conceptual pictures, documentary photographic projects with relevant social themes and stock photography. He lives and works in Cadaques, Spain. He made *Naakt zijn* in 1976.

Tajiri, Shinkichi (1923). Visual artist who uses various media – in the 1950s he made 16 mm films, including the experimental *The Vipers* (1955) and later *Bikers*. He was involved with video for a short time and was among the first Dutch artists to possess a camera. He also made *Berlin Wall* (1972) and developed a master plan for the Video sphere, a huge media tent for the Munich Olympic Games (1972). Later focused on monumental sculptures and now only uses video for documenting his work.

Theuws, Roos (Amsterdam, 1957). Began in the late 1980s using video – making abstract and minimal works which play with architectural space and the effect of light, like *Anaklasis forma lucis vi* (1989). She lives and works in Amsterdam.

Toebosch, Moniek (Breda, 1948). Studied fashion graphics at the Academy St Joost in Breda, and singing and guitar at the Brabant Conservatory in Tilburg. As well as painting, singing and her music and theatrical performances, since the late-1960s she has been the regular actress in films by Frans Swartjes. Her installations are rarely autonomous and nearly always occur as a result of a performance or theatre piece. Acquired national fame as presenter of the Dutch VPRO television programme *Aanvallen van uitersten* (Extreme Attacks) (1983). Has made *Painthouse 1,2 and 3* (1981), *Verzamelde beelden en toevallen, af- en toespraken* (1983)

Ulay (Frank Uwe Laysiepen) (Solingen, Germany, 1943). Studied photography from 1962–1968 and experimented with the Polaroid camera. Moved to Amsterdam in 1968 where he worked as a freelance photographer. Between 1976 and 1988 he made *Relation works* – performances, videos and lifesize Polaroids with Marina Abramović. Since 1998 Ulay has been teaching new media art at the Staatliche Hochschule für Gestaltung, Karlsruhe. Works include *Namen, Uiterlijkheden, Personenruil* (1975), *da ist eine kriminelle beruhrung in der kunst* (1976).

Verheyen, Marieken (Bergeyk, 1954) Made videos, experimental films and performances. Made the video *As a Woman* (1983), and with Claudio Goulart conceived the concept for the video performance *Diamonds are a girl's best friend* (1983) and the two-monitor installation *Head over Heels* (1984). She is currently making installations in public spaces.

Vleeshouwer, Co (Amsterdam, 1955). Briefly attended the Amsterdam Rietveld Academy and then worked with graphics, film and video. Since the late 1980s she has focused more on the writing and producing of audiovisuals as well as devoting time to amateur video works. Has made *Basic I, II* (1981), *Kiss and Scratch* (1981), *Voorgoed Ongeschikt* (1981).

Vos, Giny (Rotterdam, 1959). Graduated from the Rietveld Academy in 1988 in graphic design and audiovisual/theatre workgroup. Has made *Golden years* (1985), *Work to Do* (1986), *Wildebeest* (1986) and *I watch you*. In the 1990s she increasingly devoted her time to works commissioned for public spaces. Lives and works in Amsterdam.

Weide, Albert van der (Meppel, 1949) In the 1970s he fought against Apartheid, and his performances, environments, art works and writings all expressed fierce criticism against discrimination in South Africa, i.e. his video work *Africa* (1979).

Wijnen, Henk (Asten, 1950). Studied from 1969–1970 at the Den Bosch Academy of Art, from 1970–1976 at the Tilburg Academy (teacher training) and from 1977–1979 at the Jan van Eyck in Maastricht (mixed media). Collaborated on various actions in public spaces and made various videos, including *Driehoeksverbranding* (1982) and *Symfonie van een brug* (1988).

Zegveld, Peter (The Hague, 1951). Studied at the Royal Academy of Fine Arts in The Hague. Is a member of Caspar Rapak, a company making theatre and video art. He describes his work as 'sound theatre' – using objects, sound and light he brings theatrical moments alive. Various performances have been captured on video.

Analogue versus digital
Analogue and digital video are fundamentally different technologies. Analogue signals are continuous and variable, while with a digital signal the information is recorded as a series of numbers, so-called 'bits'. A big disadvantage with the analogue video signal (unlike the digital system) is that copying results in deterioration, known as generation loss.

Chroma Key Studio technique to make a composite of two video images by replacing a specific colour or brightness level in one image with the content of another. It is also known as 'blue screen imaging'.

Closed-circuit installation Installation involving a single camera and a monitor or video projector that shows the images synchronously or with a slight delay.

Cut Also known as 'hard cut'. Refers to the abrupt transition from one video image to another. Until the start of the 1970s it was almost the only way to edit.

Dissolve Studio technique in which a scene transition is effected by gradually and fluidly mixing one video image with another.

Environment Installation comprising one or more monitors in a space that is set up and arranged by the artist – the walls, the ceiling and the floor are part of the presentation.

Editing From a technical perspective, the history of video art traces the history of control over the 'temporal image'. With the 'open-reel' video tape it was technically impossible to perform editing. It was only with the introduction of the U-Matic tape (1972) and the CMX computer-controlled editing system (1974) that the possibility of editing and post-production became available.

Loop Video images edited so that there is no (obvious) beginning or end.

Master In video terminology the 'master', also called the 'mother tape', is the first-generation tape (the tape used for the original recording), and in the case of an analogue recording system it has the best image quality. The artist usually retains possession of the master, while museums and other institutions own copies (**submasters**), though these are often labelled as masters. The **viewing copies** and **archive copies** are then reproduced from the submasters.

Multi-channel video installation Installation that comprises multiple screens and possibly multiple projectors in which there is a relationship between the images.

Multimedia installation A genre in which video is one element in an installation that incorporates other media.

PAL/NTSC tapes: PAL is the acronym for Phase Alternating Line and applies to the European colour television broadcasting system, in which the image is composed of 625 lines of information that are scanned or refreshed at 25 frames per second. NTSC tapes were developed for the American National Television System Committee (NTSC) system, which is based on 525 lines scanned at 30 frames per second.

Portapak In 1965, Sony introduced the Portapak, a portable set for making video recordings, on the American market. This relatively lightweight, half-inch video unit comprised a camera and a portable black-and-white tape deck. The arrival of the Portapak in fact marked the breakthrough in the use of the video medium by artists. The equipment was relatively inexpensive and its use required little technical know-how, making it possible for a large group of artists to set to work in the medium. Nam June Paik was the first artist to acquire a Portapak.

Real time An important concept in the video medium. Because video tape can actually be played back while recording – something that is impossible with film – it is possible to show the unaltered, real time. The viewer is a witness to the actual registration of an event. If a tape is the same length as the action, then the term 'real time' is normally used. In the early years of video art in particular, artists simply recorded video tapes to the end – the 'reel time' – using the concept of 'real time' in an effort to establish direct and immediate contact between artist and viewer. The term 'real time' is in fact an unfortunate choice here, because it could be regarded as a case of the present shifted in time – the action has, after all, taken place in the past. As the technical capabilities of the video medium increased, artists started to apply more technological manipulations, and the concept of 'real time' fell by the wayside.

Single-channel video installation An installation in the narrow sense, which consists of a single videotape that must be shown in a space that is controlled, at least in part, by the artist.

183

Site-specific In contrast with video works that are exactly the same whenever and wherever they are presented, site-specific works are adaptable, depending on the circumstances in which they are shown. This means that they can in fact have a new meaning each time.

Still Term taken from the film jargon for a single frame. In video, it is also known as 'freeze frame' – a 'frozen' fragment of the moving image.

Superimpose Technique for superimposing graphics, such as letters, on video images.

Time Base Corrector Equipment that synchronizes various video input signals. A TBC is unmissable when working with multiple video signals, as is necessary for applying certain techniques.

Video format Term that is used to indicate, among other things, the size of the cassette, the width of the tape and the speed at which the tape records and plays back. Originally there was a video system based on separate reels. However, there were too many disadvantages associated with these open-reel tapes (of which the 0.5-inch format was probably the most popular) for them to reach a broad public. Sony then developed a system in which the two tape reels were housed in a single cassette: the **U-Matic** tape appeared on the market in 1972. It would become one of the video-tape systems used most by artists. In 1983 this U-Matic Low Band was succeeded by the Broadcast Version U-Matic (BVU), which has improved colour resolution. At the start of the 1980s, Sony also launched its professional **Betacam** system, based on Betamax. JVC introduced the

M-II system in 1982, which was of a higher quality than U-Matic but never really caught on. Many different formats have appeared over the years because of market competition, but by no means all of them became popular.

Video sculpture Installation with one or more monitors that displays similarities with a 'traditional' sculpture. Video is the most important medium in this form of installation, and the equipment and specifications for the presentation of the video can be critical to the impact and the meaning of the sculpture.

Video synthesizer Equipment with which it is possible to manipulate the shape and colour of images using sound impulses.

Wipe Visual effect by which a transition from one image to another is effected with a moving line or pattern.

selected bibliography

Amsterdam 1979
Gerry Schum, exh. cat. Stedelijk Museum, Amsterdam 1979

Amsterdam 1984
The Luminous Image, exh. cat. Stedelijk Museum, Amsterdam

Amsterdam 1992
Ulises Carrión, exh. cat. Museum Fodor, Amsterdam 1992

Art 1993
Art & Design Profile, no. 28 (special issue), Academy Editions, London 1993

Basel 1984
General Idea. 1968–1984, exh. cat. Kunsthalle Basel (etc.), Basel 1984

Beeren 1984
W. Beeren, 'Video and the visual arts', in: *The Luminous Image*, exh. cat. Stedelijk Museum, Amsterdam 1984, pp. 24-33

Beleid 1981
'Beleid voor Videokunst', *Informatiebulletin Raad voor de Kunst*, 12 (1981) 10, pp. 2-8

Bellinkx 2001
R. Bellinkx, *Stichting De Appel. Centrum voor performance, environment en situatiekunst 1975–1983*, thesis University of Amsterdam, 2001 (not published)

Berghaus 1995
G. Berghaus, 'Happenings in Europe', in: M.R. Sandford (ed.), *Happenings and Other Acts*, London/New York 1995

Van Berkum 1988
A. van Berkum, 'De barok is waar, het beeld is ding', *Nederland 4. De Nederlandse kunstvideo*, exh. cat. Stedelijk Museum Het Prinsenhof, Delft 1988

Bilwet 1992
Bilwet, 'Theorie van het mixen', *Media-Archief*, Amsterdam 1992

Boddy 1995
W. Boddy, 'The Beginnings of American Television', in: Anthony Smith (ed.), *Television: An International History*, Oxford University Press, Oxford 1995

Bolter/Grusin 1999
J.D. Bolter, R. Grusin, *Remediation. Understanding New Media*, Cambridge (Mass.) 1999

Boomgaard 1999
J. Boomgaard, 'Portret van een vage vriend', *De Witte Raaf*, no. 78 (March/April 1999), p. 11

Boomgaard 2000
J. Boomgaard, 'Actieve immobiliteit', *De Witte Raaf*, no. 88 (November/December 2000), pp. 4-5

Boomgaard/Van Mechelen/Van Rijsingen 2001
J. Boomgaard, M. van Mechelen, M. van Rijsingen (eds.), *Als de kunst erom vraagt. De Sonsbeek-tentoonstellingen van 1971, 1986 en 1993*, Stichting Tentoonstellingsinitiatieven, Amsterdam 2001

Bouma 1984
G. Bouma, 'Video in veelvoud', *Metropolis M*, 1984, no. 5, pp. 47-49

Burris 1996
J. Burris, 'Did Portapak Cause Video Art? Notes on the formation of a New Medium', *Millennium Film Journal*, 1996, no. 29; online available: www.mfj-online.org/journalpages/MFJ29/J burrisportapak5319.html.

Cassagnac/Fargier/Van den Stegen 1979
J.-P. Cassagnac, J.-P. Fargier, S. van den Stegen, 'Entretien avec nam June Paik', *Cahiers du cinéma*, no. 299 (1979)

Decker-Phillips 1998
E. Decker-Phillips, *Paik Video*, New York 1998

Deleuze 1990
G. Deleuze, 'Postscriptum sur les sociétés de contrôle', *L'Autre Journal*, 1990, no. 1 (May)

Delft 1988
Nederland 4. De Nederlandse kunstvideo, exh. cat. Stedelijk Museum Het Prinsenhof, Delft 1988

The Hague/Eindhoven 1977/1978
JCJ van der Heijden, publication Gemeentemuseum Den Haag, The Hague 1977/Stedelijk Van Abbemuseum, Eindhoven 1978

Desjardijn 1989
D. Desjardijn, *Voer voor miljoenen. De aktie BBK en Sonsbeek buiten de perken*, Amsterdam 1989

Dienst 1994
R. Dienst, *Still Life in Real Time. Theory after Television*, Duke University Press, Durham (etc.) 1994

Doane 1990
M.A. Doane, 'Information, Crisis, Catastrophe', in: Patricia Mellencamp (ed.), *Logics of Television. Essays in Cultural Criticism*, Indiana University Press, Bloomington/Indianapolis/London 1990, pp. 222-239

Falke 1983
L. Falke (ed.), *The Second Link. Viewpoints on Video in the Eighties*, Walter Philips Gallery/The Banff Centre School of Fine Arts, Alberta 1983

Feuer 1983
J. Feuer, 'The Concept of Live Television: Ontology as Ideology', in: F.A. Kaplan (ed.), *Regarding Television. Critical Approaches – An Anthology*, University Publications of America, Maryland 1983, pp. 12-21

Gigliotti s.a.
D. Gigliotti, *The Annotated Video Exhibition List (1963-1975)*, www.davidsonsfiles.org

Van Ginneken 1984
L. van Ginneken, 'Video in de beeldende kunst', *Kunstschrift*, 28 (1984) 4

Gribling 1982
F. Gribling, 'Kunst, Kunstenaars en de Kunstwereld in Amsterdam, 1960–1980. Feiten en samenhang', in: *Amsterdam '60-'80. Twintig jaar beeldende kunst*, exh. cat. Museum Fodor, Amsterdam 1982

Groys s.a.
B. Groys, *Media in the Museum/The Museum as Medium*, online available: www.edsvikart.com.

Haase 1983
A. Haase, 'Kunst als Möglichkeit des Lebens', in: W. Herzogenrath (ed.), *Videokunst in Deutschland 1963–1982*, Stuttgart 1983, pp. 30-40

Hall/Fifer 1990
D. Hall, S.J. Fifer, *Illuminating Video. An essential Guide to Video Art*, New York 1990

Hanhardt 1995
G. Hanhardt, 'Museum/Video Space: A Videotape program for The End(s) of the Museum, in: *Els límits del museu*, exh. cat. Fundació Antoni Tàpies, Barcelona 1995, p. 137

Kittler 1999
F.A. Kittler, *Gramophone, Film, Typewriter*, Stanford University Press, Stanford 1999

Knight 1996
J. Knight (ed.), *Diverse Practises. A Critical Reader on British Video Art*, Arts Council of England, 1996

Krauss 1978
R. Krauss, 'Video: The Aesthetics of Narcissism', in: G. Battock, *New Artists Video*, New York 1978, pp. 43-64

Krauss 2000
R. Krauss, *A Voyage on the North Sea*, London 2000

Levin/Frohne/Weibel 2002
T.Y. Levin, U. Frohne, P. Weibel, *Ctrl [space]. Rhetorics of Surveillance from Bentham to Big Brother*, Karlsruhe 2002

Ligthart/Smitshuijsen 1982
P. Ligthart, C. Smitshuijsen, 'Action replay. 20 jaar kunstenaarsverzet', in: *Amsterdam '60-'80. Twintig jaar beeldende kunst*, exh. cat. Museum Fodor, Amsterdam 1982, pp. 50-62

Linders 1979
A. Linders, 'Video de moderne kwasten van de kunstenaar', *Skrien*, April 1979, pp. 22-25

Lippard 1973
L. Lippard, *Six Years. The dematerialization of the art object from 1966 to 1972*, Studio Vista, London 1973

Lippard/Chandler 1968
L. Lippard, J. Chandler, 'The dematerialization of art', *Art International*, 12 (1968) 2, pp. 31-36.

López 2002
S. López, 'Identity, Reality or Fiction', in: *The Third Text reader on Art, Culture and Theory*, Continuum, London 2002

Luijters 1997
R. Luijters, *Een kleine geschiedenis van een medium*, Montevideo/TBA 1997

Lyon 1988
Servaas, exh. cat. Lyon 1988

Masotta 1968
O. Masotta, *Conciencia y estructura*, Editorial Jorge Alvarez, Buenos Aires 1968

McLuhan 1964
M. McLuhan, *Understanding Media. The Extentions of Man*, New York 1964

McLuhan 2002 (1964)
M. McLuhan, *Understanding Media*, London 2002 (1964)

Mignot 1984
D. Mignot, 'Video Art in Rembrandt's country', *Dutch art and architecture today*, 1984, no. 15, pp. 13-17

Mulder 2000
A. Mulder, *Het fotografisch genoegen. Beeldcultuur in een digitale wereld*, Amsterdam 2000

Nairne 1983
S. Nairne, 'The Video Mix', in: L. Falke (ed.), *The Second Link. Viewpoints on Video in the Eighties*, Walter Philips Gallery/The Banff Centre School of Fine Arts, Alberta 1983, p. 22

Omdat 1978
'Omdat het museum het niet doet', *Pulchri*, 6 (1978) 2, pp. 3-6

Perrée 1983a
R. Perrée, 'Videokunst in
Nederland. Onverstoorbaar op
weg naar Nederland 3', *Kunstbeeld* 8 (1983) 1, pp. 11-14

Perrée 1983b
R. Perrée, 'Video, het achterlijke
broertje van de televisie', *Kunstbeeld*, 8 (1983) 7, pp. 48- 49

Perrée 1985
R. Perrée, 'Introduction to an
Introduction', in: L. Bodeving, R.
Perrée, S. López (eds.), *Image
on the run. Dutch video art of
the 80's*, Amsterdam 1985

Perrée 1988
R. Perrée, *Into video art. The
characteristics of a medium*, Con
Rumore, Rotterdam/Amsterdam
1988

Rajandream 1986
M.A. Rajandream, 'Livinus en het
licht', thesis University of Leiden,
1986

Rajandream 1987
M.A. Rajandream, 'Fluxus +
Video', *Mediamatic*, 1 (1987) 2

Reedijk 1974
H. Reedijk, 'Is video kunst voor
allen?', *Museumjournaal*, 19
(1974) 2, pp. 67-71.

Reedijk/Van Tuyl 1974
H. Reedijk, G. van Tuyl,
'Video in de kinderschoenen',
Museumjournaal, 19 (1974) 4,
pp. 168-174

Reedijk 1976
H. Reedijk, 'Video in the
Netherlands. It takes a long time
to grow up and be recognised',
Studio International, no. 981
(1976), pp. 277-278

Reedijk 1984
H. Reedijk, 'De eerste
Nederlandse Video-gebruikers',
Kunstschrift, 28 (1984) 4

Ross 1973
D. Ross, 'Introduction to Art +
Cinema', Vol. 1, 1973, no. 2, p. 5

Ross 1976/1977
D. Ross, 'Nam June Paik: Overkill
als Ideologie', in: *Nam June Paik,
Werke 1946-1976, Musik –
Fluxus –Video*, exh. cat.
Kölnischer Kunstverein, Cologne
1976/1977

Rossler 1990
M. Rossler, 'Video: Shedding the
Utopian Moment', in: D. Hall, S.J.
Fifer (eds.), *Illuminating Video.
An essential Guide to Video Art*,
New York 1990, pp. 30-50

Rotterdam 1981
Cardena, exh. cat. Boymans-van
Beuningen, Rotterdam 1981

Ruhé 1982
H. Ruhé, 'Acties en performance
in Amsterdam. Overzicht van
20 jaar branche-vervaging', in:
*Amsterdam '60-'80. Twintig jaar
beeldende kunst*, exh. cat.
Museum Fodor, Amsterdam
1982, p. 41

Schoondergang 1983
R. Schoondergang, 'Schilderen
met video', *Nieuwe Revu*,
October 1983, p. 75

Sluik/Kurpershoek 1994
R. Sluik, R. Kurpershoek, *Radau.
Tatortfoto's Marinus van der
Lubbe (1933). Schuldig reizen
(1993)*, Maldoror/The Hague
1994, n.p.

Van Steegeren 1978
Th. van Steegeren, z.t., *Skrien*,
October 1978, pp. 16, 17, 39

Sturken 1990
M. Sturken, 'Paradox in the
Evalution of an Art Form', in:
D. Hall, S.J. Fifer, *Illuminating
Video. An essential Guide to
Video Art*, New York 1990

Terreehorst 1991
P. Terreehorst, 'Opkomst en
ondergang van Videokunst in
Nederland', *Kunst en beleid in
Nederland 5*, Amsterdam 1991

Trescher 1996
S. Trescher, *Die kanadische
Künstlergruppe General Idea*,
Verlag für Moderne Kunst,
Neurenberg 1996 (thesis Freie
Universität, Berlin 1994)

Tromp 1979
H. Tromp, 'Het tv-bestel en de
angst voor het experiment',
Haagse Post, 15 December
1979

Tweede 1984
'Tweede beleidsadvies over
videokunst', *Informatiebulletin
Raad voor de Kunst*, 15 (1984)
5, pp. 2-8

Velthoven 1987
W. Velthoven, 'Forever
Young/Echoes of the Death',
Mediamatic, 1 (1987)

Vostell 1973
W. Vostell, *Autopsie eines
Happenings. Befragung von
W. Vostell*, Produzentengalerie,
Berlin 1973

Webber 1996
S. Webber, *Massmediauras.
Form, Technics, Media*, Stanford
University Press, Stanford (Cal.),
1996, pp. 116-122

Williams 1990
R. Williams, *Television.
Technology and Cultural Form*,
Routledge, London 1990
(1975), pp. 92-95

Van Winkel 1999
C. van Winkel, *Moderne leegte*,
Nijmegen 1999

Wolfs 1987
R. Wolfs, 'Mediakunst: accepteren
of distantiëren, van Schouten tot
Scholte', *Beeld*, 2 (1987) 4, p. 37

188

colophon

This publication appears on the occasion of the 25th anniversary of the Netherlands Media Art Institute, Montevideo/Time Based Arts in Amsterdam.

Compiled and edited by
Jeroen Boomgaard, Bart Rutten
Authors
Jeroen Boomgaard, Ruth Bellinkx,
Anne van Driel, Heiner Holtappels,
Hinke Kappert, Sebastián López,
Marga van Mechelen, Rob Perrée, Bart Rutten,
Jorinde Seijdel
Photo research
Femke Lutgerink, Amsterdam
Artists' biographies
Sabien Schütte, Amsterdam
Technical terms
Xandra de Jongh, Amsterdam
Translation
Lynn George, Amsterdam (H. Kappert)
Victor Joseph, Amsterdam (H. Holtappels,
J. Seijdel)
Peter Mason, Amsterdam
(R. Bellinkx/M. van Mechelen, A. van Driel,
R. Perrée)
Andrew May, Amsterdam (Introduction,
Technical terms)
Arthur Payman, Bussum (J. Boogaard/
B. Rutten)
Copy editing
Els Brinkman, Amsterdam
Peter Mason (S. López)
Production
Astrid Vorstermans, NAi Publishers, Rotterdam
Graphic design
Harald Slaterus, Arnhem
Publisher
NAi Publishers, Rotterdam with Netherlands
Media Art Institute, Montevideo/Time Based Arts,
Amsterdam
Lithography
Words and Pages, Arnhem
Printing
Drukkerij Die Keure, Bruges

Cover
Livinus, *Percussion a till e*, 1973–1978
Inside front cover:
Lydia Schouten, *Romeo is Bleeding*, 1982
Inside back cover:
Servaas, *Pffft*, 1982

Credits video works and photography
Pieter Boersma **pp. 31, 53**
Marinus Boezem **p. 39**
Bonnefanten Museum, Maastricht **p. 140**
Wim Bors **69**
Miguel-Angel Cardenas, formerly Michel Cardena **pp. 60**
(photos Studio Hartland), **91, 92, 103, 116**
Jan Dibbets **p. 36**
Flatland Gallery, Utrecht (Komen/Murphy) **p. 169**
Ger van Elk **p. 37**
Pieter Engels **p. 40**
Galerie Paul Andriesse (Fiona Tan) **pp. 164, 165**
General Idea **p. 97**
Wim Gijzen **p. 42**
JCJ van der Heijden **pp. 26 below**
JODI (http://sod.jodi.org) **pp. 159, 162**
Gerald van der Kaap **pp. 155, 169**
Raoul Marroquin **pp. 29, 30, 124**
Montevideo/TBA, Amsterdam **pp. 14, 29, 30, 37, 40 top, 48, 65, 77, 81, 82, 83, 88, 89, 131, 132, 137, 141, 144-147, 152**
Montevideo/TBA, Amsterdam (with thanks to the Livinus van de Bundt heirs) **pp. 17-19, 21, 22**
Manfred Montwé, Düsseldorf **p. 24**
Peter Moore/VAGA, NYC **p. 25 top**
Jan van Munster **pp. 11, 47**
Museum Boijmans Van Beuningen, Rotterdam **p. 50**
Nederlands Instituut voor Beeld en Geluid, Hilversum **pp. 44, 120, 121**
Egon Notermans/ZEBRA, Venlo **p. 34 top**
Openbaar Kunstbezit/Montevideo/TBA, Stedelijk Museum Amsterdam (photo: Wim Riemens) **p. 39**
Rabotnik **pp. 73, 126**
Lydia Schouten **pp. 153, 154**
Bert Schutter **p. 48**
SKET **p. 150**
Stansfield/Hooijkaas **pp. 49, 94, 95**
Stedelijk Museum Amsterdam **pp. 123, 127, 128, 139**
Stichting De Appel, Amsterdam **pp. 62, 78, 85-87**
Stichting Open Studio, Lily van der Bergh **pp. 57; 58, 59** (photo: Henk Pauwels)
Shinkichi Tajiri **pp. 34, 54, 56**
Roos Theuws **p. 142**
Wolf Vostell **pp. 23, 25 below**
Vijselaar/Sixma **pp. 148, 149**
from: *Fandangos 8.9.10.11 SuperIssue!*, Spring 1978 **pp. 65, 90, 101**
from: *Fandangos on Raul Marroquin's World's TV Convention* **pp. 56, 99, 100**
from: W. Herzogenrath, *TV-Kultur, Fernsehen in der Bildenden Kunst seit 1879*, Verlag der Kunst, Dresden, 1997 **p. 32**
from: Guy Schraenen, *Ulises Carrión, "We have won! Haven't we?"*, Amsterdam 1992 **pp. 71, 74**
from: *Video Verslag*, Lijnbaancentrum/Rotterdamse Kunststichting 1973 **pp. 55, 61, 63**

We would like to thank the artists, photographers, and institutions for providing visual material and information.

NAi Publishers is an internationally orientated publisher specialized in developing,
producing and distributing books on architecture, visual arts and related disciplines.
NAi Publishers, Mauritsweg 23, 3012 JR Rotterdam, info@naipublishers.nl,
www.naipublishers.nl

This publication is also available in a Dutch edition: *De magnetische tijd*,
ISBN 90-5662-298-6

English edition:
ISBN 90-5662-299-4

Printed and bound in Belgium

This publication was partly made possible throught the financial support of

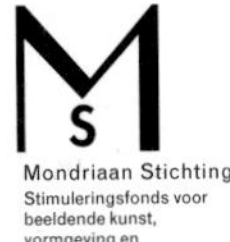

Mondriaan Foundation

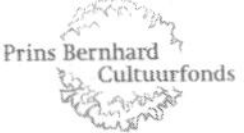

Foundation Prins Bernhard Cultuurfonds

VSB Foundation

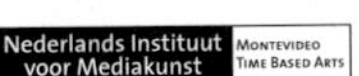